The Shape of Revelation

STANFORD STUDIES IN JEWISH HISTORY AND CULTURE

EDITED BY *Aron Rodrigue and Steven J. Zipperstein*

The Shape of Revelation

Aesthetics and Modern Jewish Thought

Zachary Braiterman

STANFORD UNIVERSITY PRESS

STANFORD, CALIFORNIA

2007

Stanford University Press
Stanford, California

Published with the assistance of the Arts and Sciences Faculty
Subvention Fund and the Department of Religion and Judaic
Studies Program at Syracuse University.

Printed in the United States of America on acid-free, archival-
quality paper

Library of Congress Cataloging-in-Publication Data
Braiterman, Zachary, 1963-
  The shape of revelation : aesthetics and modern Jewish thought
/ Zachary Braiterman.
      p. cm.–(Stanford studies in Jewish history and culture)
  Includes bibliographical references and index.
  ISBN 978-0-8047-5321-0 (cloth : alk. paper)
  1. Aesthetics–Religious aspects–Judaism. I. Title.

BM729.A25B73 2007
296.3'77–dc22   2006038220

Typeset by Bruce Lundquist in 10.5/14 Galliard Oldstyle

For my parents, Sheldon (z"l) and Marilyn

Contents

Acknowledgments

Parts of the Preface and Introduction have appeared as "Aesthetics and Judaism, Art and Revelation," *Jewish Studies Quarterly* 11, no. 4 (2004): 366–85. Parts of Chapter 1 appeared in "Der Ästhet Franz Rosenzweig: Beautiful Form and Religious Thought," *Journal of Jewish Thought and Philosophy* 10 (2000): 145–69. Parts of Chapters 1 and 5 have been reworked into "Martin Buber and the Art of Ritual" in Michael Zank, ed., *Martin Buber: New Perspectives/Neue Perspektiven* (Tübingen: Mohr/Siebeck, 2006). Parts of Chapter 3 appeared as "'Into Life'? Franz Rosenzweig and the Figure of Death," *AJS Review* 23, no. 2 (1998): 203–21. Parts of Chapter 4 appeared as "Cyclical Motions and the Force of Repetition in the Thought of Franz Rosenzweig" in Aryeh Cohen and Shaul Magid, eds., *Beginning a Reading/Reading Beginnings: Towards a Hermeneutic of Jewish Texts* (New York: Seven Bridges Press, 2002), 215–38. Parts of Chapter 6 appeared as "A Modern Mitzvah-Space-Aesthetic" in Barbara Kirshenblatt-Gimblett and Jonathan Karp, eds., *The Art of Being Jewish in Modern Times* (Philadelphia: University of Pennsylvania Press, 2006). Parts of the Epilogue appeared as "Against Leo Strauss," *Journal of the Society for Textual Reasoning* (online) 3, no. 1 (2004). I present these texts again here in altered form with permission from the publishers.

Generous sabbatical support was provided this project by Syracuse University, the Center for Advanced Judaic Studies, and the Memorial Foundation for Jewish Culture and the National Foundation for Jewish Culture's Gantz-Zahler Fund for Non-Fiction Publishing. Support for various subventions and other publication costs relating to the acquisition of images and rights to these images was provided with equal generosity by the Arts and Sciences Faculty Subvention Fund of Syracuse University, Department of Religion and Program of Judaic Studies.

I am happy to acknowledge kind guidance from friends and colleagues: Leora Batnitzky, Avi Bernstein-Nahar, Kalman Bland, Daniel Breslauer, Charles Delheim, Arnold Eisen, Yaron Elcott-Milgrom, Ken Frieden, Barbara Galli, Robert Gibbs, Peter Eli Gordon, Gail Hamner, Leah Hochman, James Hyman, Marion Kant, Gregory Kaplan, Martin Kavka, Steven Kepnes, Barbara Kirschenblatt-Gimblett, Ken Koltun-Fromm, Greg Lambert, Amy Lang, Laura Levitt, Nancy Levene, Shaul Magid, Paul Mendes-Flohr, David Meyers, David and Patricia Miller, Peter Ochs, Gesine Palmer, Einat Ramon, Randi Rashkover, Norbert Samuelson, Susan Shapiro, Alan Thomas, James Watts, Charles Winquist (z"l), Elliot Wolfson, Edith and Michael Wyschogrod, Michael Zank, Carol Zemel, and Steven Zipperstein. Norris Pope at Stanford University Press provided expert editorial guidance, while Paul Morris and Deborah Pratt skillfully tracked and handled the images that appear in this book. Jessica Nathans first pointed me toward Bauhaus architecture (from where I made my way to Klee and Kandinsky). Warmest thoughts to Margaret and Joseph Karalis (z"l), who have always displayed keen interest in me and in this project; to my mother, Marilyn, who introduced me to the world of rare book collectors and fine arts Judaica; to my father, Sheldon, who made everything possible; always to Meg, with whom I share everything; and now to Joe.

Abbreviations

Throughout the text, I use parenthetical notes to indicate primary sources. I have generally relied upon extant translations. Where the translation has been altered, or emphases not present in the original have been added, this is indicated.

ABH   Martin Buber, *A Believing Humanism*, trans. Maurice S. Friedman (New York: Simon & Schuster, 1967)

AF   Martin Buber, "Autobiographical Fragments," in *The Philosophy of Martin Buber*, ed. Paul Arthur Schilpp and Maurice S. Friedman (La Salle, Ill.: Open Court, 1967)

ANG   Martin Buber, *Alte und neue Gemeinschaft*: *An Unpublished Buber Manuscript*, ed. Paul Mendes-Flohr and Bernard Susser, *AJS Review*, no. 1 (1976): 41–56

B   Martin Buber, *Briefwechsel aus sieben Jahrzehnten,* 3 vols. (Heidelberg: L. Schneider, 1972–75)

BMM   Martin Buber, *Between Man and Man* (New York: Collier Books, 1965)

BRA   *The Blaue Reiter Almanac*, ed. Wassily Kandinsky and Franz Marc (New York: Da Capo Press, 1974)

BT   Franz Rosenzweig, *Der Mensch und sein Werk: Gesammelte Schriften*, vol. 1: *Briefe und Tagebücher* (The Hague: Martinus Nijhoff, 1976)

CW   Franz Rosenzweig, *Cultural Writings of Franz Rosenzweig*, ed. and trans. Barbara E. Galli (Syracuse, N.Y.: Syracuse University Press, 2000)

CWA   Wassily Kandinsky, *Complete Writings on Art*, ed. Kenneth C. Lindsay and Peter Vergo (New York: Da Capo Press, 1994)

DJSJ   Martin Buber, *Der Jude und sein Judentum: Gesammelte Aufsätze und Reden* (Gerlingen: Lambert Schneider, 1993)

Dn   Martin Buber, *Daniel: Dialogues on Realization*, trans. Maurice S. Friedman (New York: Holt, Rinehart & Winston, 1964)

DPK   Paul Klee, *The Diaries of Paul Klee, 1898–1918* (Berkeley: University of California Press, 1964)

EG   Martin Buber, *Eclipse of God* (New York: Harper, 1952)

EW   Leo Strauss, *Leo Strauss: The Early Writings (1921–1932)*, ed. and trans. Michael Zank (Albany: State University of New York Press, 2002)

FB   Martin Buber, *The First Buber: Youthful Zionist Writings of Martin Buber*, ed. and trans. Gilya G. Schmidt (Syracuse, N.Y.: Syracuse University Press, 1999)

FR   Franz Rosenzweig, *Franz Rosenzweig: Life and Work*, ed. Nahum N. Glatzer (New York: Schocken Books, 1961)

GB   Franz Rosenzweig, *Die "Gritli"-Briefe: Briefe an Margrit Rosenstock-Huessy*, ed. Inken Rühle and Reinhold Meyer (Tübingen: Bilam, 2002)

GMW   Franz Rosenzweig, *God, Man, and the World: Lectures and Essays*, ed. and trans. Barbara Galli (Syracuse, N.Y.: Syracuse University Press, 1998)

GS3   Franz Rosenzweig, *Der Mensch und sein Werk: Gesammelte Schriften*, vol. 3: *Zweistromland: Kleinere Schriften zu Glauben und Denken* (The Hague: Martinus Nijhoff, 1984)

H   Barbara Ellen Galli, *Franz Rosenzweig and Jehuda Halevy: Translating, Translations, and Translators* (McGill-Queen's University Press, 1995)

HMM   Martin Buber, *Hasidism and Modern Man*, ed. and trans. Maurice S. Friedman (New York: Harper Torchbooks, 1958)

IT   Martin Buber, *I and Thou*, trans. Walter Kaufmann (New York: Scribner, 1970)

IW   Martin Buber, *Israel and the World: Essay in a Time of Crisis* (New York: Schocken Books, 1948)

JL   Franz Rosenzweig, *On Jewish Learning*, ed. Nahum N. Glatzer (New York: Schocken Books, 1955)

JP   Leo Strauss, *Jewish Philosophy and the Crisis of Modernity: Essays and Lectures in Modern Jewish Thought*, ed. Kenneth Hart Green (Albany: State University of New York Press, 1997)

KM   Martin Buber, *The Knowledge of Man: Selected Essays*, ed. Maurice S. Friedman, trans. Maurice S. Friedman and Ronald Gregor Smith (New York: Harper Torchbooks, 1965)

L   Martin Buber, "Die Losung," *Der Jude*, 1916

LBS   Martin Buber, *The Legend of the Baal-Shem*, trans. Maurice S. Friedman (Princeton: Princeton University Press, 1955)

LD   Oskar Schlemmer, *The Letters and Diaries of Oskar Schlemmer*, ed. Tut Schlemmer, trans. Krishma Winston (Evanston, Ill.: Northwestern University Press, 1972)

LMB   Martin Buber, *The Letters of Martin Buber*, ed. Nahum N. Glatzer and Paul Mendes-Flohr, trans. Richard and Clara Winston and Harry Zohn (New York: Schocken Books, 1991)

LTP   Martin Buber, *Land of Two Peoples: Martin Buber on Jews and Arabs*, ed. Paul Mendes-Flohr (Oxford: Oxford University Press, 1983)

M   Martin Buber, *Moses: The Revelation and The Covenant* (New York: Harper Torchbooks, 1958)

MA   Paul Klee, *On Modern Art* (London: Faber & Faber, 1949)

MO   Siegfried Kracauer, *The Mass Ornament: Weimar Essays* (Cambridge, Mass.: Harvard University Press, 1995)

N   Paul Klee, *Notebooks*, ed. Jürg Spiller; vol. 1: *The Thinking Eye*, trans. Ralph Manheim; vol. 2: *The Nature of Nature*, trans. Heinz Norden (New York: George Wittenborn, 1961, 1973)

NT   Franz Rosenzweig, *Franz Rosenzweig's "The New Thinking,"* ed. and trans. Alan Udof and Barbara E. Galli (Syracuse, N.Y.: Syracuse University Press, 1999)

OJ   Martin Buber, *On Judaism*, ed. Nahum N. Glatzer (New York: Schocken Books, 1967)

OMH   Martin Buber, *Origin and Meaning of Hasidism*, ed. and trans. Maurice S. Friedman (New York: Harper Torchbooks, 1960)

P   Martin Buber, "Pharisaism," in *The Jew: Essays from Martin Buber's Journal Der Jude, 1916–1928*, ed. Arthur A. Cohen (University, Ala.: University of Alabama Press, 1980)

PIU   Martin Buber, *Paths in Utopia* (Syracuse, N.Y.: Syracuse University Press, 1996)

PL   Leo Strauss, *Philosophy and Law* (Albany: State University of New York Press, 1995)

PW   Martin Buber, *Pointing the Way*, trans. and ed. Maurice S. Friedman (New York: Harper & Row, 1957)

S   Franz Marc, *Schriften*, ed. Klaus Lankheit (Cologne: DuMont, 1978)

SR   Franz Rosenzweig, *The Star of Redemption*, trans. William W. Hallo (Notre Dame, Ind.: Notre Dame Press, 1971)

ST   Martin Buber and Franz Rosenzweig, *Scripture and Translation*, trans. Lawrence Rosenwald and Everett Fox (Bloomington: Indiana University Press, 1994)

TRN   Martin Buber, *The Tales of Rabbi Nahman*, trans. Maurice S. Friedman (New York: Horizon Press, 1956)

USH   Franz Rosenzweig, *Understanding the Sick and Healthy*, ed. Nahum N. Glatzer (New York: Noonday Press, 1954)

VFW   Martin Buber, "Vorbemerkung über Franz Werfel," *Der Jude*, 1917–18

Z   Martin Buber, "Zwischenmenschliche," in Paul Mendes-Flohr, *From Mysticism to Dialogue: Martin Buber's Transformation of German Social Thought* (Detroit: Wayne State Press, 1989)

Figure 1. Paul Klee, *Villa R* (1919).
Oil on cardboard. Kunstmuseum, Basel. Photo Credit: Nimatallah/
Art Resource, New York. © 2005 Artists Rights Society (ARS),
New York/VG Bild-Kunst, Bonn.

Preface: Revelation and the Spiritual in Art

The figure of revelation sits at the overlap between aesthetics-art and religion, a space explored in these pages from the perspective of Judaism by setting the modern Jewish philosophy of Martin Buber and Franz Rosenzweig alongside its immediate visual environment in early German modernism, especially German expressionism. No direct influence can be claimed for this conversation between modern Jewish thought and "the spiritual in art" articulated in the art and aesthetic theories of Wassily Kandinsky, Paul Klee, and Franz Marc. The relationship builds upon more subtle transpositions. It is based not upon common theological or aesthetic contents, but rather upon intersecting discourses of form-creation, sheer presence, lyric pathos, rhythmic repetition, open spatial dynamism, and erotic pulse. Art and aesthetics will cast religion in a new, unfamiliar light, teasing its thought away from an exclusive preoccupation with epistemology and ethics by underscoring the shape of revelation in physical sensation and the visual imagination. At the same time, philosophical theology provides historical and theoretical contexts with which to entertain and critically assess claims made about the "spiritual" dimension of art and artistic creation.

The appearance of art in this philosophical reconstruction does not conform to its usual usage in the field of art history. Most notably, heavy use has been made of the Rosetta stone provided by Kandinsky's, Klee's, and Marc's voluminous theoretical writings. I have turned to visual material and to verbal cues offered by these texts and by art historians, not to illustrate, but to articulate a set of philosophical points about the composition of religion and revelation that could perhaps not be made by discursive means alone. As Walter Benjamin remarks in

The Origin of the German Tragic Drama, art unlocks the "methodological element in philosophical projects [that] is not simply part of their didactic mechanism," even as theory triggers the creation of new art.[1] Kandinsky, Klee, and Marc used paint to create plastic works that resonate with the language of spirit, while Buber and Rosenzweig sought to conjure an image of revelation through words marked by strong visual presence. While art is the first order of art, and no revelation will add to the study of a picture's visual shape or material basis, theoretical claims and counterclaims made by artists and critics about the spiritual in art belong to a worldview steeped in philosophy and religion.[2]

Without overt religious reference, Klee's *Villa R* (1919) (fig. 1) reveals no God, no new angel with which to plumb the relationship between religion and art. In Klee's work, the affinity between the one and the other is formal and coy. Nature is no longer natural. Objects are no longer three-dimensional. The architectural structure is a construct composed of squares, rectangles, triangles, and crosslike sections. The large green "R" protrudes up against the flattened architectural space beneath a theatrically cast, moonlit mountain scene. To quote the artist's own "Creative Credo" (1920), the invisible has been made visible. Impossible to read on its own, the letter "R" is at once audible and inaudible. Its uncanny appearance disrupts the realistic perspectival depth that the red path leading into the distance might otherwise indicate. In *Villa R*, the intersection between art and religion does not depend upon extraneous theological contents external to the picture. It rests instead *within* the relationship between two disparate dimensions: organic and geometric, real and theatrically make-believe, inhuman and human, the visible landscape and the invisible presence of language. By combining physical and nonphysical elements, image and word, Klee's pictorial space provides a visual cue without religious content with which to look at religion.[3]

Like religion, the spiritual in art was a topos all but ignored by the great American masters of post–World War II high modernist art criticism. In the strict formalism of Clement Greenberg, all extraneous content is bracketed in order to highlight a painting's formal definition. In the humanism of Meyer Schapiro, the critic attends to the truest feeling and freedom of the artist. Art is thus reduced to its most objective or to its most subjective component. Complaints against

formalism and humanism in poststructuralist and postmodern theory
are by now common coin in academic circles. Formalism is rejected
because its closed-in conception of art excludes social and other extra-
aesthetic forces at work in art, whereas humanism is rejected because
it limits the meaning of a work by understanding it solely in terms of
authorial intent and individual expression. In the immediate postwar
environment, it was easy to believe that religion was no longer relevant
to culture. Today, religion is no longer irrelevant, but its exercise is no
less odious. Indeed, the spiritual in art continues to meet with deep
mistrust in those circles devoted to the practice, study, and sale of art,
aggravated in no small part by American culture wars. Even the most
open interest in religious content meets up with preconceived ideas that
religion demands dogmatic certainty and literal belief. Most art critics
and art historians do not understand that this type of religion, a caricature of pious faith, cannot account for more canny and cosmopolitan
forms of religious expression. Like the very many conservative religionists with whom they are often at odds, art critics and art historians fail
to grasp that religion at its best is already irreligious.[4]

A more basic trust than pious faith is the central philosophical problematic at the intersection between religion and art—the trust that leads
one to assert that a word or an image can manifest God's presence, a
piece of the Infinite, the Absolute, the call of Being, the face of the
Other, and so on. This trust animated the opposition of Johann Georg
Hamann (1730–88) and Johann Gottfried Herder (1744–1803), and of
the early romantics and Hegel in the nineteenth century and Heideggerian poetics and the Levinasian ethical gesture in the twentieth, to
Enlightenment philosophy. Against this trust, reason skeptically marks
out its own limits, insisting that the physical status of art objects and
speech acts reveals purely material and formal properties. Reason, however, will sometime let imagination loose. The position reflected in this
study brings a hermeneutic of suspicion and a hermeneutic of charity
to highly charged claims regarding the relationship between aesthetic
form and spiritual reality that drove German Jewish thought and the
aesthetics of German expressionism in the early twentieth century.

While Klee's painting and his theoretical writings about painting
make no dogmatic assertion about religion and religious belief, they already ask too much philosophically. The discourse of revelation and the

spiritual in art, no matter how pared-down, intensifies the philosophical tension between objects and concepts broached in Kant's *Critique
of Pure Reason*. "Without sensibility," Kant writes, "no object would
be given to us, without understanding no object would be thought.
Thoughts without content are empty, intuitions without concepts are
blind."[5] In this ambiguous circularity, sense perception requires the or-
ganizing capacity of concepts, categories, and ideas that shape it into
objects of possible human experience. Otherwise the subject cannot
see. But the clarity to apprehend any object of possible experience relies
upon a dim sense-impression without which thought is vacuous. A cu-
rious combination of sight and sound, divine appearance and the spiritual in art stand inside and outside all such categories and intuition.
The claims made about them are enhanced by the competing rigors of
critical reason, everyday ethics, and the glory of sensation.

Aesthetics, Religion, and the Spiritual in Art

Epistemologically, aesthetics marks out an important midpoint of theoretical consciousness between the rarified study of art and beauty, on the
one hand, and mere sense impression and gross sensuality, on the other
hand. Alexander Baumgarten (1714–62), who coined the term, defined it
as "the science of perception." By this he meant the ordering of jumbled
representations into sensible patterns that are neither "obscure" nor
"distinct." As one critic remarks in his reading of Baumgarten, aesthetics lacks the rigor of scientific logic and the confused nature of unfiltered
sense perception. A middle figure, it hovers between the rational and
the sensual, the ideal and the real.[6] In their relation to the imagination,
aesthetics and art thus share the zone typically occupied by religion,
revelation, miracle, and wonder. "We agree with Descartes, who regards
wonder as 'a sudden seizure of the soul, in that it is lifted into a rapt
consideration of objects which seem to it rare and extraordinary,'"
Baumgarten wrote. "[I]n the extraordinary we sense, rather than
implicitly assert, a relation to the inconceivable."[7]

I treat "aesthetic" and "art" here as two correlated terms, which
both bear on religion. The former term refers to the intentional act
that sustains contemplation of a sense impression, including art and the

impromptu appearance of that which is not art. The more one looks to the sensual constitution of any object or group of objects (a painting by Matisse, a photograph from 9/11), and the longer that look endures, the more aesthetic the attention. "Art," on the other hand, is more limited in scope. It reflects the physical form of compressed sensation. In the artwork, Buber saw a "superformation," an altered state under which the "whole optical, the whole acoustical field becomes refashioned ever anew" (*KM*, 162, 164). No matter how large the object or fleeting its presence, it maintains a condensed character in relation to the cosmos at large and to history. Art works against the ad hoc and diffuse conditions of everyday sensation, preserving a difference between art and life that radical practitioners of art seek to obliterate by means of new, unfamiliar modes of artifice. Insofar as sustained attention to sensation enters into it, religion is aesthetic without being art; yet the more religion relies upon the intentional creation of specialized spatial environments, sonic patterns, and literary sign systems, the more it resembles art in its material makeup.

Form is the indispensable link between religion and art. In Mark Taylor's keen demonstration, the word "figure" is both a noun and a verb. Qua noun, it relates to "form, shape; an embodied (human) form; a person considered with regard to visible form or appearance; the image, likeness, or representation of something material or immaterial; an arrangement of lines or other markings." Qua verb, to figure is "to adorn or mark with figures; to embellish or ornament with a design or pattern."[8] As such, ideal contents and mental assertions—beliefs about gods and God—do not exhaust religion. Religion is the sensate shape of revelation. A composition of "natural" and "supranatural" elements, religion constitutes the physically mundane place between a daemon and its people around mediating images, texts, and acts. As a composition, religion is neither static nor dynamic. The graphic and verbal images at play across the surface of its system grow more or less stable at any one geographical place and historical moment. Continually disfigured and reconfigured by collective and individual actors in response to local conditions, they form an overlap between intersecting planes, between visible and invisible bodies.

"The spiritual in art" stands in close association with "religiosity" or "spirituality"—religion without religion, without religious content or religious objects. For Kandinsky, the spiritual in art stands for that "possibility of seeing in the object . . . something less physical than the object itself, which in an age of realism one sought merely to represent 'as it is,' with 'no nonsense.'" Refusing to overdraw the difference between the natural and the supranatural, he wondered: "Is it not possible that the distinctions we draw between matter and spirit are merely degrees of matter or spirit? Thought . . . is matter too, but a kind of matter that only fine and not coarse senses can perceive. Is spirit that which the physical hand cannot touch? . . . [It] is sufficient if one avoids drawing over-sharp distinctions" (*CWA*, 138). Bound up with love and death, the spiritual in art is an invisible filament in aesthetic sensation and artistic formation, cued by gold leaf and extended notes, empty volumes, and the interval between noise and silence. Tending toward the immaterial, it points art past its own purely physical dimension. Not exhausted by strictly formal criteria of material and method, it occupies that opaque and vulnerable joint where art inevitably joins up with the in-credible language and literature of cult and revelation.

There are no religious and spiritual phenomena apart from aesthetic sensation (sight, sound, taste, smell, and touch) and aesthetic creation (architecture, music, poetry, painting) at their base. Religious environments and the experience they make possible build upon a mass of material stuff: wooden and metal objects, stories and sound, organized and reorganized by acts of custom and law. Empirically, the relationship between aesthetics and religion is the more or less self-evident subject of art history and the history of religions. At a second order of analysis, the relationship between aesthetic form and spiritual reality depends upon the presupposition that the presence of a god or God or spiritual presence is made manifest to human consciousness through sensual media, especially visual and aural form. Such theoretically fraught claims and the counterclaims made against them are of unique concern to theological speculation and philosophical analysis insofar as the spiritual in art purports to relay human consciousness past the limits of reason into the uncertain terrain of aesthetic judgment and religious intuition.

The acts of self-conscious, crude transfer all too commonly made at this juncture between religion and art are the epitome of kitsch—defined by Clement Greenberg in his seminal 1939 essay "Avant-Garde and Kitsch" as mechanical, formulaic, ersatz culture, as vicarious experience and faked sensation.[9] In many twentieth-century "theologies of culture," no sign or style, no matter how secular, is made to lack spiritual significance. With no regard to the material difference between religion and the practice of art, the latter is pressed into an obnoxious, pre-given religious point of reference.[10] The theology of culture seems to forget that an analogy depends upon the degree to which one thing and its other are both like and unlike. While no fixed border marks the difference between religion and art, a floating line continues to separate them. This line preserves for both figures a measure of autonomy, not the fiction of absolute autonomy, but rather a provisional distance without which there is no real tension or relationship. Art and religion are *virtually* identical in their appeal to the power of the imagination and to the creation of images. But the difference that remains between them resists easy proclivities to invest every human expression with spiritual significance or to see art in everything and everything as art. Analytically, religion *is* not art and art *is* not religion, even as they indelibly stain each other in the historical culture of their production.

Image/Word

Dividing the arts according to a strict spatiotemporal axis, Gotthold Ephraim Lessing (1729–81) was the first modern theorist who sought to free one art from another—in his case, to free poetic expression from plastic art. The effort remained fundamentally insecure. Lessing saw something ghastly in painting. Unable to anticipate nonmimetic painting, he retained a deep uncertainty about the visual arts, which, he thought, can only freeze suffering for all perpetuity into a repulsive, static image. Lessing's model was the classical image of the ill-fated Laocoön and his two sons crushed in the coils of three fearsome sea serpents before the gates of Troy. Unlike the pathos-laden account by Sophocles, the sculpture did not convey to Lessing the howling scream of suffering. In this strange interpretation of a truly pathetic plastic figure, the critic found only stoic heroism and serene soul. Lessing's view of the model was clearly made to fit its interpretation. Fixed in time, the danger posed by the plastic image is that it can never move past the instance of disfiguration. But Lessing also belittled the plastic arts. With no relation to the invisible, they reduce the superhuman to human size, the gods to godlike people. They limit perception to the visible, to beauty and to the body. And even here, painting depends upon inert physical appearance, not character and charm, defined by the author as beauty in motion.[11]

In his recoil from any instantiation of unnatural suddenness and fleeting presence, Lessing anticipated the power ascribed to revelation and to the image in twentieth-century religious thought and German expressionism. The spatial arts, Lessing ruled, "should express nothing essentially transitory. All phenomena, whose nature it is suddenly to break out and as suddenly to disappear, which can remain as they are but for a moment; all such phenomena, whether agreeable or otherwise, acquire through the perpetuity conferred upon them by art such an unnatural impression . . . till the whole subject at least wearies or disgusts us."[12] Inverting the canons of neoclassical taste, the face of God in German expressionism is rendered up-close and visible, the prophet's mouth is rent asunder, the earth shudders and cities topple. Everything screams or falls silent all at once. The poet Georg Heym envied painters. "Why have the heavens refused me the talent for drawing?" he complained. "Images torment me as never a painter before me." Heym wanted in poetry that optical effect by which images appear next to and within each other. Standing Lessing's axiological schema upside down, expressionism took to things simultaneously, one thing next to the other (*nebeneinander*), not one thing following the other (*nacheinander*) in narrative sequence.[13]

The dialogue in twentieth-century modernism between verbal and graphic signs has jumbled once and for all Lessing's classification of the arts into a neat division, with enormous consequences for religious discourse. As W. J. T. Mitchell has argued, the difference separating poetry and painting does not fall into strict binaries between time/space, invisibility/visibility, or culture/nature. Visual sensation is no more naturally self-evident, no less conventionally mediated than poetic form—and no less committed to the invisible. The relation between verbal and graphic image is symbiotic. From Plato's cave to Freud's interpretation of dreams, the verbal conventions provided by narrative and theory are required to create, identify, and make sense of visual images; just as visual cues are indispensable to the work of thought. This includes the language of spirit, religious narrative, theory, and thought. Mitchell's call for a "renewed respect for the eloquence of images and . . . a renewed faith in the perspicuousness of language" supports the contention that religious truth, goodness, and beauty cannot be apprehended apart from the combination of graphic and verbal images.[14]

The impact of such combinations on visual experience is no less pronounced. The art historian Wendy Steiner has traced the radical division between image and word back to the early Renaissance, when painters abandoned the narrative sequence conveyed by multi-episodic picture planes. Single-point perspective and the illusion of pictorial depth were used to mimic the optical image organized by the eye at any single moment of apprehension. It was the reintroduction of language into cubist painting that finally upended the mimetic tradition in painting. Rainer Crone and Joseph Leo Koerner have advanced similar arguments to interpret Klee's work. In *Villa R*, the temporal and invisible form of language enters into silent pictorial space. Like all writing, the letter "R" is both a verbal and a graphic mark, a piece of linguistic code that clearly does not belong to the landscape's order and dimension. Its presence there, the presence of language in painting conveys the point that there is no relation to the visible world apart from the intrusive verbal bit with which someone has already given it shape. We begin to see in painting that which is not given to the optical eye in nature.[15]

Jewish (?) (!)

The usual theoretical statements about art and aniconism in Judaism, the original place of revelation in Western religion, most often privilege word over image in the very manner faulted by Mitchell. As polemically expressed by the neo-Kantian Hermann Cohen (1842–1918) in *Religion der Vernunft aus den Quellen des Judentums* (*Religion of Reason, out of the Sources of Judaism*), plastic art constitutes nothing less than "image worship." "*[I]t is the proof of the true God that there can be no image of Him*. He can never be known through a likeness, but simply and solely as archetype, as archetypal thought, as archetypal being."[16] It does not matter if idolaters worship the phenomena represented by the image, not the image itself, since monotheism rejects the worship of any object or phenomenal power. God's uniqueness lies in the divine ideality outstripping every real thing, process, and mimetic art. Plastic art cannot even capture the human figure, much less God, who admits of no image. The ideal art of monotheism is the lyric poetry of the psalms. It "makes shame the last recourse for the idol worshipper." Poetry couples God and man into a lively connection, whereas plastic art restricts itself poorly to one or the other in fixed isolation.[17]

The shame cast on visual art belongs more to Plato and Lessing, to the tradition of Greek and German idealism, and to fin de siècle aesthetic canons than to any biblical imperative per se. For Cohen, art was the mimetic representation of visual objects drawn from nature. In the *Ästhetik des reinen Gefühls* (Aesthetic of Pure Feeling) (1912), he championed impressionism, the avant-garde of his own early years, as the optical art par excellence. Submerging individual objects in the limpid succession of everyday phenomena, light becomes its own autonomous object, an optic that awakens human persons to their true and natural humanity.[18] To Cohen, impressionism was the highest form of art in the history of Western culture but went no further than this purest object available to the human eye. This is the art-historical context of Cohen's *Religion of Reason*, posthumously published in 1919. Its conception of Judaism, insofar as that conception rests on a critique of art and the rejection of image worship, hangs precariously upon the balance of outmoded aesthetic discourse about representation, which a crop of young artists had already begun to supplant. In expressionism, color is no longer natural. The green letter in *Villa R* is spiritual and free from objects, even from matter as immaterial as light's motley play upon physical surfaces.

Standing on weak art-historical and hermeneutical feet, such philosophical pieties cannot account for the flora, fauna, and human images that grace the ancient synagogue art at Beit Alpha, Sepporis, and Dura-Europos, medieval, renaissance, and baroque Haggadah illustration, and the decoration of eastern European gravestones and synagogues. Apart from the representation of God and angels and outside the context of worship, there is no *Bilderverbot*, no prohibition of images. While the second commandment states, "You shall not make for yourself a sculptured image, or any likeness of what is in the heavens above, or on the earth below, or in the waters under the earth," it then adds, "You shall not bow down to them or serve them" (Exod. 20:4–5). One can see with the art historian Moshe Barasch that the first verse entails a comprehensive restriction banning *all* figures only in isolation. The second verse limits the restriction. Viewed as a whole, perhaps the text bans only *the worship* of figurative images. Cohen myopically supported the comprehensive curb without art-historical or text-critical support.[19]

Writing at mid-century after the triumph of modernism, a more discerning Steven Schwarzschild allows plastic art into Judaism; although once again, word trumps image in order to contrive a uniquely Jewish approach to visual art. Schwarzschild cites the *Shulkhan ʿArukh* to explain that Jewish law permits nonmimetic plastic expression. According to a gloss by Moses Isserles (1520–72), "There are those who hold that images of man or a dragon are not prohibited unless they are complete with all their limbs, but the shape of a head by itself or a body without a head is in no wise forbidden." Schwarzschild relates this opinion back to the rationalism of Moses Maimonides, who rejected any attempt to reduce the human soul, God's very image, to an appearance. As Schwarzschild puts it, "To represent physical appearance as the whole person is, therefore, a misrepresentation. The converse is also true: a 'misrepresentation' will in fact be a true depiction. . . . To represent the empirical as *tout court* is, therefore, also to misrepresent God."[20]

Deference to the authority of Jewish law notwithstanding, this stilted approach to art trips up on German philosophical idealism. Schwarzschild continues to patrol the anxious boundary separating art from reality, the ideal from the empirical. He wants to avoid that instance in which two objects, the original and its artistic reproduction, appear exactly identical. According to Schwarzschild, art is no longer art when the artwork neither adds to nor detracts from the real world. "What in truth is the difference between a pop art duplicate . . . of a soup can and the original on a display shelf? Hegel was surely right when he held that whenever and wherever the idea is believed to have become identical with the real, the 'death of art' has occurred."[21] Couched in the idealist critique of empirical reality and in a modernism already at war with postmodernism, Schwarzschild's discussion of the *Shulkhan ʿArukh* proudly concludes, "We have thus deduced two of the chief principles of twentieth-century modern art—abstraction and distortion."[22] Leaving copy realism far behind, abstract art nihilates physical semblance, whereas distortion detracts from and adds to it.

Modern art and Judaism are thereby forced to confirm each other on the basis of philosophical constructs regarding the fixed difference between appearance, representation, and reality. Mostly, the entire exercise remains fundamentally arbitrary, as seen by Schwarzschild's embrace of Rembrandt, El Greco, and Modigliani, while excluding classical Greek art, its Renaissance revival, French pointillism, and American pop art. The author seems to think that the shadows and light casting human figures in Rembrandt's paintings obviate their realistic character, while Warhol's soup cans violate the fragile boundary between real and ideal. Spurious at best, such judgment reflects a rearguard modernism, not halakhic principle. Kandinsky is far less dogmatic. "Approaching it in one way," he writes, "I see no essential difference between a line one calls 'abstract' and a fish. But an essential likeness." Line and fish are "living beings," each with latent capacities. A "miracle," these capacities are made manifest and radiant by the environment of their composition. And this despite the equally essential difference that a fish "can swim, eat, and be eaten" (*CWA*, 774–75).

Frozen by theoretical constructs set at particular points in the history of style, Cohen and Schwarzschild have no eye for art as it takes shape as an emerging practice. The following story is a case in point. In 1860, Moritz Lazarus and Zecharias Fraenkel argued about a memorial statue in New Orleans for the philanthropist Judah Touro. According to the more religiously conservative Fraenkel, it was first necessary to disfigure the sculpture in order to conform to Jewish law. He was, it seems, unconcerned by bourgeois canons of refined beauty. Comparing this to Picasso, Schwarzschild claims Fraenkel for the mid-twentieth century, saying, "The 'chaste Athena' which Lazarus admired would be regarded as embarrassingly maudlin today."[23] Yet his own hysterical response to pop art proves no less so. Having brought Jackie, Marilyn, and other "chaste Athenas" back into vogue, pop art plays with the supermediated difference between real and fake, not the one between real and ideal. Beholden to regnant styles just as they were about to go out of fashion, Schwarzschild and Cohen overlook that which is new in art or meet it with extreme hostility. The reflex stilts their understanding, not just of art and art history, but also of Judaism in its classical and philosophical expression.

Unable to strip God's revelation from human sensation, the authors of the Hebrew Bible bring them to bear upon each other. In this religious imaginary, the divine presence descends in thunder, lightning, and thick cloud (Exod. 19). Moses later warns the people: "And the Lord spoke to you out of the midst of the fire; you heard the voice of words, but you saw no form; only a voice. . . . Take you therefore good heed unto yourselves, for you saw no manner of form on the day that the Lord spoke unto you in Horeb out of the midst of the fire" (Deut. 4:12, 15). The people make out no visible form; all they saw was thundering (Exod. 20:15). God told Moses, "For men shall not see me and live" (Exod. 33:20). But Moses, Aaron, and the elders "saw the God of Israel; there was under his feet the like of a paved work of sapphire stone, and the like of the very heaven for clearness" (Exod. 24:9–10). And the prophet Isaiah is said to have said, "I saw *YHWH* sitting on a throne, high and lifted up" (Isa. 6:1). Regarding the signal difference between Isaiah and Moses, the rabbis explain: "'I saw *YHWH*' [is to be understood] in accordance with what was taught: All the prophets looked into a dim glass, but Moses looked through a clear glass" (Yevamot 49b).

Already showing discomfort with the gross anthropomorphism found in Scripture, the thought behind this rabbinic utterance draws attention away from the content of revelation toward the glassy form of an optic medium. With his own attention to the Hebrew *tzelem*, Mitchell observes how the word "image" refers most broadly to a rough idea of likeness, resemblance, and similitude, not to the precise identity feared by Schwarzschild. Art trades in *graphic images* (pictures, statues, and design) whereas literature employs *verbal images* (metaphors and descriptions). *Perceptual images* include sense data and appearances, while *mental* images embrace dreams, memories, ideas, and fantasmata. Mirrors and projections provide refracted *optical images*.[24] In this broader light, Jewish thought and culture extend across a wide range of visual bodies and objects, optical stimuli, and ideas about them. In contrast, God's image in Judaism demands a chaster visual etiquette. The intimate visual appearances of the divine presence referred to by Jewish writers are perceptual and mental, never graphic and public. They are also time-sensitive. The prophet, sage, and mystic claim to see God, but the reader never sees what they saw.

Attempts to prioritize word over image deaden both. Not one before the other, the value of the one and the value of the other sit next to each other. This principle of co-priority identifies a system of simultaneity precluding any single root of knowledge or source of value. Any asymmetry elevating one over the other is at most pragmatic, since each one subsists at the same instant, despite the temporal interlude it takes to think one after the other. The give-and-take between image and word elides a priori philosophical and theological principles and privilege, pseudo-halakhic warrants and formalist aesthetics. Just as language in the picture-frame provides broader theoretical rubrics with which to interpret visual material, religion brings to art a dimension of linguistic content that is not restricted to optical experience. For their part, art and aesthetic form open religion further out into the world of sense and sensation, into the spatial and temporal orders shared with other people, into what Kant called the "purposive purposelessness" of a system whose sole true purpose is nothing more than prolonged attention to the pleasure of its own shape. From this point of departure, the shape of revelation and its ethos ride upon "the science of perception."

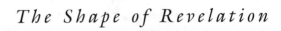

The Shape of Revelation

Figure 2. Wassily Kandinsky, *Lyrically* (1911).
In the book *Klänge* (Munich: R. Piper, 1913). Color woodcut on cream-
laid Holland Van Gelder paper. 145 x 217 mm. Fine Arts Museums of San
Francisco, gift of the Reva and David Logan Foundation, 1998. 40.60.5.

Introduction

In the epigraph to Franz Rosenzweig's *The Star of Redemption*, a verse from Psalm 45, an imperative voice tells a king to "ride in the cause of truth" (*rehav al devar emet*), as if toward a goal external to him. Better yet, "ride upon the cause of truth." Or perhaps even, "ride upon the word of truth." Truth is the vehicle upon which the rider already sits. His "tongue the pen of an expert scribe," the psalter calls to his heart "astir with gracious words." He declares himself to his king: "You are fairer than all men, your speech is endowed with grace. . . . Gird your sword upon your thigh, O hero, in your splendor and glory; and in your glory win success; ride upon the word of truth and meekness and right and let your right hand lead you to awesome deeds." A thundering passage into twentieth-century religious thought, the psalm embeds truth in a discourse of poetic beauty, declaratory love, miracle and righteousness. In the tempo of Kandinsky's *Lyrically* (1911) (fig. 2), horse and rider merge into a unified movement of black line and color forms composed of greens, blues, yellows, and blood red. While the picture works in tandem across its leftward plunge, each color remains distinct. The colors ride upon the same truth, the spiritual semblance of material reality as it begins to discombobulate.

The horse and rider in Rosenzweig and Kandinsky blend truth, goodness, and beauty into a permanent sensual source. German expressionism and German Jewish thought were simultaneously metaphysical and anti-metaphysical. Kandinsky invokes "spirit" through paint's physical medium. For Buber and Rosenzweig, an acosmic God has no reality apart from sensual form. God and that which belongs to spirit remain fundamentally other (heteronomous) to world and to "man." In this, they are meta-physical. And yet anti-metaphysical— God's presence and the spiritual in art lie at no ideal end point or "good

I

beyond being." They are already incorporated into the wholeness of being, constituting the vehicle upon which the rider already sits. Revelation and the spiritual in art are irreducibly colored by everyday life and physical sensation. We catch Kandinsky (and with him Buber and Rosenzweig) at that point at which reference and propositional content begin to dissolve. We can still see horse and rider, the face of God, but not for long. Soon there will be nothing left, just the impression left behind by the pure sound of color and linguistic tempo.

The attention that I want to call to the affinity between early twentieth-century German Jewish philosophy and the history of early German modernism is meant to accomplish two ends. It brings new philosophical perspectives with which to reframe modern religious thought and the problem of metaphysics. Art and aesthetic theory pull Jewish philosophy away from a simple focus on God, text, and community by recasting it as "form," "presence," "pathos," time," "space" and "eros." Aesthetics provides the live wire that to this day animates the modern Judaism reflected in the Buber-Rosenzweig oeuvre. I have also found that attention to art and style heightens the sense of temporal passage between their time and our own. Buber's first publications began to appear a century ago. The historical gap separating us from him and Rosenzweig is as long as the gap in time separating them from the early German romantics. Like Kandinsky's lyrical rider, their texts are stuck in a yawning historical chasm from which they continue to stimulate a terrific sense of movement. Like Blue Rider German expressionism, Buber and Rosenzweig are no longer contemporary. If their work survives the passage from Germany to the United States and Israel, from modernism to postmodernism, from expressionism to neoexpressionism, it will have done so transformed by new hermeneutical circles.

Buber and Rosenzweig

From its inception at the turn of the twentieth century, "the Jewish renaissance" was immersed in the language of plastic expression. One of its most prolific members, Martin Buber (1878–1965), a student at the University of Vienna in philosophy and art history, coined the term in conversation with the Swiss historian Jakob Burkhardt (1818–97), the Italian renaissance, and contemporary currents in the arts. Buber's published body of work spans the entire first half of the twentieth century. As a public persona, he was the very image of Jewish renewal. A 1901 article for the journal *Ost und West* explicitly links that movement to "forerunners of a great general culture of beauty . . . the artistic feeling that awakens everywhere, the development of modern arts and crafts, the infusion of everyday life with a sense of beauty, the diverse attempts at an aesthetic education for our youth, and the effort to socialize art" (*FB*, 30). The people behind the renaissance of modern Jewish life, including Buber himself, formed part of this larger development and were "electrified by it" (31). As Paul Mendes-Flohr points out, the combination of particular Jewish reaffirmations with general cultural interests formed "one seamless weave."[1]

In Buber's early work, leading up to World War I, the vogue for Nietzsche that was then current and the flowing contours of German-speaking art nouveau fused with Zionism, Jewish art, and Hasidism. *The Tales of Rabbi Nahman of Bratzlav* (1906) and then *Legends of the Baal Shem* (1908) earned Buber early literary fame. *Ecstatic Confessions* (1909) and *Daniel* (1912) further increased his reputation in the world of German letters. *Erlebnis*—experience—is fundamental to all these early works. The essence of pure experience grasped intuitively by the whole self, it extends human being beyond the relative limits and finite concepts of mental cognition. *Erlebnis* reflects the root power in the break of myth and mysticism from the rigid form of inert religion and bourgeois convention. The absolute and unconditional are made real through Dionysian passion and Apollonian form-creation: creative, organic acts at the physical center of the chaos of brute sensation. Jewish religiosity and renewal are a youth style, a *Jugendstil*, lent art's lush tonal shape and sensual texture.

In the wake of World War I, Buber looked past the stylized individual subject to highlight the life of relationship between multiple subjects. His greatest single masterpiece remains *I and Thou* (1923), the basic tenets of which he was to modify but never to abandon. A theoretical lens upon which to conceive the relation between God, person, and human community, it was the key to his mature thought on everything from Zionism, Hasidism, the Hebrew Bible and its translation, Arab-Jewish conflict in Palestine, philosophical anthropology, works of art, and the contemporary "eclipse of God." Complicating the unified shape of *Erlebnis*, the text's profoundly dualistic worldview embodies the clashing color combinations in expressionistic poetry and painting. Human intersubjectivity affirms the polymorphous I-YOU encounter. Resting upon the claim that no isolated "I" exists apart from relationship to an other, revelation transforms each figure into an ultimate and mysterious center of value whose presence eludes the concepts of instrumental language. The heteronomous revelation of YOUR presence calls ME into an open-ended relationship, a living pattern, that defies sense, logic, and proportion, whereas the I-IT relationship assumes the fixed form, the density and duration of realist painting, of objects that one can measure and manipulate.

Rosenzweig (1886–1929) was one of Buber's first critics and major collaborators. Obscuring basic lines of agreement that they came to share regarding revelation and redemption, the differences between them are at first glance easy to overstate. They concern Buber's early mysticism, his alleged antinomianism, the exact character of the IT world, and the status of Jewish law. If a dionysian image of the hasid and the drama of Zionism first drew Buber into Jewish life, Rosenzweig was drawn to the formal character of revelation and ritual. Pressed hard by his beloved friend Eugen Rosenstock and cousins Hans and Rudolf Ehrenberg to convert from Judaism to Christianity as they themselves had done, he decided to do so as a Jew, not as a "pagan." According to legend, however, a visit to an eastern European *shtiebl* in Berlin on Yom Kippur in 1913 so overwhelmed the young Rosenzweig that he sent word back, in a well-known letter to Rudolf Ehrenberg, that he was going to remain a Jew. In doing so, he left behind the laissez-faire form of middle-class German Jewish assimilation and the inert Judaism of his parents' generation. He pursued intensive commitments to learning and observance at the Freie jüdische Lehrhaus in Frankfurt, an adult education program that he directed until his untimely death in 1929 after a long bout with Lou Gehrig's disease.

At once physical and meta-physical, the amalgamation of visible and invisible elements contributes to the structure of Rosenzweig's most important work, *The Star of Redemption* (1921). Its most basic insight is that the truth that appears to human beings in this world is multiform. At first, the "elements" of God, world, and "man," which are to compose that truth, constitute autonomous components, mere figments of thought. Each one is irreducible to the others. No single figure can be said to comprise the All, to exhaust reality. Terrified by death, the human subject inhabits a broken semblance of a world—self-enclosed fragments symbolized by Mt. Olympus, the Greek polis, classical sculpture, and tragic theater. The "course" through which these silent elements then open out to one another is made real by the acoustic media of creation, revelation, and redemption. But they disappear from view. Parallel to epic, lyric, and dramatic speech, their language intensifies spiritual life by rendering it into the invisible shape of poetry. Finally, the forms of Jewish and Christian cult constellate into a metacosmos, in which all six points—the triadic form God-world-"man" and the triadic form creation-revelation-redemption—assemble into an integrated star-shaped gestalt. By the end of the text, the now visible manifestation of God's face, a palpable image of absolute truth, confronts the soul at death's border and ushers it back into life.

Meta-physical pictures saturate this peculiar philosophical thought. On the combination of triangles ($\triangle$) ($\triangledown$) that compose the "star of redemption" ($\maltese$) Rosenzweig explained in a 1918 letter to his lover Margrit (Gritli) Rosenstock-Huessy, "I think in figures" (*GB*, 124). As he was to claim later, the miracle is not, as Heidegger would have it, that something "is," but rather that "there is yet something that has form." The movement of time in "the real world" congeals into an image or a group of images that stand apart from time. About what God, world, and "man" are, we know nothing, but how they *look* in a system of revelation, "that we can know exactly." Historical flux ("the flow of events") "projects gleaming pictures onto heaven, above the temporal world and they remain." Reversing the axiological order in traditional metaphysics, Rosenzweig goes on to say about these pictures: "They are not archetypes. On the contrary, they would not exist did not the stream of reality continue to break forth out of its there invisible-mysterious sources." The "invisible mysteries," past, present, and future—that is, time itself—"become image-like in these images, and the steady course of life devolves into recurring form" (*NT*, 92–93).

For both Buber and Rosenzweig, "religion" fell short of revelation from either of two angles. On the one hand, revelation is still platonic. Pure *Erlebnis*, an I-YOU encounter, and the commandment of love underscore a palpable otherness that transcends the objective organization of things and mere subjective states of consciousness. Religion pales before revelation, unable to measure up to that which is always incommensurable to human structures of consciousness and culture. On the other hand, the beliefs and practices of religion are rejected because they are set apart from the full range of physical being. In his later work, Buber argued that rather than render reality absolute, revelation made reality more real and less fantastic. Religion must reflect "the *whole* existence of the real man in the real world of God" or else it is no better than art, ethics, and science (*ABH*, 110–11). Rosenzweig agreed: "Only we, the best of us, live entirely sober, under God, but without 'religion.'" Pagan rites turn creation and its host into gods whereas revelation restores the world to its elemental order. Heaven, earth, and water do not cease being heaven, earth, and water. Revelation "makes the world unreligious again" (*BT*, 767–68).

Expressed positively, rejecting religion for the "real world of God" entails a revelation that is both transcendent and immanent. Revelation simultaneously points beyond the human, even as it remains embedded within it. Rosenzweig took his cue from the biblical Song of Songs to declare: "Love simply cannot be 'purely human' . . . by speaking, love already becomes superhuman, for the sensuality of the word is brimful with its divine supersense. Like speech itself, love is sensual-supersensual" (*SR*, 201). Buber understood the Hebrew word *ruah* (wind/spirit) to make a similar point. Neither physical nor metaphysical, it means not one of two meanings but both together and undivided. *Ruah* constitutes a natural process, a surging, a *Geist*-ing, a wind surge that points to its divine origin in a spirit surge, a God-storm that shakes and animates the human person (*ST*, 86–87). The critique of "religion" and the turn to revelation were rhetorically brought to bear against nineteenth-century bourgeois religion, namely, the "pseudo-ethical" rationalism of Reform Judaism and the "pseudo-juridical" observance of Orthodox Judaism.

With Kandinsky and other avant-garde artists, Buber and Rosenzweig shared a lively antipathy in respect to another form of nineteenth-century culture: the canon of art for art's sake (*l'art pour l'art*). Against the "pure aesthetics" of museums, books, and theaters, their anti-aesthetic was "completely free of the typical embellishments [*üblichen Verschönerungen*]" (*BT*, 849). As Rosenzweig once observed, translating a tale about God's revelation is more challenging than telling the tale of Hansel and Gretel. In the latter case, the story only has to be beautiful, while in telling tales about God's revelation, "it is not enough that it is beautiful, but rather it must also be true." At the surface level, translating revelation only seems to have nothing to do with art. Even without embellishment, however, the translation is still aesthetic. It just belongs to a different order of beauty. Revelation is not impassive to shape and form. Rosenzweig slyly added: "It cannot be indifferent to [God] what kind of tales His children tell about him, much less the name with which they name Him" (1042).

In the history of modern art, the rhetoric of anti-aesthetics signals the passage of one style into another. Like "religion," the "aesthetic" is narrow and unreal, too pretty and too precious; it creates an artificial division between art and life that emergent avant-gardes seek to overcome with a new system of artifice. Rosenzweig recognized that the rejection of neoromantic ornament and embellishment, the critique of rarified and beautiful objects, was itself a modern art discourse. The nineteenth century, he wrote his parents in 1916, was "German," that is, Gothic, ornamental, romantic; unlike the twentieth century, which would be "Latin," that is, unromantic, formal, constructive, and unsentimental, as in the work of Thomas Mann, Kafka, and anti-Wagnerian music (*BT*, 204–5). It was expressionism that shaped what Rosenzweig once called, in reference to Hebrew Scripture, his own *unästhetisch-überästhetische ästhetik* (1153). The "unaesthetic" represents the dissonant quality in modern art that is *über*-aesthetic, that is, more than merely aesthetic. Neoromantic art-for-art's-sake aestheticism gave way to the modernism identified by Rosenzweig. In doing so, revelation remained aesthetic but no longer "aesthetic."

The important differences dividing Buber and Rosenzweig around a brace of theoretical and practical problems recede before what they had in common—an unaesthetic-superaesthetic slant to revelation and redemption as they come to press upon human expression. Rosenzweig's initial dislike of Buber belongs to that selfsame history of style. The somewhat older Buber had begun his literary career under the influence of art nouveau, the most advanced style then available across Europe in the late 1890s and early 1900s. Rosenzweig's relative youth saved him from Jugendstil, as it was known in Germany and Austria. He first began to publish after World War I, when it had already passed from the scene. By the 1920s, he and Buber were in sync both with each other and with the pathos-laden rhythm and sharply drawn dualisms of expressionism. They both thought in terms of multiform and complex patterns. And they both tried to keep pace with the cooler German styles developing in the mid to late 1920s. Their later work grew more and more *sachlich*: objective, matter-of-fact, and realistic. Indeed, the history of early German modernism, from Jugendstil through Neue Sachlichkeit, constitutes a running index to the discourse of "religion" and revelation in early twentieth-century Jewish thought.

Romanticism and Neoromanticism

The increasingly acrid character of early twentieth-century culture was fundamentally at odds with the romantic religion of nature and melancholic weltschmerz. Immersed in the dream of the faraway in place and time, the romantic subject is one who shapes the world into a vast hieroglyphic system with himself at its center. He is the absolute self, the poet who can transpose one thing into its opposite, men into stars and stars into men, nature into art and art into religion, or religion into nature and nature into art. In *The Novices of Saïs* by Novalis (1772–1801), the romantic poet divines the once-broken bond between heaven and earth out of his own diction; he masters the great cipher to which everything belongs and in which everything interconnects: eggshells, clouds, crystals, stone formations, ice-covered water, plants, beasts, human beings, and the lights of heaven.[2] But for Buber, "Authentic religiosity . . . has nothing in common with the dreamings of rapturous [*schwärmerischer*] hearts, or with the self-pleasure of aestheticizing souls, or with the pensive play [*tiefsinnige Spielen*] of a practiced intellectuality" (*OJ*, 93; trans. modified). The expression is anti-romantic. As against "superficial emotionalism," the collecting of "experiences," and "prattling about God" (154), Buber's work bears only a superficial resemblance to the romantic tale of human subjectivity.[3]

Religious thought as it first took shape in the culture of German modernism was neoromantic, not romantic. It participates in the world of Jugendstil design, the poetry of Rainer Maria Rilke and Stefan

George, the dramatic theater of Hugo von Hofmannsthal, paintings by Gustav Klimt, the music of Richard Strauss and Gustav Mahler, Wilhelm Dilthey's *Lebensphilosophie*, and the sociology of Georg Simmel. Repelled by the ugliness of modern industrial society, neo-romanticism worked to rejuvenate the conditions of human existence based on the utopian socialism of William Morris and Nietzsche's apotheosis of life and beauty. In the poetry of Rilke, one detects a similar change in relationship to the order of objects. The *New Poems* of 1907 and 1908 attach less value to the romance of self-expression than is the case with Novalis. More attention is paid to the individuated thing, to sculpted angels or swans, an image of the Buddha, the body of a courtesan, the remains of the dead, a bowl of roses. Rabbi Nahman, the Baal Shem Tov, and Daniel exercise the same thinglike status in Buber's early work. Instead of submerging the vast hieroglyph of nature around the subject, neoromantic artists isolated a single, self-contained object, tone, or color over against a blank, flattened surface.[4]

In relation to nature, the neoromantic work creates the opposite visual register to the romanticism of Caspar David Friedrich's *Monk by the Sea* (1809) (plate 1), in which the romantic subject stares out into a vast three-dimensional abyss with his back to the viewer. Receding into a distance that dwarfs the monk, the line between heaven and earth is blurred in a black belt of rain beneath the massive blue orb pressing down from above. As Robert Rosenblum remarks, "The mysteries of religion . . . left the rituals of church and synagogue and had been relocated in the natural world."[5] In contrast, the neoromantic approach to nature is anti-naturalistic. The naked boy in E. M. Lilien's *The Creation of the Poet* (ca. 1900) (plate 2), the lush floral decoration, and four angels superimposed upon the black surface are abstracted out of a two-dimensional surface. Lilien's *Passah* (1903) (plate 3) combines in a more radical fashion the blank volumes from which the stylized figures obtrude: pyramids in the shape of Egyptian statuary, a doleful and suffering Jew wrapped in thorns, and a distant sun inscribed with the Hebrew word "Zion." Objects are drawn out of nature, not into it.

The inversion of romantic into neoromantic consciousness marks a wayward line of historical, theoretical, and stylistic continuity. As traced by Rosenblum, it extends from Friedrich and Philippe Otto

Runge (1777–1810), through Kandinsky and the Blue Rider to the postwar abstract expressionism of Rothko and Pollock. In Rosenblum's estimation, Friedrich's vast seascape is "daringly empty, devoid of objects, devoid of . . . narrative incident" and thus anticipates abstract art.[6] Rosenblum's otherwise persuasive analysis underplays the rhetorical violence that propelled this "northern romantic tradition" into the twentieth century. A host of strained links tie the anti-romanticism of German expressionism to the romanticism its proponents were more likely to ridicule than not. The conceit that a moment in time can reveal eternity, the critique of Enlightenment reason and middle-class society, the weight given to the individual fragment, the disdain for instrumentalist language, the grip of myth, music, and poetic language, alongside the intense coupling of love and death are perennial romantic topoi in twentieth-century art, poetry, and religion. But this does not make the culture of early German modernism "romantic." When an art falls out of fashion, it does so piecemeal, never all at once.

Distinguishing between "form-elements," "form relationships," and "expressive quality," Meyer Schapiro's analysis of style is an important gauge of the complicated relationship between romanticism and early modernism. By "form-elements," Schapiro means an individual motif or content, while "form-relations" and "expressive quality" refer to the system of their organization and the tone it takes.[7] A single romantic form-element can thereby survive the rejection of those more systematic relationships and tonal qualities that are the sine qua non of German romanticism, for example, the relation to nature in hieroglyphic arrangements and sentimental expression. Style constitutes that more deliberate ordering, disordering, and reordering of the surface appearance that sets a subject or an object within or apart from its environment. Early twentieth-century cultural expression emerged out of distinct environments formed by the first impact of mass society, advanced capitalism, and world war. Romantic and neoromantic impulses belong to this field of reference, which quickly gave way, to a more roughly drawn set of contours. By the time *I and Thou* and *The Star of Redemption* were published in the early 1920s, revelation had begun to look more like expressionism.

Expressionism

At war with itself, the expressionism that burst onto the scene between 1905 and the early 1920s maintained a complex religious profile. The art historian Gustav Hartlaub saw in it the early herald of a dionysian Christianity, a divine essence irreducibly bound up with flesh, a resurrection that represented no otherworldly hatred of being (*Daseinsverachtung*), but rather rejuvenated human will and the sanctification of this world.[8] Works by the northern expressionist painters Max Beckmann, Ernst Nolde, Karl Schmidt-Rottluf, and Ludwig Meidner were said to realize an unprettified and anti-sentimental picture of corporeal being consumed by spirit. Their art is superreal, but not alien to reality.[9] Hartlaub realized that expressionist art was not itself religious, but at best only prereligious. Arguing against the very idea that there is such a thing as "religious style," he maintained that the most important component of religious art is religious conviction (*Gesinnung*) and religious content (*Gegenstand*), that is, nonpainterly content drawn from literary sources. Hence the antipathy in his analysis to Kandinsky, a critique that heightens the tension within expressionism between dematerialized forms of nonobjective (*gegenstandlos*) art and figurative representation.[10]

Expressionism was an uneasy hybrid, combining four basic elements. (1) The critique of impressionism and surface reality: "His sensibility is very close to mine," Klee wrote, comparing himself to Rilke, "except that I now press on more towards the center, whereas his preparation tends to be skin-deep. He is still an Impressionist, while I have only memories left in this area. . . . The perfect elegance of his appearance is an enigma to me. How are such things achieved?"(*DPK*, 317). (2) Presence and the present: the four sons in Jakob Steinhardt's Haggadah inhabit the war-torn landscape of modern Europe; the wicked son wears the spiked helmet worn by German soldiers during World War I (plate 10). The exodus from Egypt with its story of catastrophe and redemption relates a twentieth-century reality. (3) Dialogue, encounter, spiritual transformation, and the subjective in tandem with a suprasubjective element: Ernst Ludwig Kirchner describes a person who "sits across from us and we talk, and suddenly there arises this intangible something which one could call mystery. It gives to his features his innate personality and yet at the same time lifts those features beyond the personal. . . . And yet this portrait, as close as it is to his real self, is a paraphrase of the great mystery . . . a part of that spirituality or feeling which pervades the whole world."[11] (4) Hot color and burning pathos: Meidner cried to God to calm his unruly soul, but his best work shows the opposite inclination: wildly staring and distorted self-portraits and cafe scenes, exploding cityscapes, frenzied prophets and sibyls (plate 11). The short literary works he penned express both despair and faith, along with ecstatic hymns to God, paint, poetry, and international brotherhood.

Aside from Buber and Rosenzweig, the lion's share of attention in this study goes to Kandinsky, Klee, and Franz Marc, because their own theoretical writings lend verbal expression to the spiritual in art, that non-material element in art that transcends its materiality; and because their texts are more varied and sophisticated than Meidner's confessional outbursts, less likely to play themselves out or to parody than Max Pechstein's creative credo, "Work! Ecstasy! Smash your brains!"[12] Kandinsky published the famous *Blue Rider Almanach* with Marc, as well as the classic *On the Spiritual in Art*, prior to World War I. Klee's diaries, especially from his 1914 trip to Tunisia, give word to the mystery of creation and to the discovery of color. Marc's collected writings take up the problem of suffering and the promise of redemption. After the war, Kandinsky and Klee continued to produce important theoretical texts prior to and during their stay at the Bauhaus, including Klee's "Creative Credo," a lecture delivered at Jena on modern art, and voluminous pedagogical notes. Kandinsky's *Point and Line to Plane* (1926) speaks to the abiding spiritual presence in his most abstract compositional work. An intense written output, it confirms Hartlaub's claim about the literary character of religious and prereligious art.[13]

Scenes saturated by Jugendstil, French symbolism, and Russian folklore direct Kandinsky's first period in Munich. They take place in fairy-tale settings, with horsemen riding though mottled scenes from Old Russia, colorful costumes, village fairs, and country beauties. A diffuse religiosity saturates *Riding Couple* (1907) (plate 9). Two costumed lovers mounted upon a cloaked horse ride before a meandering river and a small, walled city of Russian Orthodox domes. The softly dappled coloring unifies the picture. Orange and yellow above, blue and red below intensify the neoromantic mood. Kandinsky's second period reflects the heyday of prewar Blue Rider expressionism. *Composition V* (1911) (fig. 4) and *Composition VI* reveal the semblance of horsemen with horns and trumpets, hills and mountains, angels, reclining lovers, Cossacks, spears, lances, and apocalyptic scenes of the Last Judgment. Not immediately visible, the figures blur into overlapping fields of clashing color tones. A third period perfected at the Bauhaus after the war produced an art devoid of any overt representational context. Past the overtly religious pathos of color-coded symbolism, *Composition VIII* (1923) (plate 17) is a geometrical construction whose sole spiritual content is form itself.

At once worldly and otherworldly, the image of physical reality in Klee's work was no less metaphysical. Color squares in *Memory of a Garden* (1914) (fig. 3) and horizontal strips in *Runner at the Goal* (1921) (plate 12) create ordered inorganic patterns that cast the individuated figure: arms and legs akimbo, angels, acrobats, and actors, plants and architectural features. As Marcel Franciscono explains, the abstract and figurative elements in this pictorial universe are interdependent. Uncomprehending parts of an unfathomable pattern, the individual figure is not autonomous. It does not command itself. Animating the entire system is a never-named creative, incessantly form-giving power. Apart from the garden's obvious beauty, there is nothing warm to this force—or about Klee's view of nature. "What my art probably lacks," he wrote "is a kind of passionate humanity. I don't love animals and every sort of creature with an earthly warmth . . . I tend to dissolve the whole of creation and am then on a footing of brotherliness to my neighbor, to all things earthly. I possess. The earth-idea gives way to the world-idea. My love is distant and religious" (*DPK*, 345).[14]

Klee meant to distinguish his own work from that of Marc, but the gap between them was not so vast. The main figure and flattened landscape in *Horse in a Landscape* (1910) (plate 13) are just as unnatural as *Memory of a Garden* or *Runner at the Goal*. The reds and yellow in Marc's palette are electric. They intensify the curving neck and tail and the moving fluid mass over which the horse looks. Marc was adamant. His work had nothing to do with naturalism, but rather lies in the horse and its construction, its inner animal life, and the coursing blood beneath the visible surface (*S*, 98). Marc broke with this line in 1912. He was dead by the end of the war. Already anticipating the apocalypse of war under the influence of cubism, the gentler organic rhythm was replaced by the geometric ordering of pictorial objects. Sharp, other-worldly shards of light and color slice diagonally through doom in the dark forest torn apart in *The Fate of the Animals* (1913) (plate 14).[15] Ecstatic pantheism gave way to a pessimism whose spiritual disposition was soon to die a sudden death in Weimar modernism.

Postexpressionism

As the literary critic Wolfgang Rohe remarks, no other literary movement has been so quickly shown to its grave as expressionism. In the plastic arts as well, one finds throughout the 1920s constant reference to the crisis of expressionism, the end of expressionism, the death of expressionism.[16] Wilhelm Worringer, whose *Abstraction and Empathy* (1907) had done so much to validate the turn to abstract and "primitive" art, was to call it empty and dried out, "decorative chic."[17] In "Expressionism Is Dying," Yvan Goll declared in 1921: "The spirit is a hoax in this age of profiteering. . . . The ecstatic mouth becomes bitter, very bitter." Rejecting the sentimentality of expressionism, Goll spoke to a "new power [that] seems to be coming over us: one of brain-machinery. . . . Why reach for heaven. *Heaven is also earth*, as the aviator knows."[18] Even Hartlaub soured on the possibility of a new religious art, having coined the term *Neue Sachlichkeit* in 1925 to characterize the new objectivity in postwar painting. Of expressionism, he said: "Any 'movement' bound up as it is with one generation, ages with that generation, stepping into the background at some point, perhaps later to be rejuvenated under different conditions."[19]

Uncompromisingly anti-metaphysical, the varied forms of what the art historian Dennis Crockett calls "post-Expressionism" advanced a purely material conception of art and reality. The tubes, triangles, and cubes in late Bauhaus design embody principles of rational construction. The clarity brought to function along with biting social critique and satire go to the creation of Neue Sachlichkeit art, the rise of German cinema and new graphic design, the development of photography and

montage, the origins of the Frankfurt School and Russian constructiv-
ism. Hitherto, the tension between romanticism, neoromanticism, and
expressionism had encouraged new forms of spiritual expression. The
towering figures of twentieth-century Jewish and Christian thought,
Buber, Rosenzweig, Karl Barth, Friedrich Gogarten, Max Scheler, and
Rudolf Otto made their greatest contributions to the study of religion
to the period between 1910 and 1920. In contrast, the precision that was
now brought to bear upon the visible, the public, and the here and now
was toxic to religion. There was no reason to reach for heaven in this
age of profiteering.[20]

While Kandinsky, Klee, Buber, and Rosenzweig continued to create
some of their finest work well into the decade, they grew out of touch
with the new reality. But it is Walter Benjamin who leaves the most
dispirited impression. In Benjamin's work, fully realized commitments
to the contemporary aesthetic of surrealism, photomontage, and film
sit side by side with unhappy nostalgia for mystic and cultic expression.
The new objectivity made no allowance for the melancholy illuminations of messianism, auras, and angels. Politically, the brave world of
Weimar modernism was caught in the tough middle between fascism
and communism. In a conversation with Benjamin, Bertolt Brecht
clearly had his interlocutor in mind when he called Franz Kafka "a Jew-
boy . . . a mere bubble on the glittering quagmire of Prague culture. . . .
The images are good of course. But the rest is pure mystification. It's
nonsense. You have to ignore it. . . . Depth is a separate dimension, it's
just depth—and there's nothing whatsoever to be seen in it."[21]

If postexpressionism enacts the exile of religion and metaphysics
from modern society, then Martin Heidegger was its philosophical
Nebuchadnezzar. *Being and Time* (1927) constitutes a tour de force
against Platonic metaphysics, the subject/object dichotomy, and mass
consciousness, with the visible human proposed as the best platform
from which to recover the problem of being. The text is animated by
a split personality. Its first part demonstrates great sensitivity to ontic
phenomena, to the daily equipmentality of objects at hand to human
being in the world. In comparison, the temporal analytic in the second
part remains closed in, its image of "authentic" human *Dasein* preoc-
cupied with *jemeinigkeit*, the condition of "mineness," the question of
my own being, my precious singularity, my care first for myself and

then for others, my guilt before the infinity of foreclosed possibilities, and the imminence of my own death. The problem of the other continues to go unresolved in Heidegger's existential analysis of *Dasein*. "*Being and Time* opens the question even as it evades it," Christopher Fynsk notes.[22]

As read by Jacques Derrida, spirit haunted Heidegger, although Derrida admits that it has no real place in the existential analytic of *Dasein*.[23] Its discourse came out into the open, first in the notorious 1933 rectorship address and in the *Introduction to Metaphysics*, and then most notably in a postwar essay on the expressionist poet Georg Trakl (d. 1912). Anti-metaphysical, the perception of spirit is neither not foreign to nor set apart from spatial and temporal being: "Es ist die Seele ein Fremdes auf Erden" ("Yes, the soul is a stranger upon the earth"). Derrida clarifies: "The soul is a 'stranger' does not signify that one must take it to be imprisoned, exiled, tumbled into the terrestrial here below, fallen into body doomed to the corruption of what is lacking in Being and in truth is not." He explains: "[T]he soul only *seeks* the earth, it does not flee it. The soul is a stranger because it does not yet inhabit the earth."[24] To give shape to this earth-bound spirit, Heidegger turned in his later work to the poetry of Rilke and Trakl, that is, back to Jugendstil and expressionism. Spirit sought a home in the world after World War II, eluding the new sobriety of postexpressionism and the closed-in conception of *Being and Time*.

By then it was too late. The enduring problematic in Heidegger's work over which Derrida tries to glide lies in the identification of spirit and fire. There is no mediating space around the fire, no air-breath-*ruah-spiritus-pneuma*, no dialectical gap between earth and spirit, no pause to the pyrotechnics of Being. Heidegger lost any critical traction with which he might have otherwise turned to the world by turning away from it at the precise historical moment when he needed to do so. Ensconced at the University of Freiburg during World War II, at ease in a one-dimensional cosmos, he compares unfavorably to Klee and Kandinsky, who fled to Switzerland and Paris, and to Buber who stayed in Germany until right before it was too late. Simultaneously world-friendly and world-foreign, the work of revelation and the spiritual in art occupies a more ambiguous position than Heideggerian ontology. Fire continues to this day to contaminate Heidegger's thought, a body of work in which spirit found a not uncomfortable home in Nazi Germany. He was a type of thinker who, Buber believed, "has become incapable of apprehending a reality absolutely independent of himself and of having a relation with it—incapable moreover of imaginatively perceiving this reality and representing it in images, since it eludes direct contemplation" (*EG*, 14).

Postmodernism

The grim picture of modern secularism presented by Buber in his critique of Heidegger, Sartre, and Jung in *The Eclipse of God* (1952), his last major work, hardly accounts for his own broad readership after the war. At least in the United States, it obscures the influence of liberal Christian thought exercised by Paul Tillich, Reinhold Neibuhr, Karl Rahner, Thomas Merton, and Martin Luther King Jr., the continuing attraction of Eastern religions popularized by D. T. Suzuki and Alan Watts, and the metaphysical meanderings that echo in the abstract expressionism of Mark Rothko and Barnett Newman. The Jewish thought of Mordecai Kaplan, Abraham Joshua Heschel, Joseph Soloveitchik, Emil Fackenheim, Steven Schwarzschild, Arthur Cohen, Will Herberg, and Robert Gordis testifies to an intellectual vitality that was coterminous with the rise of institutional religious life, church and synagogue construction in high modernist, international architectural styles, the religious signature of an American suburban scrawl that neither Buber nor Rosenzweig would have been able to read.

The spread of postmodern culture into the 1960s and 1970s leads us further and further away from postwar modernism, Neue Sachlichkeit, German expressionism, and art nouveau into "the society of spectacle." In deconstructing "the difference," postmodernism in art, architecture, philosophy, and religion has carved out a place between extreme forms of secularism and religious belief. Rather than restrict religious imagery, the late writings of Derrida and the art and architecture of Anselm Kiefer, Andres Serrano, Shirin Neshat, and Daniel Liebeskind seem to revel in it. If contemporary aesthetics undercuts those forms of dogmatic faith alive in the culture at large and the pieties still at work in Buber and Rosenzweig, it also upends the secular orthodoxies with which religion is rejected out of hand. Instead of building distinctions based on a binary logic or fixing religious reference to a nonreligious sediment (sociological and psychological), postmodernism has loosened up the discursive boundaries between fact and fantasy, real and fake, secular and sacred, natural and supernatural. Religion thus retains a hold on the contemporary imagination.

The ten human figures in Michal Rovner's *Merging P#1* (1997) (plate 20) blend into a single black blurry silhouette, their heads part of the grainy yellow color field into which they merge. Original Polaroid shots are rephotographed and infused with unnatural color to magnify the distance between the image and its original subject. Like loops in electronic music, the same is intensified into a monotony that borders onto something else.[25] No longer subject to the illusion of immediacy, the process of technological reproduction lifts vision out across a series of mediated displacements. Benjamin had been too quick to see in mechanical reproduction the loss of aura, that "unique phenomenon of distance, however close it may be," the "natural distance" that the painter maintains in his work.[26] As he himself perceived, "The enlargement of a snapshot does not simply render more precise what in any case was visible, though unclear: it reveals entirely new structural formations of the subject."[27]

If the language of "creation," "revelation," and "redemption," language that was integral to Buber, Rosenzweig, and German expressionism, still has a place in a contemporary work of art like Rovner's, it does so vexed by questions about the spiritual significance of aesthetic form. The naïve magic and thick, yellow substance that stick to the spiritual in art have always lent themselves to strained interpretive possibilities that are perhaps unique to religious discourse. *Merging P#1* conjures the ambiguous situation of shadowy borders and liminal flight. Earthbound and unbound, mutant figures wander in spaceless space. Nissan Perez detects the unreal and nondescript "immaterial presence of bodies," hovering in suspense on the edge of something unnamed and unspeakable, the destination of bodies "into light transcending to an unknown, new condition."[28] Drawn to tai chi and Taoism, art and art criticism enter the dubious domain of technology and the New Age. At least one critic has remarked against the "pandering heavy-duty symbolism" and the "polished, almost commercial quality" of Rovner's art.[29] Kandinsky, Klee, and Marc believed in the invisible. Do Rovner and Perez? A lighter touch might have made the symbolism *more* open to a tonic skepticism, a counterimage and counterrhetoric by which to render the spiritual in art less incredible.

Jewish Thought

Left behind in the rapid-fire succession of styles in early German modernism, Buber and Rosenzweig remained fundamentally at odds with the "new realism" that began to worm its way into their work in the mid to late 1920s. Emerging out of Jugendstil art and letters, Buber's name appears prominently at the end of Hartlaub's *Kunst und Religion* (1919) and in Hermann Bahr's monograph *Expressionismus* (1916). Rosenzweig's private transition from Jugendstil to expressionism has been less observed. In a 1928 letter to Willy Haas about his response to a questionnaire attempting to document the importance of Stefan George for the contemporary scene, Rosenzweig indicates the more important influence of Rilke upon him in 1910, of Werfel in 1918, and of Buber since 1922 (*BT*, 1191). Expressionism was to him "a pressing down upon the nerves," associated with the image of judgment. Commenting upon Kafka's story "The Judgment," he dubbed expressionism the aesthetic caricature of the religious person, comparing, as so many were to do at the time, impressionism to the natural scientist (335). Toward the end of his life, Rosenzweig distanced himself from the ultrarational style by declaring this allegiance: "I am myself, forsooth, already of yesterday, 1918, not 1928, 'Expressionism,' not *Neue Sachlichkeit*" (1191).

By the end of this study, we shall be better able to assess Buber and Rosenzweig's place in contemporary aesthetics, but I would like to say this much now. Thanks to a dedicated coterie of readers, Buber and Rosenzweig have survived the death of expressionism and entered into new postmodern environments. These environs are image-rich, awash in photography, installation art, digital design, and virtual realities. In this environment, revelation and the spiritual in art recycle, recycle, and turn into rhetoric. Artful appeals to immediate encounter call attention away from any external referent back to the artifice of their internal construction. At the same time, popular and increasingly conservative religion adapts very well to artificial environments, to technology and to the appearance of fakes, copies, and other simulacra in ways that outpace the capacity of left-wing and liberal religionists. As for Buber and Rosenzweig: to paraphrase Brecht, the images are (still) good. The image of encounter and evanescent presence finds a place in the archives and spectacles of contemporary culture. In the artificial light cast by this culture, Buber and Rosenzweig continue to open up new worlds for their readers, artificial worlds in which "something" that looks like "spirit" continues to make itself present.

Once upon a time, philosophical thought in the West promised a way out of spectacle. I mean, of course, the parable of the cave in Plato's *Republic*. With no direct access to the sun outside, the prisoners who dwell in the cave are captives to sense impression and surreal imagination. They mistake for real the shadows that flicker upon the walls. Having torn himself from this captivity, the philosopher learns to enjoy the direct apprehension of the good after painful acclimation to life outside the cave. Having expelled poetry and the mimetic arts from the ideal republic, the philosopher in his cognition proceeds from shadows, to reflections, to objects, to starlight and moonlight, and then to a blinding vision of the sun at the apex of its course. The parable trades upon the interplay across a complex set of dualisms—truth/image, subject/object, inside/outside, substance/attribute, eternity/time, mind/body. It performs a back and forth motion between the real world of ideal cognition and the everyday world, assured in its conceit that the dialectics of pure reason can momentarily rip itself from the sensual confines that restrict its operation.[30]

The rabbis offer a counterimage of a cave, their own conceit, that anticipates the metaphysics of Buber and Rosenzweig. Commenting on the verse "And Moses spoke to YHWH" (Exod. 33:12), the rabbis ask, "To what may the thing be compared? To a cave placed by the edge of the sea whose water fills it. From here on, water from the sea is delivered to the cave and water from the cave returns to the sea. So it was that 'YHWH said to Moses' and 'Moses said to YHWH'" (*Tanhuma, Ki Tissa* 14). Trading upon the motion between divine and human utterance, between outside and inside, the rabbinic parable is one in which human consciousness encounters truth inside its own limit. Inverting the move made by Platonic philosophy from inside to outside, revelation moves deeper into the confines of sensation and the imagination represented by the cave. Water in the cave (the voice of Moses) remains distinct from the seawater outside (the voice of God). But the two waters mingle. In this motion between inside and outside, Jewish thought does not seek to separate the formal shape of revelation from liquid sensation.

Figure 3. Paul Klee, *Memory of a Garden* (1914).
Kunstsammlung Nordrhein-Westfalen, Düsseldorf. Photo Walter Klein.
© 2005 Artists Rights Society (ARS), New York/VG Bild-Kunst, Bonn.

One   Form

Reading Kandinsky's *On the Spiritual in Art*, the northern expressionist sculptor and dramatist Ernst Barlach complained: "I will believe
this honest man when he claims that for him, points, spots, lines, and
dabs . . . create profound spiritual shocks, i.e., they have effects that
are more than ornamental. Yes, I will believe, and then—good by."[1]
Barlach did not share the naïve trust in graphic or linguistic form that
was an essential component in the work of Kandinsky, Klee, Buber,
and Rosenzweig. He failed to see how the transposition of bare formal
elements into complex compositional networks might take shape as the
human correlate of supersensual creativity. In the lines drawn between
the graphic and verbal nodes of expression, our own definition of
"form" as found in the discourse of revelation and the spiritual in art
refers to two discrete phenomena: the isolated points, spots, lines, and
dabs parodied by Barlach versus the broader form pattern, the *Gestalt*
into which they morph. Formation is genesis. Points, spots, lines, and
dabs do not "represent" the world of visible objects. In Klee's *Memory of
a Garden* (fig. 3), they are world-creating, the elemental building blocks
of what Rosenzweig called a super-cosmos (*Überwelt*), the transfiguration of this empirical world.

The difference between Barlach and Kandinsky about the spiritual
status of form and form-creation reflects the foundational dispute in
German philosophy between Kant and Hegel. For Kant, human cognition relies upon aesthetic forms of intuition (space and time) to receive
sense impressions, which are organized by concepts of the understanding and ideas of reason into an ordered whole. Form—the points,
spots, lines, and dabs of human consciousness—has no determinate
reference apart from its own operation. Time and space, concepts and
categories, are not real per se. They are only forms of intuition. As for

the ideas of reason (God, world, and soul), these are referents whose existence we can only postulate, since they stand beyond the limits of possible human experience. Hegel placed much greater faith in form than Kant did. Spirit unfolds logically through art, religion, and philosophy. The third term in Hegel's dialectic always combines the partial truths that precede it into a more complete Idea. Intermediary cultural forms, even those said to be one-sided, are thus necessary for truth to present itself—qua simple sense impression, qua religious imagination, qua philosophical reason. Graphic and linguistic marks are not just decorative. Their significance oversteps into the truth of Spirit's self-unfolding. After Kant, all claims regarding revelation and the spiritual in art presuppose, to one degree or another, Hegel's second naïveté.

The free shape of form in twentieth-century aesthetic theory enjoys this advantage over its predecessors. In German idealist aesthetics, intellectual and the spiritual form ride roughshod over empirical reality and content. Creative activity dominates physical content. "In a truly beautiful work of art," Friedrich Schiller writes in the *Aesthetic Education of Mankind* (1795), "the content should do nothing, the form everything. . . . Therefore the real artistic secret of the master consists in his *annihilating the material by means of the form*."[2] The "unrestrained freedom" of the formal impulse allows the artist to "join what Nature sundered . . . and sunder what Nature combines."[3] Twentieth-century aesthetics is inflected by a more fluid tension between form element and form pattern than Schiller's strict opposition of spirit to nature and freedom to necessity. There is no fast and firm distinction between form and content. Individual and isolated elements can be epistemological (sense impressions, concepts, judgments), historical (drawn from art, religion, philosophy, politics), theological (God, world, soul), dialogical (I, YOU, IT), or painterly (points, spots, lines). In a formal analysis, one looks at how they combine, splinter, and recombine into "compositional" frameworks (cognitive, institutional, pictorial, textual, sonic, performative).

Fluid, transactional conceptions of form dominated early twentieth-century German culture. Anxious to distinguish the humanities and the social sciences (*Geisteswissenchaften*) from the natural and mathematical sciences, German scholars at the turn of the century used the freedom of "form" to establish their own work on a firm but nonpositivist basis. As understood by Georg Simmel, form is not static and thinglike. Based upon flowing lines of relationship, form is an activity, not an object. Central to Simmel's sociology is an overriding interest in formal acts of sociation that organize elemental physiological and psychological drives, interests, purpose, inclinations, and movement. Focused upon the *Fluidum* created between form elements, not the individual element itself, society "certainly is not a 'substance,' nothing concrete, but an *event*—it is the function of receiving and effecting the fate and development of one individual by the other."[4] Seen as such, form is "the mutual determination and interaction of the elements of an association."[5]

The expressionist generation was to make greater claims about form than did Simmel. In line with Kant, Simmel restricted his analysis of it to strictly intellectualist terms. A very important essay, "Religion" (1912), indicates no metaphysical interest whatsoever. Attention shifts from doctrinal elements and ritual contents to what Simmel calls "religiosity," an organic rhythm based on formal relationships that lack a fixed set of objects.[6] Simmel made it clear that "his intent was [to] show the structural meaning of religion as a mental-spiritual phenomenon." Following Kant, he would not discuss the suprapsychological existence of its objects outside the subject's own apprehension of them.[7] While there is much to be said for Phillip Hammond's claim that Simmel was religiously musical, especially in comparison to Weber, he was positively tone-deaf compared to the expressionists, whose creative work was based upon the almost occult conceit that every form—each individual element, and the patterns they shape—resonates with a spiritual presence whose reality transcends the real world of visual objects and form-creating human subjects in which it is seeped.[8]

In early twentieth-century Jewish thought in Germany, form represents the vital medium that embeds revelation in the creaturely character of physical existence and symbolic expression. Form is central to the spiritual status ascribed to material objects, myth, ritual (i.e., law), the aesthetics and anti-aesthetics of creation-revelation-redemption, and the linguistic form of Scripture and its translation. Buber and

Rosenzweig were distinctly modern, rejecting romantic and post-romantic totalities and tonalities that fuse individual parts into a larger, rhythmic harmonization of opposites dominated from one single point in the system. The picture that emerges from their work is one in which existence breaks down into autonomous elements, which are reconstituted into a complex, even jagged, relational unit. An irreducible stress situated *between* the total whole and the individual element interrupts the extremes of objectivity and subjectivity represented by totalitarianism and nihilism. Form constitutes the linchpin of encounter, the in-between place without which there is no revelation in this world. Trust in form brought Buber and Rosenzweig close to art and lends sensual shape to the image of revelation in their work.

I

Form/Gestalt, Composition, Creation

The sarcasm Barlach directed against Kandinsky works only by isolating each point, spot, line, and dab as a set and separate form-element; as if to say that each black line or color volume constitutes an absolutely autonomous object bearing no relation to any other formal element. In fact, the emphasis placed in Kandinsky's art upon the unique and free single detail in its relation to a larger form-totality is much more ambiguous. Kandinsky defined pictorial composition as the "creation of the individual forms that are related to each other in various combinations, while remaining subordinate to the whole" (*CWA*, 167). However, the whole also remains subordinate to the part. The slightest change in composition, the act of altering one single form element, affects the spiritual sound made by that very same whole. With its own lithe life, form is not a static monolith. "The same form always produces the same sound under the same conditions," Kandinsky argued. "Only the conditions always differ; which permits us [to conclude]: [1] the ideal sound changes when combined with other forms. [2] It changes, even in the same context . . . if the direction of the form changes." Composition depends "upon the variability, down to the tiniest detail, of every individual form."[9]

Each separate color form or geometric shape is said to register its own unique sound. The reader learns in Kandinsky's *On the Spiritual in Art* that the sound of blue is bold and spiritual; yellow, warm; green, peaceful; red, intense, immense, and powerful; white resonates with a great spiritual, silent "other" that is alive with possibility; black sounds a dead nothing, without possibility; and so on (*CWA*, 177–88). Geometric forms later come to constitute the elements of composition, combining and recombining into more or less complex patterns. In Kandinsky's *Point and Line to Plane*, the process begins with the "point." An introverted element, it burrows into the surface, alienated from its general environment, establishing itself for all time. Ultimately, it takes an unnamed force to break open the point and to force it to emerge. In the process, a new life is formed, a new entity created: the line. The direction that a line takes within the picture frame conjures up different possibilities. "Above" and "left" reflect rarified, free, and spiritual movement. "Below" and "right" signify a state of being that is dense, bound, and material (*CWA*, 639–45).

A painting's compositional combinations constitute an act of world-creation, compared by Kandinsky to "a thundering collision of different worlds that are destined in and through conflict to create that new world called the work. . . . The creation of the work of art is the creation of the world" (*CWA*, 373). While earlier works such as *Composition V* (fig. 4) and *Composition VI* more obviously suggest the semblance of a physical world, allusions to physical space remain in the late work as well. The text *Point and Line to Plane*, written at the Bauhaus, begins by comparing the picture composition to a street, inviting the viewer to "emerge from one's isolation, immerse oneself in this organism, actively involve oneself in it, and experience its pulsating life with all one's senses" (*CWA*, 532). Art no longer mimics life, but rather vice versa. The natural world is itself compared to "a self-contained cosmic composition, which itself consists of innumerable, independent, hermetic compositions, getting smaller and smaller, and which—large or small— were ultimately created from points" (554). A discussion of line includes a nod toward crystals, plants, animal tissue, and skeletons (536).

"Art does not reproduce the visible but makes visible," Klee proclaims in his "Creative Credo" (*N*, 1: 76). Whereas in the art of earlier times visible things appear in visible form, "[n]ow the relativity of all things is made clear, the belief expressed that the visible is only an isolated case taken from the universe and there are more truths unseen than seen" (78–79). The sheer joy of victory is expressed in the green arms and brown-red legs of the *Runner at the Goal* (plate 12), a bulbous head with no face, inscribed with the number "1," with a geometric pattern defined by horizontal lines from grays to browns and black superimposed on his entire being. These formal features subvert physical semblance even as they suggest it. Rough analogues of the natural order of objects as one ordinarily sees them, they "console the mind, by showing it there is something more than the earthly and its possible intensifications." Klee adds: "[E]thical gravity coexists with impish tittering at doctors and priests. For, in the long run, even intensified reality is of no avail. Art plays in the dark with ultimate things and yet it reaches them" (80).

From the time of his 1914 trip to Tunisia, Klee's *Memory of a Garden* (fig. 3) speaks to the process of genesis and growth, to the study of creation, to the formation of an ordered cosmos, a liminal space caught somewhere between the invisible world of spirit and the visible world of physical sensation. Robert Kudielka comments that for Klee, "genesis is not just an unlimited flux, but a force continually moving between formation and dissolution. And indeed that interplay can be articulated."[10] As in Kandinsky's composition theory, the symbol of chaos starts with the "point." Neither white nor black, but rather both at the same time, it indicates a state in which particulars cannot be distinguished from each other. The cosmogenetic moment occurs when this point is jerked into the realm of an order that radiates out in all directions (*N*, 1: 3–4). In the beginning, things moved freely, neither in straight nor in crooked lines, but simply for the sake of moving, without aim or will. The tension between points gradually yields line as objects gradually orient themselves in the distorted, three-dimensional field of pictorial space. Deep beneath the surface exterior, our knowledge of the object's inner being amplifies and intensifies in appearance. In pictorial dimension, the object grows beyond the limits imposed upon it by our optical view of its outward appearance (39–47, 63–66).

Generating growth, the force that jerks "the point" into line is an impetus from without, the plant's relation to earth and atmosphere, and a slumbering tendency toward form and articulation that awakens according to an underlying logos, idea, word implanted from the beginning. Seed and root strike downward, the plant grows upward, driven by "space hunger and juice hunger." Gradually, the plant's articulation grows more and more ramified. To illustrate this process, Klee had his students put sand on a thin plate and then vibrate the plate with a violin bow. The sand rearranged itself according to the rhythmic order set by the bow. An invisible vibration was thus transformed into a material event, into a visible expression that took the form of newly arranged material (*N*, 2: 25–45). It can be compared to the process at work in *Memory of a Garden*. The use of color evokes a physical scene that is lush in texture and wildly unmannered, whereas the geometric ordering of blue, yellow, and purple planes and the use of abstract dots, dabs, and lines to indicate plant life remain fundamentally alien to the organic world. Color has transformed the invisible geometry into a material event.

The creative power manifested by *Memory of a Garden* and the movement of the bow was ultimately metaphysical and mysterious. Klee remained convinced that matter derives its own life from this creative power, acquiring order in its minutest particles. Human beings are charged by it, move toward its source, and manifest it in their physical functions. Klee speculated that this invisible creative power might itself be a form of matter, but one that our senses cannot perceive as they can more familiar kinds of matter (*N*, 2: 63). Elements are shaped into new order and form, into images that enjoy their own objective existence. Art extends the human eye into other possible worlds, like future worlds and worlds in other star systems. This renders the exterior physical appearance of our own world arbitrary and relative. The artist attempts to apprehend the "central organ" (*Zentralorgan*) of all time and space, the brain or heart of creation. The act of creation adds more spirit to the seen, more spirit to a garden scene or to a runner at the goal. It makes secret visions visible (*MA*, 49–51).

Klee's whimsical speculation rests upon a theory of vision and a part-whole logic tracing back to Kant's conception of the mathematical sublime, that judgment made by human subjects about objects and scenes too vast to comprehend in a single glance at a single moment. In the *Critique of Judgment*, apropos of a comment by the French traveler Claude Savary on the impact of Egyptian pyramids or the sense one has upon entering St. Peter's basilica in Rome, Kant speaks of "the feeling that . . . imagination is inadequate for exhibiting the idea of a whole." It will seem that "imagination reaches its maximum" even as "it strives to expand to the maximum."[11] The sublimity of the human subject lies in its attempt to subsume a totality beyond its visual limit. Klee understood with Kant that finite human consciousness lacks the means by which to comprehend or express a number of different dimensions simultaneously. Human vision begins with single parts in their manifold detail, never losing sight of the multidimensional whole compressed into the diminutive picture frame (*MA*, 15, 47, 49–51). Klee's paintings are very small in scale. A mere 25.2 x 21.5 cm, *Memory of a Garden* is infinitesimal compared to an Egyptian pyramid or St. Peter's. And yet his spiritual universe was vaster than Kant's, less given to the visible in nature.

The spiritual element in Klee's pictorial universe lies in the invisible presence as it enters into view. The world no longer looks the same as it does in Renaissance and realist painting, in which pictorial composition acquires a purely visual register. The world of creation in its totality is one composed of variegated elements, a green graphic sign set in the mock-up landscape of *Villa R*, the corporeal figure in *The Runner at the Goal* with the number "1" marked on its head, the inorganic grids, marks, and dabs of *Memory of a Garden*, which are more signlike than strictly vegetable. Visible and acoustic forms interpenetrate, as if to suggest that the exercise of language and other forms of symbolic expression provides essential components without which the visible world of physical objects could not exist. Visible sensation is, if not subject to language, coterminous with it. Klee used language to denaturalize the material world and thereby undermine the mimetic realism in which the world's true visage is identified with the image recorded by the physical eye. *Memory of a Garden* evokes spiritual shapes of visible sensation, caught at the very moment of creation before its solidification into raw matter.

Rosenzweig's understanding of creation shares the same variegation in which an invisible logic intersects with the world of visual objects. He named it the "grammar of the logos." Prior to the act of creation per se, an archetypal language of mathematical signs provides a semblance of voice to the elements God, world, and person. At this moment, each figure resembles the willful, dumb, aimless points in Kandinsky's and Klee's composition theory. They only become real and terrestrial through living speech and sound (*SR*, 109–10). In the act of creation proper, adjectives are identified as root words that lead from the inaudible archewords "Yes" and "No." Judgment constitutes the first act of speech. Declarative statements like "beautiful!" and "good!" provide the first real building block of an intelligible universe. Not unlike *Memory of a Garden*, the created world is all attribute. At this level, the thing itself, that which bears the attribute, remains a pure abstraction. The world of created objects acquires its own solidity through the *definite article*, which designates a recognizable and completed individual. Only now does the object attain substance, defined on its own, over against its Creator. The world, just a moment ago a chaos of attributes, is now replete with things. The object's temporal location is finally defined by the verb form, its spatial location by the noun form. In the past tense, everything stands at rest, anticipating the perfect tense, which is death. The identity of a thing is not fully fixed and realized until it finally falls silent (125–31).

In its totality, the world of created form remains fundamentally ambiguous. On the one hand, spoken language constitutes the organon by which our perception of visible objects acquires a measure of stability; but the sensation of stability relies upon language and its invisible presence. On the other hand, the spoken word transforms the physically tangible world into something meta-physical. At first, language is non-referential. It can express judgment and indicate attribute, but it represents no substance external to its own operation. Having once assumed the perfect tense, the now visible sign no longer belongs to this world, although it continues to inhabit it. Crowned by death, even verbal signs soon fall silent as they acquire physical density and duration, despite the revelations they offer in the interim. An ultimately dead form in the midst of the world, language in Rosenzweig's text ultimately gives

way to vision, a vision of God at the border separating this world from
the next. The uncanny presence of language, its relation to this world
and to another world, bears not a little resemblance to the thick, green
graphic sign in the unreal, moonlit landscape of Klee's *Villa R.*

Unlike the image of language in Rosenzweig's text, Klee's world-
signs are always already silent by virtue of their graphic character. To be
sure, one can read out loud paintings like *Once Emerged from the Gray
of Night* (1918) and *Let Him Kiss Me with the Kisses of His Mouth* (1921).
Graphic marks are inscribed into grids of colored squares to form into
the poetry of Hölderlin and the biblical Song of Songs. But the com-
pression of the letters into each other renders each poem difficult to
read. As Joseph Leo Koerner notes, paintings like *Document* (*Urkunde*)
and *Legend of the Nile* are impossible to read. In the one, linear rows
of signs written onto a vertical, brownish-white rectangle evoke hieroglyphs on ancient papyrus. In the other, orange-brown signs surround
pictographs of an oarsman, boat, and fish. Such sign-paintings imply
message and narrative, while providing no interpretive key with which
to decode them. The sign has become "pure" insofar as it does not carry
the otherness that meaning could give it.[12] Klee's cosmogenic theory of
composition presents sign worlds that have turned visible, but inaudible
and illegible. At the level of pure sensation, the words that compose the
world ultimately reveal nothing beyond their own creaturely, thinglike
character.

II

At first glance, the tenuous stability provided to the object by the verbal
and graphic sign does not suggest itself in Buber's work, if only because
the privileged *topoi* in his work—the unconditional, the absolute, and
the I-YOU encounter—elude the limits imposed by the objective world
of fixed form and I-IT consciousness. Rosenzweig was among the first
to complain. "In your setting up the I-IT, you give the I-YOU a cripple
for an opponent," he wrote Buber after the publication of *I and Thou*
(*BT*, 824). "You make of creation a chaos, just good enough to provide
construction material [*Baumaterial*] for the new building" (825).[13] This

misses the mark. Rosenzweig's critique and others like it overlook the place of form in Buber's work. Despite the animus for what he saw as the stiff character of law (an issue of particular concern to Jewish philosophy) and the realist form of discrete objects (of concern to aesthetics and art history), Buber's approach to the natural order belies any such claim that he "crippled" the physical universe. The simplistic binaries between religiosity and religion and between YOU and IT are ones that he himself consciously rejected. Indeed, the importance he ascribed to *Gestalt* calls into question his own inability to see law and realist objects as flexible, plastic shapes.

Law

In his earliest writings on the Jewish renaissance, rigid form and the free countenance of art chafe against each other. On the artist Lesser Ury, Buber wrote in 1903 in the *Jüdische Künstler* series: "Form does not say anything about reciprocal relations, the reciprocity of things. . . . Form separates, color unites. Only color can tell about air and sun, fog and shadows: it puts the thing in context" (*FB*, 65). Restraining the "energy of Judaism," law appears equally thick and thinglike in "The Jewish Cultural Problem and Zionism" (1905). The law is "ornate" and "distorted," a "hard, petrified imperative . . . removed from reality, which falsified and destroyed everything that was intuitively bright and joyous, everything that thirsted for beauty and all flights of fancy"(177). The problem with law lay, then, not in its substance but in its art, in its formal resemblance to the ornamental styles rejected by the youth culture of the fin de siècle. In its resistance to change, law's brittle shape dams the flow and flux of mystical *Erlebnis*, of landscapes painted by artists working under the influence of impressionism and Jugendstil. In Buber's writings, the form of Jewish law is almost always so rigid. It lacked organic capacity for him.[14]

In German, the words *Form* and *Gestalt* are not identical, although in English translation, it is easy to confuse the one with the other. By 1912, *Gestalt* assumed a central and positive meaning, in marked contrast to the term *Form* in the 1903 Lesser Ury piece. Commenting upon a work by Michelangelo, Buber looked to the form submerged in raw material. The artist struggles to overcome the dead block, not because art is somehow inadequate, but rather on account of a more fundamental opposition between the formative (*Gestaltende*) and formless (*Gestaltlosen*) principles. The tension between them, we now learn, lies at the source of all spiritual renewal, raging within every human soul as the creative, spiritual act subjugates unformed, physical stuff (*DJSJ*, 239). It is the free play of *Gestalt* that quickens the dead rigidity of form. As Klee was to observe, form occludes the idea of path, while *Gestalt* signifies "something more alive," an underlying mobility, a "form with an undercurrent of living functions. A function made of functions, so to speak. The functions are purely spiritual. A need for expression underlies them" (*N*, 1: 17).

Great victories of the formative principle over the formless principle do not remain pure *Gestalt*. Hence the need for the formless principle to break up ossified and institutional forms of normative order. This impetus drove Buber's utter and absolute rejection of Jewish law and ritual practice, bound up as it was with neoromantic proclivities for the hazy atmospheric of "air and sun, fog and shadows." And yet the power of formation (*Formung*) must continue to push back that border between spiritual creation and the unformable in its twofold struggle. It struggles dialectically against the formless principle, even as it works in league with it to undermine the kingdom of rotting *Gestalt* (*DJSJ*, 240). A complex unity impulse composed of contrasting vectors, the formative principle is central, not just to all creative activity, but to the very lifework of prophecy. Moses built upon the potent rhythm of a twofold movement between forming a unified people versus the people's straining against the formative idea. Jeremiah struggled for the unity of *Gestalt*, a faith in the ability to form (*gestalten*) the formless, to mold the people into the kingdom of God, a divine *Gestalt* (241–43).

Law explicitly acquires an "undercurrent of living functions," ascribed to *Gestalt,* as against *Form*, at least twice in the Buber oeuvre. In "Herut" (1919), an address on the openness of youth and the malleable power of religious symbols, Buber welcomed "the man who with his total being adheres to its commandments and prohibitions." He admitted: "Observance of commandments because one knows or feels that this is the only way in which to live in the name of God has a legitimacy all its own" (*OJ*, 164, 165). As in the famous rabbinic word-play, God's writing is simultaneously inscribed and free (*harut/herut*) on the tablets of the law. The forces of renewal seek to restore "the blurred outlines" of this freedom on the second tablets of teaching and law (169). A more radical revision appeared in "Pharisaism" (1925). Against Christian critics, Buber defended the early rabbis for having inserted the law's "rigid letter" into world events, having reinterpreted it in order to cope with "streaming reality" (P, 226). The relative openness to law proves largely rhetorical. In "Herut," a life of law required a literal certitude about its divine origins that the author knew most modern Jews would have to reject; and the apologetic purpose of the latter essay was, not to renew the form of law in the present, but rather to defend the good name of the distant Jewish past.

Rosenzweig was correct when he wrote to Buber: "[A]fter liberating us and pointing the way to a new teaching, your answer to the other side of the question, the question concerning the Law . . . should leave this Law in the shackles put upon it . . . by the nineteenth century" (*JL*, 77). The more consistent antipathy toward the law derives from the inability to see it as a lively and organic patterned activity, or *Gestalt*. Regarding the practice of *mitzvot*, Buber was for the most part myopic. All he recognized was the rotten form of thinglike "form-elements." The failure of vision, however, and this Rosenzweig did not understand, was practically, not theoretically, conditioned. From the hindsight of a 100-year perspective, one can today recognize the historical conditions accelerating the breakdown of traditional Jewish life at the start of the century and the rigid response to that crisis, particularly in relation to the revolutionary impact of Zionism, by the ultra-Orthodox establishment in eastern Europe and by the modern Orthodox in Germany; not to mention the failure of Reform Judaism to meet the demands of post-Emancipation society in respect to the performance of "ceremonial law" in anything other than its dullest bourgeois aspect. In this hindsight, Buber deserves at least some license. At the turn of the century, law had not yet acquired its modern idiom, not before the renewal of Jewish thought and teaching spearheaded by Buber, a renewal in which *Gestalt* and the world of objects play an essential role.

We are perhaps in a better position today to see how law retained a residual and more ambivalent place in this approach to form than would have appeared to Rosenzweig at first glance. Writing in 1922, on the evening of Yom Kippur, Buber expressed it to him this way: "But I must still tell you something serious: that in spite of everything, I feel in my innermost heart that today is the Eve of Yom Kippur. This may be so because (if I may add an autobiographical note) between my thirteenth and fourteenth year (when I was fourteen I stopped putting on my Tefillin) I experienced this day with a force unequalled by any another experience since . . . my body already reacting to the fast, became as important to me as an animal marked for sacrifice. . . . So you see I had not originally been exposed to 'liberal' influences in my religious education." As if to dispel the air of nostalgia that sticks to a childhood memory, Buber concluded: "All this is not only past but present, and yet I am the way I am: with much imperfection, yet nothing is felt to be missing anymore. May your good heart understand me!" (*JL*, 110–11). The heart occupies the ultimate seat of judgment. There is no longer a place for the form of law that Buber continues to feel in his very flesh.[15]

Objects

The problem of form in the philosophy of religion rests upon complicated arguments about "realism" and the status of objects. Realists will argue that human cognition performs reliably at base, that the reality of these objects fundamentally coheres with the formal constructs with which we perceive them. They represent the clear, objective order that began to buckle under the abiding impact of Kant's critical idealism, postimpressionist painting, and the new physics. In Jewish philosophical circles, it has been long argued that Buber was unable to ward off the relativism that permeates the notion that human concepts and judgments play an active role in forming the world of possible human experience. Building on Rosenzweig's complaint against Buber's epistemology, Steven Katz called for a "realism" that affirms the rich world of stable objects. It is still widely assumed—in fact, falsely—that in his critique of the I-IT form of relationship, Buber rejected the world of object forms in toto.[16] In doing so, Buber's critics overlook the empathy with which he turned to the material form of I-IT existence and the degree to which the I-YOU encounter penetrates patterns of formal signification rooted in the time-space continuum.

Most critics overlook the careful literary construction of *I and Thou*. If, in part 1, objects register disappointment, it is because the I of the basic word I-IT is "surrounded by a multitude of 'contents.'" Insofar as a human being makes do with the things he experiences and uses, he lives in the past, and his moment has no presence. He has nothing but objects" (*IT*, 63–64). No longer melancholy, the discussion of form is positively hostile in part 2. The institutional IT is a "golem," an "incubus, " a "gigantic swamp phantom" (93–94, 96, 102). The particularly harsh characterization does not, however, exhaust the world of real objects. Referring to just one type of organization, namely, the modern culture of capitalism, a quantifiable order in which people and objects are reduced to thinglike units, part 2 of *I and Thou* reflects the rhetorical nadir of Buber's three-part text. Rosenzweig and Katz fail to see that the vociferous rhetoric in part 2 is penultimate. With less to say against the world of objects per se, it anticipates the power of revelation in part 3.[17]

No dead thing, a tree described in the first part of the text indicates the most fluid form of I-IT life. "I can take in [*aufnehmen*] the tree as a picture. . . . I can perceive it [*verspüren*] as movement" (*IT*, 57; trans. modified).[18] The scientist assigns it a species class with an eye to its constructions, dissolved into a pure relation of numbers. Alternatively, an artist can register the tree as a rigid pillar in a flood of light and green flash. IT takes form as motion, flowing veins around sturdy core. This lovely description—Rosenzweig found it "bewitching"—suggests the impressionist, whose work captures the shimmering quality of perception, the first impressions made by light hitting the eye and its object; the flowing veins recast the sensual undulating line found in floral Judgendstil. Buber went on to lament: "Throughout all of this the tree remains my object and has its place and its time span, its kind and condition" (*IT*, 58; cf. 57–58). Not fixed and frozen, but precisely the opposite, it is subject to the flow of time and place (64). Buber mimics the expressionist complaint against impressionism. Over against a shifting and dappled surface, a more enduring and eternal visage was sought beneath the object's visible exterior.

The value of the IT-world hangs upon the status of the so-called thing-in-itself, the *Ding an sich*, the object par excellence. As proposed by Kant, an object exists in its own independent right even if human beings enjoy no privileged understanding of it apart from the aesthetic forms of intuition and the relatively static order of concepts that limit consciousness. In contrast, Hermann Cohen insistently denied the very notion that any pre-given thing exists prior to logical cognition, ethical will, and aesthetic feeling. Nature is the object (*Gegenstand*) generated by pure thinking. "Man" forms the object generated by pure will. Aesthetics combines the object generated by the logic of cognition (nature) and the subject generated by ethics ("man") into a new and complex form: the human person as a flesh and blood creature situated in nature. Cohen sought to preserve the autonomy of thought over against feeling (*Empfindung*) and representation (*Vorstellung*) to highlight the activity of reason, not the origin of sense impression. No objects (understood qua object of possible experience) are given, not even in the restricted sense allowed by Kant. Objects of possible experience are not given; they are produced by "the logic of pure cognition," "the ethic of pure will," and "the aesthetic of pure feeling."

Against Kant, Cohen rejected the view that the ordering of impressions according to concepts constitutes the content of thinking. That would have meant that formal concepts act as containers that shape the sense of preexisting objects, whose independence from thought Cohen sought to deny. The very first content of thinking is its own autonomous, self-referential activity. This activity takes the form of intellectual separation (*Sonderung*), unification (*Vereinigung*) and conservation (*Erhaltung*).[19] The real object (*eigentliche Gegenstand*) appears when objects of the mathematical sciences combine with objects of the descriptive sciences.[20] In the mathematical sciences, the object subsists as a system relation within a series of movements between points that remain mere geometric and mechanical abstractions. In the descriptive sciences, however, we apprehend concrete forms of nature, including and especially the individual life-form.[21] Ultimately, the individual object differentiates itself from the abstract and mathematical system of movement in order to constitute a new type of object: a unitary object (*Einheitsgegenstand*), an essence (*Wesen*), an organism.

This weighty negation of the primacy of physical substance goes to the heart of Buber's understanding of objects. The person who lives in the IT-world "perceives the being [*Sein*] that surrounds him, plain things and beings as things [*Wesen als Dinge*]; he perceives what happens around him, plain processes and actions as processes that consist of moments, things that consist of qualities [*Eigenschaften*] and processes that consist of moments, things recorded in terms of spatial coordinates [*Raumnetz*] and processes recorded in terms of temporal coordinates [*Zeitnetz*], things and processes that are bounded by other things and processes and capable of being measured against and compared with those others—an ordered world, a detached world" (*IT*, 82). In this description of objects, one finds not the mechanistic universe presupposed by Kant, but rather something more like the smooth curve and process posited by Cohen in the *Logik der reinen Erkenntnis* (Logic of Pure Cognition), a theoretical model of the universe based on the separation, unification, and conservation of thought.

Rosenzweig could not have been more wrong about Buber's approach to the world of created objects, as a second look at the 1903 essay on Lesser Ury confirms. The rejection of fixed and rigid line in Ury's impressionistic landscapes constitutes a rejection of the Newtonian cosmos writ large. "Here, all is given in the natural-material as mutual effect [*Wechselwirkung*]," and the "soul of the landscape . . . reveals itself in the reciprocal effect [*Auseinanderwirken*] of its elements, in the reciprocal shadings, mistings, intensifications, and deepenings." Ury's landscapes provide a "moment in which one thousand life streams mix" (*FB*, 67–68), a view of the world that recasts a neo-Kantian order, what with its fluid and dynamic exchange of reciprocating energies. Field, lake, sky, and tree in the undated *Untitled* (*Landscape with Lake*) (plate 7) are still separate in the incandescent haze of color. They present a world composed of soft, autonomous color fields right at that precise moment prior to either their ossification into distinct units or the complete dissolution of any object-like order. A world apart from the stable substance of realist landscape, it is one step away from the complete reorganization of space into the color grids of Klee's *Memory of a Garden*.

If the appearance of mathematical and empirical objects represents an exciting and hard-fought apex in Cohen's logic of pure knowledge, to Buber, it registers disappointment. IT receives only grudging due in *I and Thou*. IT is "somewhat reliable." IT has "density and duration," without which "a human being cannot live" (*IT*, 82, 85). But this does not mean that IT is something dead, since to call it only somewhat reliable already shows the elusively unreliable quality that it shares with YOU. The critique of the isolated object in a society motivated by materialism and means-end relations relies upon a more fundamental confidence. No dead chaos, the world of objects at its most precious proves as richly textured as the universe implied in Cohen's *Logik*, an impressionist surface, a floral Jugendstil pattern, or a landscape by Ury. Nor does it remain impervious. Something will happen to the object that goes beyond our perception of IT as an ordered thing. As the place of revelation, the world as object will catch fire and become presence.

Forms Bear Revelation (Early Buber)

Buber's privileging of "religiosity" and myth as against "religion" in the early lectures on Judaism contributed to his reputation as a mystic who was hostile to the stability of form. "Religiosity" refers to the "sense of wonder," the "ever anew articulation" that transcends conditioned being, while religion is the unalterably binding sum total of prescriptions and dogmas. The binary is not, however, that simple, in that religion remains true when religiosity continues to imbue its expression (*OJ*, 80). The key dynamic at work in their interchange is the formal act of "realization" (*Verwirklichung*), that is, the act of making "real" (*wirklich*). Form makes real. Intentional acts of perception transform the divine presence into a sensual shape subject to sensation. The essence of religiosity starts with the unconditional human act of decision that breaks the human state of spiritual inertia and works to "realize" divine *Gestalt*. An action below effects action above. Citing midrash and Zohar, Buber drew upon the human capacity to imitate God, intensify His reality, and redeem His presence (*OJ*, 83–86). The absolute deed makes divine reality real by providing *visible* form to the invisible Godhead. Recalling the reference to Michelangelo, Buber declared: "The countenance of God reposes, invisible, in an earthen block; it must be wrought, carved, out of it. To engage in this work means to be religious—nothing else" (93).

In myth, "to make real" is defined by its opposition to the ideal. To follow Klee, realization "does not reproduce the visible but makes visible." Once the divine hero of His people in the earliest biblical strata, God is "unsensual" (*Unsinnliche*) in later prophetic literature. No longer a sensual reality, God is now an ideal figure devoid of shape and form. *YHWH* turns into the God of the universe, the God of mankind, the God of the soul who no longer walks to-and-fro in physical concourse with human beings and material reality (*OJ*, 102).[22] The renewal of myth was meant to restore that sensual character, to reveal the invisible divine form pattern in things. "*YHWH* Himself can no longer be perceived, but all His manifestations in nature and in history can be so perceived. . . . Sensual reality is divine, but it must be made real [*verwirklicht*] in its divinity. . . . The *shekhinah* is banished into concealment; it lies tied, at the bottom of every thing, and is redeemed in every thing by the man, who, by his own vision or his deed, liberated this thing's soul" (*OJ*, 105–6).

Religiosity and myth have less to do with God and gnosis about the divine nature than with the human power to *perceive* in figures the spiritual significance of natural events and objects. "We must name as myth every tale of a sensually real event that is perceived and presented as a divine, an absolute, event," Buber explains (*OJ*, 103). Myth is the response to those rare and intense moments in which perception transcends the natural law of cause and effect. One now sees a worldly event (earthquakes, floods, wars, revolution, mass migration) as supercausal expressions of some never-named central intention (*Sinn*) that no conceptual thought can grasp. The event remains open to the wide-awake power of the senses as a "vividly perceptual [*anschauliche*], multifaceted reality" (104), a unified composition composed of many elemental and discordant parts, points, dots, and dabs that combine into a unified visible figure or form pattern. While myth does not preclude understanding a natural or historical event in causal terms, it was supposed to disclose a fuller truth. Again, form is central to Buber's understanding. The human act of mythmaking "opens up . . . the very being of the beloved, blessed figure [*Gestalt*]" (104–5).

Ultimately, Buber's attempt to see World War I through the prism of mythic patterns proved to be an utter, embarrassing failure. Writing the lead essay in the new journal *Der Jude,* he sought to see in the war an opportunity for the modern Jew to forge out of the chaos of rupture a feeling for community, connection, a new unity, a unified *Gestalt* that would restore the Jewish people to a condition of wholeness (L, 1–3). For the anarchist Gustav Landauer, Buber's close friend, such thoughts were "very painful . . . very repugnant, and border on incomprehensibility. Object though you will, I call this manner aestheticism and formalism and I say that you have no right . . . to try and tuck these tangled events into your lovely wise generalities [*schönen und weisen Allgemeinheiten*]: what results is inadequate and outrageous" (*LMB,* 189; trans. modified). Writing to Buber, he argued: "Historical matters can only be talked about historically, not in terms of formal patterns [*formalem Schematismus*] . . . I gladly grant that behind this is the desire to see greatness; but desire alone is not sufficient to make greatness out of a confused vulgarity" (190–91). Landauer's challenge to the grotesque fusion of *Erlebnis, Gemeinschaft,* and *Gestalt* out of world war and mass slaughter put an end to the aesthetic of religiosity and myth in Buber's work.[23]

Revelation Takes Form (Late Buber)

The relation between form and revelation underwent a fundamental transformation. Whereas before the war, Buber had promoted an aesthetic of unity and unification, revelation and form creation now received the rougher visage of an elemental dualism. Human spirit grew more passive in the process. Revelation now precedes the act of form-giving. It happens. It no longer constitutes an object of Promethean will, an effect by which unconditional human deeds make the divine presence real in a unified sensual shape. No longer the sole product of human activity, revelation will create its own form. The human person has to be called, its mouth but a sounding board. While the person is open to the revelation he or she receives, the subsequent activity of form creation that mediates revelation depends upon the prior act of reception. Revelation is the first active agent. It is revelation that now "seizes the whole ready [human] element in all its suchnesss, recasts it and produces a form, a new form of God in the world" (*IT*, 166).

Buber's critics continue to miss a fundamental theological distinction. The divine *essence* may bear no IT-like character, but the divine *presence* maintains an abiding relation with the forms that shape around it. In what seems to be a complaint, Buber observes: "And yet we reduce the eternal YOU ever again to an IT, to something, turning God into a thing, in accordance with our nature." This statement is immediately followed by a caveat usually ignored in the critical literature: "*Not capriciously*" (*IT*, 161; emphasis added). Buber then affirms: "In truth, the pure relation can be built up into spatio-temporal continuity only by becoming embodied in the whole stuff of life" (163). A pure relation outside time and space has by right a paradoxical place in the spatio-temporal world. Form is not dead when it contains a mixture of IT and YOU (167). Living forms are permeated by YOU-encounters (163). Indeed, "God is near his forms as long as man does not remove them from him" (167). Historically, cult and cosmos crumble only when "religions" extinguish God's "countenance," that is, the formal dynamic element that has been the subject of this chapter.

Understood as a visual composition, Buber's text is one in which persons, physical objects, spiritual creations, and God are reduced to three graphic signifiers: YOU, IT, and I. They are the elemental, open variables whose combinations and recombinations stamp the history of spiritual consciousness. Individuated elements persevere in relation, forming into patterns that burst into life, grow, die, and revive. The composition forms a complex structure based on a few simple elements. I, YOU, and IT are the philosophical correlate to the continual crisscross between circles, half circles, squares, triangles and trapezias, and straight lines in the pictorial universe of Kandinsky's *Composition VIII* (plate 17). As observed by Magdalena Dabrowsky, the balance between linear and circular elements and the use of horizontal, vertical and diagonal lines distributed throughout the picture enliven its surface, floating forms within an undefined and infinite light-colored background, symbolic of the absolute, the cosmic, and the highest spiritual plane.[24]

Alert to the elemental polarities that shaped Buber's thought as early as the Lesser Ury piece, Avraham Shapira has tracked how color stands in tension with but tends toward form, distance toward relation, vortex toward direction, the moment toward eternity. Indeed, the emphasis placed in most of the secondary literature upon color, vortex, and the moment have reinforced the false impression that Buber's work resists form and structure.[25] Certainly Buber did not want to pin revelation down to *one* particular theophany, law, form, or set of forms. His thought is "anti-form" in this most limited sense. But the term does no justice to a thinker whose thought assumed such pronounced formal character. Goethe once claimed to be a pantheist in relation to science, a polytheist in art, and a monotheist in ethics.[26] Buber too was a "polytheist" when it came to religion. His approach to form-elements and form-patterns suggests that he was neither nomian nor antinomian, but rather polynomian.[27]

III

A tentative association between theological content and aesthetic sensibility already appears in a 1905 letter that a young Rosenzweig wrote to his cousin and confidante Gertrude Oppenheim (née Frank). Rosenzweig recounted the pleasure he took in drawing lessons, how beautiful he found the life of "perpetual receptivity [*fortwährender Empfängnis*] . . . : eyes, ears, and understanding." In the very next breath, he went on to joke about how his own beloved God had turned into a weather-maker and humorously noted the backward evolution. Ordinarily, wind and weather gods like Wotan and Zeus turn into an ethical *melekh ha-olam* (king of the universe), whereas the reverse had happened in his own conception (*BT*, 10). In this quite funny account, bourgeois ethical monotheism gives way to wild, pagan impression. What young Rosenzweig may or may not have meant by wind and weather gods or *melekh ha-olam* is beside the point. Reflecting precocious wit, not definite theological content, the letter rests upon an unstated formal logic binding aesthetic life, pure reception, and theological discourse.

In tracing the trajectory of Rosenzweig's aesthetic, Annemarie Mayer-de Pay has pointed to the Jugendstil style that characterized the period of his youth, an art that did not serve as an end in itself but as a means to individualize and beautify the human environment.[28] In doing so, she undercuts the surface impression created by the author's own critique of "art" in *The Star of Redemption*. The move made from Greek paganism and cold plastic art into the lively world of revelation depends upon a methodology according to which the artist fragments the picture plane into stubborn compositional elements, which he then reintegrates into a variegated whole. Revelation is thus made to reenact the formal contrast between Renaissance and baroque art drawn by Rosenzweig's teacher from Berlin, the famed art historian Heinrich Wölfflin, as well as the break Hegel defined between classical sculpture and romantic painting and music. Viewed from this perspective, later works like *The Star of Redemption* and the Bible translation resemble works of art that are neither postromantic nor art nouveau. They reflect a type of anti-art, an artwork-that-is-more-than-a work-of-art in its formal arrangement.[29]

Method: Beautiful Detail and Pure Vision

Rosenzweig's "way" remained remarkably consistent in its compositional structure, despite changes in its tonal character over time. In a diary entry for May 25, 1906, he wrote: "To fall in love with beautiful details—for example, a beautiful forearm, the tumble of the raiment of one on his knees, the landscape in the background of a picture, the hushed entrance of the Rhine daughter at the conclusion of the *Götterdämmerung*." The next entry for that same day reads: "From the *detail* to seizing the *whole*—that is my way in many respects; intensive in *the beginning*, general and superficial *afterwards*" (*BT*, 45). From the very start, Rosenzweig's aesthetic was one in which reality is first broken into fragments and then reassembled. In another 1906 diary entry, Rosenzweig contrasts two ways in which one might look at an object, the theoretical and the aesthetic. The theoretical view breaks up the object into parts, whereas the aesthetic allows one to look upon it as a unity. The union of all theories would yield a view of the object in its highest sense (35).

As Cordula Hufnagel observes, Rosenzweig felt in art a wholeness missing in real life.[30] The same is true of religion, as is evident in a letter to his parents from a 1906 trip to Venice. Alongside Tintoretto's paintings and rococo interior design, he takes particular note of Giorgione's *The Tempest* in all its "wonderful details" (*wundervollen Einzelheiten*): a man with a woman with a child before a thunderstorm, his clothing, her movements, clouds, a well, branches before the female figure, a city, and houses in the background.[31] After sitting for a couple of minutes, "a miracle" (*ein Wunder*) occurs. Everything disappears. All the details vanish and "you see without knowing what you see; you become total vision [*ganz Sehen*]. Without passion, without agitation, without thoughts, without knowing about anything else or even about yourself: total vision. It is absolute art, as one speaks of absolute music, a music of nothing, representing pure, complete nothing [*rein gar nichts*]. . . . It is something so inexplicable [*Unbegreifliches*] that one could found a religion upon it" (*BT*, 47–48).

Hyperbaroque

Young Rosenzweig in Italy provides a fitting point from which to address the total compositional structure of *The Star of Redemption*, the dizzy detail, luscious language, soaring architecture, and undulating passions that course through the entire text. From Wölfflin, Rosenzweig would have learned how to make out the difference between Renaissance "linear" modes of rendering subjects qua solid, tangible bodies versus baroque "painterly" values that allow such bodies to merge; or the formal contrast between Renaissance composition across "horizontal" planes versus baroque composition along receding and ascending diagonal planes; and the distinction between the "absolute clarity" of Renaissance and the "relative clarity" of baroque. Most important will have been the move from a "closed" form of art to an "open" form and the difference between the Renaissance "multiplicity" of self-standing detail and the integrated baroque "unity" of parts.[32]

Expressionism in religion, painting, and poetry is hyperbaroque. As discerned by Walter Benjamin in his study of *The Origin of the German Tragic Drama*, they share the same "vigorous style of language," the "violence of world-events," the "contraction of adjectives and substantives into a single block," the "desire for a new pathos," "arbitrary coinings," and "archaisms in which it is believed one can reassure oneself of the wellsprings of linguistic life."[33] The contrast between Rosenzweig and Benjamin's baroque, however, could not be greater. Benjamin illuminates the ruined fragments and minutely isolated detail in German tragic drama.[34] These ruins figure prominently in his melancholy late reflections on the "angel of history" (a melancholy that shows none of the humor evidenced by Klee's *Angelus Novus*, which inspired Benjamin's essay "Theses on the Philosophy of History"). In contrast, Rosenzweig's mood was dark-bright and arrogant. He took more from Italian painting than from German tragic drama, from the detail in its relation to the endurance of a multiplex whole. Despite the author's own claims to the contrary, a careful look at *The Star of Redemption* shows that he never quite quit Wölfflin, whom he called "the god of my youth" (*BT*, 941). Aesthetics and aesthetic theory define a text whose elemental parts course into the total form of a six-figured *Gestalt* that renders almost everything that he has said against "art" virtually irrelevant.

Critique of Art

The aesthetic of *The Star of Redemption* is an anti-aesthetic that trades upon a crude caricature in which the visual art of Greek paganism is used as a negative foil with which to maximize the potency of revelation. In part I, the totality of existence fragments into three coeval, elemental components: God, world, and "man." No one single image can redeem the human subject from the overpowering fear of death. Like the point in Kandinsky and Klee's composition theory, each individual shard creates a closed figure completely disinterested in the existence of anything external to it. Rosenzweig took his cue from Greek religion, art, myth, and philosophy. The internally vital gods of Olympus and Aristotle's god show no concern for the world or love for the human person, whereas "Hellas" forms a social world that knows nothing of a god standing over against it (*SR*, 30–40, 61). Lastly, pagan "man" is reduced to a defiant tragic hero. The closed pagan character proves unable and unwilling to step out of the introverted confinement that keeps it from becoming soul (78–82). Plastic art was ready-made to fit this entirely overwrought, polemical program. The silent figure rendered visible, the hero who evokes terror and compassion, spectators alienated from each other: these represent "the world of art."

The caricature of art is a straw man at work in revelation. If art shows no transcendent connection, if it retains a purely internal coherence of part/whole tension independent of any external reference, then the artwork requires a revelation with which to extract it from the closed circuit out of its own self-possessed orbit (*SR*, 60, 81–82). The critique of art is a broadside, which by its very nature is limited to a very narrow consideration of art-for-art's-sake art tracing back to the impressionism of Manet and the hothouse poetry of George and Rilke. It obscures the deep desire expressed in Jugendstil architecture and design to break down barriers between art and life, and ignores the obsession with spirit and spiritual renewal in expressionist circles. More critically, the broadside cannot account for the fact that its own understanding of form already mimics the fancy found in Wölfflin and Hegel, according to which the plastic work of art seeks to press past its own frame or material limit.

Hegel was supposed to have epitomized everything that Rosenzweig rejected, a classic philosophical tradition, a single-point system of totality in which an absolute spirit subsumes all forms of consciousness under the wings of its own expansive rubric. I am not sure whether Rosenzweig ever saw that his own critique of art in relation to revelation reiterates Hegel's critique of Greek art and sculpture in the *Lectures on Fine Arts*. Hegel himself had already criticized the closed and self-subsistent character of classical art.[35] The self-referential form of Greek art sublimates the abstract spirituality of the "oriental" sublime by showing free spirituality in the form of determinate individuality.[36] Yet the gods dissolve in the face of fate.[37] Spirit *must* consequently surpass the self-enclosed character of classical art.[38] In Greek sculpture, Hegel recognized a rich and vital internal configuration of parts and wholes, before which he was ultimately unmoved.[39] More at home in painting, the first "romantic arts," he felt here the life and breath of our own existence; the divine appearing as a living subject in direct relationship with the community; the possibility of communion and reconciliation between the individual and God.[40] Rosenzweig could not have described revelation any better.

Addressing the shift from closed to open tectonics, Wölfflin developed Hegel's critique of Greek sculpture. The closed construction of Renaissance art gave way to the open a-tectonic quality in baroque art. In the former, every detail points back to the self-contained picture whereas the latter does not stabilize around a central axis. Baroque figures are thrown along ascending diagonal lines that veil the picture's rectangularity. In doing so, the artwork points beyond itself so as to appear infinite.[41] Wölfflin admitted that all works of art are finite objects that must therefore share a self-contained quality.[42] He thereby indicated the degree to which the baroque overshot the limits that define all works of art. And this bolsters my own argument about the critique of art in *The Star of Redemption*. Revelation in its relation to paganism marks the shift from one kind of art to a new kind of art, from the Renaissance and impressionism into baroque and expressionism, a type of art that is fundamentally aesthetic in rejecting what was perceived to be the narrow "aesthetic" of purely horizontal systems of organization and meaning.

Epic, Lyric, Drama

True to Lessing's seminal distinction between painting and poetry, the emphasis in part 2 of *The Star of Redemption* is placed upon what Rosenzweig was to later call "speech thinking," the late German post-idealist notion that truth only takes shape through temporal order and linguistic form. The visual elements of God, world, and "man" now co-relate through acoustic media. Creation is the narrative art of epic poetry, revelation the dialogue of lyric poetry, and redemption the choral song of dramatic poetry. Despite this heavy premium placed upon poetry, however, the "theory of art" running through part 2 reiterates the difference in the history of painting between the Renaissance "multiplicity" of self-standing detail and the baroque "unity" of parts. That a theory that so radically eschewed plastic expression depended so heavily upon Wölfflin's work in art history only contributes to the impression of an aesthetic that remains rhetorically overwrought and profoundly obscure.

Creation is epic, a sweeping exposition of a rich world of detail through which the whole is realized and from which the individual emerges (*SR*, 193–94; cf. 191, 242–43); the epic is a world of creation crowned by death. And revelation is lyrical; the opus comes to life, vitalized by the artist's love; the individual detail now forgets its own integrity and the multiplicity of things; immersed in a complete oblivion that inspirits it, revelation gives speech and soul to the mute self, just as the immediacy of lyric poetry inspires the individual detail with sound and life (191–95, 198). And redemption is dramatic; in redemption, the epic fullness of material unites with lyric immediacy as it enters into the public sphere (244–45); anticipating the concluding refrain of *The Star of Redemption*, the work of art spills "into life" through the spectator (248); the aesthetic of redemption achieves an animated and significant interconnection, complete and conclusive (242–43). In its completed compositional construction, the reconstitution of totality recalls the method described in Rosenzweig's 1906 diary entry or in his approach to paintings by Tintoretto and Giorgione.

Renaissance is to baroque for Wölfflin as paganism is to revelation for Rosenzweig. In the Renaissance, Wölfflin argued, the individual detail remains isolated. It speaks for itself, just as the isolated fragments refer only to themselves in part 1 of Rosenzweig's text. In baroque composition, however, the separate elements are no longer isolated. This too resonates with Rosenzweig's understanding of the detail in the aesthetic theory of creation. In a unified exposition of detail, parts work together to form a whole. Rubens was said by Wölfflin to weld individual figures into a homogeneous mass from which the individual figure cannot detach itself.[43] Then something happens, like the revelation that will happen in Rosenzweig's text. A main motif emerges from a mass of forms so strongly that it focuses the eye like a lens intensifying a ray of light. It speaks with double energy through the whole picture.[44] By converging on single striking effects, the painting is bound up with an acute concentration upon the momentary. Time contracts. The picture grasps only the brief consummation of the action.[45]

Religion is itself a compositional form in which a variety of figures take up a position vis-à-vis each other. It too is subject to the same formal analysis as a work of art. As in baroque paintings, a main motive, whatever it be, dominates its system. Perhaps the single figure of love/revelation constitutes that main motif. Or perhaps the motif forms around the interplay between three figures (God, world, and person) or the interplay between six figures (God, world, person, creation, revelation, redemption). This too suits Wölfflin, whose own example of a main motif includes Rembrandt's *Landscape with Three Oaks*. It need not matter whether the main motive is a monothematic or a polythematic figure. Rosenzweig created a pattern and Wölfflin analyzed compositions in terms of parts taken up into a total form: Rembrandt's three oaks, the figure of revelation, or the six-figured star of redemption. As Norbert Samuelson notes, *The Star of Redemption* compares to a painting a "picture of reality" or composition in which each part contributes to a complete, interconnected whole.[46]

Face

In the reconstitution of totality, Judaism and Christianity reflect enlarged form patterns in which the visible, elemental parts that compose the system have coursed through an aural network into a new, now visibly manifest *Überwelt*. In its overlap, a distinctly suprasensual, supranatural super world remains part of and apart from this physical world and its history. Judaism and Christianity are mirrors that focus the mediated miracle by which God, world, and soul meet in the speech-acts of creation, revelation, and redemption. To repeat Wölfflin's observation, in baroque art, the main motif emerges from a swirl of forms so strongly that it concentrates the eye the way a lens does to a ray of light. God, world, "man," creation, revelation, and redemption are mediated by the ritual cycles of synagogue and church.

And then, at the very end of the text, the figure of absolute truth, God's very face, will loom over both. The image of God's eye, ear, nose, and mouth combines into a spiritual synaesthetic that leaves behind the narrow world of "art" and the partial form of "religion."

The intensely visual character of the face ultimately undermines any critique of "art" proposed by the author. As described by Rosenzweig: "Nose and ears are the organs of pure receptivity. The nose belongs to the forehead; in the sacred tongue it veritably stands for the face as a whole. . . . Over [the first triangle [composed of forehead and cheeks] is now imposed a second triangle composed of the organs whose activity quickens the rigid mask of the first: eyes and mouth. . . . [W]hile the left [eye] views more receptively and evenly, the right one fixes its glance sharply on one point. Only the right one 'flashes'—a division of labor which frequently leaves its mark deep in the soft neighborhood of the eye-sockets of a hoary head" (SR, 423). As described by Wölfflin: "A head is a *total form* which the Florentine Quattrocentists, like the early Dutch artists, felt as such—that is, as a whole . . . in any detail we at once become aware of the whole. We cannot see the eye without realizing the larger form of the socket, the way it is set between forehead, nose, and cheekbone, and to the horizontal of the pair eyes and mouth the vertical of the nose at once responds."[47]

Did Rosenzweig take this face from Wölfflin? At the formal level, God's countenance and a baroque head demand the exact same features: eyes, forehead, nose, cheekbone, and mouth. A minor point, to be sure, since these comprise the main features of any face—unlike the very specific feature of the eye socket, not an obvious feature that immediately suggests itself. Both descriptions link forehead, nose, and cheek into one organizational structure and contrast that triangular form with another tri-thematic structure of eyes and mouth. Both highlight the mobility of a face whose features flash in a back and forth response. And both authors privilege the nose. By "total form," Wölfflin meant a *spiritual* form. He explained: "The form has a power to awaken vision and to compel us to a united perception of the manifold which must affect even a dense spectator. He wakes up and suddenly feels quite a new fellow."[48] Wölfflin's spectator becomes new. In Rosenzweig's text, the soul encounters this ecstatic vision of God's face and then shifts back "into life." In both accounts, the vision of the face constitutes a formally united perception of manifold detail that rejuvenates the souls of those who come to apprehend it.

The vision of the face intensifies lingering tensions that attend the relationship between truth, art, and aesthetics. On the one hand, Rosenzweig paid deference to the second commandment of Judaism, dutifully quoting Scripture, "You heard the sound of words but perceived no shape" (Deut. 4:12). Truth is the divine face alone. And we recognize this face, this truth, as it is, as it is in God. We do not recognize it figuratively (*uneigentlich*). On the other hand, the face remains a figure, a figure of truth. "The Eternal had become figure [*Gestalt*] in the truth. And the truth is none other than the countenance of this figure." Now, toward the end of his system, Rosenzweig boldly exclaims: "Yea, we now recognize the Star of Redemption itself, as it has at last emerged as figure for us, in the divine [face]" (418). Truth is not a figure in its own right, hovering freely (*für sich frei schwebende*). The *Gestalt* does not "represent" the face of God, but only because it constitutes it. Truth does not stand over against aesthetics, does not stand like a referent over against the sign that represents it, since truth *is* always already an aesthetic figure.[49]

In later work, Rosenzweig came to invert the classical part-whole dynamic of form. The divine figure discombobulates. Parts do not combine. One continues to see, but not too much. In the notes for a 1922 lecture on "The Science of God," Rosenzweig wrote: "Form [*Gestalt*] is always a binding of individual traits to a whole. Precisely this is forbidden in the case of God. . . . *That's how* the anthropomorphisms of the Bible are. God has a nose, eyes, ears, everything one wants. He cries, pleads, repents, *anything* one wants, but always from instance to instance. . . . He never has two attributes *at the same time*—that would already be form" (*GMW*, 47). The same argument was pursued six years later in "A Note on Anthropomorphisms" (1928). Hebrew Scripture prohibits naturalistic descriptions of God that combine two or more attributes into a single and fixed image. The image of God is disfigured by the entry into the creature's "momentary bodily-spiritual reality," into the "equally concrete momentary corporeal and ensouled meeting" between them (144).

These two short essays are as close as Rosenzweig came to break-ing once and for all with the form of totality. At the end of the *Star of Redemption*, God's face has appeared with all its features intact, combined into a single figure. "The Science of God" and "A Note on Anthropomorphisms" demonstrate a rougher sensibility. Stylistic and theological factors account for part of the difference. To use the expres-sion coined by Rosenzweig in reference to the Bible, the overall concep-tion is "unaesthetic-überaesthetic" in its reduction of a figure to one single attribute of character.[50] The theology is also different. "The Sci-ence of God" and "A Note on Anthropomorphisms" are rooted in this world, and we know from the Bible that one cannot see the face of God and live. God's face is an extraordinary figure whose image resists total figuration. Its integrated appearance in *The Star of Redemption* does not belong to the physical world. Hovering at the border between life and death, it no longer belongs to the concrete, created world.

The Bible

The Bible translation project's frame of reference belongs much more to this world than does *The Star of Redemption*.[51] Dissatisfied with the existing translations of the Hebrew Bible into German by Luther and Mendelssohn, Buber and Rosenzweig began translating the Bible in 1924. (Buber was to complete the project in Israel on his own after World War II.) Although Rosenzweig disdained art for art's sake, his view of the Bible diverged from his 1906 description of Giorgione's *The Tempest* in only one sense. The young Rosenzweig had felt no ambivalence in regarding an art object in aesthetic terms, whereas he was to later say that the Bible translation was more than a work of art. And yet, Rosenzweig and Buber's entire approach to the Bible and its translation remained no less aesthetic. In a May 1906 diary entry, Rosenzweig expressed love for the beautiful detail as a preliminary step toward grasping the whole. The Bible translation follows suit. Rosenzweig and Buber began their translation with the formal detail of word repetitions, etymological renderings, and breathing units in order to grasp the Bible as a unified whole, like a work of art pressed against the limits of "art." The intent was nothing less than to create the technical means with which to reproduce the sound of revelation in German as recorded in the original text.

A century before, Friedrich Schlegel had called Scripture a "system of books," an "infinite book," the absolute book." This was the romantic model upon which he understood, not just Scripture, but classical poetry as well. A network composed of individually coherent but inseparable works forms into "an organic whole." According to Schlegel, a literary canon constitutes "a single poem, the only one in which poetry itself appears in perfection."[52] Our own translators saw eye to eye with each other and with the early romantic theorist on the unitary character of revealed and inspired tradition. However, they radicalized Schlegel, for whom it was the poem and the book that constitute the individual fragments that forms into a whole. For Rosenzweig and Buber, it was not just the individual poem or book, but the individual word. This made their translation of scripture much less "aesthetic," opening it to harsh, odd-sounding effects. No less than Rosenzweig, and much more than Schlegel, Buber rejected any approach to Scripture detached from everyday life.

Rosenzweig did not want the translation to be seen as *just* a work of art. Translators had to respect the truth as it took shape in its original form (*BT*, 1037, 1041–42, 1052). At the same time, the Bible translation was still a kind of art. In a 1927 letter to Ludwig Strauss, Rosenzweig asked, all things being equal, which possible translation of a verse from the book of Samuel he found most beautiful (1177). Writing to Buber a few months earlier, he had insisted: "Whoever expects a piece of art cannot understand us; even though it is one. But it is perceptible as such only for those who do not seek [art] in it. Just as the elegance of a mathematical proof [is perceptible] only to those who approach it with mathematical interest, not to those who seek elegance." Rosenzweig clarified that subject matter dominates one's approach to any art form. However, he went on to suggest that his and Buber's own aesthetic and aestheticism, and by this he meant their interest in form, blocked their path to even the most ordinary work of art (*Kunstwerk*) and not just to that which is a more-than-a-work-of-art (*Mehralskunstwerk*) (1171). Much more than simply "more than a work of art," the *Mehralskunstwerk*, based as it is in the German construct form, preserves the link to art even as it severs it.

Another 1927 letter, this one to Gertrude Oppenheim, indicates how the art of literature shapes the image of God. The main body of the letter concerns the authorship of the two biblical accounts of the Balaam legend. In Numbers, the gentile prophet Balaam is called against his will by the king of Moab to curse the Israelites at his border but instead obeys God's command to bless them (Num. 22–23). This text suggests a stage in the history of Israelite monotheism when biblical authors recognized pagan prophets, whereas the authors of Deuteronomy blame this very Balaam for provoking the Israelites into the sin of sexual fertility rites. Rosenzweig speculated that a single author might very well have entertained conflicting opinions. He continued, "the people who wrote the Bible to all appearances thought of God similarly to Kafka. I have never read a book that had so strongly reminded me of the Bible as his novel *The Castle*. Reading it is therefore also no pleasure" (*BT*, 1152). It is modern literature, not classical medieval philosophy or Jewish tradition, that articulates a sense of the inscrutable God whose form appears in the Hebrew Bible.

This is "The Secret of Biblical Narrative Form." Rejecting any notion that form has no role to play in creating content and meaning, Rosenzweig opposed Goethe's call to translate Shakespeare into German prose. This would have meant sundering content (prose) from aesthetic form (poetry). But poetry and prose are not separable. With Hegel in *The Science of Logic*, Rosenzweig argued that content cannot exist without form.[53] It is therefore impossible to distinguish religious content from aesthetic form without reducing religion to the "prose of bare content," to a specialized, cutoff religious subculture separate from broader currents of consciousness. Religious content must therefore "sound all tones," retaining all connections with reality, including aesthetic reality (*ST*, 129–31). Luther, according to Rosenzweig, had respected the particularity of Hebrew expression only in those relatively rare instances where he detected the living word of God, a content. In contrast, Rosenzweig and Buber preserved the formal peculiarities of Hebrew and biblical style, convinced that one must remain open to the possibility of hearing God's revelation in every scriptural passage (48–

50). They could not profess to know beforehand from which words, from which elemental *parts* of the Bible, teaching and comfort might one day come (59).

Rosenzweig and Buber consequently took meticulous care rendering Hebrew linguistic form. While epic narrative form contains a verbal stimulus (*Stichwort*), but no point; and while anecdotal narrative style has a point, but no specific verbal stimuli, biblical narrative form contains both point (in this case, teaching or *Botschaft*) and particular verbal stimuli that tie the different frame stories into a whole. "Verbal stimuli" refers to Hebrew idiom, wordplay, and repetitions, the interconnections between words throughout the text. A great deal has been said against the effect that such attention to the Hebrew original creates when trying to recreate it in German. The idiomatically awkward etymological renditions chosen by Buber and Rosenzweig in their word choice come especially to mind. And yet that was precisely that unnatural, unbeautiful result intended by the translators, not to mimic ordinary language but to stretch out revelation like a line in a composition by Kandinsky or Klee.[54]

The particular words used by Buber to illustrate his essay "On Word Choice in Translating the Bible" create a theological tour de force. The discussion starts with *qorban*. Not a sacrifice, it reflects no idea of renunciation, but rather a *Darnahrung*, a near-bringing, a there-bringing, a "term of relation" that implies the "existence of two persons . . . one of whom seeks to diminish the distance between himself and the other in approaching it by means of the *qorban*, which he 'brings near' the other." The *olah* is no burnt offering, but an "ascending," "that is what ascends in its glowing-embers on the slaughtersite," a literal reading of the term *mizbeah* that the more neutral "altar" does not convey. *Kipper* does not "atone" and "expiate" as much as to cover, cover over, and protect. It is that which protects from *negef*, not a plague, but rather a "stroke," that which strikes down. In this system, holiness, that which is *kodesh*, is "not a static but a dynamic concept, not a condition but a process," a process of hallowing, on a "ground of hallowing," in "garments of hallowing," on "festivals of hallowing." Hallowed objects are set apart for ritual exclusion, whereas the opposite of *kodesh* is *hol*, not "unholy," but more simply that which is "surrendered" for ordinary use. The goal of all this is to apprehend God's *kabod*, not God's majesty, but rather his "appear-ing," the "manifestation of invisible *majestas*, its becoming-apparent—glory, but glory as the radiation of 'force.'" The translation appeals to the "immediacy of linguistic perception in the reader," the perception of God's *ruah*, not wind or spirit, but rather surge, and to *YHWH*, not "the Lord," not a concept but a name, translated by Rosenzweig and Buber as a pure pronoun as I/MY, YOU/YOUR, HE/HIS, depending on the context (*ST*, 77–87).

Buber's conceptualization in this essay is priestly, not prophetic. The precise order of the word choice moves the readers into the tabernacle space in order to bring them near to the divine manifest, up to the very name of God. The form of repetition is nothing less than the *Botschaft* of Scripture at its most cultlike, to quote Klee, an underlying *Gestalt* that is "something more alive," an underlying mobility, a "form with an undercurrent of living functions. A function made of functions, so to speak. The functions are purely spiritual. A need for expression un-derlies them." Ritual is not rigid, but rather sinuous in the repetition of key terms that insinuate themselves through a prolonged passage. The effect is at once musical and visual:

> So *Aharon is to bear*
> the names of the children of Israel
> on the *breastplate of Judgment*
> *over his heart,*
> *whenever he comes* into the Holy-Place,
> for remembrance *before ME,*
> *regularly.*
> And you are to put
> Into the *breastplate of Judgment*
> the shining-things and the planing-things
> that they may be *over the heart* of Aharon,
> *whenever he comes before ME.*
> So *Aharon is to bear*
> The Judgment of the children of Israel
> *before Me*
> *regularly.*

Scripture highlights the act of bearing; the heart; the breastplate; Judgment; entrance before *HIM*; regularly. The repetitive form of poetry and the presence of a name combine with the breastplate and shining-things and the planing-things over the high priest's heart. The repetition of words illuminates the dramatic feature of revelation as it appears in the form of ritual, its inherent regularity (*ST*, 36–37).

Verbal stimuli in the Bible reflect a world of beautiful detail, the same unified world of beautiful detail that Rosenzweig had once apprehended in painting. There is no substantive difference between the parts merging into the experience of "pure vision" before Giorgione's *The Tempest* and the discordant parts that comprise the different verbal stimuli in the Bible, a unified literary document. As Rosenzweig wrote to one Orthodox reader, Jakob Rosenheim, he and Buber translated the Bible as one work, the work of a single mind. Neither translator believed Moses to have been that author. And yet, the appellation "R," by which modern biblical scholars designate the text's redactor, took on the authority and status of *rabbeinu*, the traditional honorific ascribed to the prophet (*ST*, 22–23). For Rosenzweig, the Bible translation was the last development of the aesthetic method from 1906, in which a host of harmonious and unharmonious details combine into a whole that is no longer limpid and lovely or set apart from everyday life. Super-aesthetic and even unaesthetic, it forms into a "more-than-a-work-of-art."

IV

If revelation takes a half-step from art, then art, like creation, is but a half-step removed from nature. The art of creation and the creation of art are always already permeated by judgment. "It is good," "it is very good." Reorganized into grids, each is unique, each in tandem with the others. In religion, the apprehension of divinity hangs upon the play of word and color, the physical world of objects, and complex acoustic and literary constructions. Rosenzweig was right to observe that without attention to aesthetic form, there is the risk of religious content turning into bare content. Revelation does not exist apart from the order, disorder, and reordering of creation, from the form of part, whole, mass, color, tone, touch, and taste, from individual points, lines, spots, and dabs. It fits into creation, which is a type of composition, a kind of art, a that-which-is-more-than-a-work-of-art in its formal constitution. Such claims rest upon a logic whose fundamental premise is that no aesthetic frame can isolate formal expression from everyday human life and existential mysteries. So-called isolated art objects manifest larger contextual nexuses that situate them, and therein lies their social significance and spiritual status.

In opposition to Buber and Rosenzweig (and also to Kandinsky and Klee), two points may be made in favor of provisionally holding on to the notion of an isolated art object. First, definite epistemological over-reaching haunts any claim of theological or spiritual significance for a poem, painting, or scripture. Expressionism in religion and art begins to creak under very little critical scrutiny. At the simplest level, isolated art objects, scriptural compositions, and ritual acts neither reveal nor constitute God's living word or any spiritual presence. Viewed suspiciously, the luminosity they generate speaks to the elaboration of their own performance. As for art objects, they remain subject to the intense ethical vagaries of cultural capital and class privilege while providing simple, quotidian pleasure to those who enjoy them. Art forms are the attendant fetish to political and cultural domination, but on their own, they are not worth the price of institutional bloodshed.

In the acute attention paid by modernist writers to formal artifice, the literary critic Robert Alter identifies the residual belief that they could outdo the proponents of nineteenth-century realism in registering psychological, social, and even historical reality through the form of fiction.[55] Revelation and the spiritual in art take this residue one step further. Pat contentions that "art" does not trust language turn a blind eye to the fact that Kandinsky and Klee placed the same trust in the visual media of color, line, and volume that Buber and Rosenzweig placed in the linguistic form of revelation. If this trust proves ultimately misguided, it is not because the claim that physical form can reveal a spiritual super world is inherently ridiculous, but rather because such constellations are insufficiently problematized. The instability that stamps all acts of formal signification, especially in relation to religion and revelation, undercuts the trust in spiritual good with which one might otherwise invest them. When form makes mystery manifest, it does so with the raw force of a subtle nullity that is impossible to verify.

Figure 4. Wassily Kandinsky, *Composition V* (1911). Private Collection, Switzerland. © 2005 Artists Rights Society (ARS), New York/ ADAGP, Paris.

Traditionally grouped around a set of acoustic and visual contents, revelations are, by their very nature, incomplete. The prophet Ezekiel beholds an image of God upon His throne, but only at the threefold distance lent by the "appearance of the semblance of the glory-of-God" (*mareh demut kavod-YHWH*) (Ezek. 1:28). The invisible essence of the divine name stays hidden from view, cloaked in the visible appearance-semblance-glory of its presence. In their tug away from realist representation, it is the infinitesimal gap between "something" and "nothing" in revelation that in the twentieth century acquired a visual register in "abstract art," that is, art without objects (*gegenstandslose Kunst*). In Kandinsky's *Composition V* (fig. 4), the use of colors and geometric shapes vaporizes realist space and physical contour as the painting's overt religious reference begins to burn away. A painterly analogue to the pared-down external reference in the religious thought of early German modernism, art without objects illuminates revelation without content. At the apex of art and religion, expression seeks to surpass, to burn up the formal elements and patterns upon which it simultaneously feeds.[1]

In his call for "more realism" in revelation, Steven Katz rejects the rare, fleeting character invoked by Buber in the I-YOU encounter. Such conceptions entail an insubstantial notion of self, thing, and God, which cannot explain how identity endures over time. Space and time ground knowledge. This includes the identity of a revelation, which has no significance apart from intuitive contexts and conceptual contents. According to this view, revelation without content fosters religious subjectivism and ethical relativism.[2] Recognizing the problem, Buber took to a more realistic orientation vis-à-vis concrete existence after *I and Thou*. "Since then," he declared in 1929, "I possess nothing but the

63

everyday out of which I am never taken. I do not know much more"
(*BMM*, 14). And yet for all that, his approach to revelation always fell
short of the determinate content or fixed form demanded by the realist
critic. The rarified nothing of revelation does not easily give way to the
mundane something of everyday life.

In Buber's defense, "realism" ill suits a body of thought with roots in
the heady milieu of Jugendstil ornament, neo-Kantian philosophy, expressionism, abstract art, theoretical physics, and Bauhaus architecture.
The image of revelation reduced to nearly nothing—to quote Robert
Alter, "the 'zero point' of revelation, revelation pushed to the brink of
nihilism"—was not unique to Buber.[3] In *The Star of Redemption*, revelation signifies the expression of love, an imperative so pure as to lack all
descriptive contents beyond its own command. Early twentieth-century
Jewish thought and abstract art share this turn toward paring down
verbal and visual signs. In doing so, art without objects intensifies the
logic of modern religious expression, a discourse about presence that
does not pretend to say too much about its object. In radical opposition
to the visual mediations of naturalism and materialism, abstract art respects the elusive shape of revelation in ways that realist philosophy and
art cannot.[4]

Revelation and the spiritual in art depend upon the degree to which
that which is thing and that which is no-thing are dialectically enmeshed in their separation. As defined by Theodor Adorno, "spirit"
is that intangible quality by reason of which artworks "are more than
they are." An immaterial surplus supplements the unique physical characteristics that condition their material existence in a back-and-forth
motion. "What appears in artworks and is neither to be separated from
their appearance nor to be held simply identical with it . . . is their
spirit. It makes artworks, things among things, something other than
thing by becoming a thing."[5] What Adorno was to call autonomous art
reflects critically back upon its own thinglike character and upon the
world of objects that it seeks to outshine. Immaterial forms composed
of physical paint on material canvas manifest a spiritual pulse, a mysterious presence. In doing so, the recondite represents the transformation
of the material object, a transfiguration that acts upon the everyday that
is its own most genitive character.

The spirit of autonomous art and religious expression maintains a critical distance from the material forms they inhabit, at once simultaneous to an appearance with which they are not identical. Adorno rejected any attempt to collapse that distance. Against Heidegger, he opposed the formulation of a care, commitment, obligation, and identity too completely stuck in its own self. Against Buber, he complained: "Theology is tied to the determinations of immanence, which in turn want to claim a larger meaning. . . . In this process, nothing less is whisked away than the threshold between the natural and the supernatural."[6] The distance between thing and non-thing, which Adorno sought to preserve, is essential to his hallmark critical approach. The "jargon of authenticity" brings transcendence too close to everyday reality.[7] Not unlike Katz, however, Adorno failed to see that in Buber's work, the revelation of presence, like the autonomous art he himself championed, is neither separate from material existence nor simply identical to it. In this way, it preserves the distance from objects sought by Adorno.

I

Art Without Objects

A countersystem that derives maximum significance from minimum content, art without objects constitutes a fundamental critique of systems of representation that objectify persons and things into rigid, objectlike form. In Jugendstil circles at the turn of the century, the term "abstraction" referred to the act of highlighting a physical motif by superimposing it against a ground composed of empty volumes devoid of any inessential detail. Sometimes called "stylization," the method draws attention to a main figure or group of figures whose pose and presentation is ornamental and symbolic, not natural per se.[8] In Hermann Obrist's *Whiplash* (1895) (plate 5), all that matters is the main figure itself, the physical mix of pain and floral motion, a curvature of silk on a blank wool background. Works by Kandinsky, Malevitch, and Mondrian are still more radical. Rather than highlighting a single object or group of objects, abstract art at its most intense will begin to obliterate all form drawn from nature to heighten the luminosity of color and to quicken the activity of line.

In German idealism, this rough approach to the visible order is traced back to the Hebrew Bible. For Kant, the second commandment was "[p]erhaps the most sublime passage in the Jewish Law." Purging image from cult purifies and elevates consciousness, while precluding the fanaticism in "*wanting to SEE something beyond all bounds of sensibility.*"[9] Objects are of as little interest in Kant's aesthetic as they are in his reading of Scripture. To say as he did that art is "disinterested" means that art has no stake in any extra-aesthetic reality external to its own constitution. In this rococo interpretation of art, the subject enjoys nothing more than the sinuous line's free movement through space. Hegel paid no less respect than did Kant to the sublimity of Hebrew poetry in relation to physical reality. In his reading of the Psalms, Hegel confessed, "What we most are amazed at is the power of spiritual exaltation which suffers everything else to fall away that it may declare the unique Almightiness of God. . . . Light, heavens, clouds, the pinions of the winds, each and all are here nothing by themselves, merely an external; vesture, the chariot or messenger in the service of God."[10]

The art historian Wilhelm Worringer looked even further back, past oriental poetry to "primitive art." Setting the theoretical stage for expressionism in his seminal *Abstraction and Empathy* (1907), he identified two basic typologies. "Empathy" is that style in which one delights in the organic shapes of nature, the purpose of which is not to copy nature but rather to enjoy one's own nature and its mysterious power of organic form. Renaissance art marked a high point in this, after which empathy was said to fall into the mere imitation of copy realism. "Abstraction," on the other hand, is life-denying and inorganic, reflecting archaic fears in response to physical decay. Projecting a contemporary European mood onto non-European cultures, Worringer tried to explain that "primitive" people turn to abstract patterns "because [they stand] so lost and spiritually helpless amidst the things of the external world, because [they experience] only obscurity and caprice in the inter-connection and flux of the phenomena of the external world." For this reason, "the urge is so strong in [them] to divest the things of the external world of their caprice and obscurity in the world-picture and to import to them a value and necessity and a value of regularity."[11]

Despite its now universal usage, we should treat the term "abstraction" with some hesitation. In philosophy, the word signifies a lifeless form of expression empty of sensual or spiritual content. It barely appears in modern religious thought and always negatively. Kandinsky preferred the term *gegenstandslos* (without objects) for the same reason. I have kept the term only to elucidate a critical approach to objectlike data of consciousness that are earthbound and inert; and to associate revelation with more ambient forms of sensation that resist fixed-point location. For Buber, a formless presence binds the relationship between I and YOU. For Rosenzweig, a grammar of eros reveals the God who commands the human soul to love "Him." Devoid of content, presence is pure. Something happens about which one can know nothing except to say that something has happened. Describing the actors on stage in a play, Buber's protagonist in *Daniel* recalls, "When they appeared to me, they came from the edge of being, and when they went, they died away into the void, as a tone dies away. They announced to me nothing other than their presence. And they did this with the precision of a shadow" (*Dn*, 103).

II

Daniel

With its mix of art nouveau stylization and expressionist pathos, Buber's *Daniel* provides an excellent starting point from which to consider the empty form of revelation. Set up as a series of dialogues between the poet-seer and his friends, the text opens in the mountains with a discussion "On Direction." Daniel speaks to an unnamed woman about tearing one's own direction out of a formless abyss composed of infinite possibilities. The benumbed bourgeoisie surrenders itself to inherited traditions, whereas the commanding soul enters the whirlpool, which it forms around its own intentionally crafted direction (*Dn*, 56). In the dialogue "On Reality," Ulrich learns that the real is not pre-given; it refers neither to the unformed essence of pure experience (*Erlebnis*, the absolute and unmediated experience of the world) nor to the world of experience structured by the concepts and contents of human experience (*Erfahrung*). The real is the creative human act that transforms *Erlebnis* into the form of symbolic works and acts (65–67). In the dialogue "On Meaning" that follows in the garden, Daniel advises Reinhold to descend into the abyss of pure experience in order to create unity out of its thousandfold duality. The unity of form out of chaotic duality provides the first step from empathy to abstraction.

The dialogue "On Polarity," after an excursion to the theater, is the text's high point: the revelation of a god from out of an empty space. Daniel recounts how *"something took place* before me in a way that seemed unusual and astonishing. In a space that was lifted out of the context of space and no longer had any connection, neither with the above nor with the below, neither with the right nor with the left, neither with the being nor with . . . but yes, a single specific connection with this before where I was" (*Dn*, 102–3; emphasis added). The first act of the performance revealed the free polarity of human spirit. Two actors personify two godlike, competing primal powers surrounded by the mediating chorus of the ensemble. Act 2 draws attention to the palpitating, quivering community of spectators who confirm the drama that occurs onstage. Act 3 hits the climax as the youth in the Bacchus play conjures up the god. Suddenly, Daniel looks up above the stage to perceive "a man of high stature" standing before him, "Nothing any longer veiled me from his being; he was the son of venture and polarity; and he was beautiful" (119–20). Daniel compares the poet to Enoch transformed into fire. Like the angel in the legend, the poet is reduced to two single attributes, eye and wing. Fire burns up everything extraneous, presenting an abstract field bearing no tangible shape.

The combination of revelation and art nouveau in the god's appearance brings the drama of religion back to its base in perception and the organization of objects. The position of the Bacchus youth in relation to the surrounding milieu shares the shape of the young boy in Lilien's *The Creation of the Poet* (plate 2) or Obrist's whiplash shape. They are superimposed upon the blank space of the theater stage, a black backdrop, or an empty field. The empathetic approach to fluid form in the lush organic look complements the tendency to simplify that is the signature of abstraction. The coiling vegetal design simultaneously excludes any extra, naturalistic detail that might otherwise clutter the picture. The Bacchus boy personifies the epitome of aesthetic perception. Daniel tells an interlocutor, "Look at the ground, at the shadows of the trees as they stretch themselves over our path. Have you ever

seen . . . a branch so outlined, so clear, so abstract as here?" (*Dn*, 103).
As in Japanese screen art, the tree branch and the god stand out against
a bare, flat surface.[12]

Only stylized, the abstraction here is incomplete. An empty volume
highlights the central figure or group of figures. The larger, surrounding world of objects has disappeared, but only to isolate the titanic
forces onstage, the community of spectators who confirm their act, and
the beautiful god who has risen above the stage before Daniel's eyes.
The god hovers above and beyond the actual stage. Something real has
happened; he has been made real and visible. All else belongs to the
"edge of being," to the void from which these figures emerge and into
which they fade. The god who appears before Daniel is silent; the word
belongs solely to the poet who has conjured up its presence. In distinct
contrast, the more dialogical picture of revelation becomes more abstract in *I and Thou*. I and YOU have less tangible character than the
Bacchus boy, more pared down, more like a dot or line by Kandinsky or
Klee than like flesh. Individual figures carry less value than the relationship between them. The shape of revelation thus retains less form, while
remaining purer. In its active character, the content of its presence will
have lost all physical semblance.

Presence

If the Jugendstil of Daniel forms around a world of precious objects,
I and Thou plays at the hard-edged oppositions of expressionism. The
sculpted figures onstage are stripped down to four bipolar elements:
I-YOU, I-IT, reduced to the barest possible significance in order to
underscore the more fundamental interchange between presence
and object (*Gegenwart* and *Gegenstand*) (*IT*, 63). The latter stands for
that real entity, a physical and material substance, while the former is
indeterminate by definition. Although a separate, sensual I and YOU
constitute the sine qua non of relationship, neither figure exercises the
center of gravity. A place of metamorphosis, the axiological center of
relationship occupies an *in-between* space as objects lose their character as solid matter. Objects dematerialize into presence, a bare surge
between two parties, impossible to define, a mode of pure relating
unsullied by determinate, space-fixed, time-bound feelings, contents,

and objects. In the syllabic gap between *Gegenwart* and *Gegenstand*, "something happens" to IT.

Derrida and others have argued that in the history of Western philosophy, the value ascribed to presence comes to exclude sign, sense, and sensibility. An index to self-presence, transparence, auto-affection, and metaphysical closure, "God is the name and the element of that which makes possible an absolutely pure and absolutely self-present self-knowledge," according to Derrida.[13] "Pleasure *itself*, without symbol or suppletory, that which would accord us (to) pure presence itself, if such a thing were possible, would be only another name for death."[14] But that was never Buber's point about presence. In place of presence, Derrida identifies a counterlogic that approximates the I-YOU relationship, a supplementarity "which is *nothing*, neither presence nor an absence. . . . It is precisely the play of presence and absence, the opening of this play that no metaphysical or ontological concept can comprehend."[15] Insofar as an I must say YOU to HIM, the divine presence is never self-identical. Revelation is the impossibility of a self-proximity unmediated by the signs (I, YOU) to which it cannot be reduced. "[I]ncompatibilities are simultaneously admitted," Derrida asserts.[16] The empty quality of presence demands the dialogical play of signification. A destabilizing figure, presence flickers between I and YOU in the empty volume defining OUR difference.

"Things" Catch Fire

To assert that IT can turn into YOU contributes first and foremost to the disordering of realist perception. Ordinarily, an object appears within a visual field, determined by a spatial nexus defined by other objects to which I selectively attend. IT stands next to IT, which stands next to IT and so on. To grasp this nexus means to apprehend the interaction of each unit in relation to and upon one another. IT is impressionism, for example, Lesser Ury's *Untitled* (*Landscape with Lake*) (plate 7), color blending into color into color. But something happens to this order of perception when any one such thing or figure assumes YOUR exclusive status. No longer "a dot in the world grid of space and time. . . . Neighborless and seamless, he is [YOU] and fills the firmament. Not as if there were nothing but he; but everything else lives in his light" (*IT*, 59). The image reflects a gigantism in its break with the copy realism of mimetic representation and the relative shadings of impressionism. The distorted image of a single thing fills the field of perception to occupy the sole focus of MY attention. Ripped out of context, a gigantic dot assumes a value in whose light everything else now transpires.

The "world-order" that YOU now subsumes stands over against the world of ordered objects oriented around the determinate center provided by the Kantian cognitive subject, the romantic poet, the boy in Lilien's *The Creation of the Poet*, or the titanic powers and the beautiful boy-god that Daniel saw onstage. The YOU-thing has lost its sculpted, objectlike character. It constitutes a singular essence, and I approach it exclusively. "[M]an encounters . . . always one being [*Wesenheit*] and every thing as a being [*Wesenheit*]. Nothing else is present except this one cosmically [*welthaft*]" (*IT*, 83). The one single thing becomes an exclusive world (*Welt*) unto its own when IT turns into YOU. The exclusive relationship takes place outside ITS ordering nexus of process, time, and space. YOU are unruly, uncanny. YOUR presence fills the picture plane. YOU destabilize the concepts, judgments, and time-space coordinates of realist representation. YOU threaten the ordered world of objects (83–85).

The aesthetic of revelation surpasses Kant's account of the sublime in the *Critique of Judgment*. In Kant's account, the concepts of the understanding falter before the superiority of reason over "the nature within us and the nature without." The center of this *moral* universe actually thrives upon threats posed to it by massive and overwhelming objects. Disorientation being only penultimate, cognition sticks to the world of visual phenomena and to the judgments proper to the IT-world; and nothing "happens" outside the sublimity of the subject's own reason, which will recognize "in his own attitude a sublimity that conforms to God's will."[17] Revelation, on the other hand, implies a more severe failure in the order of objects and subjects. Disorienting encounters and events elide the entire range of visual perception. Presence constitutes an *invisible* order that overthrows the ordered world of perceived objects and perceiving subjects. It shoots past the object, causing IT to dematerialize in the empty zone between I and YOU.

The notion that a thing can assume a YOU-like status is trademark fin de siècle fantasy. In Hugo von Hofmannstahl's *Lord Chandos Letter* (1902), the order of words and objects has just collapsed. The protagonist explains to the renowned empiricist philosopher Francis Bacon that he had exemplified the romantic virtues. At one with the hieroglyphics of arcane and inexhaustible worlds, he spoke forth from them in tongues. Existence was one vast unity with his own self at the center, in which everything was a metaphor, each key a key to the next. Now that this romantic world breaks into irreducible fragments, Lord Chandos has lost the ability to think or to speak coherently about anything at all. In the end, he turns away from this chaos and crisis to cherish those blissfully quickening moments that ineffably fill some arbitrary feature of his everyday surroundings, to simple things like a watering can, dogs, a church manifest. And so on his daily rounds, he continues to seek that one single object of unprepossessing form whose simple mute existence can trigger nameless delight.[18]

Like Lord Chandos, Buber held that one must remain open to the presence of any one, single, everyday thing, be it ever so mute—a horse, a cat, a tree, the one dumb creature that might lift itself toward the I, demanding absolute and exclusive attention. They both turn against the descriptive, content-laden, context-heavy language of instrumental reason. The ordered universe falls apart, be it the mechanistic system ordered by the rationalist or the romantic world of mysterious ciphers. In this pared-down universe, the subject encounters single things. The difference lies in this: Buber's philosophy of dialogue does not privilege mute creatures and inanimate objects; it does not actively set out to seek them like a connoisseur in the pursuit of art objects. It champions intersubjective partnerships, whereas Lord Chandos remains morally alienated from his wife and the members of his personal staff, who do not seem to share the sublime capacities of a watering can.

Reflecting upon the transformation of objects, Rilke's *Duino Elegies* (1922), a late neoromantic masterpiece, reiterates the same crisis of language in relation to the object. The poet-protagonist grasps for words, humbled before terrible angels. Lamenting the loss of serene, godlike figures and submerged in the chaos of sex, he suffers the ill effects of divided human consciousness and lost childhood. Then suddenly, in the seventh elegy, the poet picks himself up to declare, "Being-here is splendid" (Hiersein ist herrlich). The poet remains aware of human insecurity in the world, the inability to order the world as it and we disintegrate. In the ninth elegy, he nevertheless upholds the vocation of saying simple things: house, bridge, fountain, gate, jug. He now wants to show the angel some such simple thing, to make it leap with ecstasy, to praise the world: "Say things to him" (Sag ihm Dinge). In a 1925 letter to his Polish publisher, Rilke explained that our task is to transform visible things into invisible word-vibrations, to let the earth take refuge in the poet's inner world from the onslaught of modernity, technology, and America. The angel, we now learn, represents that creature in whom the transformation of the visible thing into invisible vibration already appears complete.[19]

Buber's conception of revelation lends itself to a comparable logic of invisibility. Objects combust. Presence burns. One cannot live in the pure present. "It would *consume* us if care were not taken that it is overcome quickly and thoroughly." Moving past neoromantic reverie, the word "consume" evokes the clash of competing destructive powers, an *Apocalyptic Landscape* (1912–13) (plate 11) in which cities explode under the force of a godlike presence. Buber remained confident that "whatever has thus been changed into IT and frozen into a thing among things is still endowed with the meaning and destiny to change back ever again." The most dramatic moment is this. "*[T]he object shall catch fire and become present*" (*IT*, 90; emphasis added). In its most rotten form, the IT-world resists the burning presence of the I-YOU relationship. Buber therefore mocked romantics and neoromantics who turn inward, as if this could "*thaw* or explode" the institutions that press upon the modern person (94). In this same light, a picture of Napoleon represents the demonic person to whom others say YOU. Everything "*flames* towards him while he himself stands in a *cold fire*" (118). The invisible force of revelation, the dangerous power to reduce objects to air and ash, comes from without.

What then remains visible in revelation? Theodore Ziolkowski has observed how Rilke in his own life withdrew from the urban geography of modern life to live in castles and towers.[20] Poetically, he extends the same refuge to the earth by drawing the visible world into a deeply personalized *Innenwelt*. Objects enter the invisible world of words, where they hide; nothing shows itself in the process. The obverse occurs in the case of Buber. As visible objects disappear, an invisible presence reveals itself in a fleeting, visible form. Deeds redeem from the oppressive force of causality. Buber evoked the *fiery* matter of our capacity to will, the alluring glance of potentialities *flaring up*, plunging both hands into *the fire*, where the YOU who intends the I is hidden. There, on the threshold, naked before an unnamed countenance, the spirit is *kindled* again and again. The eyes of fate, once severe, are now full of *light* and look like grace. The free person who meets fate now returns into the IT world, carrying the *spark*. He no longer feels oppressed by causal necessity. In dark times, original encounters and the *glowing deeds* of solitary spirits keep this spirit alive (*IT*, 101–3).[21]

The fire of revelation insinuates around the object. At the moment when IT is present as YOUR world-order, "Then the tone is heard all of a sudden whose uninterpretable score the ordered world of objects is. These moments are immortal; none are more evanescent. They leave *no content* that could be preserved, but . . . the *radiation* of its force penetrates the ordered world and *thaws* it again and again" (*IT*, 82; emphases added). The "ordered world" generates objects that thaw, catch fire, and become presence. They radiate and burn IT up, turning IT into YOU, object into presence, matter into spirit. Fire and light show YOUR presence in a visible but ever-shifting form relieved from the oppressive density and duration of solid matter. YOU form a bulwark against the ever-encroaching, modern IT-world. But I can never quit IT. The presence between I and YOU is not, to quote Derrida on spirit, an "auto-affective spontaneity which has need of no exteriority to catch fire or set fire, to pass ecstatically outside itself."[22] Revelation has never not required the anterior, exterior organization of raw material.

Revelation

In Exodus, real flesh-and-blood human creatures enter into a covenant defined by practical terms regarding the ordering of what purports to be an actual society. These are *real* contents, without being *realistic*. Buber knew that the scene where this contract unfolds does not jibe with the scientific and historicist canons of critical culture. His own understanding of revelation lacks "real" substance, while assuming less fantasy, fewer contents that might otherwise strain critical credulity. The image of revelation is pared down. As such, it appears more "realistic" by virtue of its empty character and minimal claim. It would have been unrealistic to demand more content without accepting the tradition recorded in Scripture of God handing Moses Torah at Sinai as an exact historical fact. Logically, as soon as one begins to doubt that account's strict historical veracity, one must begin to abstract its contents, more or less like Buber. As this thought matured into the 1920s, revelation took on even greater realism. No longer supernatural, it lacks the dualistic contrasts of *I and Thou*. More and more, revelation now forms part and parcel of the natural world.

The essay "People Today and the Jewish Bible" (1926) sits halfway between supernaturalism and naturalism. Buber rejected conceptions of revelation in which the "natural" sequence of events is torn apart by "the incursion of something incomprehensible." Moving past the rhetoric of mystery in *I and Thou*, revelation is now the "verbal trace of a natural event, i.e. an event having occurred in the common sensory world of humankind and having fitted into its patterns." Yet even here, one notes the continuing hold of the supernatural. "It happens," Buber writes, "that we unexpectedly notice a perception in us that was missing just a moment ago. And whose origin nothing can enable us to trace." The turnaround is crude and apologetic. It was the only way to defend the reality of revelation against the counterclaims made by psychology. The "celebrated unconscious" explains nothing. "No—what has happened to me was precisely otherness, was being taken hold of by something other." Contradicting his own critique of supernaturalism from just earlier, Buber says: "On the premise that revelation is perceived, creation and redemption become perceptible. I begin to understand that when I ask about my origin or my end I am asking about something other than myself and something other than the world" (*ST*, 10–11).

The more consistent naturalism in *Moses* (1945) is one in which image still continues to trump data. Sifting through the biblical text and contemporary scholarship, Buber sets out to isolate a genuinely historical kernel preserved in saga, defined as the nearly contemporaneous recording of the revelation-event. He then tries to separate saga from the mythic and editorial accretions added by later generations. What really happened at Sinai? There is simply too little evidence to say, forcing one to concede: "*There can be no certainty* of arriving by this method at 'what really happened.' However, even if it is impossible to reconstitute the course of events themselves, it is nevertheless possible to recover *much of the manner* in which the participating people experience those events. We become acquainted with the meeting between this people and a vast historical happening that overwhelmed it. . . . Insofar as the saga begins near the event, it is the outcome and record of this meeting" (*M*, 16).

Revelation must contend with an incomplete record about which nothing is certain, not even the historical evolution of the people who came to carry it. Buber is again forced to admit: "*We do not know*, to be sure, the names of the tribes referred to here, *nor can we judge* which of them were and which were not identical; those whose names have been preserved by tradition. *We do not know* which sects or clans were united by Moses as one tribe, nor to which clans grown large he gave the character of tribes. *But we may rest reasonably assured* that he, and none other than he . . . educed the tribal system of Israel from out the natural structure of the national material" (113). A deep epistemological modesty is evident here. The biblical account reflects a national and natural reality about which the author can know nothing beyond its being a historical postulate. Buber accepts its veracity only by reducing its historical contents to a bare minimum. This reduction yields a sparse outline of a leader and the raw material of a people; and nothing more. Without real historical sequence, Buber retains at least that image.

Attempts to ascertain the historical event of revelation exacerbates an already sketchy empirical record for which there are no supporting data. Any reliable reconstitution will also have to bracket determinate content, even as it pivots around the world of normal phenomena. What then is the referent of the Sinai saga? Buber assumes that it refracts some real event, rather than reflect sheer make-believe. But the lightning and thunder in Exodus 19 refer to no extraordinary natural event, to no thunderstorm or volcanic eruption. "[E]very attempt to penetrate to some factual process which is concealed behind the awe-inspiring picture is quite in vain. We are no longer in a position to replace that immense image by actual data" (*M*, 111). Buber therefore rejects the sequence of "tremendous scenes" from Exodus 19 in which Moses runs up and down Mt. Sinai in order to mediate between God and the Israelites (138–39). Here again, the attempt to ascertain the text's historical veracity begins with a firm caveat. The evidence simply does not exist to substantiate the biblical account.

The memory of revelation at Sinai hangs upon image, not data. The result is inspired speculation. Moses and company

> have presumably wandered through clinging, hanging mist before dawn; and at the very moment they reach their goal, the swaying darkness tears asunder (as I myself happened to witness once) and dissolves except for one cloud already transparent with the hue of the still unrisen sun. The sapphire proximity of the heavens overwhelms the aged shepherds of the Delta, who have never tasted, who have never been given the slightest idea, of what is shown in the play of early light over the summits of the mountains. And this precisely is perceived by the representatives of the liberated tribes as that which lies under the feet of their enthroned *Melek*. And in seeing that which radiates from Him, they see Him. . . . He allows them to see Him in the glory of His light, becoming manifest yet remaining invisible. . . . The word *hazah* used in the prophetic field of experience for "seeing," bears less relation to an objective exterior, is more interior, than *raah*, to see. It should be understood as more or less "the inner appropriation of that which is seen." As the sun rises higher the primal blue grows paler; but the heart of the hallowed eaters of the hallowed food remains full of the primal blue, such as it had been (*M*, 117–18)

In this image, revelation represents neither a supernatural event nor an exceptional natural event. It elicits instead a penchant against "fantastic scenes." Revelation has nothing to do with an "objective exterior," with a discrete and physically solid object like sun, moon, stars, animals, or trees. The presence of God becomes manifest through nothing more than ordinary, unsubstantial light.

Recourse to light indicates Buber's debt to and distance from romantic and neoromantic aesthetics and metaphysics. The protagonist of Novalis's novel *Heinrich von Ofterdingen* sets off on a quest following a dream in which the hovering delicate face of his future beloved reveals itself within the corolla of a blue flower. In its fairy-tale ambience, the tale invokes "the higher world. . . . We are already living in it here, and we perceive it most intimately interwoven with earthly nature."[23] In Stefan George's *Der Siebente Ring* and *Der Stern des Bundes*, the divine is

manifest in the beautiful form of an ill-fated youth named Maximin. "Do
you still invade forbidden/Spheres with tangled hair and pray/That you
may approach the Hidden?/See him in his earthly day/Dust through
which a flame is ridden!"[24] This appearance of primal powers revealed
by tangled hair and dust is part of an art nouveau metaphysic that resists
solid form. As Robert Schmutzler notes, the life force is the élan vital in
the philosophy of Bergson that flows through the stylized organic form
of lilies, swans, peacocks, mermaids, marine life, and a dizzy cornucopia
of lower biomorphic forms.[25] The image in *Moses* inclines toward light,
color, and fire, lending an even less solid shape to revelation than the one
governing romantic and neoromantic aesthetics.

A marine or floral Jugendstil index to the divine presence would have
stood in too great a tension with the second commandment. Light se-
cures revelation a place within the world of phenomena while providing
it a more shifting visual presence. The biblical God is a way-God leading Moses through the wilderness. "[C]louds, smoke, fire, and all kinds
of visual phenomena are interpreted by Moses as manifestations" from
which to decide his course. And yet, God remains the Invisible One
who only allows Himself to be seen "in the flame, in 'the very heavens,'
in the flash of lightning." The anthropomorphic figures that poke in
and out from behind these light-filled signs never jell. No fixed-formed
icons, they reveal a formless God, an ambient presence that escapes any
single manifestation, much less any natural or human shape. The cher-
ubim crafted by Bezalel and placed over the ark of the covenant in the
Holy of Holies bring art into an imageless cult whose law is meant to
"subdue the revolt of fantasy against faith" (*M*, 126–27).

Both faith and fantasy require careful lighting. In the twofold effect explored by John Rupert Martin in baroque art, human subjects
are rendered with the greatest possible verisimilitude, while the supernatural is set into a visible form.[26] In Caravaggio's system of lighting,
circumambient darkness highlights the force and meaning of the light
that illuminates a central figure.[27] For his part, Buber rejects the traditional account of revelation in Exodus 19, but sticks to this bare image:
"If we wish to keep before us a sequence of events possible in our human world, we must renounce all such tremendous scenes. Nothing
remains for us except the image, capable of being seen only in the barest outline and shading, of the man who withdraws to the loneliness

of God's mountain in order, far from the people and overshadowed by God's cloud, to write God's law for the people" (*M*, 139). In contrast to baroque verisimilitude, Buber presents no closeup, no realistic detail, no feet, hand, raiment, expression; and no determinate commandments; just the bare outline, a trace human figure overshadowed by the chiaroscuro of God's concealing cloud. The shape of revelation lies in the way the scene is lit. It presumes an exotic desert-mountain scene, but leaves something less than a landscape, something less real, solid, and stable. Light and blue and cloud have dematerialized the scene of revelation by removing all exterior figures from it.

What then happened at Sinai? All one can say about revelation is that "something happens to man. At times it is like feeling a breath and at times like a wrestling match; no matter: something happens." In *I and Thou*, Buber quotes Nietzsche: "One accepts, one does not ask who gives" (*IT*, 158). In "People of Today and the Jewish Bible," Buber returns again verbatim to this quotation to underscore its importance. That is all one can say with any reasonable confidence. Revelation is the content of revelation. What then is the purpose of revelation? "The purpose of relation is the relation itself—touching the YOU" (112–13). Like genuine relationship, it has no point outside itself. Then who reveals? Again, "That which reveals is that which reveals. That which has being is there, nothing more" (160). Revelation has no content or purpose outside the bare fact of revelation itself. On the one hand, revelation has that thermal capacity by which physical objects dissolve into pure intangibility. On the other hand, it enjoys shifting physical form. Something happens, the subtlety of which demands simplicity of expression, tautological elegance, intellectual clarity, and epistemological modesty. One avoids impossible premises and promises regarding the nature of this God or the destiny of that people by reducing the content of revelation to its own event.

III

Nothing/Something

Although it might appear, especially in comparison to *I and Thou*, as if *The Star of Redemption* is rich in revealed content, the substance that remains stands next to nought. Rosenzweig begins by negating the known character of God, world, and "man." One knows nothing about them except to affirm each figure as something (*Etwas*), something distinct, one from the other, neither everything (*Alles*) nor nothing (*Nichts*). This adds no definite content to one's store of knowledge. As Norbert Samuelson explains, the something that we know about God, world, and person remains indefinite and undefined.[28] Likewise, the world of speech and revelation does not contribute much by way of determinate content. Revelation provides minimal content at best. In *The Star of Redemption*, it refers simply to the commandment to love. Even less content is ascribed to revelation in the later writings. The image of revelation in Rosenzweig's work begins to resemble the image Buber presents. First, because even Buber senses that in revelation, "*something* happens." And even Rosenzweig recognizes that this "something" ultimately refers back to nothing more than the pure presence of encounter.

Love

Presence distills into expression without content, the entire content of revelation to the shape of God's commandment to love Him. In the "grammar of logos," the creation of a fixed and intelligible world begins with a chaos of attributes offering no stable substance; the world of real objects is generated by the gradual introduction of the definite article, verbs, verb tense, and nouns crowned by death. It will take a new "grammar of eros" to reveal a human soul. A defiant "I" declares itself to be a subject, to be this-way and not otherwise. With this declaration, the defiant self is drawn into confrontation. God responds, "WHERE ART THOU?" to which the subject must finally declare, "Here I am." The self is now "wholly receptive, as yet unlocked, only empty, without content, without nature, pure readiness, pure obedience, all ears" to the divine utterance (*SR*, 176). She waits to hear "that one commandment which is not the highest, which is in truth the only commandment, the sum and substance [*Sinn und Wesen*] of all commandments ever to leave God's mouth," the commandment by which God declares, "LOVE ME!" The self must confess, "I have sinned," "I am a sinner." Confident in His love, she declares to God, "I am yours," to which God replies: "I HAVE CALLED YOU BY NAME." The soul now cries, "my God My God" and pleads and cries for the coming of the kingdom, for this groundless miracle to repeat itself (173–85).

Love transcends objective and objectlike content. It cultivates instead the space between two stylized figures: God and the beloved soul. Everything else, the entire gamut of society, moral community, and the world of objects, remains outside the unfolding dialogue. At this precise moment, nothing else matters, only the deep presence of its expression, a language of love without any descriptive or determinate content apart from its own declaration. The content of revelation has been reduced from 613 mitzvot and their possible interpretations and counter-interpretations to the one single commandment, the essential sum and substance of all commandments: "Love Me!" Moses demands, "You shall love the Lord your God with all your heart and with all your soul and with all your might" (Deut. 6:5). To Rosenzweig, this imperative form represents a "wholly perfect expression, wholly pure [*ganz reine*] language of love" (*SR*, 177). A distilled, minimum core to revelation, barely a content, the commandment contains but two words.

Art may not be revelation, but revelation is art. Barely a content, the commandment has no purpose, no specific meaning apart from its own utterance, no ostensible end apart from its own general purposiveness, the purpose of which is to sustain itself over time. Akin to aesthetic judgment, revelation is subjective because it cannot rely on *determinate* concepts. There is no way that you and I can come to an agreement about love, because there are no definite concepts by which to adjudicate conflicts about it. At the same time, the event is objective because we share our judgment with others. Kant combined both aspects under an *indeterminate* concept, a "purposiveness without purpose." The general purposiveness of a beautiful presentation has nothing to do with content per se. Rather, it lies in our wanting to sustain this presentation, to extend the duration of its play in time, to linger before the object at hand, to share it with others. The eye follows the meandering line of a wallpaper design or is absorbed by the play of fire or the motion of water, which have no purpose other than their own beautiful movement. This then is the sum and substance of revelation, "namely to keep [us in] the state of [having] the presentation itself, and [to keep] the cognitive powers engaged [in their occupation] without any further aim."[29]

Prayer enjoys the same lack of purpose, caught between the purely subjective and the socially objective, between nothing and something. At its purest expression, one prays neither to receive reward nor for anything relevant to ethical or social import. Already its own fulfillment, prayer remains entirely without purpose. It belongs solely to the moment of its own utterance. The soul "prays to be able to pray" (SR, 185). For what, though, does she pray? She prays for God to repeat the call to her, to extend its presentation into the future, and to do so in public. "God must do it 'again' one day, but this time 'in the eyes of everything that lives.'" In this view, "The soul prays for the future repetition of this miracle, for the completion of the once-founded structure, and *nothing more*" (185; emphasis added). She wants to linger before the miracle of love and to show it to others. This wholly private language of love will enter into the public sphere that it works to redeem. Yet the song sung by the community of souls is just as empty. "Communal singing does not take place for the sake of a content; rather one looks for a common content for the sake of singing communally. If the root-sentence is to be the content of a communal chant, it can only appear as a rationalization of such a community. 'He is good' must appear as 'for he is good'" (231).

Rosenzweig himself understood that revelation finds its visual correlate in abstract art. The reader is reminded, of course, that painting forms the language of that which is otherwise still unpronounceable prior to enunciation (SR, 190–91). A trite claim, it reiterates the neat neoclassical division according to which the mute plastic arts belong to the fragmented "pagan" world, whereas the verbal arts dominate the world of revelation. Contradicting the author's own critique of art, revelation is compared to the artist who works to displace the natural object, to minimize the field of natural reference, in order to heighten artistic effect. "The 'natural impression' has to be completely crowded out . . . in order to make way for the vision to burst into flame." Echoing modernist tenets of abstract art, artistic vision is nonrepresentational. "The picture exists in the artist at the same moment that he ceases to see the subject and sees instead a whole freed from any nature and made up of directions, proportions, intensities, or, to use the jargon of the studio, of 'forms' and 'values'" (196). Revelation originates in the individual soul's simple perception of its being loved. At this moment, that is all it knows about God or anything else.

Eluding the representation of empirical reality and material substance, the dialogue between God and soul in the "grammar of eros" will repeat itself in Rosenzweig's analysis of the Song of Songs. The biblical love song par excellence, it declares the only thing that love can know outside its own self. Love is stronger than death. "This," according to Rosenzweig, "is the only thing that can be stated, pre-dicated, re-counted about love. Everything else can only be spoken by love itself, not stated 'about' it. For love is—speech, wholly active, wholly personal, wholly living, wholly—speaking." The Song of Songs reinforces the pure character of love in its intense activity. A lover's voice, God bears down in a "downpour of imperatives," not descriptive contents. "Draw me after you, open to me, arise, come away, hurry—it is always one and the same imperative of love." And the lover "lifts his love above the fleeting moment," out of and beyond the temporal context of flux, decay, and death. So now she knows at least this, that "he is mine." By itself, love is not "real." It demands the reality of "the street" (*SR*, 262–63). But this only makes the point about revelation without real content. Unreal, love lacks content at its highest pitch.

Law

Somewhere between God and soul, the intermediate figure of law creates a much lower pitch, which is why Rosenzweig was bound to fail in his debate with Buber about its revealed status. He had himself already distinguished in *The Star of Redemption* between commandment (*Gebot*) and law (*Gesetz*). Only the commandment "Love me!" constitutes revelation. Rosenzweig calls it "pure presence." He goes on to say that "while every other commandment could equally well have been law . . . , the sole commandment of love is simply incapable of being law; it can only be commandment. . . . All other commandments can pour their content into the mold of the law as well. This one alone resists such recasting" (*SR*, 177; trans. modified). Law is to content as commandment is to form. But if commandment cannot become law, how can law become commandment? In an open letter entitled "The Builders," Rosenzweig tried to soften this distinction in order to persuade Buber that "[l]aw must again become commandment which seeks to be transformed into deed at the very moment it is heard. It must regain that today-ness [*Heutigkeit*] in which all great Jewish periods have sensed the guarantee for its eternity" (*JL*, 85; trans. modified).

The todayness of law affords revelation no determinate content. Quite the contrary. The law remains human insofar as it is the loving human heart, not God's word, that transforms legal content into the form of revealed command. As such, the extent of an individual's obedience to the law depends on his or her inner ability to obey. Rosenzweig has to admit that "whether much is done, or little, or maybe nothing at all, is immaterial in the face of the one and the unavoidable demand; that whatever is being done, shall come from that inner power" that constitutes the commandments' true compelling force" (*JL*, 86). The well-placed critique of Buber's all-or-nothing approach to the law begs a more fundamental problem, however. No law worthy of the name depends for its observance upon an "inner power" that leaves one free to embrace only that which one can embrace, either a plenum rich in content or nothing at all. Law consists instead of carefully drawn legal contents that lend some stability to the type of relationships that one seeks to regulate by its practice. Rosenzweig's understanding of revelation resembles art more than law in the freedom to choose between much, little, and nothing.

An exchange of letters following the publication of "The Builders" confirms the sense that Buber got the better of Rosenzweig. In 1924, Rosenzweig wrote: "For me too, God is not a Law-giver. But he commands. It is only by the manner of his observance that man in his inertia changes the commandments into Law, a legal system" (*JL*, 116). Here again, Rosenzweig tries to split the difference between *Gebot* and *Gesetz*. Unsatisfied, Buber pressed on. Is the law God's law? In a 1925 letter, Rosenzweig again had to cede that revelation was "certainly not Law-giving. It is only this: Revelation. The primary content of revelation is revelation itself. 'He came down'—this already concludes the revelation; 'He spoke' is the beginning of interpretation" (118). This position reappears in the Halevy commentary: "God reveals this in revelation always only just this—revelation. In other words: he reveals always only Himself to the human, to the human only. This accusative and dative in its union is the peculiar content of revelation" (*H*, 188). All determinate laws that proceed from this encounter constitute the product of human interpretation. God reveals no object, no law, not even the simple commandment to love. Revelation reveals only revelation, nothing but a tautology.

No matter what the medium, the tendency from something to nothing took time to develop. At first, in *The Star of Redemption*, revelation enjoys at least some stylized content: the commandment to love binding God and soul; whereas in the exchange with Buber and in the Halevy book, revelation contains no real or realistic content beyond its own presence. Elsewhere, in the prettified art nouveau stylization of Kandinsky's *Riding Couple* (1907) (plate 9), the viewer can clearly see something: the two lovers, the horse upon which they ride, a city in the background, the dabs of autumnal color. The objects in Kandinsky's *Composition V* (fig. 4) require more time to register. One is at once struck by color and shape. One must look more closely to discern boats, angels, and other figures. In *Composition VIII* (plate 17), however, there is nothing but line. The geometric forms represent nothing apart from their own sheer presence in the vis-à-vis between each other. The something between object and nothing in abstract art and the language of love is not, however, the sole provenance of the individual subject. It exists in subtle tension with the material world and a shared social order. Neither subjective nor objective, revelation and the spiritual in art are superobjective.

IV

Against art for art's sake aestheticism, Kandinsky believed that art is revelation, a "power that has a purpose and must serve the development and refinement of the human soul. . . . It is a language that speaks in its own unique way to the soul about things that are for the soul its daily bread, which it can only obtain in this form" (*CWA*, 212). In *On the Spiritual in Art,* he compares art's emergence to an ascending triangle, a mountainlike form, at whose apex the avant-garde of any generation stands. The mass of people occupies the base of the triangle, historically arriving at the height achieved in the preceding generation. Ascending the triangle at any particular historical moment ultimately frees one from what Buber called "density and duration," from the fear and insecurity that define the material world; but not before an intervening experience of great commotion and anxiety. The further one ascends the triangle, the more tumult, deafness, and blindness; old graves open and the sun darkens. But fear no longer terrifies at the highest level, where matter itself is subject to doubt (*CWA*, 141–42). "Invisible, Moses comes down from the mountain." He comes down from the triangle and "sees the dance around the golden calf. Yet he brings . . . new wisdom." It is like a revelation, "an inaudible voice" that the artist cum prophet is the first to perceive (137).

At their apex, both revelation and the spiritual in art look past the visible dimension of human subjectivity, physical sensation, and material content. The pure sound of color stands apart from the human subject, both the one who creates it and the one who comes to observe it. From the edge of being, its origin is spiritual, not just supraobjective, but suprasubjective as well. Kandinsky insists that the artist "obeys that categorically imperative voice which is the voice of the Lord before whom he must humble himself and whose servant he is" (*CWA*, 400). Artists do not set their own tasks. These are set for them, as if revealed. "[A]n artist working under an impulse *from within*, must go in a way that in some mystical manner has been laid out for him from the very start. His life is nothing but the fulfillment of a task set for him (*for him, not by himself*). . . . Talent is not an electric pocket lantern, the rays of which one may direct now hither and then thither; it is a star for which the path is being prescribed by the dear Lord" (*CW*, 405). As late as 1929, Kandinsky describes his own creative process in terms of an order that one has to obey. "In such cases, one just has to let it happen" (739).

"Something happens" in *Composition V* (fig. 4), subtitled *Resurrection*. Grayish tone and muted reds, greens, and blues are intersected by a crude black whiplash figure. The painting's flat, volumeless surface indicates no illusion of perspective. Angels in the upper left, indicated by the semblance of a wing, blow a trumpet outlined in black and highlighted with blue. An angel in the upper right blows a shorter trumpet highlighted with red. Above the black whiplash, a walled city with towers. In the middle right, red burning candles held by praying figures. Dimly visible figures of the dead at bottom. *Composition VI* (1913), subtitled *Deluge*, also veils dimly visible figures dissolved into abstract space. Dark tones in the upper-left quadrant surround intense white, pink, yellow. Colliding forms, vaporized color intersected by strong diagonal and vertical lines suggest torrential rain. The semblance of a boat with oars appears on the lower left.[30] Combining bright color and dark volumes, the sound of revelation is a dissonant one as it enters into the picture frame. The color volumes indicate the intensity of matter about to dissolve. In this transfiguration, force descends from above as the figures that remain begin to float.

Will Grohmann notes that Kandinsky was a lifelong member of the Greek Orthodox Church, but the painter did not pretend to be a theologian.[31] Commenting upon the subtitles *Resurrection* and *Deluge* given to *Composition V* and *Composition VI*, he explains: "One needs a certain daring if one is take such outworn themes as the starting point of pure painting. It was for me a trial of strength, which in my opinion has turned out for the best" (*CWA*, 398–99). He had carried a picture for *Composition VI* in his mind for over a year. After an exact description of the process by which he formally attacked the canvas, Kandinsky explains: "[T]he original motif out of which the picture came into being (the Deluge) is dissolved and transformed into an internal purely pictorial, independent, and objective existence. Nothing could be more misleading than to dub this picture the representation of an event" (388). Already in 1913, "deluge" and "resurrection" belong to an iconographic system of reference whose overt expression the artist was soon to leave behind.

Not revelation, but the relation between object and form was the principal theoretical problem with which Kandinsky grappled. Seeking to justify his decision to abandon physical representation, he began with the free use of color without regard for perspective. In earlier work, he had retained the object, but only in distorted form. This led to the next logical step. "It seemed to me," he writes, "that if one physical realm is destroyed for the sake of pictorial necessity, then the artist has the artistic right and the artistic duty to negate the other physical realms as well. . . . [Pictorial elongations and anatomical distortions] would not and could not be for me the solution to the question of representation. Thus, objects began gradually to dissolve more and more in my pictures" (*CWA*, 396). In flattening the picture plane, that is, abandoning realist canons of depth and fixed perspective, the spiritual in art gives extra impulse to the idea that revelation transcends the phenomenal world of spatial coordinates and the depth and density of realist art.

As physical objects begin to dissolve, as they lose spatial and material structure, abstract objects hover in the air. The pink and white forms in *Composition VI* "seethe in such a way that they seem to lie neither upon the surface of the canvas nor upon any ideal surface. Rather, they appear as if hovering in the air, as if surrounded by steam. This apparent absence of surface, the same uncertainty as to distance can, e.g., be observed in Russian steam baths. A man standing in the steam is neither close to nor far away; he is just somewhere" (*CWA*, 387). One has lost all perspectival depth enabling one to locate the bather in spatial coordinates vis-à-vis other persons and objects. He is neither close nor far. All Kandinsky could say was that he is "somewhere," as minimal a claim as the play between "something" and "nothing." Neither here nor there, the bather no longer belongs to the world of ordered objects. Understood graphically, revelation is flat, the sudden collapse of depth into the pure height of surface.

Kandinsky's analysis in *Point and Line to Plane* allows one to see how revelation might look like "something." The I is a graphic point. Forced into motion by the "line" that upsets my self-repose, I seek a place within a picture plane bifurcated into four quadrants. "Above" and "left" conjure images of rarification, what Buber called presence, as they tend toward YOUR lightness and freedom. "Below" and "right" conjure density, what Buber called object and the IT-world as they tend toward weight and bondage. Movement to the picture plane's left means a movement toward freedom, toward that which stands far away from human environments and conventions (*CWA*, 639–45). In *Composition VIII* (plate 17), the bases of all of the triangular forms face toward the bottom of the canvas. Their peaks press upward, an ascent that carries with it the small yellow and blue and purple circles, unimpeded by the burnt-out purple and black ringed circle at upper left. The "[p]oint that burrows its way into the surface is likewise capable of freeing itself from the surface and 'floating' in space" (670–71).

Ethics

But what moral right allows one to float above the material world and the creatures who suffer in it? Should we not side with Steven Katz in his stand against the ethical relativism and epistemological nonsense that he sees as threatening religious discourse without content? According to Adorno, Kandinsky's "justified revolt" against Jugendstil sensualism blurred the distinction between a legitimate belief spirit and "superstition."[32] The textual record, however, supports neither critic. Adorno ignores the basic fact that, as a painter, Kandinsky was occupied with physical objects composed of canvas and paint; and Kandinsky's position at the Bauhaus, an institution devoted to a left-leaning program of social renewal not too unlike Buber's and Rosenzweig's commitments to religious renewal and community renaissance. But I am more intrigued by the footnote ending *Point and Line to Plane*, where Kandinsky explains, "the *transformation* of the material [pictorial plane] into an indefinable space affords the opportunity of extending the dimension of time" (*CWA*, 671; emphasis added).

The words "transform" and "extend" assume spiritual and ethical significance. The pictorial elements in *Composition VIII* (plate 17) do not simply dematerialize and float away from before a morally disinterested subject. They maintain an abiding relation to that pictorial surface of the canvas. "The street may be observed through the window pane," Kandinsky observed, "causing its noises to become diminished, its movements ghostly. . . . Or one can open the door: one can emerge from one's isolation, immerse oneself in this organism, actively involve oneself in it and experience its pulsating life with all one's senses" (*CWA*, 532). These words belong to the opening paragraphs of *Point and Line to Plane*. The street alludes to the surface that Kandinsky seeks to transform by the end of the text. Just as for Buber, YOU thaw IT, the material picture plane requires someone or something to animate the "pictorial element" and force it to float free, to "transform" the "picture plane." To "extend the dimension of time" is to float past temporal limit and, in doing so, redeem the picture frame from stasis and death. The "miracle" of abstract art requires this social confirmation.

Preferring a dark art whose primary color was black, Adorno himself saw the ethical gravity of abstract art in the dialectical relation it posits between its own autonomous presence and the reality of human suffering.[33] In the name of "accumulated, speechless pain," Adorno contrasted the autonomy of art with cheerful art and entertainment.[34] Autonomous art is not indifferent. It maintains a paradoxical relationship to the empirical being from which it simultaneously disassociates and with which it secretly connects. Even the most sublime work of art takes up a definite position vis-à-vis material reality by stepping outside of its spell, not once and for all, but dialectically.[35] Autonomous art thus couples keen awareness of reality with an equally acute sense of alienation from it. The desire for distance is not in itself neurotic insofar as the brutality of social reality warrants the desire to escape.[36] All works of art are polemical. Severing ties with the empirical world generates a desire to change it.[37] Art without objects, YOUR presence, the pure imperative of God's love, the bare "something" that happens "somewhere" between I and YOU in a Russian bathhouse remain fundamentally free from, yet critically connected to, "the street."

Logic

Somewhere between determinate (scientific, systematic, synthetic) knowledge and the mere rhapsodic play of representations, expression without content sustains revelation and the spiritual in art within the limits of Kantian reason. For theology to constitute "knowledge," it must determine distinct things about God: namely, that God has this or that attribute (omnipotence, omnibenevolence, omniscience) and that these attributes relate to each other in such and such an order. For Kant, such knowledge remains beyond finite human understanding. "For the predicates—'very great,' 'astounding,' 'immeasurable,' in power and excellence—give no determinate concept at all, and do not really tell us what the thing is in itself." The grandeur of creation "can indeed lead us to the point of admiring the greatness, wisdom, power, etc., of the Author of the world, but can take us no further."[38] The argument from design does not permit one to attribute omniscience, omnipotence, or omnibenevolence to God. (These are taken up by the so-called ontological argument, which Kant dismisses for the simple reason that existence does not designate a predicate of an object). By his own account, Kant's critique does not bear upon pared-down religious discourse.

Unlike classical theists, Buber and Rosenzweig restricted themselves to a more indeterminate set of claims about God. Claiming to know nothing more about divine revelation than that "something happens" saved them from having to argue about the precise nature of God, about God's power, justice, goodness, foreknowledge and providence, especially as these relate to the limits of human cognition and to the problem of evil. Buber and Rosenzweig never address these questions. God's love and presence are evoked without claiming to know anything about them. The play of signs, light, and love sufficiently manifest a bare divine presence that yields no more than its bare presence. The zero-sum of revelation thereby skirts around the limits of critical reason, which it continues to respect. Theological minimalism represents more than mere rhapsody, while avoiding the higher bar set by scientific proof. That these signs provide no determinate knowledge goes precisely to the point pressed by Buber and Rosenzweig against theological realism.

Expression

Circumventing Kantian epistemology, zero-sum revelation participates in a classic topos of eighteenth- and nineteenth-century aesthetic theory, the critique of instrumental language. The ability of language to convey human/spiritual reality suffers serious doubt once it is understood that all acts of human signification are accidental, arbitrary, limited, and prone to error. Enlightenment and romantic theorists therefore privileged the nonmimetic arts of poetry and music over against sculpture and painting, which were still closely tied to realist canons of representation. Although poetic and musical signs lost the capacity to represent objects, they were able to conjure up more subtle states of consciousness. In the age of postimpressionism, color gradually came to assume the same nonmimesis. The art of Van Gogh and Cézanne inspired the poetry of Hofmannsthal and Rilke. By the time of the *Lord Chandos Letter*, language had been reduced to a sign as mute as color; although even here, Moses Mendelssohn had already anticipated the poetic power of sheer silence.[39] As Kandinsky puts it: "[T]here will always remain something extra that cannot be expressed by words. . . . For this reason, words are and remain mere indications, somewhat external labels for colors" (*CWA*, 191).

Abstraction gives pictorial expression the utmost concision. Having freed color from the clutter of mimetic representation, Kandinsky conveys a spiritual atmosphere in terms of actions, thoughts, feelings, and intangible examples that remain secret, unuttered, unexpressed (*CWA*, 633, 192). What Rosenzweig calls the act of "crowding out the "natural impression" cuts out "frills" that muffle inner sounds. Excluding accidental features from the picture frame highlights the exclusivity of authentic encounters. By definition, the exclusive encounter brackets superintending elements. It sets them out of the picture. Traditional claims about God and revelation are pared down, eliminating elements that distract one from the main point defining spiritual life: the overpowering presence that marks the high point of encounter. Love demands such expression as reflects those flickering epiphanies that otherwise escape the grasp of realists who describe fixed objects and substantial referents by means of instrumental reason and its language. In the pure flash of color, philosophies of revelation that seek to transcend instrumental language, cognitive concepts, and physical objects in order to instantiate the sheer power of presence and the pure presence of love finally find their visual register.

Beyond the Subject

The heteronomy informing the creative process as described by Kandinsky mitigates the notion that abstract art and modern religious thought represent nothing but the artist's or author's own subjective presence. This was the view of Meyer Schapiro, who affirmed the power of abstract art to express human subjectivity. Writing on the "Humanity of Abstract Painting" in 1960, Schapiro makes no reference to the occult or to the spiritual in early twentieth-century abstract art.[40] When contemplation and communion occur, they revolve around "the work of another human being, the sensing of another's perfected feeling and imagination."[41] Schapiro had no ear for the ambiguity of the creative subject, entrenched in his or her own subjectivity, who seeks to transcend that very nature. In a more recent study, the art historian Johanna Drucker plumbs the exaggerated image of human subjectivity represented by the mythic-modern genius-artist. She argues that the dispersal of activity across vast picture planes precludes the kinds of unities and boundaries that make for clearly delineated subjects. The abstract art of Kandinsky, Rothko, Pollack, Newman, and others vaporizes the very subjectivity that they themselves lauded.[42]

To reject material objects does not automatically render one's work subjective. Buber, we already know, constantly downplayed the importance of feelings and experience. In *I and Thou*, he calls relation a "primally simple fact" (*ureinfachen Faktum*) (*IT*, 126). It does not belong to subjective, dreamlike states and reverie. Both he and Rosenzweig repeatedly rejected the subject-centered tenets of romanticism. This same anti-romantic tendency appears in Kandinsky, for whom art means more than inner states or feelings. In his observation, the artist does not express himself, but rather tries "to give expression to the object being represented" (*CWA*, 166). More than once, Kandinsky complains about "superficial readers [who] conclude that I paint psychic states—in particular, my own." His own psychic states, he thought, were of no concern or interest to others. Although art cannot do without psychic states and other subjective factors, these pale before a more important point: is the artwork alive or dead? Does it have its own "independent, intense, life"? (345, 400).

The "orgy of emotional self-indulgence" that Max Scheler saw in expressionist art and poetry was in his view but the first stage, the raw material for the true architect of religious renewal.[43] Adorno makes a similar claim about Klee and the Bauhaus. Modern art "breaks out of the sphere of the portrayal of emotions and is transformed into the expression of what no significative language can achieve."[44] It gropes toward a latent language of things, for which the human subject is but a vehicle. Adorno goes so far as to argue that "the total subjective elaboration of art as nonconceptual language is the only figure, at the contemporary stage of rationality, in which something like the language of divine creation is reflected."[45] He did not share Walter Benjamin's despair about the fate of the artwork in the age of mechanical reproduction losing its "aura," the charisma conferred upon the work by the authoritative mystery of distance. He points to the "plus" by which natural beauty consists in appearing to say more than it is, a surplus that art seeks to wrest from its contingent, accidental setting in nature. The modern rebellion against aura and atmosphere "has not meant the simple disappearance of the crackling noise in which the more of the phenomenon announces itself in opposition to this phenomenon."[46]

That mysterious crackling noise signals a transcendence that is neither objective (insofar as it does not belong to objects) nor subjective (insofar as it does not belong to human subjectivity). It is situated between an objectivist approach that reifies God's presence into an object and a subjectivist approach that turns it into a psychological delusion. Rejecting both extremes, Buber writes: "Life before the countenance is . . . the only true 'objectivum.'" (*IT*, 167). Creation, revelation, and redemption refer to something real, the crackling play of which transcends the static reality set by the world of objects. Revelation enters into and out of the world, betwixt and between the forms that constitute it. The precise nature of that "objectivum" and its locus in the spatiotemporal order are unclear by definition. Revelation thus lacks stable, objective determinants, but we cannot ascribe them simply to "psychic states" either. The revelation of presence subsists between I and YOU, shows itself in love, and manifests its own autonomous pulse. It belongs neither to the world of fixed objects nor to the world of willful subjects. Revelation overlaps into the world of objects and the subjects who order them into the spatiotemporal matrix.

Still Life

Steven Katz is right to argue that Buber's understanding of revelation and the relationship between YOU and I does not capture the full richness of religious life in its broad, everyday character. Religious cultures generate an ordered world of clashing contents. Physical acts, material things, and moral obligations inhere in time and space, like the *mishkan* (tabernacle) in the biblical books of Exodus and Leviticus. Buber obscures the order of objects that define its cult. The brazen copper altar, the golden altar and candelabra, the tent pegs, the dolphin skins, and the linen garments recede from view. We lose the sacrificial gesture, the bleating sound of goats, the smell of incense, and the feel of cutting meat. Yet Buber's account of revelation unintentionally registers the immaterial quality of this very same cult, one that builds upon the physical order to conjure up that sensation set apart from objects, from space and time. It insinuates itself into a sacrificial cult where objects arranged on altars lose their solid, material character and turn into smoke. It opens out into fire, into flashing sapphire light. To require revealed content from such bright, burning stuff and the cries they provoke would be like demanding a still life from Kandinsky.

Figure 5. Franz Marc, *Yellow Cow* (1911).
Oil on canvas. Solomon R. Guggenheim Museum, New York. 49.1210.

Three Pathos

In the arts and religion of German expressionism, "pathos" and "pathetic" transcend strong, personal feeling. Pathos forms the terrible bind between one person, one tone, and one color together with another. Sound and silence clash in tandem with redemption and death. The old pathos identified by Stefan Zweig in his essay "Das neue Pathos" (1913) was the barely verbal cry of the *Urgedicht* (primal poem), an address to the collective mass that grew increasingly lonely, more "lyrical," and less "pathetic" with the advent of writing. Only a new pathos could now restore the broken bond between poetry and the people. Rudolf Kayser sought to free the term "lyrical" from "pseudo-romantic sylvan solitude *[Waldeinsamkeit]* and meadow fragrance *[Wiesengeruch.]*" The lyric of the modern age was said by Kayser to be religious, and by this he means something strong, something distinct from the neoromantic poetry of George, Rilke, and Hofmannsthal, with their finely aching feeling (*schmerzlich-feinen Fühlen*) and relativistic-nihilistic thinking.[1] This was a screaming moral pathos of visionary storm, beating a path to a pagan-Christian God promising deliverance and redemption.

Subverting neoclassical clichés about mute painting and nonreferential music, the media arts critic Douglas Kahn argues that works of plastic art are tied up with sound, despite their manifest silence. Indeed, he claims, twentieth-century visual culture becomes more "mellifluous and raucous," that much more animated, with the inclusion of this hitherto muffled region of art.[2] The same can be said for the form-construction of revelation and its texts. The place of sound will include its image in myth and color, not just sound itself, but also ideas about sound; not just sound itself, but silence. Revelation is, as it were, a body that emits a sound. "It is only when [Scripture] is freed from the monotonous gray of the usual piano reduction," Rosenzweig writes, "that this whole wealth of voices and tonal colors [*Klangfarbe*] becomes, precisely through this notation of it in full score, audible, legible—and *audibly legible*" (*ST*, 66; emphasis added). In the text of revelation par excellence, sound and color, voice and score, audibility and legibility are inscribed into one another.

The relation between sound and silence is key to the interval between revelation and redemption. Individual moments of pure, lyric presence spread out into the future in a musical line. The tonal color of revelation as it enters into the world, redemption is only complete at the hush that follows upon its terminus. Therein lies the importance of three thematic foci dominating Kahn's discussion: the vibration, inscription, and transmission of sound.[3] The sound of revelation vibrates, its trace transcribed and transmitted. When the musical line concludes, as conclude it must, revelation juts into the silence that anticipates the ultimate silence of death. The challenge of recording this sound is a central component in the Buber-Rosenzweig oeuvre. Choral form, the hasidic tale, the Bible, and their transmission and translation are inscription technologies with which to sound out the element of revelation, extending its duration into the future.

The lyric pathos of revelation straining toward redemption is caught by expressionism at its most anti-romantic. In Caspar David Friedrich's *Monk by the Sea* (plate 1), the stormy sound evoked by the sea is a rhythmic back and forth, with chords that are as thick and full as the gloom that envelops the horizon; the pale blue that hangs above the cloud lends a naturalistic counterpoint used to make a larger harmonic whole. Franz Marc brought different tonal color to suffering and death. Compositionally, *Horse in a Landscape* (plate 13) bears a pronounced formal resemblance to Friedrich's painting. A figure viewed from behind looks out into the landscape. But the tonal color belongs to an entirely different score. The yellow, green, and red vibrate with static electricity, an ecstatic glow from out of this world. A radiant note, this pathetic element ultimately undermined expressionist culture in both religion and the arts. Like the old neoromantic bathos ridiculed by Zweig and Kayser, hysterical, hymnlike pathos had no place in the "new sobriety" of Weimar culture after World War I.

I

Revelation

In his *Theory of Harmony* (1911), Arnold Schoenberg called tone "the material of music."+ Tonal color also forms the stuff of revelation. In the *Tonkunst* of lyric poetry, Rosenzweig heard the aesthetic of revelation, "the 'lyric' beauty of the moment which becomes possible in the whole of the work of art only as this whole immerses itself wholly into the moment, unto complete oblivion" (*SR*, 194). Buber expressed it this way: "Then the tone is heard all of a sudden whose uninterpretable score the ordered world of objects is." Like revelation, musical tones are not objectlike, but they enjoy temporal duration. "These moments are immortal [*unsterblich*]; none are more evanescent," Buber explains. On the one hand, time quickly relegates revelation to the evanescent past; on the other, these moments are undying—they perish and yet they do not perish. "[Q]ueer lyric-dramatic episodes [*wunderliche lyrisch-dramatische Episoden*]," their sound is "altogether uncanny" (*IT*, 84). Lyric pathos trades upon this deliberate paradox. What is the future of revelation if at its most recondite, the revelation of pure presence lives and dies in the very moment of its articulation?

Metaphorically, the conundrum unravels clearly. The profoundly isolated tones that constitute revelation endure in one of two ways: as a vibrating echo or as a recorded inscription. In the first case, revelation consists of sound, or a sound and its interpretation; in either case, a formal pattern. It belongs to a precise moment even as it passes into the future as an echo. Kandinsky knew that art learns rhythm, abstract construction, the repetition of color tones, and motion from music (*CWA*, 154). "[A] sympathetic—or even an unsympathetic—vibration," he writes in *On the Spiritual in Art*, "cannot remain merely empty or superficial . . . such works prevent the soul from being coarsened. They maintain it at a certain pitch, as do tuning-pegs the strings of an instrument" (*CWA*, 129). "Color is the keyboard," he continues, further conflating the difference between sight and sound. "The eye is the hammer. The soul is the piano, with its many strings. The artist is the hand that purposefully sets the vibrating by means of this or that key" (160).

The vibration of color at perfect pitch persists beyond its own immediate enunciation. As a key to the future and to the phenomenon of duration, the idea of sound thereby meets the challenge posed by the event of revelation as pure presence. Such moments are indeed immortal. "We have perceived redemption [*Erlösung*] but no 'solution [*Lösung*],'" Buber writes. "The eternal source of strength flows, the eternal touch is waiting, the eternal voice sounds, nothing more" (*IT*, 160; trans. modified). Nothing less either. The guarantee of duration lies in the degree to which revelation resonates throughout objects in the IT-world, "so that the holy basic word sounds through all of them" (163). Paul Mendes-Flohr argues that notwithstanding the evanescent character of the individual I-YOU encounter, it is not "devoid of continuity." For Buber, the eternity of God's presence endures. "The voice of God, refracted through the fluid, shifting situations of existence, is continuously resounding."[5] The sound of revelation pours into the time-space continuum as a vibration.

A "tone color" will "echo" in the after-image of itself. A case in point from Buber's reading of the Bible is the sapphire image that Moses, Aaron, his children, and the elders apprehend atop Mt. Sinai in Exodus 24. In the previous chapter, we saw how revelation assumes the status of a blue color tone, the primal intensity of desert light. When the revelation concludes, it still endures, not qua doctrinal or legal content. No communication rich in content or any other audible message reverberates. All that remains is the lasting impression of color. The blue color sounds, nothing more, but nothing less. "The heart of the hallowed eaters of the hallowed food remains full of the primal blue, such as it had been" (*M*, 118). The revelation and its memory is a primal blue "sound," which keeps the soul in a state of tension. Like a piano key, it hammers the eyes of Moses, Aaron, and the elders, and its echo persists in their vibrating hearts as they eat.

A twofold effect observed by Kandinsky in viewing colors speaks directly to our interest in the problem of revelation and endurance. The first is physical, superficial, and fleeting. The satisfaction it yields does not persist past its own event. Beauty charms the eye. Forgotten once the eye turns away, the optical effect leaves no lasting impress. That is precisely the kind of impressionism for which Buber has been faulted by his critics. But color, according to Kandinsky, can register more durable effects; and for these, the critics never accounted. Color does more than meet the physical eye. It registers a lasting impact on the entire human constitution, spiritual and physiological (*CWA*, 156–57). Buber has this to say about these types of revelation: although "they leave no content that could be preserved, . . . their force enters into creation" (*IT*, 82). In its purest form, presence does not hang together over time; but insofar as a trace echo sounds through in every living form, it enjoys duration. The primal blue of God's presence retains an original charge as it continues to ring throughout the IT-world. The pure sound of revelation reverberates in the ear and eye open to the visual and aural signs that manifest its presence.

Dialogue testifies to the power of lyric expression to sustain itself over time through a variety of possible modulations. A recurring dream described by Buber, "the dream of the double call," always begins with some extraordinary event. A sound reveals the presence of someone or something, and a small animal resembling a lion cub tears at his flesh. The pace of the dream unfolds at a furious tempo, which then suddenly abates. The dreamer cries out. Although the affective contents of that cry vary, the form remains constant: "[E]ach time it is the same cry, inarticulate but in strict rhythm, rising and falling." When his own call ends, his heart stops beating. And then he hears a countercall, not the mere echo of his own voice, but rather a true rejoinder, tone for tone, not repeating his own (*BMM*, 1–2). "The response is no more capable of interpretation than the question. . . . Each time the voice is new. But now, as the reply ends, in the first moment after its dying fall, a certitude, true dream certitude comes to me that *now it has happened*. Nothing more. Just this, and in this way—*now it has happened*" (2). All that happens is the repetition of a call-response type of rhythmic form, which Buber claims to recognize. And then it ends. Lyric tone and the anticipation of death create a certainty that eludes descriptive content and cognitive expression.

Hasidic Pathos

The sound and song of lyric pathos and the silent image of death take on more torrid expression in Buber's early hasidica, namely, *The*

Tales of Rabbi Nahman (1906) and *The Legend of the Baal Shem* (1908). These works were a protean form of "translation," a device used to retranscribe "spirit," not reconstruct history. The art nouveau stamp is obvious. The curvilinear shape in Hermann Obrist's *Whiplash* (1895) (plate 5) and on the title page of the 1908 edition of Nietzsche's *Also sprach Zarathustra* designed by Henry van de Velde (plate 6) bear no direct resemblance to any real natural form. They do not really belong to this everyday world. In music, art nouveau recalls the lush sensuality of Debussy, Richard Strauss, and Mahler, whom Adorno called "a late link in the tradition of European *Weltschmerz*."[6] The same exotic line and tone in the Nahman and Baal Shem Tov tales came to inform avant-garde Jewish culture in the first decade of the twentieth century. In tune with the time, the new pathos was a youth style, a Jugendstil that combined beauty, drama, music, and death. A new basis upon which to reimagine Judaism, it underpinned German Jewish culture up until World War I.[7]

The Jugendstil élan is distinctly otherworldly. The libretto of Mahler's *Das Lied von der Erde* (1907–9), adapted from Sung dynasty Chinese poetry, moves from life into death. "The Drinking Song of Earth's Sorrow" that opens the cycle is dire. "Dark is life, is death," a male soloist mocks three times, once hard, followed by a furious trill of trumpets, then soft, then hard on a sudden, flat trumpet tone at the end of the song. The middle songs to autumn, youth, beauty, and spring are alternatively melancholy, soft, gay, and careless. And then, the final, famous song, the two-part "Farewell" that marks the sun as it goes down. Cool shadows, dreams, the moon rising, rest and sleep, the song softly ends, "eternally, eternally." Rilke's "Swan" from the 1907 *New Poems* performs the same elegant movement from one world into the next. Everyday life is the lumbering of a swan on land, death the grace of its movement as it enters the water. "And dying—this no longer grasping/of that ground, on which we daily stand/like his nervous settling himself—:/into the water, which received him gently, and which, so happy in its passing, draws back under him, wave after wave/while he, infinitely still and sure/and ever more confidently and majestically/and serenely deigns to glide."[8] As Rosenzweig suggested of Mahler's *Kindertotenlieder* (1901–4), it raises "the question that certainly confronts the questionability of all art and that we, were we only always really moved, would have to ask always: the question whether suffering—may become beauty for us" (*CW*, 134).

Buber's early hasidica are bound up, not with the past, but with the future of mystical pathos. "[T]he inner destiny of Judaism seems to me to depend on whether—no matter if in this shape [*Gestalt*] or another—its pathos will again become deed," he writes in the introduction to the Nahman tales (*TRN*, 34). This was a pathos that ultimately negates the here and now. Coveting the higher soul that descends on the Sabbath, Nahman perceives nothing. He wants to die. "He wanted to expire in order to behold, but he saw nothing." Quiet tears reinforce the pathetic scene. "Then he opened his eyes, which the weeping had closed, and the candle flames of the prayer house beat against him like a great light and his soul grew peaceful in the light." Nahman experiments in asceticism, but soon returns to nature, overwhelmed by "the power of growing things." He begins to hear nature sing to God. The "ardent love for all that is living and growing" segues immediately into death. "When once in the last period of his life, he slept in a house that was built out of young trees, he dreamed that he lay in the midst of the dead" (21–25).

The Jugendstil effect is heightened in *The Legend of the Baal-Shem*, a stylized focus upon the spiritual "biography" of a single *zaddik*. Extraneous figures are crowded out to reveal this one titanic figure, Israel ben Eliezer, the Baal Shem-Tov, known as the Besht. "The Revelation" relates the tale of one Rabbi Naftali who begins the story unaware of the Besht's powers. Rabbi Naftali is put off by his simple appearance and bare blond (?!) locks. Declining an invitation to spend the Sabbath with him, Rabbi Naftali attempts to take his leave a number of times. Something prevents him each time. First, he is perplexed by the whirling disorder of things. Then he is stopped in his tracks by their fixed and frozen order. Each time, the Besht leads him back to his mountain abode. Six days pass. That Sabbath eve, the Besht reveals himself. Blue unstable fire underneath turning red and black enthrones an unchanging white fire that hovers over it. An art nouveau image, the Besht's head stands set apart in the white light that gradually crowds out the blue, in "a hidden light that was free of all earthly aspects and only in secret revealed to the beholder" (*LBS*, 72).

The introductory essay to *The Legend of the Baal-Shem* suggests that, despite the different style that separates them, Buber's neoromantic hasidica entertain a supernatural impulse that was in fundamental sympathy with classical hasidic mysticism. Material reality (the color, landscape, and pathos infusing Buber's tales) does not constitute an end in its own right, but merely sets the stage, a glorious throne for the presence that ultimately annihilates it. Ecstasy (*hitlahavut*) is not restricted to any temporal and spatial constraint. It constitutes a destructive force of renewal in which time and space shrink. The ecstatic individual is a fugitive soul who encounters the *shekhinah*, God's indwelling spirit. The "holy men who detach themselves from being and ever cleave to God see and comprehend Him in truth, as if there was now the nothing as before creation. They turn the something back into nothing." Service (*avodah*) will bring the *zaddik* back into the phenomenal world of time and space. All deeds, physical and spiritual, become one in the light cast by proper intention (*kavvanah*). They unite God, world, and "man" by raising sparks to the nothing from which the something of a new creation can emerge. Humility (*shiflut*) represents that last facet of hasidic religiosity in which the self is itself annihilated. This counters the arrogance that would otherwise attend the subject's power to negate the world of objects (*LBS*, 15–50).

In this theoretical dramatization of mystical experience, material existence reflects a penultimate good consummated by death. Confirming the power of speech, "He who knows the secret melody . . . who knows the holy song that merges the lonely, shy letters into the singing of the spheres, he is full of the power of God, 'and it is as if he created heaven and earth and all the worlds anew'" (*LBS*, 39). In the redemptive act of prayer and song, "all will be resolved of itself, and his own suffering too will be stilled out of the stilling of the higher roots" (27). Stillness alludes to death. Members of the community on Yom Kippur stand "like dead men in the clothes of the dead and prepared themselves to look into the eye of eternity" (196). A king's son warns his bride: "It happens at times, in moments of ecstasy, that my body lies as if lifeless and looks like that of a dead man" (128). Rabbi Nahman receives death as "an ascent to a new stage of great wandering, to a more perfect form of total life" (*TRN*, 31). As he dies, the Besht sees "an angel with shining forehead who now also laid the other arm around his neck and kissed him. He recognized the prince of death and of rebirth" (*LBS*, 208).

This final image of rebirth complements the image of the Besht revealed in white light. More than a decorative device, it provides a cue by which to restate the problem that has bothered historically minded critics of Buber's hasidica. Revelation requires a "technology" with which to record and retransmit its presence. Alluding to the storage of words and sounds, Kahn has made this claim regarding the historical origins of print: "[I]t was in the printed book that one could find an affinity for recording and the perpetuity of voices. With printing still in its infancy . . . the *black teeth*, as they were called at the time, . . . gave words a more certain objecthood and permanence."[9] The problems that scuttled Buber's early hasidica bespeak the problematic character of book culture. On one hand, the printed word lends permanence to sound. On the other hand, script remains subject to the ephemera of style. In a 1915 letter to Buber, the younger Hugo Bergmann complained that his generation had acquired its relationship to biblical and hasidic Judaism "aesthetically" (*B*, 1: 388). Four years later, Bergmann was to reject a merely "literary," "third hand Judaism," a "Judaism of speeches" (*LMB*, 249). Too art nouveau, the aestheticism of the early hasidica lacked the high fidelity with which to record and reproduce revelation.[10]

The Bible

The Bible translation project comes closer to validating Kahn's remark about the affinity between the written text and the perpetuity of voices. The early hasidica are too precious and pretty, the scene of their discourse is too remote from the essential voice they are supposed to convey and from the political realities they were supposed to meet. Their mettle was to fade. And if *I and Thou* is informed by a grittier, more explosive expressionism, its pathos likewise extinguished itself. In contrast, the Bible project, both the translation itself and the accompanying essays, reflects something of the new sobriety. Undertaken during the mid 1920s and into the early 1930s, it was a more technically sophisticated attempt to distil the sound of revelation. In its very appearance, down to the jacket design and typography, the project was ultramodern, neat and unadorned, without a trace of art nouveau decoration or German *Fraktur*. Gershom Scholem complimented the final, revised version of the translation for its "extraordinary urbanity."[11]

The ultramodern style is a prose style achieved at the expense of lyrical poetry. As Rosenzweig drew the difference, prose is marked by regular and rhythmic speech, poetry by discrete individual pulses. In this view, "the language of every child is originally lyrical and magical, the enraptured outburst of feeling and the powerful instrument of desire. . . . But the child becomes an adult when through his *Ursprache* there breaks the unlyrical and unmagical fullness of the word. . . . The Bible is the hoard of this language of the human being because it is prose, prose in the enraptured song of the prophecy and in the powerful declaration of the law" (*ST*, 45). While the distinction between prose and poetry no doubt remains tendentious, it marks an important shift in modern religious thought in the move toward the everyday and the prosaic. The project of recording revelation in a written format was now seen to require a technical precision that shifts revelation down from the intensity of the masterworks for which Buber and Rosenzweig are still best known.

Despite the mark of a "new objectivity" in their work, neither Buber nor Rosenzweig quit the lyric pathos of expressionism. The poet Alfred Mombert thanked Buber for the translation of Isaiah, whom he called "[that] gigantic prophet and mysterious volcano, the greatest 'expressionist' the world has ever seen" (*LMB*, 375). As Rosenzweig suggests, the spirit of the translation extends well beyond the overt pathos expressed in prophetic literature and down into the prose of law. Even Buber came to see this: "We read legal and ritual prescriptions of the driest, the most concrete casuistic precision; and suddenly they breathe out a hidden pathos," he writes. "We read psalms that seem to be nothing but the cry for help lifted upwards by a man in torment; yet we need only listen carefully to see that the speaker is not just any man but a man standing in the presence of revelation, and witnessing revelation even in his cries and shouts" (*ST*, 27). As if they were ready-made for each other, the shouts and cry of expressionism survive in Buber and Rosenzweig's Bible work.

This abiding expressionism is responsible for the project's single most false note, the peculiar word choices. In trying to retransmit the original force of revelation recorded in Scripture, the translators turned *mizbeah* into "slaughtersite" (instead of altar), *amei ha'aretz* into "folk of the earth" (instead of all the world, all the lands), *kedesha* into "cult-maiden" (instead of whore or concubine), *nabi* into harbinger (instead of prophet). Such renditions struck one early critic, Siegfried Kracauer, as reactionary ur-German, reminding him of Stefan George and Wagner. In response, Buber and Rosenzweig argued: "[T]he reviewer's objections to our translation are all in fact objections to the Hebrew text" (*ST,* 157). Even though etymologically correct, Buber conceded, such translations would seem "harsh" to contemporary readers (78). The fact that Kracauer was himself ignorant of Hebrew does little to improve upon the pseudo-primitivism that stamps the project.[12]

These word choices were a bizarre aspect of a more basic experiment that lies at the heart of the translation. In the attempt to inscribe sound, to record its presence, the project presumes the priority and superiority of speech to writing. It participates in what Walter Ong—tracing a linear development from sound to script to the electronic—has dubbed "the technologizing of the word."[13] Everett Fox, who has himself begun to translate the Bible into English according to the Buber-Rosenzweig principle, compares the project to a performance by Arturo Toscanini, "the record of an extraordinary reading" (*ST,* xxvi–xxvii). "Martin Buber has discovered this secret of biblical style in translating [biblical narrative], and has taught us how to *reproduce* it in translation," according to Rosenzweig (131; emphasis added). Translation is technology, an example of what Kahn calls "phonography." In this capacity, more than a technical device for recording and reproducing sound, the phonograph constitutes "an emblem for a dramatic shift in ideas regarding sound, aurality, and reality."[14]

"The phonograph" encapsulates the overriding anxiety about script expressed by Buber and Rosenzweig. If sound is primary and pure, the open medium of revelation, then script is secondary and subject to culture and corruption. As Kahn presents it, phonographic technologies inscribe "the voice of presence . . . into the contaminated realm of writing."[15] This goes to a central ambivalence about written language in modern culture. The voice, Rosenzweig writes, wants to be free, not enclosed in any space, "not [in] the inner sanctum of a church, not in the linguistic sanctum of a people, not in the circle of the heavenly images moving above a nation's sky" (*ST*, 56). Referring to the "sensation" created by the original Luther translation, Rosenzweig called it a "trumpet call in the ear of those who had fallen asleep happy in their possession of the 'received and certified text'" (57). In regard to script and translation, Buber claimed: "The holy text is . . . an orally transmitted text . . . even where it coexists with a highly cultivated secular repository of writing. It is *recorded* only when its uncorrupted presentation has . . . become difficult" (75–76).

In fact, the distance between sound and script is not so vast. Both constitute sign-systems, subject as such to the ironies and boredom that complicate all acts of mediation. The possibility that revelation is already mediated prior to any graphic inscription softens the anxiety about script upon which the translation project trades—as does the conceit that a literary translation might reliably record a spoken word's original rhythm. Rosenzweig placed great trust in musical and visual reproductions over against the original work of art:

> People who hardly have any idea how an etching is made would nevertheless . . . sooner bite off their tongues than admit that the page from the national printer's is just as beautiful, or even . . . more beautiful than the "authentic" Rembrandt out of the engraving cabinet. In truth, as long as there is a certain, not too low, minimum quality . . . , the work alone is the deciding factor. The same applies to reproducing artists . . . Beethoven remains Beethoven even when the concertmaster of the local orchestra is playing the violin and kitsch remains kitsch, even when [Fritz] Kreisler plays it. (*CW*, 123)

The comment betrays none of Walter Benjamin's "anxiety in the age of mechanical reproduction." Nothing threatens a work's original aura, the authority of its distance or the transmission of its duration, not even a parochial reproduction by the local orchestra or a phonographic recording.

Faith in reproduction is part of a larger trust in the power of a graphic technique to extend the sound of revelation. By introducing visually cued breathing units (*cola*), Buber and Rosenzweig broke the biblical text into discrete linear units. These indicate to the reader when to set a pause into the flow of sound. Against the translators' own claim regarding the prose character of the new work, the most immediate effect is to make the biblical text *look* more like poetry than it usually does when formatted as a continuously running block of script. The linear form, according to Rosenzweig, "mirrors directly the movements and arousal of the soul itself in its gradation of energy and above all in its gradations of time" (*ST*, 43). Speech is temporal, broken into units by the simple need to breathe. Graduated speech is marked by breath-renewing silence. Reading aloud and the need to rest set the text into discrete, rhythmic units. Trusting the traditional vocalization, not the handed-down punctuation, the translator must listen to the breathing movement of the word in establishing cola and respect the meter of its poetry (43–44).

The line is at once a graphic and metrical sign, a unit of measurement the introduction of which is one of the most distinguishing contributions to the discourse of revelation. Despite the privilege ascribed by both Buber and Rosenzweig to speech, the relation is not so clear-cut. While in the biblical account, speech precedes creation, the use of line in translation suggests how "[t]he bond of the tongue must be loosed by the eye" (*ST*, 42):

> God spoke: Let there be light! There was light!
> God saw the light: that it is good
> God separated the light from the dark
> God called the light: day! And the darkness he called: night!
> There was evening and there was morning: one day (Gen. 1:3–5)

In providing a visual cue to the recitation of Scripture, the translators bring great clarity to the text of revelation. "God-saw-the-light-that-it-is-good" creates a complete unit of meaning that is distinct from the line that precedes it and the line that follows it. The words "light-day" and "darkness-night" are balanced across the same string. An alternative measurement, for instance, a decision to break up the components parts into short, choppy bits would have altered the sound, constructing a more oppositional contrast.

The even rhythms formed by the breathing unit recall the movement of *ruah* (spirit, wind, *Geist*), translated by Buber and Rosenzweig as *Braus* (tumult, rustle, uproar). As tumult, "spirit" assumes a rustling quality, and in this, a relationship to the empirical world. Kahn rejects the claim that music transcends meaning and sociality. Certain sounds may be "inexpressible," as ineffable as the revelation of presence, but this demands no superb isolation. Nor is it true that some sounds are "mundane" and others transcendent.[16] Kahn seeks to show instead how in modern art and art music, sounds glance upon the ground as they dissipate into the air. This ambiguity of sound, one whose motion is both earthbound and transcendent lends a supple sound to revelation and to *ruah*: a rustling wind/spirit/breath sound surging back and forth between here and there. It is the musical line, the cola in the Buber-Rosenzweig translation that brings "down sound from its astronomical heights to etch audible events physically . . . onto the surface of the earth."[17]

II

Yellow Cow

This terrestrial surface is a physical place of noise and violence. Redemption is its metamorphosis. Franz Marc, who was killed at Verdun on the Western Front, was a tragic figure to those who memorialized him. Writing his obituary in the *Berliner Tageblatt* on March 6, 1916, the poet Else Lasker-Schüler called her friend "a mighty biblical figure about whom there hung the fragrance of Eden. Across the landscape he cast a blue shadow. He was the one who could still hear the animals speak; and he transfigured their uncomprehended souls."[18] Marc's 1911 *Yellow Cow* (fig. 5) is physically and spiritually lyrical. She undulates soundfully. The art historian Klaus Lankheit spots instinctive, joyous, animal-like being. Frederick Levine finds security and harmony along with exaltation. Both refer to Kandinsky's color symbolism. Yellow is placid, cheerful, and sensual, the blue on the cow's flank is spiritual, as are the mountains in the distance. Levine notes how the creature has begun to float above the ground.[19] Standing in for redeemed existence, like the Baal Shem Tov, she is "free of all earthly aspects" (*LBS*, 72).

A visual marker to the tonal stuff of redemption in relation to death, the yellow cow's joyful lilt betrays signs from a different symbolic register than that of simple sensual joy. Pathetic, her image evokes the ecstatic change of status that only death can bring just before the material order dissolves into immateriality. Four obtruding black vertical shapes, an axis of doom, frame the main figure. The line of her throat, the motion with which she has stretched it out and up, is the secret movement toward her own slaughter. It is the same gesture performed by the blue deer in Marc's *The Fate of the Animals* (plate 14), her throat curving into slashing shards of orange, red, and black light from the dark, right side of the forest. Both are premonitions of death. *The Fate of the Animals* is only more violent in its expression. "It is artistically logical to paint such pictures before wars, not as dumb reminiscences afterwards," the painter wrote to his wife in 1915.[20] Levine hears the more obvious plea for redemption in *The Fate of the Animals*, but the same cry can already be heard in *Yellow Cow*.[21]

The same complex of expression, the fear of death and its embrace, the combination of visual form and sound, preoccupies Marc's *The 100 Aphorisms/The Second Visage* (1915), a programmatic statement on war and death, the purification of things and the resurrection of Europe. At the end of an era dominated by nineteenth-century materialism and naturalism, Marc rejected the notion of relativity, confident that every single thing had its shell and kernel, appearance and essence, mask and truth. To only experience the former is to miss its inner definition. Marc quotes the Christian mystic Angelus Silesius: "Man becomes essential because when the world dies, the accidental falls away and the essence remains" (*S*, 185). The sound was intentionally anti-romantic. This was the struggle for the new Europe unfolding on a new battlefield, not in the dreams of German music. Marc died before he could sour on what he and so many others perceived to be the essence of Germany's war aims, "to unloose the spirit of the hour from out of raging din" (187).

Art constitutes the second visage of a thing, music its second tone, and thought its second sense. "The day is not far," Marc prophesied, "when the great pain of his formlessness will suddenly fall upon the European. . . . Then these tormented ones will stretch forth their arms and be form-seekers. They won't seek the new form in the past, and also not in the external, in the stylized façade of nature, but rather to construct the form from within according to its new knowledge, one that has transformed the old world-tale [*Weltfabel*] into a world-rule [*Weltformel*], the old worldview [*Weltanschauung*] into a *seen through* world [*Weltdurchschauung*]" (*S*, 195). Marc witnessed an art of pure forms in a vision, claiming to have seen "stern, wretched forms, black, steel-blue, and green, thundering against each other [so] that my heart cried out for woe. Because I saw how everything was at odds and painfully disordered" (206). Then Marc saw another picture, "many small leaping forms, which arranged themselves over whizzing and whirling lines into tone-figures." Everyone who saw this singing image laughed with joy. Marc professed to have seen in a third vision how "[t]he forms whirled themselves around a thousand sides back into the deep. . . . All who saw this picture cried out of longing" (207).

The created object is a living form that sings the catharsis of material being in thunder, whiz, and whirl. Still another vision: "I went around and about the things and those I looked at transformed themselves and showed their wretchedness and fled their untrue being. A tree that I looked at began to groan excruciatingly and broke apart. Its green leaves fluttered singing off through the blue sky." A message written in the sand stood where the tree had been read: "He who redeemed me from stern tree-being, he does not seek my soul in the core of the apple or will to form, but rather in the distress of tree-being alone, in the sorrow and compulsion of false form. The artist should not sing the praise of our ugly being but rather our dryadic will for being other. That we appear to you as sap and wood and form is our misfortune." And a chair, there it stands still, or rather held. "Otherwise it would fly and bind itself to spirit." Just as Hermann Bahr said, the song is a cry for redemption. "At best, one should feel a great sadness for nature, as for a prisoner. There is nothing sadder than the buds of small flowers or the inner burden of the unhappily reeling sea in its distress" (*S*, 95).

Religion, art, and death dovetail in the pathos of redemption. Marc proclaimed that space, time, color, sound, and form are only modes of intuition rooted in the mortal structure of our spirit. The dead do not know space, time, and color. They are "redeemed from all partial sensations [*Teilempfindungen*]. With death begins the genuine being around which we the living swarm, like moths to light. The longing for indivisible being, for the liberation from the illusions of our ephemeral life is the basic disposition of all art. Its great goal is the dissolution of the entire system of our partial sensations in order to show an unearthly being that dwells behind everything" (*S*, 117–18). There is no great and pure art without religion. Or so Marc claimed in an article titled "Religiöses" (1912–13).The more art is authentically artistic, the more religious it is, but the more artistic the age, the less religious it is. Referring to an unreligious age, one dominated by science and technology, Marc sincerely hoped that one day people would tire of technology and science and turn to spiritual goods (*S*, 111).

The struggle for religion and the pathos of redemption in an irreligious age drove Schoenberg's music as well. "For a long time," he wrote Richard Dehmel in 1912, "I have been wanting to write an oratorio on the following subject: modern man, having passed through materialism, socialism, and anarchy and, despite having been an atheist, still having in him some residue of ancient faith (in the form of superstition), wrestles with God . . . and finally succeeds in finding God and becoming religious."[22] No soothing balm, as in the case of Mahler and Rilke, death and eternity are heightened in atonal music by rupture and rapture. The female protagonist of the tone-poem *Erwartung* (1909) finds the corpse of her beloved in a dark forest. In *Die glückliche Hand* (1910–13), another one-act monodrama, a man loves a woman whom he will never have. Religion does nothing to settle the desolation. In the unfinished oratorio *Die Jakobsleiter* (1917–22), instead of renouncing dissonance, the archangel Gabriel pushes the human spirits who have come before him "further, further." *Moses und Aron* (1930–32) retells the drama of Sinai around the clash of two diametrically opposed opposites. Moses represents the law that resists all attempts at representation; Aaron is the priest who fails in a misguided attempt to find a form with which to mediate revelation. There is no peace between them, not in the librettos and not in the musical score, which refuses to resolve the dissonance that pulls the ear toward that which lies beyond its reach.

The expressionism of Marc and Schoenberg was "Christian" in the very limited sense sketched polemically by Max Brod. It was a point of view that "sees divinity in the image of a denial of this world, and it strives after the dissolution of the visible world and hopes for the invisible one."[23] The idea may have come from Karl Barth's *Epistle to the Romans* (1919), a classic text of twentieth-century Protestant neo-orthodoxy.

Barth draws the sharpest possible line separating the invisible kingdom of God in His ultimate majesty from the night of this visible world and the sinful things that fill it. Buber and Rosenzweig were, if we follow Brod's crude schema, more "Jewish." In their expressionism, which neither affirms nor denies the world, God is not as utterly other.[24] Although Rosenzweig's embrace of death as a good is no less intense than Marc's, the difference between him and the painter lies in the fact that Marc's lyric pathos drives desire out of the world. Rosenzweig's approach is more dialectical. Jolting between the fearsome, created death of creaturely existence and terrestrial life, the soul shoots toward redeeming death and eternal life and then backs into death-crowned life.

III

Your Brother

Death obsessed Rosenzweig, and he never turned his eyes away from it. The choral pathos of redemption yields to the silent figure of death in a deference that should startle those who would otherwise want to underline philosophical commitments to everyday life, social ethics, and physical love. At the end of the short treatise *Understanding the Sick and the Healthy*, Rosenzweig writes: "[One] must direct [one's] life to no other goal but death. A healthy man has the strength to continue towards the grave. The sick man invokes death and lets himself be carried away in mortal fear." The healthy understanding knows that death will strike down life, but it takes comfort in knowing that death will accept it with open arms. In the end, eloquent life falls silent as the eternally taciturn one speaks, saying: "Do you finally recognize me? I am your brother" (*USH*, 91). In his notes to the English translation, Nahum Glatzer, somewhat aghast, it seems, responds: "This concluding chapter—on death—stands in a striking contrast to the final passage of *The Star of Redemption*." To offset the mordant tone, Glatzer then quotes verbatim the paragraphs that end on the rousing refrain "into life."[25]

Silence, light, and spectacular vision are the three nonaural markers that provide the key to identifying the figure of death throughout Rosenzweig's work. The association of life with eloquence and of death with silence occurs not just in *Understanding the Sick and the Healthy* but throughout *The Star of Redemption*. Revelation and redemption render terrestrial life vocal through dialogue and choral song, while death and eternal life are "silent." Light is also silent. Apocalyptic, it represents the visual correlate of spectral silence. These are the cues that accompany the appearance of redemption, capped by God's final word of judgment, the silent non-word of light that marks off terrestrial time. "God himself must speak the ultimate word which may no longer be a word. For it must be the end and no longer anticipation, while any word would still be anticipation of the next word. . . . In [God's] They, the We and the Ye sink back into one single blinding light. Each and every name vanishes" (238). In the end, noisy life falls back into the silence of the punctiform godhead.[26]

Song

Redemption is bound up with form and the problem of temporal endurance, expressed as the basic opposition between "existence" and "life." The age of Enlightenment left the world disenchanted. Conceived by science as momentary existence (*Dasein*), with no ability to stand on its own, the world evaporates into mere representation. "For creature to become *Gestalt*, to be of the kingdom and not merely existence tied to the moment, it must acquire essence, it must acquire durability for its momentariness, for its existence—well what?" (*SR*, 221; trans. modified). Momentary existence must emerge as imperishable individuality. "Life," then, is that individuality delimiting itself from out of itself, which is not delimited by anything external to it. To be truly alive means to be "a form of one's own, forming itself from within and therefore necessarily enduing" (222). Life applies to organic being, institutions, communities, feeling, things, and works of art. It registers the durability of the world itself, "an endless duration, able to take its place beneath the constantly momentary existence to form its basis . . . , a substance of the world beneath the phenomenon of its existence." In redemption, the profusion of phenomena turns into something "enduring, structured, fixed within the living." Real living beings are those that wish "to persist in their structure" (223).

The problem of temporal endurance takes form as song, "the grammar of pathos," the lyrical sonic of redemption intensified by the silent face of death bonding one living being with another. The grammar of pathos begins with dissonant percussion. From the side of the soul and the side of life comes "a knocking on the locked door of the future," into which both want to endure. "Life presses towards the world in a dark growth which defies all calculation; the soul, sanctifying itself, seeks the way to the neighbor in the hot outpouring of the heart" (*SR*, 227). From an inarticulate knock a duet develops. "The redemption of the world through things, of things through soul, occurs in one breath, in the duet of both, the sentence which resounds together [*zusammenklingt*] out of the voices of both words together" (229; trans. modified). The archetypal chant is "He is good," always the chant of several parties, always communal, the chant to which all creation is exhorted to join. "At its beginning, the individual voices had summoned one another, antiphonally. . . . Now they unite in the mighty unison of a 'we,' . . . This the concluding stanza of the chant of redemption begins with the We. It had begun, in the cohortive, summoning the individuals who emerged from the chorus thereto; it continued, in the dual, with a fugue for two voices, joined by more and more instruments; finally everything gathers, with the We, in the uniform choral tempo of the multivoiced finale" (236–37).

In this performance, the single harmony of redemption's "grammar of pathos" resolves the dissonance at the end of revelation's "grammar of eros." Revelation concludes with a cry (*Schrei*) as the beloved soul pleads for the future repetition of the miracle of God's love. "The prayer for the coming of the kingdom is ever but a crying and a sighing, ever but a plea." At the moment of supreme fulfillment, the soul "rises in new unrest from a new depth which we have not yet recognized. It sobs beyond the proximity of the lover, unseen but felt, and into the gloom of infinity" (*SR*, 185). The *Schrei* that concludes the "grammar of eros" morphs into the percussive knocking that opens the "grammar of pathos." That grammar, the grammar of redemption, now ends with the individual cry bound up together into a single rhythm and harmony (203–4), transforming the *Schrei* into a "triumphal cry" (*Triumphsgeschrei*). The soul no longer sobs, but shouts in the We of its own eternity. "Life becomes immortal in redemption's eternal hymn of praise" (253). A sonic theodicy, it sets the stage for the silent word of God's judgment, which it has just now already vindicated.[27]

Song turns the soul, not away from, but toward destruction and death, condemning all those who do not join the chorus: "The We encompasses everything it can grasp and reach or at least sight. But what it can no longer reach or sight, that it must eject from its bright, melodious circle into the dread cold of the Nought: for the sake of its own exclusive-inclusive unity, it must say to it: Ye" (*SR*, 237; trans. modified). The melody is harmonious, the judgment dissonant. The silence in which their combination ends anticipates God's last word that finally comes to annihilate the beings who long to persist in the penultimate order of momentary existence. God's ultimate judgment is that one single blinding flash of light in which "each and every name" must vanish (238). The concluding finale of the "grammar of pathos" predicts the ultimate image of redemption. Death might lie vanquished, but not in this world. At this bright second midnight, on the day of God, the day of the Lord, the chorus does not shame death as much as it is bedazzled by the silence of that which lies past sound.[28]

No less than Marc's *Yellow Cow*, the chorus is a singing form. An alien presence in the world, it articulates the overlap between sound and silence, life in death, and death in life. It "stands there unique, detached from its originator, uncanny in its vitality which is full of life and yet alien to life. Yes, it is truly uncanny" (*SR*, 243). The reality of the image cannot reside with the artist who created it. It enters into life as its own distinct life. It acquires duration when others come to recognize its own separate being, although we know "this life is, after all, completed by death and as such in the power of death from creation on." Life enjoys neither existence in this world forever nor the last word in the choral "He is good." The chorus that sings Psalm 115, the psalm from which these words are taken, vaults over against the death that crowns creation and the love that redeems it prior to its annihilation in the cacophony of divine light. Art, song, and revelation—unlike philosophy, which depends upon language—feed upon the silence before which all sounds fall.

Love Conquers Death?

A welter of speech—command and song—first affirms life and love in revelation, an intimate love that then assumes comprehensive reality through the choral medium of redemption. In the end, however, "The *created death* of the creature portends the revelation of a life which points us beyond the creaturely" (*SR*, 155). There are two types of death and dying, the one that revelation defeats and the one before which it is quiet. In a 1922 diary entry, Rosenzweig claimed that revelation "overcomes *created death* and sets up the right of *redeeming death*. Whoever loves no longer believes in death and only in death" (*BT*, 778; emphasis added).[29] This text, we see, only seems to contradict the proud proclamation from the Song of Songs that "love is as strong as death." Combining the two texts yields the following interpretation. Love conquers the fear of created death in order to greet the fraternal figure of redeeming death, namely, the death that catapults the soul into eternal life. "The dialogical love of revelation overcomes the physical death imposed by creation, but that love itself is overcome by the spiritual death experienced in redemption, which results in the reintegration of the self in the oneness of God," Elliot Wolfson explains.[30]

The following passage would seem to buttress the argument made by Else-Rahel Freund that the move from death to everyday life constitutes the meaning of Rosenzweig's thought. Describing the final swell of the communal choral song of redemption, our author bursts out: "The We are eternal: Death plunges into the Nought in the face of this triumphal shout of eternity. Life becomes immortal in redemption's eternal hymn of praise" (*SR*, 253). Death does not, however, rest vanquished in the sense intended by Freund. Her reading suggests that choral form renders everyday life immortal. Like many others, she points to this worldly, messianic character of Rosenzweig's thought. But redemption is not exhausted by the everyday life that it has come to intensify. "[T]he kingdom may build its growth on the growth of life. *But in addition* it is dependent on something else, something which first assures life of the immortality which life seeks for itself" (225; emphasis added). A surplus bears upon the ordinary life to which it adds. In relation to life, death is a "supplement"—as thematized by Derrida, a dangerous capacity to invert the value of the identity with which it comes into contact.

In this way, the conclusion to Rosenzweig's discussion of redemption holds no surprise. Immediately after the passage quoted by Freund, the text cites the rabbinic sage Rav: "For only thus did the Rabbis dare to describe the eternal bliss of the world to come, which differs from that ever renewed peace which the solitary soul found in divine love: the pious sit, with crowns on their heads, and behold the radiance of the manifest deity" (SR, 253). So ends redemption, not in this world. Eternal life in the world-to-come combines the trope of light with the promise of spectacular vision. The luminous appearance of a deity become manifest (*offenbargewordene Gottheit*) does not belong to this world. To borrow the language of *Understanding the Sick and the Healthy*, it suggests that life and love propel the beloved soul toward the goal of death and the radiant vision described by the rabbis. As we are now about to see, the holiday structure constitutes the mirror with which the beloved soul prepares itself. The recourse to silence and light in this discussion will anticipate the collapse of eloquent life into silence before its brother death in *Understanding the Sick and the Healthy*. It recalls this allusion to the light that illuminates the righteous in the silence that concludes the worldly hymn of praise.

Back into Life?

The beloved soul has leapt from the gradual growth of the terrestrial kingdom to a radiant vision of eternal life. It must now be led back into life. Rosenzweig warned against fanatics who jump straight to the final end-goal, only to perish in the void. To counter this danger, the kingdom must grow in earthly, social time. Love must proceed gradually, loving always only the most proximate person (*der nachste*) and then the next one, without concerning itself with the next-after (*der übernachste*) (SR, 270–71). In a 1920 letter to Rudolf Hallo, Rosenzweig makes this very point, using identical language. One should only look at the next moment (*der nachste*) and forget the fact that one can die at the next-after-moment (*der übernachste*). Death stands before the human person, forcing him or her "into life" (*ins Leben*) (*BT*, 662). *The Star of Redemption* ends with the same refrain. After the premature premonition of death, the ritual cycles of Judaism and Christianity and the historical trajectory of Christianity gradually grow the kingdom of God from one moment to the next. As Robert Gibbs discerns, they turn the soul back to the social structure of terrestrial life.[31]

The turn, however, remains only partial. A supplement that adds on to the growth of life, death haunts the ritual cycle. Liturgy's main component consists of the silent common gesture, not the common word. Ritual signifiers at their most primary are visual and inaudible. "They are the light, by which we see light. They are the silent anticipation of a world gleaming in the silence of the future" (*SR*, 295). Rosenzweig compared liturgy to a reflector in which the light of eternity is focused into the small cycle of the year. It prepares the soul for the ultimate silence of perfect union (308–9). The light shines like a face, "like an eye which is eloquent without the lips having to move. Unlike the muteness of the [pagan] protocosmos, which had no words yet, here we have a silence that no longer has any need of the word. It is the silence of consummate understanding. One glance says everything here" (295). This creepy silence runs throughout the holiday cycle. The Sabbath sermon demands unanimous silence (310). It puts an end to the chatter and noise of the workweek (314). The festivals of Passover, Shavuot, and Sukkot are epitomized by festival meals—eating that prepares the soul for the ultimate experience of common silence (315–16). Having once met at the festival table, people greet each other silently. Echoing what the literary critic Russel Berman calls "fascist modernism," redemption is symbolized by the army, the common spirit, the knowledge of belonging to the whole, the flag—situations in which everyone knows everyone and they greet one another wordlessly (321–22).[32]

Sabbath and festivals leave only veiled allusions to light, perfect union, and ultimate silence. Death is now palpable as the silent ritual cycle turns to the apex of Yom Kippur. The Jewish man wears a *kittel*, a white shroud. Worn on Passover and on one's wedding day, this is a visually tactile rebuke to death, signifying eating, drinking, and joy. But on Yom Kippur, the *kittel* represents "the true attire of death"

(*SR*, 326). Alone before God on the Day of Judgment, the holiday cycle has reached its crescendo. "On the Days of Awe . . . he confronts the eyes of his judge in utter loneliness, as if he were dead in the midst of life . . . beyond the grave in the very fullness of living. . . . God lifts up his countenance to this united and lonely pleading of men in their shrouds. . . . And so man to whom the divine countenance is lifted bursts out into the exultant profession: the 'Lord is God:' this God of love, he alone is God!" (327). From the spectacular vision of Yom Kippur, the yearly cycle returns to the mundane insecurity evoked by the holiday of Sukkot. It reinstates the reality of time in order to "neutralize" Yom Kippur's foretaste of eternity (328). Everyday life does not represent the high point of the calendar. Sukkot is anticlimactic. It follows Yom Kippur as a diminuendo follows a crescendo. From the border of death, the ritual cycle has forced the beloved soul back into life, back into the decrescendo of daily terrestrial existence.[33]

The Face

The sonic intensity of "The 'Lord is God': this God of love, he alone is God!" is the great human cry of redemption, but God's final word is silent and threatens to take one out of life. The vision of God's face constitutes the final, silent crescendo to *The Star of Redemption*. A pictogram of absolute truth, it puts an end to all sound, to all speech, and to the life that speech animates. The most silent figure, it remains the most lyrical. On Yom Kippur, the soul catches a glimpse of the divine eye. Now the soul apprehends eyes, ears, nose, and mouth. The life of this face is gathered in the mouth. In the end, the mouth signifies, not speech, but ultimate silence. "The mouth is consummator and fulfiller of all expression of which the countenance is capable, both in speech as, at last, in the silence behind which speech retreats: in the kiss." The vision concludes, "But for Moses, who in his lifetime was privileged only to see the land of his desire, not to enter it, God sealed this completed life with a kiss of his mouth" (423). Not the eloquent refrain "into life" but silent vision occupies the apex of redemption.[34]

The coupling of death and God's face has marked previous high points in the text. Allusive references to divine presence and divine countenance conclude the redemption chapter with the reward of the righteous in the world to come. A divine countenance appears again at the apex of Yom Kippur in the Judaism chapter. The consummated vision now at the very end of the text concludes with God kissing Moses on the mouth (*SR*, 423). Moses dies in the land of Moab at God's command (Deut. 34:5). In the midrash, Moses refuses to die. He resists the angel of death. Since Moses will not yield to death, God must come to draw out his last breath, and He does so with a kiss. For Maimonides, the kiss of God represents the highest state of prophetic-philosophical consciousness. The soul dies and leaves behind the material veil that has obscured its apprehension of the Active Intellect.[35] By turning to this image, Rosenzweig links the spectacular vision of absolute truth with death's advent. He has already associated light with the reward of the righteous in the world-to-come. Once again, now, at the very end of the text, the figure returns. The vision of the face appears before "the gate which leads out of the mysterious-miraculous light of the divine sanctuary in which no man can remain alive" (424).

Into Life?

From this climactic and silent vision at the border of life and death, the soul is led back down into the diminuendo of noisy life's surface. Miraculously, the vision vouchsafed there is none other than the one mirrored here in the midst of life, in the word to the prophet Micah, "to do justice and to love mercy and to walk humbly with your God" (*SR*, 424). On a personal note, Rosenzweig explained to Buber in a rather pious 1925 letter that "into life" had come to mean for him married life with Edith Hahn and work at Frankfurt's Freies Jüdisches Lehrhaus (*BT*, 1062). "Into life" means everyday life, but just because these are the last words of the text does not mean that "life" represents the highest good in Rosenzweig's system. In the same way that the melancholy of Sukkot follows the spiritual apex of Yom Kippur, "into life" follows the climactic vision of God's face like a decrescendo. Death, light, silence, and a spectacular vision of the truth represent the highest good. In a 1923 letter, an already ailing Rosenzweig reassured his mother that he could never commit suicide. A brutal pull toward life and an unbounded ability to enjoy preclude that option. However, his life for him is but the second highest good. Only in the tranquility with which he looks forward to its end does he really feel that it is not the highest good for him (921–22).

Rosenzweig did more than meet death with stoic resolve. He called it good and took pleasure in this, his illicit love. In a 1922 letter, he tried to reassure his cousin Gertrud Oppenheim, who was not able to be with him, writing that just as one can accompany a passenger only as far as the railway station, one can only accompany the dying person so far. Then the whistle blows and the train disappears. Those left behind feel only sorrow. However, the person actually departing also feels a "dark joy," awaiting that which is to come (*BT*, 788). Glatzer renders "dark joy" (*dunkle Freude*) as "obscure anticipation"—a translation that does no justice to the expression.[36] This peculiar translation recapitulates the translator's discomfort with the mordant conclusion of *Understanding the Sick and the Healthy*. The joy betrays a deep quietistic strain. Rosenzweig did not face the inevitability of dying with sober poise. Rather, he contemplated his own demise in the high pitch of deep affect.

The lure of life and beauty is of a piece with death and the grotesque, one more link between religion and a sensual aesthetic committed to the body, in this case, to a body that must perish. In a 1920 letter, Rosenzweig's cousin Walter Raeburn confided that he had always recoiled from Rosenzweig, regarding him with "a kind of horror as something morbid and uncanny." He remembered having laughed at his "morbid speculations" and "senseless little worries" (*BT*, 684). In response, Rosenzweig denied being melancholy and alienated from life and then countered that he had no right to privilege life over morbid speculation. Raeburn's own hatred of speculation was itself too speculative. He therefore counseled him to fear neither Rosenzweig himself nor his own talents, going on to suggest that our talents are not our fault (685–86). The attraction to death included his own.

The dark joy in death feeds into the jokes of a precocious wit. In one 1907 diary entry, Rosenzweig considered the philosophical possibility of denying death. Responding to a hypothetically posed question, "What do you think about death?" he curtly noted, "That it is a bad symptom to think anything about it." He went on to remark how strange it was that he had absolutely no relation to the topic. Now clearly into the joke, the young Rosenzweig proceeded to offer a pseudo-Kantian argument to support the notion of immortality. Qua physiological phenomenon (in this case meaning inert, raw stuff), the human person does not die, because he or she is already dead. Qua noumenon (in this case referring to that eternal part of the soul that constitutes one's own immortal essence), the human person does not die because he or she has never lived in time (*BT*, 74). Best not to think about death, but Rosenzweig did so nonetheless. Humor is used to entertain a subject about which one cannot seriously claim anything.

The jokes are not limited to one diary entry. Consider Hermann Badt's 1908 account of Rosenzweig's morning ablutions. Coming to visit late in the morning and finding his friend still in bed, Badt proceeded to tease him about the length of time he took getting up. Rosenzweig's response was a half-serious, half-joking lecture about the moment of daily awakening from nocturnal death being the greatest and holiest part of the day. One could never dwell too long on this daily renewal. He described as truly happy not only he who consciously experiences this daily reawakening but he who remains conscious even at the moment of death, stepping from this world into the beyond (*BT*, 85). Reflecting the light of eternal life into the narrow prism of temporal life, ritual directs the soul in its journey toward the goal of death. Its practice heightens daily renewal and prepares one for the ultimate step. In this early source, ritual and death coalesce in the light-hearted jokes of an indolent student.

Raeburn was right to have recoiled. Rosenzweig joked about death and moved toward it with a dark joy because he found it beautiful. A 1911 source demonstrates a contemplative approach to old age and death. While working on his dissertation in Berlin, Rosenzweig wrote to his maternal grandfather, Amschel Alsberg, on his seventy-fifth birthday, fondly calling the latter a living document of the nineteenth century and the age of Bismarck. Playfully rebuking his grandfather—who, like "all old people," complained about old age—Rosenzweig said he actually looked forward to it as an opportunity to experience a new relationship to things, because it promised a detachment that would enable one to feel that "all this really doesn't concern me" (*BT*, 121–22). Old age and the proximity of death form part of an aesthetic distance from terrestrial life, as if one might one day enjoy the act of dying even more than life itself.

Rosenzweig reflected on a similar sensation during the war. In addition to his stint as a wartime tourist traveling to exotic locales while on leave from his military duties, letters from the front show him reading, preparing articles, giving lectures to members of the officer corps. In a 1922 letter to Oppenheim, the now mortally stricken Rosenzweig alluded to these pleasures, describing his daily routine of lectures and reading. He admits that the following observation sounds comical. During the war, he had sometimes felt the same way, but not frequently. Now he perceived this to be simply true: dying is more beautiful than living (*BT*, 785–86).

Reflecting a deeply promiscuous spirit, another letter shows the love that marked Rosenzweig's approach to death, no less than to life. Attempting to console his mother on the death of her husband, his father, he reminded her how during the war she had written him how her life would cease if something ever happened to him. Unlike her, however, he could imagine no present or future loss that would alienate him from life. While every loss makes us more familiar with our own death, no loss can bring us closer to it. No loss can expel us from the "house of life." In the face of death, Rosenzweig stubbornly upheld his "I" and the unfathomable and surprising tasks that each day newly brings. Every loss, by familiarizing one with death, makes one more prepared for life. The letter evokes a love of life and an extraordinary sense of self. "The less I fear death, *indeed the more I love it*, the more freely I can live," he writes. "Happiness and life are two different things, and it's no wonder that men finally came to ascribe bliss to the dead alone. In any event, it is not the portion of the living" (*FR*, 67; emphasis added). Rosenzweig loved death like the brother identified at the end of *Understanding the Sick and the Healthy*. The strange letter of condolence to his mother in 1918 predates the story of its author's disease.

Judah Halevy

The formation of sound and redemption around a core of silence and death reemerges in the commentary to Rosenzweig's translation of the medieval poet Judah Halevy. No scattered miscellany, the poems and commentary are organized around a masterfully arranged theological exposition.[37] They reveal the same philosophical acuity and heady lyricism that attract readers to *The Star of Redemption*: the attention to language, the dialogic play of revelation, passionate descriptions of the love binding God and human souls, the turn toward community. The Halevy commentary also reveals the same preoccupation with dying, the notion that the soul is bound to death within life, and plots the joyful motion toward that death. In the poems organized in the first chapter ("God"), the poet takes up revelation, the knowledge of God, and religious praise. Qualifying the choral shout from *The Star of Redemption*, Rosenzweig recognized the moral danger when too many hallelujahs drown out the reality of evil and individual suffering. Whoever wants to forget this has no right to praise God (*H*, 202–4).

Once again, however, the attention to suffering is penultimate. God must shake the world until it collapses into a confusion of body and soul. In place of proud spiritual order, the soul finds religious confidence amidst a chaos of humiliation (*H*, 208). The chapter ends on the certainty of divine help to restate the restrained joy that we are not gone, but live. The reader is left with two kinds of certainty. The first is the easy certainty belonging to one for whom help has been given. The deeper certainty belongs to those who have reached such deep despair that the memory of past help has choked them. When help has become unbelievable, it can only come from the farthest source (211–12). The revelation of divine presence, the certainty of divine help rests on suffering, dread, and despair as a condition of possibility. This faith in the cathartic power of suffering to transform human consciousness and reveal the presence of God does not represent a unique trust in modern religious thought. The same idea and its rhetoric attend the work of Buber and Barth. They too predicate divine encounter on suffering and shock. What sets Rosenzweig apart is his excessive preoccupation with this.[38]

The second chapter, entitled "Soul," makes the move from despair to triumph, the exact same motion made in *The Star of Redemption* from *Schrei* to *Triumphsgeschrei*. As promised, this confidence does not come from turning away from death. Judaism couples a sensual this-worldly understanding of good with otherworldly anticipations. The poet apprehends life in the midst of death and longs for worldly, sensual reward. This "blending" of the two worlds finds its boundary at the point of death. While eternity may here and there "break into every moment," only "the clasp of eternity" allows the soul to grasp life as a real, present, perfected whole (*H*, 219–23). The chapter on the soul concludes with the same confidence in *Understanding the Sick and the Healthy*. Death does not frighten the soul. A "floating away of imme-diate musical power" introduces the motif of death into a poem dedi-cated to life. The calm certainty of death lends intensified exuberance to the refrain of life. And finally, the call "into life" with which the soul greets earthly life allows it to enter into the "community of souls." The poet has turned from "the today and here" to that which is "there and always" (231–33). In the next poem, he glances out from temporal life into the life of eternity at the day of death. The soul surveys both worlds (233). Finally, in the chapter's concluding note, Rosenzweig summarizes all the songs of the soul: the longing for a vision of God, the certainty of death, the heavenly origin of the soul and its desire to go home (234–35).

While one can share Glatzer's discomfort with the figure of death at the end of *Understanding the Sick and the Healthy*, there is simply no sup-port to the claim that Rosenzweig's conception rests completely within this-worldly frames of reference. The last poems in the final chapter, entitled "Zion," recapitulate Judah Halevy's departure from Spain, his sorrow, anticipation, and ultimate confidence. The poet has overcome lament and longing. Dole breaks into delight. If it was true that only those who dare not forget suffering and death are allowed to praise, now this very forgetting evokes bright, manly consciousness and clear, inspired vision. The greatness that will crown Zion at the end of days overwhelms the memory of suffering. And so the poet forgets in or-der to rejoice. In a joy that points beyond messianic trust, Rosenzweig concludes on this jubilant song carried by the poet to his very death (285–86). This crowning image of the 1927 Judah Halevy commentary ends on a note of pathos and "dark joy," which readers like Glatzer have refused to translate.

Into Life

Thrown into historical time with its face pointed back toward the ruined past, the angel of history painted by Walter Benjamin in his "Theses on the Philosophy of History" is a melancholic creature that flies with its back toward the future terminus of historical time, its eyes absorbed by the accumulating storm of human suffering that blows it forward. Having already anticipated the end point of personal time, Rosenzweig's pathos of redemption makes the reverse movement and exhibits the obverse sentiment. He seems to have loved death a little too much and life perhaps a little too little. The dazzle of death leaves him too wide-eyed. The soul moves from the silent gates of death "into life" without ever turning its eyes from them. She has jumped ahead and reached the apex of human consciousness, the vision of God's face. She does not want to die. She wants to live. With nowhere left to go but through the luminous gate, the soul steps back into life. But she does not turn away from death and fly face forward back into life. Instead, she backs back into life, her face pointed with a dark joy toward the spectacular light to which she speeds.

IV

Romantic and Unromantic

The pathos binding sound, silence, and death constitutes the point where Rosenzweig, Marc, and Buber simultaneously veered toward and away from the early German romantic tradition. In *Hymns to the Night*, Novalis celebrates the night, which he associated with love, death, and eternity. The first hymn ends with a wedding night that lasts eternally. Cursing the day that always returns, and with it unholy and measured busyness, the poet longs for the night's timeless, space-less reign. "Ewig ist die Dauer des Schlafs," he intones (Eternal is the duration of sleep.)[39] As in *The Star of Redemption*, the hymns speak to the problem of temporal endurance. They assume a forward-driven, eschatological thrust, toward the final morning when the light will no longer frighten night and love away. When the poem turns to the figure of Jesus in the fifth hymn, the poet sings, "In death, eternal life is made known."[40] This removes death's sting. The pagan worlds symbolized by classical Greek antiquity and the German Enlightenment fear the night and the dream-image of death. In contrast, the death of Christ shows the struggle of the new world's birth with the old fear of death. Resurrection shows "life striding into eternal life. An eternal poem—and all our sun's God's face."[41]

Novalis's poem presents the entire ensemble of Rosenzweig's text: eternity and eternal life, love, the fear of death and its embrace, redemption and the countenance of God.[42] But this surface resemblance only amplifies the degree to which the larger culture of expressionism remained unromantic, the difference most intense precisely at that point where they draw so closely together. Fin de siècle neoromanticism, especially art nouveau and Jugendstil, separates the masterworks of German Jewish modernism from Novalis and early German romanticism. Already modern, art nouveau and other kindred styles formed a critical response to late nineteenth-century life conditions. Their late, decadent pathos could not keep up with the rapidly accelerating pace of urbanism and industrialism, advances in the natural and social sciences, and world war, which gave a new, harder tone to both art and religion. The imagery associated by Rosenzweig with death inverts that employed by Novalis. Death is now marked not by night so much as by light. Like the colors in Marc's palette, harsh daylight hurts the optic nerve, not night, which soothes the eye by obscuring clear line and difference.

Expressionist pathos contradicts the natural order that is the precondition of romantic weltschmerz. Even Lankheit, who pays so much attention to the affinities between the painter of *Yellow Cow* and the romantic tradition, observes the increasingly acrid tone. The interest in science follows suit. Scientific discoveries were said by Marc to reorient the spiritual eye. One day, he thought, we shall split apart nature and join it back together according to our own will. One day, we shall see through matter as we see through air. No mystic ever saw the perfect abstraction of the modern thinker, even in the most ecstatic hour in which he saw the heavens open (S, 199). Marc rejected the old romantic pathos of sentiment, as did Rosenzweig and Buber. To make that difference perfectly clear, his last aphorism ends on this note: "He who sees the old weltschmerz in our compassion and horror of the ugliness of natural things understands us poorly. We don't want to pity, but to transform, to create something different." Marc eschewed romantic dreaminess. "We live in a severe age," he claimed. "Our thoughts are severe. Everything must become still more severe" (212–13).

Such hard modern pathos is dead set against romantic pathos. For all their own dissonance and attention to the grotesque, the romantics had sought to sublimate and harmonize. As Barth complains against Novalis: "We wonder where death is now, a figure full of menace, warning, and promise. . . . Has not death, after all, been resolved in a play of harmonies? And can it be thus resolved?"[43] The same can be held against Rosenzweig, who "resolved" death with rhythm and light. Rosenzweig understood that musical taste was relative, and that his belonged to a previous era. His own musical development stopped with the neoromanticism of Richard Strauss and Mahler, and he did not care for "the new music" of Schoenberg, Berg, and Webern. "Truly, I can certainly not go along with the new music," he wrote to Gertrud Oppenheim in 1925. "I lack the basic ability to find beauty [in it], as in our youth we had [found it] in the harshness of the late Brahms or the daring of R. Strauss, which to old ears was too harsh and too daring. I mean the entirely basic harmonic, still more primitive, what my wife calls caterwauling [*Katzenmusik*]. According to contemporary reports, Mozart had also indulged in dissonances" (*BT*, 1042).

Rosenzweig's rejection of the new music obscures a basic affinity between his work and it. During its expressionist phase, the rhetoric of new music retained at least the idea of tonality. Harmony still assures order in a musical world, even if all such order is nothing but an expedient.[44] In fact, at this still early point in his musical development, Schoenberg denied the existence of *non-harmonic* tones. So-called non-harmonic tones only appear that way. He defined harmony in the broadest possible way, as "tones sounding together [*Zusammenklänge*]," as "everything that sounds simultaneously."[45] There is a strong eschatological element to these thoughts, a speculative note about the creation of musical patterns out of pure tone-colors—subtle and unheard-of things.[46] Deferring harmony to a point after time, Schoenberg expressed the hope that "[t]here must be, somewhere in our future, a magnificent fulfillment as yet hidden from us. . . . Perhaps that future is an advanced stage in the development of our species. . . . Perhaps it is just death; but perhaps it is also the certainty of a higher life after death. The future brings the new and that is perhaps why we so often and so justifiably identify the new with the beautiful and the good."[47]

In contrast to the choral harmony at the heart of redemption, which creates a distinctly romantic impression, the "Jewish understanding" of God, world, and person as conceived by Rosenzweig is bipolar, nonsequential, and distinctly atonal. Divine justice stands in tension with divine mercy. The person who loves God is at odds with the person who loves her neighbor. The world of creation juts up against the "life that grows toward and into the kingdom." These collisions allow no resolution. Hence the phraseology: "inextricably twinned," "cannot untangle," "over against," "teeming with contradictions," "side by side" (SR, 306–8). The antinomies rending Jewish life are explicitly distinguished from the harmonies of redemption. "Up to now," Rosenzweig wrote in reference to Judaism, "we regarded all these separations not as separations but as a sequence of voices taking up the theme in the great fugue of God's day. Up to now, we regarded as essential not separation but union, the union into one harmony" (306).

The repetition of the phrase "up to now" is there to reinforce a basic opposition between sequence and simultaneity, union and separation. The element of time in redemption allows no lasting contradiction. One tone follows the other within a temporal order, resolving such tensions into its great fugue. But the visual appearance of eternity in Judaism leaves behind the course of linear time. "Now, for the first time, now that we are preparing to see eternity as something present at every hour . . . these synthesizing voices appear as antitheses." God, world, and person can no longer "pass one another, to interweave in contrapuntal motion; they oppose one another with inflexible rigidity" (SR, 306). The silent cycle of calendar time will help sort through this "maze of paradoxes" into an "orderly pattern," a "visible illustration" that will "[exceed] all visual estimates" (308). All will one day reemerge back into the unity of the godhead and its blinding light. Meantime in this world, Judaism typifies the dissonance according to which two or more opposite figures stand starkly opposed, side by side, one over against each other. Nothing could be less romantic than this "inflexible rigidity."

Played Out

Such pathos could not endure over time. In a letter to Buber about the Bible translation, Scholem complained, *"What fills me with doubt* is the excessive *tonality* of this prose, which leaps out almost uncannily from the particular wording (this word is wrong; I mean the *niggun* of your translation). If the narrative of Genesis fairly bursts with pent-up pathos . . . I dare not think of the *niggun* that *prophetic speech* will have to assume in your translation" (*LMB*, 338). The letter dates from 1926. Its use of the Yiddish term for melody recalls the wordless tunes made famous by the Hasidim. Scholem was to repeat the argument in 1930 with the publication of the Isaiah translation, observing that, "for the reader of this translation, the problem of pathos is truly flagrant" (*B*, 2: 371). The problem with the translation was sonic. This, according to Buber, was the only serious objection to the Bible project (*B*, 2: 375). If the tonal force starts so high in the relatively prosaic epic of Genesis, it has to explode by the time one gets to prophetic literature. One can ratchet up the pathos only so high and sustain such a pitch only so long.

All Buber could reply to Scholem was that the Bible in its sacral spokeness is a "pathetic" and "hymnic" work composed of many grades of pathos (*B*, 2: 375). But this only begs the question about how to extend such tone. In fact, the pathos had already begun to play itself out by the time that Scholem and Kracauer leveled their respective critiques. The essays in *Scripture and Translation* lack the clamor of harmony and dissonant pathos of *I and Thou* and *The Star of Redemption*. They are supposed to evoke sounds more like a stutter and stammer than a song and shout (*ST*, 12, 13). In particular, Rosenzweig's late translation-essays indicate pronounced fatigue with his own rhetoric of eternity. The mouth that speaks "becomes weary, and so accepts the alteration of day and night. . . . but the book is indefatigable, cares nothing for day and night, has no sense of the human need for relaxation and change" (41). Hence the importance ascribed to breathing. In the essay "Scripture and Word" (1925), "breath renewing silence" restores life, since, after all, one "cannot speak more than twenty, at most thirty words without taking a deep breath."

"All these words" (Exod. 20:1). The rabbis comment, "Scripture hereby teaches that God spoke the ten commandments with one utterance—something impossible for flesh and blood creatures." The trumpeting blare of God's voice at Sinai grows louder and louder over time, while the human voice runs out of breath (*Mekhilta de Rabbi Ishmael*, tractate *Bahodesh*, chap. 4). Rosenzweig seems to have grown tired of eternity's bathos, a fatigue that suggests itself at the end of an important essay from 1929 on Moses Mendelssohn's translation of the Tetragrammaton. Rosenzweig objected to translating *YHWH* as "the Eternal." Alluding to the concluding refrain to Mahler's *Lied von der Erde*, he argues that the word "eternal" leaves God in heaven. This remains "a genuine human sound." But the God of the Hebrew Bible "quiets this longing—not, however, by fulfilling it or promising it fulfillment, but precisely by quieting it, bringing it to silence." As if commenting on his own work, he writes: "The longing for eternity passes away from those who experience and hope God's becoming present in this world and time. . . . In the face of living time, the human desire for eternity learns to fall silent" (*ST*, 112). Tragic elements of limit and force mark the passage. The human voice can only accomplish so much, and the soul learns to fall silent.

Ludwig Meidner's *Apocalyptic Landscape* (plate 11) suggests what happens to pathos. Meidner drew and painted many such scenes between 1912 and 1916. In *Apocalyptic Landscape*, a naked young man out in the mountains lies ecstatically prone before the exploding natural and social order. Eternity erupts shardlike into the space of time. The scene is charged with energy—dirty brown, black, and blue. But then what? The young man will either burst into the ether or pick himself up and get dressed, as the sound of eternity fades into memory. Quite suddenly, in the early 1920s, Meidner himself eschewed that very pathos in order to paint objects and embrace Orthodox Judaism. As one scholar has observed of him, one cannot be an expressionist all one's life.[48] Nor can one maintain the intensity of the hasidic legends, *I and Thou*, and *The Star of Redemption*. Scholem's doubt stands. The success with which Buber and Rosenzweig sustained that pitch for as long as they did hinged upon a subtle sense of time and timing.

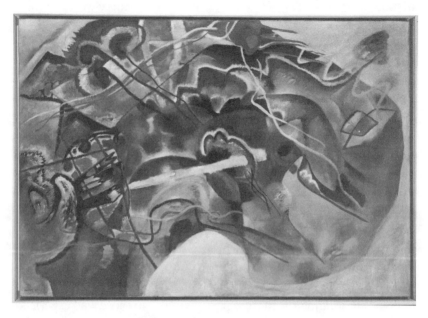

Figure 6. Wassily Kandinsky, *Painting with White Border* (1913).
Oil on canvas. Solomon R. Guggenheim Museum, New York. Gift,
Solomon R. Guggenheim, 1937. 37.245. © 2005 Artists Rights Society
(ARS), New York / ADAGP, Paris.

Four Time

"Of the various choices offered me, I have chosen the Propaganda Committee, because that is what I love: communicating movement," Buber wrote his wife Paula from the Third Zionist Congress in 1899 (*LTM*, 66). In her reply, she denounced the torpid bourgeois spirit. Consciously echoing Nietzsche, Paula proclaimed: "[D]ivergencies, movement, life. We don't want to sleep. O you hobbling, you lazy, you used-up people!" (69). Even as the exchange indicates an impatient, forward-looking élan typical at the turn of the century, Paula's letter neglects the static, circuitous time-conception at work in modern culture. Transforming figures loosely drawn from non-European and pre-modern cultures, works by Gauguin, Picasso, and Kirchner reflect a distinctly modern primitivism. As one scholar suggests, the presence of the past in twentieth-century painting was an elective affinity to its own modernity, fostering a radically new and more profound duration.[1] Modernism in both art and religion looped the past into a progressive impetus, self-consciously timed between stasis and flux, repetition and difference, rest and renewal, eternity and the moment.

Setting theoretical essays about art and music alongside an eclectic range of graphic art, *The Blue Rider Almanach* demonstrates how a trace of the distant past constitutes a disordered time element. Anonymous votive art, drawings by children, a Bavarian glass painting, and works by Henri Rousseau and Arnold Schoenberg grace Kandinsky's essay on "The Problem of Form." Paintings by August Macke, Kirchner, and a sculpture from South Borneo accompany Marc's essay on "The 'Savages' of Germany." Grouped in no historical or geographical order, the images are nonsequential. As Buber comments on his own work on Hasidism, the interest in the past was neither ethnographic nor biographical: "I do not report the development and decline of the sect; nor do I describe its customs . . . I also do not enumerate the dates and facts which make up the biography of the Baal-Shem" (*LBS*, 9). The point was not to reproduce the original context in which a tale originated or in which an artifact had been crafted, but to conjure up eternity as it lifts out of the past and echoes into the present (10).

Still too ethnographic, *The Blue Rider Almanach* and Buber's early hasidica were tightly bounded by external points of temporal reference. In contrast, Kandinsky's most abstract works, like Buber's *I and Thou*, hide the time element almost entirely. Buber abstracted the main idea of relationship and presence from any direct reliance upon traditional Jewish or German philosophical source material. Allusions are made by way of paraphrase without direct reference. *Composition V (Deluge)* and *Composition VI (Resurrection)* work over motifs drawn from Christian and pagan cultures in the same way. Such ties grow more tenuous in *Painting with White Border* (1913) (fig. 6). Kandinsky's account of its composition calls attention to the presence of two formal color volumes in the middle of the painting and the massive white, wavelike border that loops around them (*CWA*, 389–91). The description reveals none of the iconographic content identified by most critics, in whose estimation St. George is "represented" by the large blue circle in the middle-right quadrant, his lance the bright white line extending leftward as it drives into the body of the serpent, the whiplash of whose thin black tail extends back toward the right. Color has so completely overwhelmed historical reference that not even the painting's title identifies the central figure, whose heroic presence is left invisible.[2]

By "modernity," Charles Baudelaire meant the kaleidoscopic consciousness of the flâneur, "the ephemeral, the fugitive, the contingent, the half of art whose other half is the eternal and the immutable." "The painter of modern life" enters into the crowd as if stepping into "an immense reservoir of electrical energy." With his eye on the fashion of texture and weave, on crinoline or starched muslin, "pleats . . . arranged according to a new system," he "[makes] it his business . . . to distil the eternal from the transitory." Such distillation complicates any simple break with the past. It points instead to the "thrilling originality in which any vestiges of barbarousness or naivete appear only as new proof of his faithfulness to the impression received, or as a flattering compliment paid to truth."[3] The collision between old and new is basic to the culture of early modernism. In the image of the new set alongside the presence of the past, time steps out of the time into which it is drawn.[4]

Lending graphic conception to three distinct models of time in modern culture, Robert Gibbs ascribes a "messianic epistemology" to the line, circle, and dot. The line represents the neat chronological sequence from past through present to future. Associated with nineteenth-century liberal idealism, it possesses a fundamentally progressive, temporal grandeur, which lies in the sublime infinity along which human subjectivity proceeds, but whose goal recedes forever beyond its finite grasp. If the line ultimately surrenders to melancholy, the circle and the dot exhibit much greater verve. Past and future collapse into a circle of pure presence whose rhythm repeats the motion of a prescribed course. Or time is reduced to the sudden appearance of a dot, that image of the past as it flares up in the visage of what Walter Benjamin called now-time (*Jetztzeit*). The most dangerous face of modernism, circles take on an intensive velocity that excludes those outside the circuit. Dots—"blasted out of the continuum of history," the incarnation of Rome in the French Revolution—echo with the staccato burst of gunfire.[5] In the culture of modernism, these temporal figures tend toward the violence of closed systems and cycles.

I

Kulturpessimismus and Anti-Historicism

In his late essay "The Conflict in Modern Culture" (1914), Georg Simmel saw that, under normal conditions, culture consists of formal patterns that become autonomous; they assume a fixed condition, which then fades before the impress of new, more vibrant forms. The "conflict in modern culture" lay in its having radicalized life's struggle with structure. Modernity reflects, not the ordinary tension between old forms and new forms, but a struggle of life against form as such. A member of the old guard, Simmel perceived a signature lack of shape in modernity, particularly in expressionism, a uniquely negative impulse undermining shared ideals and values. In the jaundiced opinion of a late impressionist, expressionism only manifests inner emotions, resisting aesthetic conventions imposed from without. Simmel shied away from the frenetic pace of the day's youth, its commitment to unrestrained expression, its disdain for anything formal, the penchant for mysticism. Observing only decay and degeneration, not regeneration, "[W]e gaze into an abyss of unformed life beneath our feet. But perhaps this form-lessness is itself the appropriate form for contemporary life."[6]

"Historicism" represented one such broken form. With roots in the eighteenth-century Sturm und Drang of Herder and Humboldt, its conception of history drives the philosophy of Hegel and culminates in Ranke's dictum that historians must present history "as it really was." As Georg Iggers notes in his study of "the German conception of his-tory," historical time was seen as a state of incessant flux in which tenta-tive centers of stability coagulate. Each person, nation, institution, or epoch retains an inner structure that supports its metamorphosis. His-toricism has two connotations. On the one hand, it enables one to say that all forms of being, truth, and value are radically temporal. They are confined to the distinct historical periods, which unfold in a neat linear sequence. Each generation strands the truths of the ones that came be-fore it. On the other hand, the proponents of classical historicism were optimistic, believing that all cognition and historical value reflect the expression of real value and even divine will; that history unfolds teleo-logically toward some good end, toward progress understood as cos-mopolitanism (*Weltbürgertum*), toward formative culture and education (*Bildung*), the Absolute Idea, the German nation state, and so on.[7]

The so-called crisis of historicism, with its immediate origins in the 1890s, shattered the confidence that history and its empirical study can reveal value, purpose, or direction. The historian Jörn Rüssen has traced it back to arguments in opposition to Karl Gottfried Lamprecht's positivist thesis that one can study culture and its history with the same precision enjoyed in the mathematical and natural sciences. The crit-ics of historicism were to posit a fundamental distinction between the methodologies pursued in the natural sciences (*Naturwissenschaften*) and those in the humanities (*Geisteswissenschaften*). Charles Bambach pins the philosophical origins of this crisis further back, on the col-lapse of Hegel's speculative idealism. Hegel's far-flung system, one that sought to draw all historical phenomena under one single dialectical rubric, collapsed under the weight of an ever-expanding record of empirical data and scholarship. Likewise, Iggers posits the rise and fall of positivism as contributing to the crisis of historicism at the fin de siècle. Positivism destroyed the metaphysical image of the world upon which the optimism of Herder, Humboldt, Hegel, and Ranke rested, only to pale under the light shed by Nietzsche and Freud on the irrational side of human existence.[8]

Pointing to the great confidence in science and civilization at the time, as well as to the search for objective methods by which to study historical phenomena, Iggers reminds his readers not to overdramatize the spirit of pessimism at the turn of the century. Wilhelm Dilthey assumed that "life" constitutes a common substratum that objectivates itself into historical forms. As such, history was not simply an arbitrary artifact. These forms are grasped, not through conceptual systems and ideas, but through intuitive acts of understanding afforded by immediate experience of *Erlebnis*. Dilthey welcomed the "transformation of the world into the apprehending subject." Citing Novalis, he concluded, "Every time the mind seems to succeed in perceiving the subject of nature itself, free from all its veils, what it actually finds there is—itself."[9] Unlike Dilthey, the neo-Kantian Heinrich Rickert refused to identify value with subjective experience. Although empirical history had lost its character as a real, meaningful process, he affirmed the existence of timeless values and norms. Even if historians do not paint a picture of reality, they transform and simplify the image of historical phenomena by distinguishing essential from inessential elements.[10]

Radically sundering the relationship between fact and value, the *Kulturpessimismus* associated with the crisis of historicism found more radical expression in the writings of Max Weber and Oswald Spengler. In "Politics as a Vocation" (1919), Weber argues that politics reflects no moral values and norms, but only the exercise of raw power. In "Science as a Vocation" (1919), academic scholarship is reduced to the endless accumulation of facts without order or value. Norms are at most imposed from without. Resting on a purely mechanical foundation, the "victorous capitalism" of Weber's *The Protestant Ethic and the Spirit of Capitalism* (1904–5) no longer needs the support of religion. The care for external goods, once stripped of religious and ethical meaning, constitutes the "iron cage" in which we all live.[11] Spengler's magisterial *The Decline of the West* (1918–22) offers an even grimmer prognosis in its view of the morphological relationships inwardly binding all cultural forms (mathematical, ornamental, architectural, philosophical, political, etc.), undermining linear models of history. Humanity has no aim, idea or plan, any more than a butterfly or orchid might possess one. A zoological expression, an astonishing wealth of actual living forms, history exhibits nothing more than a picture of endless formations and transformations. Cultures bloom and die to no particular end. They ossify into civilizations dominated by world cities inhabited by nomadic elites driven by money, without religion or tradition. The modern West was soon to meet its doom. Its future was not limitless, but strictly limited and defined as to its form and duration. Spengler set its decline between the years 1800 and 2000.[12]

At the surface, the dominant currents of expressionism could only have confirmed the pessimism of Simmel, Weber, and Spengler; the embrace of insanity, death, and destruction in the poetry and prose of Heym and Trakl; the manic line in Meidner's graphic work; "the night" that darkens Barth's *Epistle to the Romans*; the nervous tick brought into painting and music by Kokoschka, Schiele, and Schoenberg. The pessimists belonged to an older generation, unable to see the point argued by Donald Gordon that in expressionism, "renewal was always the outcome of decline, creation always the goal of destruction."[13] The critics of modern life missed the underlying impulse toward regeneration, the promise that, in falling apart, organic form generates spiritual growth, that the past as it loops into the present creates something new and unfamiliar. In early twentieth-century Jewish thought, this hope builds upon the trust put in the power of revelation to redeem life from rigor mortis. Its battle cry was neither history nor degeneration, but rather eternity and renewal.

Eternity

Standing over against history, which can only produce time-conditioned and relative truths with no meaning or telos, "eternity" was the new anti-historicist figure par excellence. For Rosenzweig, the Jewish people already stands outside of time in the rhythm of its own blood and calendar. Loyal to that revelation, the life of Israel constitutes an eternal form impervious to historical decay and linear sequence. The anti-historicist bent in Buber's thought is no less pronounced. Zionism and Hasidism free the Jewish people from the flow of exilic time. I and YOU remain free from the temporal-spatial order of chronological sequence, the contingent reality of objects and historical reference.[14] Eternity admits of no power subject to the vicissitude of time overcoming the brute force of historical flux. And so it dams up the forward flow of time. Stéphane Mosès explains that, for Rosenzweig, eternity does not constitute an indefinite stretch of time. It refers to motionless time, to immobilized time, a state of perfect equilibrium, a duration compacted into a point without beginning or end.[15] To cite Paul Mendes-Flohr, "a passion to master time—temporal finitude, death, history" animates the discourse of revelation.[16]

Repetition is one method by which to master time and to make it stand still. A single element threads like a musical note through the composition of a text or painting. Cyclical motion—we shall return to this later in the chapter—liberates the element from any one single temporal point of meaning and reference. Alternatively, two figures appear simultaneously. Simultaneity signifies eternity by undermining the succession of historicist time, the order by which one element follows another in a temporal sequence of discrete now-moments. Eternity takes shape as one thing and another, especially its opposite, appear at the very same moment. All parts subsisting all at once, combined into a single figure, God, world, soul, creation, revelation, redemption, each over against the other, form into the instant image of God's face. Or two figures, I and YOU, stand together all at once, together at this single moment, not one before the other. In a state of "mutual" or "counter-sided" tension, they betray no logical or axiological sequence by which the priority of the first orders the second according to its own use and purpose.[17]

As the literary critic Walter Falk remarks, expressionism revolves around the image of a person whose deepest being (*Wesen*) is bound up with powers that are supranatural and supraindividual, powers that have their homeland in a place beyond time. Tongue in cheek, he calls the younger generation represented by Trakl and Heym *Aeter-nisten* (Eternalists).[18] Highlighting the simultaneity of temporal tense in modern poetry, Franz Werfel addressed the sense of déjà vu. In the "I have already experienced that," the poet anticipates what the theologian might call "the all temporality [*Allzeitlichkeit*] of God. The time that passes in the verse has already fulfilled itself prior to its having elapsed."[19] Regarding the need to eliminate the time element from motion, Klee writes of "[y]esterday and tomorrow as simultaneous." He goes on to say: "Polyphonic painting is superior to music in that, here, the time element becomes a spatial element. The notion of simultaneity stands out even more richly" (*DPK*, 374). As drawn by Kandinsky, the graphic point demonstrates utmost conciseness, great and eloquent reserve. It belongs to speech even as it indicates the silence that ends the sentence (*CWA*, 538). Static, an utter lack of impulse to move will reduce to a minimum the time it takes to perceive it. This excludes the temporal element from its perception. Mixing the idea of sound back into the graphic image, Kandinsky compares the point to a short musical note or a woodpecker's staccato noise (549).

The simultaneous staccato noise represents a signature feature in twentieth-century aesthetics. It appears in Ernst Bloch's *Spirit of Utopia*, in Benjamin's essay on Baudelaire, and in Kracauer's writings on cinema, its function always to disrupt conventional consciousness and to move human culture toward some revolutionary purpose. In *Point and Line to Plane*, Kandinsky observes how children learn to recognize the point's practical and external significance. While this obscures the symbol's inner sound, any extraordinary external disturbance can shake us from our dead state into living experience: not just sickness, misfortune, and war, but also the more prosaic event of entering onto a street with open eye and ear. To cultivate this effect, one must liberate the punctuation point from the narrow sphere of its customary activity. One transfers the point from its practical function to one that is non-purposive and alogical by moving it to various parts of a sentence where it does not ordinarily belong; then by entirely moving ● it outside the sequential chain of the sentence. There, in the middle of a blank page or picture plane, it acquires a large and empty space, which intensifies its presence (*CWA*, 538–41).

The aesthetics of shock and simultaneity carry over into modern theology to mark key points of transition and passage. In *I and Thou*, the passage from part 2, the nadir of I-IT consciousness, into the discourse of revelation in part 3 is forced by the parable of a double midnight panic. In the parable, philosophical thought paints two pictures: the universe and the soul. "One and all," the same banner reads under both. In the first painting, the world is everything (one and all) and I am nothing. The world is all that really matters. With no firm existence, my individual life has no real consequence, so there is no reason for me to worry. In the second image, the self is everything. The same logic holds. I have no real reason to worry, since the world cannot harm me if it does not exist. But the moment will come when the human person "[will look] up and in a flash [see] both pictures at once." The two paintings cancel each other out, disrupting the provisional equilibrium maintained by each one on its own. Consciousness is brought to a rude halt. "And [the self] is seized by a deeper horror" (*IT*, 120–21). The sudden appearance of two logically incongruous images arrests the reader, intensifying a sense of crisis, which is the only way out into the renewal of revelation that follows.

The arrest of time defines revelation and the reading of Scripture, their reception situated between the meaningless flow of historical time and eternity. In line with a broadly conceived anti-historicism, Buber argues that history for modern people has no origin and no goal. "[H]istory eddies towards their feet—history foams past. And what lies between has become so violent and trivial an interval!" (*ST*, 9). That same violence of expression attends the image with which Buber tried to open modern people to the possibility of belief, to reading Scripture without preconditions, free of "sham concepts and sham propositions." This requires readers who "open themselves up to this book and let themselves be *struck* by its rays wherever they may *strike*," to a force that comes "without anticipation and without reservation." Revelation confounds the difference between past and present. It takes one by surprise like a slap across the face. We never know "[from] what speech, from what image the book will take hold of them and recast them, from what place the spirit will surge up and pass into them" (7; emphasis added).

In the cultures of German modernism, holy writ is an anti-historicist figure, since neither revelation nor its reception in the reading of Scripture represents a single "datable point." A spiritual surge, they do not move in neat, continuous linear sequence. Scripture is like a strobe light circling along a curving track. The moment at which the light flashes remains simultaneously both temporal and eternal. Whereas the biblical authors fixed the origin of that revelation at Mt. Sinai, the rabbis stretch it into the past and into the future. If, in rabbinic lore, the Torah preexists the world's creation while embracing the entire chain instantiated by the rabbis' own teaching, it is because revelation is caught "somewhere" between creation and redemption at no precise point in time. Reading Scripture today can form into its own revelation. Like revelation at Sinai, the temporal juncture at which it strikes the modern reader is at "the midpoint between origin and goal." At this juncture, "Scripture puts not something that happened once and in the past; rather it sets there, as a moving, circling, indeterminate center." The circling center that constitutes the reading of Scripture is "my moment, mortal and eternal at once" (*ST*, 8).

II

New, Now, "Primitive"

Scripture's place in early twentieth-century religious thought is part of a more general turn to the so-called primitive in modern art and culture. Forever young, the primitive represents eternity in time, the vanguard of consciousness against the ruins of nineteenth-century historicist canons of progress and clear chronological sequence. An image lifted out of the past into present, the primitive creates a juxtaposition with which to judge the modern life it comes to renew. It stands, never on its own, an orphan to history, but always in relation to "my moment, mortal and eternal at once." In his article "The 'Savages' of Germany," Marc associates the "primitive" with the struggle "to create symbols for [one's] own time" (*BRA*, 64). The primitive image or scriptural utterance brings out the new in relation to it most recent history. In the essay "Two Pictures," also from the *Blue Rider Almanach*, Marc

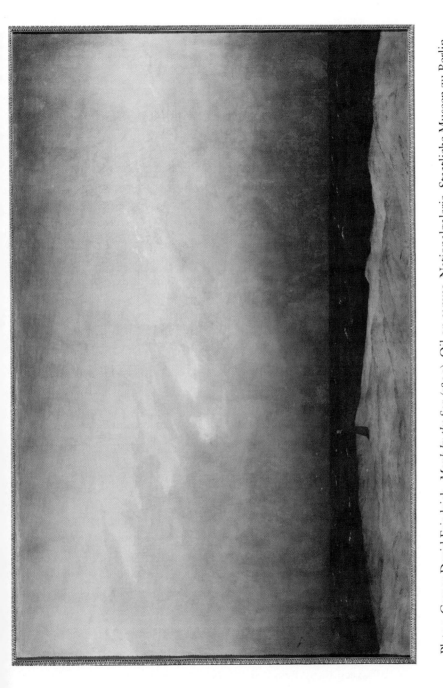

Plate 1. Caspar David Friedrich, *Monk by the Sea* (1809). Oil on canvas. Nationalgalerie, Staatliche Museen zu Berlin. Photo Joerg P. Anders. Photo Credit: Bildarchiv Preussischer Kulturbesitz / Art Resource, New York.

Plate 2. Ephraim Moshe Lilien, *The Creation of the Poet.*
Ink drawing illustrating *Juda: Gesänge von Börries Freiherrn von Munchhausen*
(Berlin: Egon Fleischel, n.d. [ca. 1900]). By permission of the Jüdisches
Museum, Berlin.

Plate 3. Ephraim Moshe Lilien, *Passah.* Ink drawing illustrating *Lieder des
Ghetto* [Songs of the Ghetto], by Morris Rosenfeld, trans. Berthold Feiwel
(Berlin: S. Calvary, 1903). By permission of the Jüdisches Museum, Berlin.

הקונגרס החמישי של הציונים בבזל־תרס״ב

והחזינה עינינו בשוברך לציון ברחמים

Plate 4. Ephraim Moshe Lilien, *Dreaming.*
Delegate card and souvenir from the Fifth Zionist Congress, 1902. Pencil,
india ink, and white gouache on white paper. Bibliotheque de l'Alliance
israélite universelle, Paris. Photo Credit: Snark/Art Resource, New York. By
permission of the Israel Museum, Jerusalem.

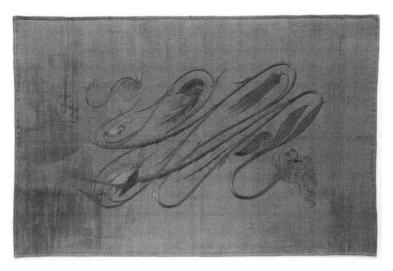

Plate 5. Hermann Obrist, *Whiplash* (1895). Silk embroidery on wool.
By permission of the Münchner Stadtmuseum, Munich.

Plate 6. Title page from Nietzsche's *Also sprach Zarathustra*
(Leipzig: Insel, 1908), illustrated by Henry van de Velde.
By permission of the Wolfsonian Museum, Miami Beach, Florida.

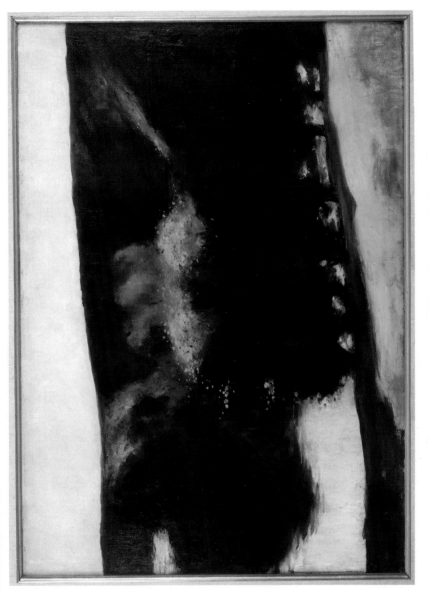

Plate 7. Lesser Ury, *Untitled* (*Landscape with Lake*) (n.d.).
Oil on canvas. Collection of Olga Bineth. By Permission of Bineth Gallery, Tel Aviv.

Plate 8. Lesser Ury, *Jeremiah* (1897).
Private Collection, Connecticut. Photo (c) The Jewish Museum, New York.

Plate 9. Wassily Kandinsky, *Riding Couple* (1907).
By permission of the Städtische Galerie im Lenbachhaus, Munich.

Plate 10. Jakob Steinhardt, *Four Types* (ca. 1921).
Woodcut. © Jüdisches Museum, Berlin.

Plate 11. Ludwig Meidner, *Apocalyptic Landscape* (1912–13).
Oil on canvas. Nationalgalerie, Staatliche Museen zu Berlin. Photo: Joerg P. Anders. © Ludwig Meidner-Archiv, Jüdisches Museum, Frankfurt am Main. Photo Credit: Bildarchiv Preussischer Kulturbesitz / Art Resource, New York.

Plate 12. Paul Klee, *Runner at the Goal* (1921).
Watercolor and pencil on paper, bordered with gouache on the cardboard
mount. By permission of Solomon R. Guggenheim Museum,
New York. 48.1172.55.

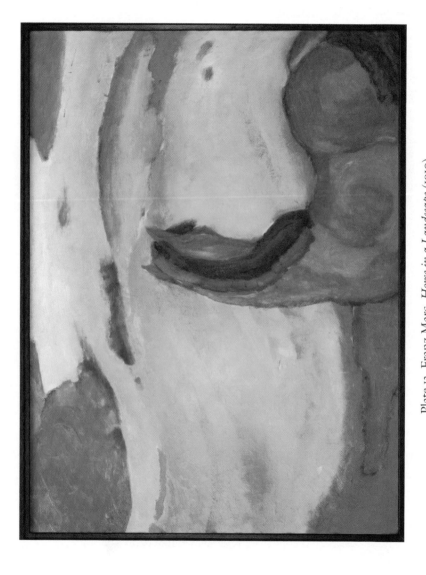

Plate 13. Franz Marc, *Horse in a Landscape* (1910).
Photo Credit: Erich Lessing / Art Resource, New York. By permission of Folkwang Museum, Essen.

Plate 14. Franz Marc, *The Fate of the Animals* (1913).
Photo Credit: Art Resource, New York/ Öffentliche Kunstsammlung, Basel.

Plate 15. Lyonel Feininger, *Cathedral* (1919).
Woodcut on gray-blue newsprint. Los Angeles County Museum of Art,
Robert Gore Rifkind Center for German Expressionist Studies. Photograph
© 2005 Museum Associates / LACMA.

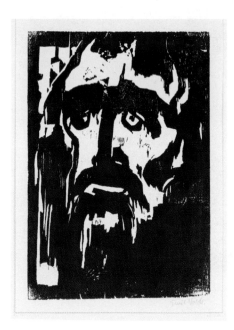

Plate 16. Emil Nolde, *Prophet* (1912). Photo Credit: Erich Lessing /
Art Resource, New York. Kupferstichkabinett, Staatliche Museen zu Berlin.
By permission of the Stiftung Seebüll Ada und Emil Nolde.

Plate 17. Wassily Kandinsky, *Composition VIII* (1923). Oil on canvas. Solomon R. Guggenheim Museum, New York. Gift, Solomon R. Guggenheim, 1937. 37.262. © 2005 Artists Rights Society (ARS), New York/ADAGP, Paris.

Plate 18. Oskar Schlemmer, *Bauhaus Stairway* (1932).
Oil on canvas. Museum of Modern Art, New York. Courtesy U. Jaïna
Schlemmer. © 2005 The Oskar Schlemmer Estate and Archive,
IT - 28824 Oggebbio (VB), Italy. Photo Archive C. Raman Schlemmer,
IT - 28824 Oggebbio (VB), Italy. Digital Image © The Museum of Modern
Art/Licensed by SCALA/Art Resource, New York.

Plate 19. "Oskar Schlemmer as the Turc II in the Triadic Ballet" (1922).
The Oskar Schlemmer Theatre Estate/Bühnen Archiv Oskar Schlemmer.
Courtesy Secretariat Schlemmer, Oggebbio, Italy. © 2005 The Oskar
Schlemmer Theatre Estate and Archive, IT - 28824 Oggebbio (VB), Italy.
Photo credit: Photo Archive C. Raman Schlemmer, IT - 28824 Oggebbio
(VB), Italy.

Plate 20. Michal Rovner, *Merging P#1* (1997). Chromogenic color print.
Whitney Museum of American Art, New York.

addressed the need to vindicate works of modern art by comparing a painting by Kandinsky to an illustration of a Grimm fairy tale from 1832. Modern art confronts the old order in order to "[pave] the way for what is new and already standing by" (65). Anyone who perceives the spiritual quality of an old Grimm fairy tale today, Marc thought, will find a modern exemplar in Kandinsky (67–68).

Like an image of St. George or an old fairy tale, Scripture represents only the most emblematic time element in a more basic temporal conception. The emphasis placed upon the present tense in modern culture is fundamentally anti-romantic. It stands against the nostalgia that imbued Novalis, whose essay "Christendom or Europe" begins like a fairy tale: "There once were beautiful, splendid times when Europe was a Christian land." Once upon a time, the inhabitants of Europe enjoyed beneficent might, childlike trust, mysterious churches, inspiring pictures, sweet scents, and uplifting music. Christendom was Catholic. Protestantism and Enlightenment represent the present tense, the decay of wonder and of mystery, against which romantic irony heralds the renewal of religion, the dawn of a new age, and the resurrection of Europe.[20] As Peter Szondi notes, romanticism presupposed a sense of time in which a magnificent past and the promise of the future turn the present into a relative, melancholic interval between "a no longer" and "a not yet."[21]

Almost a full century after Novalis, the neoromanticism of Jugendstil demonstrated only the most attenuated nostalgia for the historical past. Leading proponents like Hermann Obrist and Henry van de Velde rejected stuffy nineteenth-century Greek revival, neo-Gothic, Moorish, Italianate Renaissance, and French Empire styles. In their use of sinuous line and empty space, they wanted to create objects uniquely designed to suit the new century. In *Neue Möglichkeiten in der bildenen Kunst* (New Possibilities in the Plastic Arts) (1903), Obrist expressed great contempt for the current state of public taste, for carpets that were cretaceous or powdery brown and patterns copied from long-ago times. If one went to a store selling luxury items, one found cut glass, rococo porcelain, and a confusing mass of statues and bronzes. It was impossible to find a simple lamp in a lamp store.[22] Obrist set these criteria for the new style: design must not reproduce extant styles; every piece must be made according to a purpose, subordinating ornament to construction; the object must be singular without being bizarre or odd; and it had to be simple and not too expensive.²³ There was no reason to be hypnotized by the past, no reason to copy styles that were not one's own. One should create unconsciously, truthfully, without a thousand stimuli and diversions. Although he rejected the idea of progress, Obrist believed in new possibilities. With an eye to the "savages" of the South Sea Islands and to children, he insisted, "We must again become that which men once were: creative."²⁴

This faith in new possibilities contributes to a more fundamental turn to the past than the one represented by romanticism and nineteenth historicist styles. The goal was to transform the present on a prehistorical, ahistorical basis, not to mimic the historical past. This confidence propelled Buber's early lectures on Judaism against "Jewish inertia (called 'tradition')," as well as against the adaptability of a "soulless" liberalism (*OJ*, 13). Buber set the "renewal of Judaism" in opposition to liberal ideologies of evolution and progress. The sentiment was revolutionary—no middle-class plodding and piecemeal gradualism. Renewal is "something sudden and immense—by no means a continuation or an improvement, but a return and a transformation . . . a moment of elemental reversal, a crisis and a shock, a becoming new that starts down at the roots." The circular motion of return is "not merely a rejuvenation or revival, but a genuine and total renewal" (35, 36). It breaks into temporal existence. A creative spark from outside one's own historical time, renewal puts an end to temporal sequence.

The incursion of "the primitive" in *I and Thou* is one such eruption. "Consider the language of 'primitive' peoples" Buber advised. It represents the "wholeness of a relation." Our own formulas for greeting those we encounter—words like "Hail!"—are worn out compared to the "eternally young, physical, relational greeting of the Kaffir, 'I see you!' or its American variant, the laughable but sublime 'Smell me!'" (*IT*, 69–70). "*Mana* is that which is active and effective, that which has made the moon person up there in the sky a blood-curdling You," a palpable energy that animates physical existence. Memory preserves the impression of its original stimulus after it has already hardened into the optical impression of the moon-object. Disrupting the linear sequence of modern historicist consciousness, causality in the primitive world "is not a continuum; it is a force that flashes, strikes, and is effective like lightning, a volcanic motion without continuity" (72). At the dawn of human consciousness, primitive relation stands at a far remove from the modern world. And yet, *mana*'s "flash" and "strike" anticipates the staccato force that Buber will ascribe to the reading of Scripture. The *mana* that animates the Hebrew Bible strikes a trace in the memory that remains open to it.

The ubiquitous presence of the Bible in expressionist art was part of the same primitivism. Relatively static works like Karl Schmidt-Rotluff's *Nine Woodcuts* (1918) isolate individual scenes and figures from the New Testament—the road to Emmaus, cursing the fig tree, Christ before the adulteress, Judas, and the Virgin Mary. Combining the myth of creative origins and the pathos of suffering, single images from the books of Genesis and Job were particularly popular. More narrative works set the biblical figure in dramatic motion. Kirchner's *Absalom* (1918), a portfolio of eight color woodcuts, chronicles the conflict between David and his son. The first picture presents the rebellious Absalom, the last reenacts the king's lament at his ignominious death. Other works are capable of ritual use. A triptych composed of nine separate scenes, Emil Nolde's *Life of Jesus* (1911–12) is an altarpiece. Max Pechstein's twelve illustrations of *The Lord's Prayer* (1921) and Jakob Steinhardt's *Haggadah* mix image and word. A unique blend of piety and impiety, the darkened image of Scripture in expressionist art reflects upon the unsettled angularity of physical existence in extremis.

The archaic biblical element confronts contemporary consciousness with the most direct and intense form of revelation prior to its mediation in the history of Western culture. Nolde's *Prophet* (1912) (plate 16) has been hailed by one sympathetic critic as a "programmatic work of German expressionism," and by another as "the icon of a new art."[25] Neither Christian nor Jewish, the prophet who stares out just over the viewer's left shoulder evokes the suffering servant in Isaiah, the lamentations of Jeremiah, and the passion of Christ. Art at its most sculptural, prophets are "primitive." The masklike Hebrew visage is composed of strong vertical lines. Lending a tough, earthy countenance to Scripture, a darkened face cut into wood reveals a drawn-out face melting under the force of human suffering and the *mana* of divine pathos.

Revelation at the moment of its impact is rough and unrefined. Nolde understood that his critics preferred the "sweet biblical painters of the Italian and German Renaissance," compared to whose work his own was derision and blasphemy.[26]

The Christendom in Novalis's essay, the lonely monk and ruined cathedrals in Friedrich's paintings, and the Egyptian hieroglyphs in Novalis's *Novices of Saïs* reflect sad relics from the distant past. As for the French symbolism of Gauguin or the expressionism of Nolde and Pechstein, their primitives exist now and have done so forever. So too Klee's Tunisia or the *Ostjuden* from Poland, whose aristocratic mien appealed to a race-conscious German Jewish avant-garde around World War I. Past and present are not polar opposites if "yesterday and tomorrow [are] simultaneous." The presence of the past does not remove their work from the modern pantheon. It does not make their work romantic or unmodern. Scripture, not just in modern Jewish thought, but also in the art of German expressionism, adds a pseudo-Hebrew temporal element to the modern play of images drawn from Gothic, African, Native American, Islamic, South Sea, and East Asian art and sculpture.[27]

The encounter between "primitivism" and modernity was made possible by the troubled cultural politics of race and colonialism. In the Orient, European people had come face to face with faraway cultures deemed simple and static, unchanging and without history. As explored by the art historian Jill Lloyd, colonial attitudes combined with a voyeuristic aestheticization of other people.[28] Alert to the dangers that characterize the appropriation of styles, periods, and people for artistic ends, Lloyd's critique complicates Ludwig Meidner's complaint in "An Introduction to Painting the Metropolis" (1914). "Let's admit that we are not Negroes or Christians of the early Middle Ages! That we are inhabitants of Berlin in the year 1913, that we sit in cafes and argue, we read a lot and know quite a bit about art history. . . . Are these crude and shabby figures that we now see in museums really an expression of the complicated spirit of modern times?!"[29] Lloyd reminds us that the difference between "primitivism" and modernity was itself undone by the history of European colonialism. From at least the time of Delacroix and French romantic painting, modern art has been steeped in the cultures into which it has forced itself.

In expressionism, the presence of the "primitive" does not compromise the modern culture it comes to correct. In its rejection of *the most recent past*, the early twentieth-century avant-garde used the primitive as a tool with which to dislodge the nineteenth century, its idea of history and linear progress, philosophical idealism, aesthetic realism, and bourgeois morals. Lloyd's discussion of Nolde's painting *Mask Still Life III* (1911) makes clear that the image drawn from "primitive" cultures endures in a dialectical tension with the modern world. If Meidner's impatience represents one side of the modern/primitive divide, *Mask Still Life III* contests historicist claims that modernity makes a radical break with a past that it can now judge from the safety of its own belatedness. Isolating the image in time and space, the masks hang in an empty blue background, a cohesive composition counteracting what would have been an otherwise "realist" dependence on temporal or geographic context. As Lloyd maintains, objects are extracted from the museum display in order to juxtapose them in a new, expressive constellation. A counterimage to modern industrial production, the painting evokes the living quality of an unalienated object.[30]

The image of the past in both art and religion is most radical when it remains invisible to the naked eye, like the image of St. George identified by Peg Weiss in Kandinsky's *Painting with White Border* or the classical Jewish source material in *I and Thou*. Textual allusions appear at random. YOU floats over IT, like the divine spirit "over the face of the water" in the first chapter of Genesis (97). The "train" or "hem" (*Saum*) of the eternal YOU that fills every sphere brings to mind Isaiah's vision of the edge of God's robe in the sanctuary (57, 150). From the rabbis, Buber learned to say that one knows in the womb the world's secret, that one serves God with the evil impulse as much as with the good, that redemption remains bound up with "return" (76, 101, 106). As in the tabernacle and Temple cult, lonesomeness constitutes a "place of purification" before one can enter the "holy of holies" of relation (152). And the word of revelation echoes God's appearance before Moses at the burning bush in Exodus 3:14—"I am that I am" (160; trans. modified).[31]

Kandinsky understood the uneasy coexistence between history and eternity, caprice and necessity, the subjective and the objective. He also understood the mechanism by which the one gradually gives way to the other. In *On the Spiritual in Art*, Kandinsky identifies three moments in art's temporal dynamic of art. The first two are the most obvious. They are the individual artist and the age in which he or she creates. These are subjective factors that are time-bound in nature. The "principle of internal necessity" constitutes a third, nonsubjective element that drives art beyond these contingent origins. It is that principle by which an ancient Egyptian sculpture might move us today much more than it may have moved its contemporaries. Subjective factors of personality and time at work at the time of origin mute the work. "For this reason, centuries must sometimes elapse before the sound of the [artwork] can reach the soul of men" (*CWA*, 173–74). Although external, subjective factors go into the act of creating art, the "inner sound," not that of the artist, but of the work's internal constitution, grows more "pure" as the truly artistic element frees itself from temporal limits.

As Steven Kepnes indicates, the passage of time makes the Bible more strange, not less, by increasing the distance between text and reader.[32] In their historical setting, the original biblical texts that were to become Scripture fit into contemporary genres and familiar mores. Drawn out of context, the work is harder to interpret, more mysterious, more startling than when its parts were first authored and assembled. Buber knew that "[n]o doubt the biblical world will seem to such [modern] readers in many ways linguistically sharper and more vivid than it did to those who inhabited it; concepts will in the translation be distanced from the familiar, and will accordingly present their concrete fundamental significance more emphatically than they do in the original" (*ST*, 77). This was precisely the point made by Kandinsky about Egyptian sculpture. While this does not make "slaughtersite" a good translation for the Hebrew *mizbeah* (altar), its primitive expression disrupts the inertia of preconceived pieties tracing back to the "sweet biblical painters of the Italian and German Renaissance."

The use of words in the vein of "creation," revelation," and "redemption" is deliberately canny because it simultaneously marks and masks time. While they draw upon tradition, their meanings grow increasingly rarified as they pass into the present. Creation no longer means the creation of the world in six days; revelation no longer refers to the law disclosed to Moses at Sinai; redemption points to no real end-time.

This transformation goes beyond the obvious truism that traditional words are imbued with meanings that are no longer indigenous to their own time, place, and thought. Throughout most of part 1 of *I and Thou*, revelation is therefore invisible. When it appears toward the end of the chapter, it does so as "a force" that "enters into creation," a force that relates back to "the history of the individual" and to "the history of the human race" (*IT*, 82). Part 2 leads revelation into its weakest ebb and ends at a moment of great horror, so that the presence of God, divine countenance, and revelation reemerge, as if from out of nowhere, in part 3. Revelation returns with a difference. No longer latent, the spiral image of revelation concluding *I and Thou* points "the way" forward into the future, from YOU to IT and back to YOU.

Revelation works in a circle that spirals forward into the future. The last words of *I and Thou* read: "History is a mysterious approach to closeness. Every spiral of its path leads us into deeper corruption and at the same time into more fundamental return. But the God-side of the event . . . is called redemption" (*IT*, 168). The spiral is used to juxtapose the extreme sensitivity to decay observed by the severest critics of modern society alongside the hope in radical renewal. History does not unfold in a neat sequential order. Instead of moving neatly ahead, each forward move along the line propels one back into horror. While the motion is profoundly circular, the spiral plot allows the circle to move forward into the future of redemption. Time is unstuck. With each return-point further along, moving deeper and deeper into doom is the condition for a fundamental renewal. Revelation is the motor that drives the spiral's "savage" rhythm between creation and redemption.

III

In his study of *The Star of Redemption*, Stéphane Mosès points out that the "movement" that *creates* "stasis" is circular.[33] Indeed, the movement through time and into the future is based, not on the line, but on three different circles. The first circle is blood, an embodiment of identity that reconstitutes itself by the regular flow of its substance through the circulatory system and sexual procreation. The ritual calendar forms a second cycle, one that ends and begins anew on a regular basis. It is not the *content* undergirding any particular ritual, but the *formal* structure of repetition that defines the cycle as such. The third cycle is the least visible. In the previous chapter, we traced the intimate embrace of God's love, a blinding flash of light, the luminous image of the pious in the world to come, Yom Kippur, and the appearance of God's face. They manifest the recurrence of the same figure, an eternity in time that transcends time, an apex from which the soul loops circuitously back into the form of temporal life.

The new in revelation will always depend upon the creative force of repetition for the introduction of difference, change, and the transformation of consciousness. As Gilles Deleuze puts it: "We produce something new only on condition that we repeat—once in the mode which constitutes the past, and once more in the present metamorphosis. Moreover, what is produced, the absolutely new itself, is in turn nothing but repetition: the third repetition, this time by excess, the repetition of the future as eternal return."[34] Revelation clearly picks up where it began, with new blood at a new year before the gates of death. The cyclical process will have transfigured all three. New blood creates new life. The form of calendar-time includes the new content that intrudes into each turn of the clock. As for death, the return proves more radical. By the end of the exposition, it is practically unrecognizable. Love's intervention in the circle is the revelation that constitutes the force of repetition at its most intensive.

Blood

In *The Star of Redemption*, "blood" refers not to race and soil, but to sex and propagation. Only the blood community is eternal, Jewish birth and being, the bond between grandfather and grandson. Rosenzweig calls it a "linked sequence of life," explaining that "[f]or such a community only, time is not . . . a foe it may or may not defeat. . . . For it alone the future is not something alien but something of its own, something it carries in its womb and which might be born any day" (*SR*, 299). What assures the people's abiding endurance? Not native land. Jews trust blood and abandon soil. Not language. They trust silence over language, the visual sign of writing over speech (302). And not law. All civil laws and political nation-states come to pass (304). It is blood that constitutes what Kandinsky dubbed "the principle of internal necessity," the first source of eternity in time. The carnal existence of the Jewish people across time and space transcends local factors of land, language, and law. In Judaism, these elements are holy, set apart from the historical sequence by which other nations come into being and perish over time. As for the Jews, "[W]e are still living, and live in eternity. Our life is no longer meshed with anything outside ourselves. We have struck roots in ourselves . . . deeply rooted in our own body and blood. And it is this . . . that vouchsafes eternity" (305).

Qua circle, blood plants eternity into a viscous substance composed of its own internally autonomous flow. Or as Klee extends the image in a diary from his trip to Tunisia, "Human animal, timepiece built of blood," adding a few entries later, "I want to go beyond pathos and order motion." The second entry after this starts: "Genesis as formal motion is the essential thing in a work" (*DPK*, 310). Klee elsewhere called creation a complex, intricate construction. Over time, the limits to human perception prove elastic, which eliminates the subjective and relative factors that go into the creative process. We carry a circulatory system of similar nature within us about which we are unaware: the circulation of blood. Like the creative act itself, the movement of this substance does not depend upon relative differences in altitude or and phase, but on a central motor, the myocardium, built into us. It works according to a rhythmically repeated movement of contraction and relaxation, tension and relief. The blood propelled by an action center pervades the entire organism as increasingly intricate side streams break off into a network of branchings through capillary vessels. Good blood is returned to the heart, while bad blood requires a further circulatory system. Sent to the lungs, it is collected for a second time and brought back to the heart (*N*, 2: 99–107).

In the autonomy of its own procreation, the Jewish people is a "timepiece made of blood," a complex, intricate constriction, composed of a network of branches that spread out far and wide over history and time. The "ordered motion" of its physical substance does not depend on the relative factors of time or place, "altitude" or "phase," land, language, or law. It follows instead the internal motor of its own sex. As already traced by Buber in the essay "Judaism and the Jews," it is the "blood community," the "round of begettings and births," that exhibits lasting substance. It was Buber who first embraced the fact that, in exile, the Jew's land, language, and mores do not belong to the community of his blood, that the "confluence of blood" directs one's vision beyond the span of the individual's life toward something greater and far more enduring (*OJ*, 14–17). Of one mind, both thinkers ascribed the eternity of Israel and the abiding fact of its physical endurance to blood; and both sought to "plant" eternity back into time. The difference between the two was Zionism. Buber sought to set the people in the space of its land, whereas Rosenzweig sought to plant that blood in the temporal rhythm of a ritual calendar.

Calendar

Alongside the circulation of blood, holiday points in religion and art are rhythmic circles that recur throughout the year on an even basis. Art, according to Klee, speaks to ultimate things, ethical gravity, spiritual consolation, something more than the earthly and its possible intensifications. It then returns to the workaday world. At its highest pitch, art provides a change of air and viewpoint that empowers the inevitable return. One continues to look forward to new holidays when the soul will sit down to feed hungry nerves, to fill tired veins with new sap (*N*, 1: 80) In this, art shares the same temporal structure provided by the cyclical movement of daily prayer and Sabbath observance brought into the yearly cycle. As understood by Judah Halevy, they offer regular opportunities at which to free oneself, the more so "as necessity brings [the soul] into the company of youths, women, or wicked people." Itself a circulatory system, the body "repairs" itself from "waste" as it prepares for the week ahead.[35] In doing so, the holiday cycle anticipates death, eternal life, and other ultimate things as it feeds the body back into everyday life.

Ritual circuits revolve around their own internal regularity. According to Rosenzweig, the human institution of the week "is meant to regulate the service of the earth, the work of 'culture,' *rhythmically*, and thus to mirror, in miniature, the eternal, in which beginning and end come together, by means of the ever repeated present, the imperishable by means of the Today" (*SR*, 291; emphasis added). "The cycles of the cultic prayer are repeated every day, every week, every year, and in this repetition faith turns the moment into an 'hour,' it prepares time to accept eternity, and eternity, by finding acceptance in time, itself becomes—like time" (292). The line between the apex of Yom Kippur and the festival of Sukkot forms a circular pattern, from which "it is difficult to imagine that a way can lead back from here into the circuit of the year" (327). The soul has reached a high point from which it must now return. "To neutralize the foretaste of eternity, the Feast of Booths *reinstates* the reality of time. Thus the *circuit* of the year can *recommence*, for only within this circuit are we allowed to conjure eternity up into time" (327–28).

The regular motion of a circle does not, we have seen, simply repeat itself. It does not stand still or move backward, but rather moves forward. Unlike the motion of a bicycle or automobile wheel, which are propelled by the rider's action, calendar time is pulled forward by a heteronomous power. Explaining the forward tow of repetition, Rosenzweig writes: "The future is the driving power in the circuit of its year. Its rotation originates, so to speak, not in a thrust, but in a pull" (*SR*, 328). The consciousness that redemption is nevertheless not yet gives the year the power to repeat itself and in the process links itself into the linear chain of historical time. On one hand, history remains unredeemed. Therefore the cycle must repeat itself. On the other hand, this circular movement represents no historical growth of development, progress, and change. Since the Jewish people is eternal, it must *always already* have reached or anticipated its goal in time (328). The image of the circle allowed Rosenzweig to have it both ways. Ritual cycles move on, pulled forward into the flow of unredeemed time, just as the circle runs according to its own predetermined diameter.

The circuitous motion into the future requires not just time but timing. Since the kingdom of God must grow step by step, Rosenzweig opposes the zealot who seeks to leap to this end point without taking the requisite intermediary steps (*SR*, 265–71). With Goethe, Rosenzweig acknowledges the importance of temporality and temporal life. "Life, and all life, must first become wholly temporal, wholly alive before it can become eternal." But then he continues: "An accelerating force must be added to it" (288). This dimension of speed complements the image of a circle. Circles spin, but how fast is too fast and how slow is too slow? The fanatic proceeds too quickly toward the end, while Goethe does not move fast enough. So prayer must speed life along. Liturgical prayer quickens the wheel toward redemption. In its "plea for eternal life," it "supplements the nonbeliever's devotion to pure temporal life" (288).

Circles combine temporal flux and duration. The soul seeks eternity today in an infinite now that will not perish, but whose instance remains fleeting. "The moment which we seek must begin again at the very moment that it vanishes; it must recommence in its own disappearing; its perishing must at the same time be a reissuing." The importance of the hour lies in this:

> Because it is stationary, the hour can already contain within itself the multiplicity of old and new, the fullness of moments. Its end can merge back into its beginning because it has a middle, indeed many middle moments between its beginning and its end. With beginning, middle, and end it can become that which the mere sequence of individual and ever new moments never can: a circle returning in upon itself. In itself it can now be full of moments and yet ever equal to itself again. . . .
> This recommencement, however, would not be possible for the hour if it were merely a sequence of moments—such as it indeed is in its middle. It is possible only because the hour has beginning and end.

Having once struck, the hour recommences, exactly like the one that has just ended. "In the hour, then, one moment is recreated, whenever and if ever it were to perish, into something newly issued and thus imperishable, into a *nunc stans*, into eternity" (*SR*, 290).

Stasis does not, however, preclude historical change and spiritual nova. While the ritual cycle ultimately binds beginning and end, it nonetheless stays open to new moments in the middle interval. The hour is "equal to itself" inasmuch as it retains its *formal* identity with every other hour. But that formal structure is "full of moments," new and variegated *contents*. The combination of "formal" identity and variable "content" sustains identity over time, while introducing change. Calendars share the same feature as the hour. The static rhythm of Sabbath and holidays takes on the "surge of joy and sorrow, of anguish and bliss that the feasts bring with them." Steady flow does not contain or still this surge as much as it constitutes the condition of its possibility. Both Sabbath and creation are "renewed throughout the year, week after week the same, and yet week after week different, because of the difference in the weekly [Torah] portions" (*SR*, 310–11).

The balance between repetition and variation is brought into much greater clarity in the afterword to the Judah Halevy translation, where Rosenzweig observes:

> In the recurrence [the words of the liturgical poem] are the variable, but because . . . they are bound nevertheless to recurrence, they are necessarily forced into a certain similarity. . . . For this recurrence in the year is after all the *essence* of the festival. As in the final analysis, *repetition is altogether the great form* which man has for expressing what is entirely true for him. In these poems one can find the always renewed words of humility and devotion, of despair and trust in redemption, of world-aversion and longing for God. . . . That [the heart] does not become tired of saying anew this always One again and again testifies to [the poem's] enduring power. In the mouth of the lover the word of love never becomes old. (*H*, 183; emphasis added)

Ritual enjoys its enduring hold thanks to the play between "repetition" and "recurrence," "anew," and "renewed." Reading the liturgical poem year after year creates a loose identity over against time, but the passage of a year will introduce change into its meaning. The "great form" of repetition is a circle that allows the heart continuously to express the affect that is truest to it. Necessarily subjective and contradictory, its expression will vary as it spins forward into the future.

In its critique of essentialist notions of identity, the short treatise *Understanding the Sick and the Healthy* provides a further cue with which to explicate this dialectic between stasis and change. In Rosenzweig's analysis, a stick of butter resists any attempt to locate any single, substantive unity underlying the surface variations in taste and texture between this one stick and any other stick of butter. No underlying essence—no "butter in itself," no "idea of butter"—makes the butter that I eat today identical with the butter that I remember from yesterday. "The butter remembered, the butter desired, and the butter finally bought, are not the same" (*USH*, 36). All that links the possible varieties of butter is the word "butter." Human beings maintain the identity of butter over time through the formal repetition of a name. The same theory holds true for personal identity. A person's identity shifts over time. A man named John proposing marriage today is not the same person to whom his lover will consent or whom she will reject. Nor is the woman who accepts or rejects the proposal the same woman as the one to whom he proposed.

Since "time must elapse, the answer is unavoidably given by another person than the one who was asked, and it is given to one who has changed since he asked it." By what right then do people marry? How can one know that one's partner will remain the same through time? "[T]he lovers dare not deny, not even Romeo and Juliet, that changes, involving both of them, will inevitably take place. Nevertheless they do not hesitate. . . . They cling to the unchangeable. What is the unchangeable? Unbiased reflection reveals once more that it is only a name." At the further reaches of philosophical inquiry, the vagaries of temporal change cast personal identity into considerable doubt. In the name of healthy understanding, Rosenzweig calmed his reader: "But as soon as the 'person' becomes 'John'—well defined by his name—the doubt disappears" (37). As surely as a circular motion defines the holiday form, the *repetition* of a name establishes the identity of a person or thing who will change over time.

Static identity does not exclude historical difference, in that no *single* name can exhaust the identity of a person or thing. Rosenzweig did not ignore the variations introduced by the forward pull of cyclical time. He understood the point made by linguists in the wake of Ferdinand de Saussure that the relationship between name and referent, signifier and signified, remains arbitrary and conventional. There is no real affinity to the relation between the word "butter" and the stuff one eats. More to the point, things have many words. They receive new names that sit alongside old names. Old names are appropriated and translated into new ones. Therein lies the secret of human continuity (*USH*, 60). The object can change, the person can change, but they retain their identity by the repetition of a name. Names change, new names enter the historical record, and yet the thing still retains its identity by the act of human memory repeating old names along with new names in the process of transmission.

"Formal" repetition includes new "content," since an ostensibly static cycle must generate difference within its ambit. Changed contents are worked into an otherwise closed formal structure. As a structure, the holiday can thereby include historical variation. Historically, the biblical Yom Kippur bears but a cockeyed resemblance to the same event in ancient Babylonia or medieval Germany, even as the latter recall the former by name. Still they share the same name and place on the calendar, a nominal identity that retains the name of each festival within a predetermined order. Identity is preserved through language, through the formal repetition of names, not through any ideal or essential content. The calendar sets the course into a circle whose *precise* content remains subject to historical and geographical innovation. The festival cycle's formal repetition trumps any set of particular prayers, *piyyutim*, *kavvanot*, gestures, customary observances, or theological interpretations. Identity lies less in exact historical specifics than in the repetition of the names "Shabbat," "Sukkot," "Passover," "Shavuot," "Rosh Hashanah," and "Yom Kippur." It is this formal repetition that reflects and recreates eternity in time, understood as an enduring identity in the face of change, especially in the face of death.

The circle between difference and repetition is the circulation of blood and contributes to "health." The repetition of a name and the way it compounds with new names constitute the linguistic condition for the duration of an object or subject's nominal identity vis-à-vis the decay brought on by temporal change. The holiday cycle is a symbol of eternity whose continuous passage back and forth reflects the workday's sleep and wakefulness. "The holiday moves steadily from one to the other, and then back again—it is in continuous change. This movement is identical with that which governs the workday. Here we discovered that waking and sleeping, tension and realization alternate" (*USH*, 87). The holiday trains sick reason in the art of living. Respecting the "rhythmic movement" of the holiday structure allows one to yield to the week's rhythm. It compares to breathing, the signature of good health. "What rhythm dominates everyday occurrences? What pulsation appears in even the minutest phase? Throughout the day in every single breath, inhalation gives way to exhalation; work is replaced by rest" (85).

Death

The momentary rest formed by the holiday structure looks forward to that ultimate rest when all breath stops. Love reflects an eternity that takes the form of a static repetition in which the flow of time stands still within the linear sequence of a life-history.[36] In doing so, it mirrors that final stasis that lies beyond the line separating life and death. Temporal alteration stops at those moments when the human subject anticipates its own death. From death-crowned creation, love lifts the soul out of time and then sets it back into the world, which the soul seeks to redeem. The ultimate end rests in the annihilation of all finite names. Repetition is the sine qua non of redemption. Rosenzweig wrote, "Redemption lets the day of the world end beyond creation and beyond revelation with the same stroke of midnight with which it began. But of this second midnight, it is true, as it is written, that 'the night is light with Him.' The day of the world manifests itself at its last moment as that which it was in the first: as day of God, as the day of the Lord" (*SR*, 238). The last day is like the first, but its repetition commands one basic difference. In their return, all names disappear within the void of God's totality, a "dark" and terrifying midnight turning into one glorious flash of blinding light.

The shift from dark into light veils the presence of death. As Gilles Deleuze remarks, "The death instinct may be understood in relation to masks and costumes. Repetition is truly that which disguises itself in constituting itself. It is not underneath the masks, but is formed from one mask to another . . . from one privileged instant to another, with and within the variations."[37] Outside life, repetition is here understood to be the condition for the transvaluation of value. Throughout *The Star of Redemption*, the appearance and reappearance of its figure create for death a new mask. At the beginning of the text, death terrifies the human creature. No face illuminates the creature's terror. By the end of the text, the soul opens out into a luminous pictogram of absolute truth. We are no longer afraid of the death before whose gate we stand. The intervention of love is the difference. Revelation is stronger than the "creaturely death" that had terrified the human creature at the start. Love yields "redeeming death," transforming the fear of death into the spectacle of vision.

Repetition is key to this transition. In *The Star of Redemption*, death is pure sign. Its formal constitution is no different than that of any other significant sign. Its meaning lies in the alteration of its appearance. As Derrida has argued, a sign constitutes an iterable mark that can be "grafted" into an infinite number of contexts. "Every sign, linguistic or nonlinguistic, spoken or written . . . , in a small or large unit, can be cited, put between quotation marks; in so doing it can break with every given context, engendering an infinity of new contexts in a manner which is absolutely illimitable. This does not mean that a mark is valid outside of a context, but on the contrary that there are only contexts without any center or absolute anchorage."[38] In the process of this dissemination, the meaning of the sign changes. Its significance at t_2, that is, the moment of time and context in which we hear or read it have changed since the time of its inception at t_1. Because of the graft, death's first appearance does not resemble its last. From the original context of fear, death is now bound up with signs of passionate love. The figure is barely recognizable. No longer a visible sign, death is veiled by light, face, and "kiss." Reinscribed within a radically new context, love turns death into a redeeming figure, not an object of creaturely terror.

For the early Derrida, grafting and the generation of new meaning occur within a purely semantic framework that remains immanent to discourse. In contrast, Kierkegaard left open the possibility of a transcendence sitting midway between the first and second appearance of a figure. In Kierkegaard's *Repetition*, one Constantin Constantius sets out to advise a young poet how to break off an engagement with a young woman, a plan that involves a pretence by which the young poet would seem to carry on a love affair with another woman. This would then allow the engagement to end with the young woman's honor intact. The poet, however, seeks to uphold his own honor. He flees to Stockholm where he prepares himself for some thunderstorm from God. He hopes to acquire the necessary ethical attributes that would make him a suitable husband. But the thunderstorm occurs differently than imagined. The young woman marries another man in the meantime, a fortuitous change in circumstances that allows the poet to preserve his original aesthetic nature. He writes his older friend, "Is there not, then, a repetition? Did I not get everything double? Did I not get myself again and precisely in such a way that I might have a double sense of its meaning?"[39] Like Job, he stands by his own honor, is met by a thunderstorm, and receives back double everything he had lost.

Repetition rests upon a fundamental trust that one can master time. Constantin Constantius had himself once believed in repetition, but he abandons the faith. Having failed in a farcical attempt to make the same trip to Berlin twice, he now discovers that one cannot recreate the myriad, fortuitous circumstances that constitute any single sequence of moments. The poet, on the other hand, learns the secret of repetition, first from the book of Job and then from the recovery of his true poetic nature. In Kierkegaard's work, repetition reflects a critique of Platonic stasis and Hegelian mediation, a pressing forward, the preservation of identity, the actualization of eternity by virtue of the absurd. It is made possible only by the incursion of a foreign and unexpected element—the thunderstorm in Job, the good news that the poet's estranged fiancée has married another man. Rosenzweig's repetition occurs at a more sublimated level, but remains no less absurd. The incursion of eternity in time is the difference between the figure of death at the beginning of *The Star of Redemption* and its altered reappearance at the end. They subsist in the thunderstorm, the revelatory intervention of love that stops time.

IV

Circles are not typically associated with Judaism. Writing after World War II, Jewish theologians assumed that the natural wheel of birth, death, and renewal permits no transcendent standards by which to distinguish good from evil. The meaning of the circle was said to remain immanent to the cycle itself, as if pagan gods belong exclusively to nature, whereas the transcendent God of Israel is the unique God of history. Read in sequence, the line stretching from creation through revelation to redemption gave time an ultimate, suprahistorical dimension. "If ours is not a history according to nature," Arthur Cohen writes in *The Natural and the Supernatural Jew* (1962), "then it must be considered a history of God."[40] In their late appeal to transcendent value, postwar liberal Jewish thinkers ignored the nonlinear temporal orientation whose introduction into the culture of avant-garde modernism was meant to solve problems posed by strict linear accounts of time. This was Judaism entirely without rhythm.

Like a beating heart, a circle is more potent than a line, which can only extend out into a dead infinity. Inside the line, the past that appears in the present represents but a distant atavism, for which the line cannot otherwise account. Linear historical sequence strands revelation in the past, whereas the circle brings it into the present. In the variation of its repetition, the circle ingeniously combines temporal difference with the intensity of static duration. To return to that which once was is to highlight the change that has transpired in the meantime. Just as the circulation of blood brings oxygen throughout the entire capillary network, the circle transforms the image that it lifts from the past. Calendar time recurrently returns one to that need or event that is most important. One comes back to death in order to come back to life. The circle repeats itself, the entire system remaining the same in its alteration. It is happy in its oblivion to the historical pressures brought to bear upon it from outside. Contents are subject to the dynamic variegation of acculturation, while the form of tough circular motion ensures one's own right to be left in peace. Refusing to assimilate, there is no life, no autonomy, to revelation without a circle of its own.

But circles and other "primitive" geometries address the alienations of historical consciousness at grave potential cost to the free individual and to open sensation. As understood by Adorno, Stravinsky's music submerged the individual element back into the circle of the blind, integral tribe from which it had just emerged. Symbolized by the human sacrifice, the musical note in *The Rite of Spring* dances herself to death in a tempo that is both demonic and dull. "This submissiveness, in the final analysis, consigns what was previously sensational to a boredom which is in no way greatly different from the boredom which Stravinsky later methodically developed," Adorno quipped.[41] Only a naïve faith in new possibilities can save the force of repetition from a self-possessed tempo and from the utter tedium with which it threatens those who stand outside the circle.

Naïve in the confidence of its course, the circle is at once warm and bellicose. In his own analysis of *Painting with White Border*, Kandinsky overlooked the work's most violent graphic features. A phallocentric shaft of white line extends from the right of the blue circle in a furious motion toward the left; just as the white border crests and falls at the bottom center, to climb again up the right hand side of the canvas from which it disappears, only to crash again downward from the upper left corner. The white shaft belongs to the blue circle, the spear to St. George. A circle within a circle, the plucky blue figure is a motile element enveloped within the greater swell of the white border's loop. It is the color of the surrounding border that measures the painter's own naïveté. According to the color symbolism in *On the Spiritual in Art*, white is an open, spiritual register of a silent apocalyptic, ascribing hope to the action of the image. In its place, a black border would have signaled the enveloping doom that surrounds both St. George and the evil upon whose death he is so intent. As a closed figure, circles are exclusive. The invisible blue rider is immersed in the violence from which it would free us.

In his autobiography *From Berlin to Jerusalem*, Scholem recalled: "Every encounter with [Rosenzweig] furnished evidence that he was a man of genius." He added: "and also that he had equally marked dictatorial inclinations." These tendencies were associated with the "intense Jewish orientation" also observed by Scholem.[42] The intensity brought by Rosenzweig to revelation was the intensity of a circle. And so it is with caution that we read Russel Berman on the "rise of the German novel," where he notes the recurrence of such cycles and the tension between development and permanence. Not all circles are vicious. Berman observes how the convergence of theology, composition, and temporal structure inverts damnation into hope in Thomas Mann's novel *Doktor Faustus* (1947).[43] Berman also, however, remarks upon a type of cycle in which repetition resists change, a plethora of interchangeable episodes, the recurrence of destruction and destiny, an alliance between the archaic and the futuristic. In works of "fascist modernism," nothing new is uttered as a spectacular image comes to transfix the helpless and uncomprehending viewer.[44]

Rosenzweig drew a very tight circle whose repetition includes not much else beyond the difference of its own temporal distention. Short shrift is given Hinduism, Buddhism, and Islam. What revelation "can no longer reach nor sight . . . it must eject from its bright, melodious circle into the dread cold of the Nought." It does so "for the sake of its own exclusive-inclusive unity" (*SR*, 237). Pluralism extends only to Christianity in a very limited extent and only insofar as it yokes the nations of the world under revelation's rule. *The Star of Redemption* shares many of the best features of twentieth-century art and literature. Rosenzweig, most notably after World War I, and especially Buber remained liberal in their basic political disposition. In their work, revelation preserves the individual integrity of both partners who are party to it; and if, for Rosenzweig, God takes the last and final word before which the individual ultimately falls silent, that is because people die and God does not. But Deleuze is right to insist, "The greatest danger is that of lapsing into the representations of a beautiful soul." He warns in particular against "the release of a power of aggression and selection which destroys the beautiful soul by depriving it of its very identity and breaking its good will."[45]

In his conception of time, Rosenzweig, much more than Buber, failed to guard revelation from the danger posed by intensive, exclusive rhythms. The circle in *The Star of Redemption* remains too confined to the narrow synagogue space and to the place of death. In contrast, Buber's thought is far more open to the others with whom we share historical time and political space. It reflects the Zionism whose "movement" he sought to communicate in his letter to Paula. Their Zionism was a left-leaning variant whose proponents sought to make room for competing Jewish and Arab national claims to the same territory. This was the Zionism of German-speaking Jewish intellectuals, which Buber shared with Scholem, Hugo Bergmann, and Ernst Simon, who immigrated to British Mandate Palestine before the outbreak of the World War II, the Zionism of *Brit Shalom*. In the next chapter, we shall see that Rosenzweig gradually left behind the intensive, insularity of his magnum opus. The period between the date of its publication and his death in 1929 attests to a more open worldview whose spatial dynamic expands in critical counterpoint to its own closed, temporal structure.

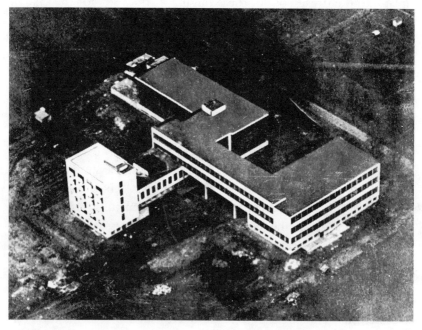

Figure 7. Walter Gropius, Bauhaus, Dessau, Germany (aerial view), 1926–27. Photo Credit: Foto Marburg/Art Resource, New York.

Five Space

As much icon as edifice, the Bauhaus building built by Walter Gropius at Dessau in 1926 conveys the quintessence of redemption (fig. 7). Contrasting it to Frank Lloyd Wright's earthbound structures from his Chicago period, the architecture historian and critic Sigfried Giedion pays special attention to its signature glass curtain. The horizontal white strip at the bottom and top of the building are "mere ribbons, supporting nothing." The effect is "not to anchor them to the ground but to have them float or hover upon the site." As for the ground plan, the building "lacks all tendency to contract inward upon itself; [on the contrary] it expands . . . and reaches out over the ground." It performs "a movement in space that has been seized and held." The Bauhaus crystallized "a hitherto unknown interpenetration of inner and outer space," which has "forced the incorporation of movement as an inseparable element of architecture."[1] Giedion's enthusiasm about the Bauhaus calls to mind Buber and Rosenzweig's "new space conception" of the kingdom of God. Collapsing the optical distinction between inside and outside, both structures spread out to shape the horizontal axis over which they hover.

The messianic kingdom figures as the temporal end point at which religious desire attains a space of complete consummation. As conceived by Georg Simmel, the kingdom is a constellation where "individual elements merge together. . . . This is the only way of expressing the relationship between the deity and the spatial-empirical world and the heterogeneous multitude of souls."[2] In the formal coordination of elemental nodes into a plastic unit, Simmel's picture anticipates the modern space conception dominating German Jewish thought in the 1920s. Revelation and redemption assume a spatial location concomitant with the move made from out of the ghetto and into the modern metropolis, to the varied types of space generated not only by *Gemeinschaft*-community but also by *Gesellschaft*-society; not just in synagogue, but out on the street, in Palestine and in Frankfurt am Main. In its layout, redemption follows the new space conception. A dynamic, urban space expanding from the inside out, with enough room for everything and everyone, its centrifugal motion was to collapse under the centripetal vortex of fascism, nationalism, and communism.

In contrast to the ethical challenge posed by spatial organization, the image of cyclical time remains self-focused in the integrity of its individual autonomy. Exclusive attention to one's own death, to one's particular substance—rhythmically patterned according to day, week, month, and year—propels one elemental unit after the next round-about like clockwork, always in the diameter around its own center. As Rosenzweig came to see, "the independence of the Jewish world" is best preserved through "the Jewish 'sacred year,' as fixed by the Jewish calendar" (*JL*, 31). Space creates a different ethical focus. The simultaneity of spatial configuration—one thing standing over against another at a single moment—demarcates the relation of one being to that which is not self. Reaching out past the locked gates of a clique, ghetto, church, or *Volk*, an expansive ethics of space will encompass a myriad of moral, social, political, and spiritual problems in relation to one critical question: How to maintain, as an open border, the difference upon which identity depends?

Buber defines "utopia" as the ideal vision of rightness realized in the image of "perfect space" (*PIU*, 8). In twentieth-century thought and culture, the dream of perfect space looks past the intimate, small-scale, face-to-face complex of family-village-town theorized by Ferdinand Tönnies in his influential study *Gemeinschaft und Gesellschaft* (1887). For as much as he idealized it, Tönnies knew that *Gemeinschaft*-community is an unattractive space, a constricted form of social life based upon the image of a circle, circles within circles, and rigid oppositions between inside and outside. "For there are," he wrote, "only a few who will confine their lives within such a narrow circle; all are attracted outside by business, interest, and pleasures, and thus separated from one another."[3] That place of private interest, *Gesellschaft*-society is epitomized by the big city and by impersonal forms of economic exchange: commodity, capital, credit, contracts, convention, and commerce. Tönnies had to admit that urban people stand in contact with each other, exchange, and cooperate, even without *Gemeinschaft*.[4] In *Gesellschaft*, there is community outside of the *Gemeinschaft*, upon whose ruins it builds.

In early twentieth-century Jewish thought, intensive commitments to small-scale *Gemeinschaft* increasingly took their place alongside big-city life, the street, stage, office, and technology. Inexorably, the image of *Gesellschaft* inflects revelation and redemption, a change in theoretical direction at work in Wagner's ideal of the *Gesamtkunstwerk* (total work of art) as modified in Jugendstil design and Bauhaus architectural theory. A variegated discourse, its members shared an interest in the renewal of forms that were social and spiritual as well as theatrical, musical, and architectural. Renewal was based upon an elastic space in which internal and external walls grow more and more permeable as it opens out toward the outside into which it juts. The new space conception coordinates the greatest possible number and most varied types of phenomena within a single space. While initially marked by a backward-looking *Gemeinschaft* rhetoric in Wagner's case, these attempts inexorably turned toward the modern urban world and its society.[5]

In the utopian vision laid out in "The Artwork of the Future" (1849), Wagner had envisioned a total work of art by which to bond the separate arts of architecture, painting, sculpture, music, and poetry under the form of operatic drama. Harking back to the ancient Greeks, he sought to recombine the arts in order to unite science, life, man, community, and nature. Some seventy years later, Gropius built the Bauhaus on the same theoretical basis, except here, "the ultimate aim of all visual arts" was the building-frame, not dramatic content. A total work of art, the Bauhaus had a twofold purpose. First, to gather under one roof an expansive array of plastic expression, ultimately combining painting, sculpture, theater, photography, dance, weaving, and architecture. To this end, Gropius recruited Kandinsky and Klee, by now the old guard of German modernism, and rising stars like Oskar Schlemmer, László Moholy-Nagy, and Josef and Anni Albers to teach at the Bauhaus. The second goal was to combine fine art and applied handcraft. In his four-page manifesto from 1919, Gropius dreamed of a classless guild of craftsmen whose members would "desire, conceive, and create the new structure of the future . . . which will one day rise toward heaven from the hands of a million workers like the crystal symbol of a new faith."[6]

Illuminating the front cover of Gropius's manifesto, Lyonel Feininger's *Cathedral* (1919) (plate 15) is the perfect crystal symbol. Bright shafts of intersecting vertical and diagonal light shards indicate ascent. The building shoots upward into a triangle formed by two strong diagonal beams of light. In its first years, it was the painter Johannes Itten who best epitomized this medieval, mystical strain at the Bauhaus. In charge of the preliminary course, he sought to apply beliefs and practices loosely derived from ancient Zoroastrianism about the material world and the battle between good and evil. Along with formal instruction in the use of texture, form, color, and tone, the regimen introduced by him at the Bauhaus included meditation, controlled breathing, physical exercise, macrobiotic diet, regular fasting, and other methods intended to purify the body. After Gropius finally forced Itten to resign in 1923, the original craft ideal gave way quickly to the functional aesthetic for which the school is most famous. When one looks toward the forms that typify the age, Gropius now argued, "the world of the architects, academicians, and artist-craftsmen disappear[s] from view." Instead, "the world of forms which emerged from and in company with the machine asserts itself: the new means of travel (steam-engine, aeroplane), factories, American silos and things which we use daily that were produced by machines."[7]

Modern trends in art, architecture, and design evinced a complicated relationship to the hurly-burly of *Gesellschaft* technologies. Already evident in Jugendstil circles, this approach swung between standoffish reserve and sheer delight. Rejecting the vulgar and the ordinary along with the production of cheap, ugly factory-made stuff, Hermann Obrist's call for a return to handicrafts was a snobbish voice against science and technology.[8] Jugendstil design theory combined Wagner's idea of the total work with the arts and crafts social utopianism of John Ruskin and William Morris. According to Obrist, the purpose of design was to refine sad bourgeois reality, to make life less toilsome, to unite the entire people—citizens, princes, critics, scholars, women, and artists.[9] Expressing similar reservations about the quality of industrial design, Henry van de Velde took a pronounced interest in new industries, in small electrical apparatuses, telephonic and telegraphic equipment, and electric bulbs.[10] He turned his gaze upon the restless journalist, upon the lawyer whose profession demands that capacity to locate oneself in all the drama and passions of modern life, commerce, and industry.[11]

Buber and Rosenzweig met these passions to the best of their ability. The types of space evoked in their work are varied, some real, others metaphorical and theoretical. Most mixed real and imaginary qualities. Rosenzweig's interest in space included the Christian cathedral, the theatricality of synagogue life, the spontaneity ascribed to Tel Aviv, and the utopian vision that drove his later work, not just at the Freies Jüdisches Lehrhaus, but also in his understanding of translation and of the challenge of "Germanism and Judaism." Buber's conception began with the need to orient the human body in the abysmal space represented by modern crisis consciousness. An architect of community, he later came to embrace the city street, the heart of modern *Gesellschaft*, as a locus of encounter. Politics was an integral part of his blueprint. The collision between fascism and communism and the dream of a binational, Jewish-Arab confederation in Palestine were first and foremost spatial problems. A *Gesamtwerk* in its own right, the life of dialogue was meant to draw the most diverse gathering of people possible into a perfect common space free from domination.

I

The original walls set out by Lessing between time and space, poetry and plastic art were forced by Rosenzweig to carry the additional weight of an immutable difference between Judaism and Christianity. Having withdrawn from the stage of history, "the Jew" conveniently hands it over to "the Christian." Obscured from view is the degree to which, in Rosenzweig's own work, space dominates the one form just as much as it does the other. At once ocular and invisible, like the distant stars over Feininger's cathedral, the star of redemption is a multiform configuration, a *Gestalt* that floats out there in space above the kingdom of God. But if the synagogue enjoys spatial reality, it does so hidden from view, which may have been Rosenzweig's point. In the privilege exercised by time, the view of Judaism is crimped, at least in *The Star of Redemption*. In contrast, a more cosmopolitan conception, a "hitherto unknown interpenetration of inner and outer space," began to shape a space in which the religious and secular jostle, Jewish and gentile platforms imbricate, the spiritual and natural space overlap. The streets feeding into and out of the kingdom of God belong to Judaism as much as to Christianity.

Christianity

The division of labor in *The Star of Redemption* between Judaism and Christianity according to a strict time-space axis effectively turns the historical contingency of Jewish Diaspora minority status under Christian hegemony in Europe into a metaphysical privilege. Eternity is reserved for the Jew and Judaism, confined to the constrained spatial limit of bloodline and synagogue. Already home at the goal, Judaism enjoys the family intimacy of lyric poetry, pathos, and prayer; with no immediately visible art, architecture, and dance; and no street life, state authority, or territorial extension. Historical time and its plastic stage are said to be exclusively Christian. While the kingdom of God remains incomplete without one or the other rival revelation, the détente between them proves insecure. Christian space undermines itself. Fundamentally unfirm, the utopia of Christianity and the perfection of its hegemony lie in its refusal to recognize any borders, including its own. In this version, the messianic path of Christianity grows out of shape, trumped by the Judaism that supersedes it.

As understood by Rosenzweig, Christian space construction is expansive and militant. The period of its first historical expansion into Europe, "the Petrine Church," is a form that "no longer imposes any external limits on itself." As a matter of doctrine, it "acquiesces in no border." It is one from which "none may remain isolated within its lap." Unabashedly imperialist, "[t]he expansion of the externally visible structure, the enlargement of the external borders takes place in the love of the missionary for those still dwelling in darkness." It "creates a visible body" for itself and for the entire world (SR, 279). However, this unity disintegrates under the "Pauline Church." With the advent of Protestantism, Christianity ignores the body in its inward turn toward the soul. The Christian world fragments until the third phase, the "Johannine Church," which begins with the rise of German pietism in the eighteenth century. The Church now subsumes the entire human person, in both its corporeal and spiritual aspect. A truly plastic space, the Johannine Church brings the Eastern Orthodox Church back into the orbit of Christendom, while admitting the Jew into gentile society. As it builds itself out into the world's vast expanse, Church space creates a social whole that collects the greatest possible aggregate of peoples under one common roof, while at the same time respecting the individuality of each member. It overcomes the hostility between nations, the cruelty of gender, the jealousy of class, and the barrier of age (even as man remains male, woman female, the aged old, youth young, the wealthy rich, the poor impoverished, Romans Roman, and barbarians barbarian) (344, 346).

The applied arts of Church architecture, Church music, and the miracle play perform a pronounced role in this utopian construction. Whereas fine art is a "prison" spatially set apart from everyday existence, the applied arts create real space and real time. They bring man "into life." Applied art is the "good wife" who prepares a man for public life, not a "demanding sweetheart." Church architecture redeems art's prisoners from ideal space. Painters decorate walls, sculptors adorn columns and cornices, draftsmen illuminate holy books. Church space is uniform, pure and simple in its orientation around one major room, in contrast to residential, commercial, official buildings, assembly halls, theaters, and inns, which are subdivided according to particular specialized purposes. Joining beauty and function, the basilica shape is "beautiful of form and yet for a purpose." The single room creates the desire for community by anticipating the "feeling of unification in every individual even before this unification itself has been established" (SR, 354–57). In Rosenzweig's scheme, Church music then comes to elevate that "initial togetherness" into a conscious and active togetherness. Architecture creates the space filled by the chorale sung by all in mighty unison. Words and feelings lose their arbitrary character; they become necessary and durable. The person "speaks, but what he says are not his words but the words set to music which are common to all" (362, 362–63).

Up to this point, the spatial dynamism suffers from a dystopian edge. The space seems at once too aggressive and too immovable, the moral communion of fellowship much too thunderous. The Church would form into a new prison, an imperious space, a brightly colored sonic trap, except that in the Johannine Church, its consummate phase, Christianity no longer constitutes a built structure. Its hegemony finally complete, Christian space turns "amorphous," "unestablished" (SR, 285). Once fixed and rigid, cathedral walls dissolve in the miracle play. " [T]he space separating man from man falls away." Gesture will now "burst the space into which architecture had placed a multitude of others, and whose interstices music had filled in and bridged." This recalls the poetry of dance, festive processions, parades, tournaments, and pageants, Cologne at carnival, Olympic stadiums, and the Bayreuth stage—fascism, were it not for the glance, the simplest gesture, which has "the power to dissolve all that is rigid." Opening the circle, dance bursts the locked gate as the procession proceeds out of the closed Church compound and into the secular city (370–73).

The Synagogue

A gross distortion, the strict time-space axis according to which Rosenzweig divided Judaism and Christianity overlooks how, in his own work, the spread of Christianity leads to its ultimate dissolution in firm, fixed space, while ignoring how Jewish life has always revolved around the architectural formations of a microspace within a larger gentile macrospace. The idea that the people are not supposed to "while away time in any home" (SR, 300) is true, but only to a very limited point. Even without a land of its own, Judaism has historically required the spatial definition provided by a "platform"—not just the synagogue and study-house, but also the mikveh, not just the home but also the market. Unable to account for Jewish space systematically, Rosenzweig reduced Judaism to its cultic dimension. In his eye, the ritual objects that fill the synagogue counteract temporal flux. The synagogue walls stretch without snapping. Ironically, however, these scattered hints regarding synagogue space appear, not in the chapter devoted to Judaism, where they belong, but in the discussion of Christianity, where they work to undermine the hegemony of its space.

Common to both Christianity and Judaism, Rosenzweig's discussion of liturgical expression is focused around the metaphor of house, room, and optical technology. Cultic space builds the house, forcing "the exalted guest" to move in (SR, 292). Prayer is the "searchlight" with which to illuminate the kingdom (293). The kingdom does not lie in the future. An eerie structure, it already looms out there now. Unlit and in the dark, it requires lighting. The "star of redemption" shares the same quality. Like the kingdom, the star assumes spatial locus, floating out there, simultaneous with our own existence, a "material point which moves in space." Only after "telescope and spectroscope have brought it to us do we now know it as we know a tool of our daily-use or a painting in our chambers: in familiar perceptions" (295). The kingdom and the star of redemption are ocular phenomena that subsist spatially, forms invisible to the naked eye that are brought into view by the technology of prayer.

In comparison to the kingdom and the star, which are perfect, Judaism and Christianity are only partial forms of truth. That Rosenzweig clearly privileged Judaism relates to time. Christianity remains always along the way, en route to the end point already reached by Judaism. But the judgment against Christianity is also spatial. Whereas Christianity never comes into view in the Judaism chapter, Judaism appears repeatedly throughout the Christianity chapter. To press the polemical point that Christianity depends upon Judaism and not vice versa, the orientated character of Church architecture requires the prior image of "Zion and all the world, Bethlehem-Ephrathah and the 'thousands of Judah'" (SR, 355). Geographically, Zion stands over against, set apart from, but in the midst of the nations of the world. Bethlehem and Ephraim form a circle within a circle, amidst the myriads of Judah. Thus conceived, Jewish space is the kingdom patterned upon the image of a circle of its own with a fixed center, stuck in the midst of Christian world-space.

It is only in the chapter on Christianity that we come to see how plastic objects and spatial extension shape Jewish life. In tandem with the ritual calendar, the static ritual object overcomes time. Resisting every change in form, ritual objects "achieve essentiality as objects." Their appearance remains stable and fixed. Preserved in ancient parchment, the Torah scroll and scroll of Esther do not change, transforming that which is material, subjective, and personal into an abiding, eternal form. The same holds true for cultic garments. In ritual, the body does without the expression of personality. One "dresses according to the rule of the space which unites him with others" (*SR*, 356). Again, the first reference comes from "the ancient garb in the Jewish ritual" before going on to Catholic and Eastern Orthodox cultic vestments. Christian liturgical space thus depends upon the synagogue and the enduring objects that first fill it.

Jewish ritual space continues to insinuate into Christianity as the discussion moves toward gesture. Announced in the first person plural, "our festival of redemption," intrudes at the very point devoted to Christian dance. An aggadah cited by the author recounts the regular occurrence of a miracle on Yom Kippur when the Temple still stood in Jerusalem. The crowds would gather so closely that there was no more room left to stand but, at the very moment when those who were standing had to prostrate, "there was endlessly much room left over" (*SR*, 372). The Temple confine stretched its space. "The gates of our Jewish houses of worship may remain closed, for when Israel kneels, there is suddenly room for all mankind in what was hitherto a confined space." In the view expressed here, dance is a cultic act in Judaism. Other examples include the holiday of Simhat Torah, when observant Jews dance with the Torah, and "the dance of the Hasid who 'praises God with all his limbs'" (373). Dance shatters the walls of the church as the festival procession proceeds into life. In contrast, the synagogue space is elastic. It includes all humanity, an infinite number, within a narrowly circumscribed space, the true universal Church.

In its ideal form as perfect space, the synagogue manifests a magnetic quality enjoyed by any performance space. To apply Kandinsky's analysis of "Abstract Synthesis on the Stage" to the synagogue: "That building (architecture), which can be nothing if not colored (painting), and which at any given moment is capable of fusing divisions of space (sculpture), sucks in streams of people through the open doors and lines them up according a strict schema. All eyes in one direction, all are tuned to a given source. The highest receptive tension waiting to be discharged. This is the outward power of the theater, which only has to be given new form" (*CWA*, 505). The "outward power" of cultic space lies in its abstract stage synthesis. Like theater, the cathedral and synagogue fuse the arts (sculpture, architecture, music, dance). At their best, they suck in streams of people to generate a "receptive tension waiting to discharge," directing the eye in one direction and tuning the ear to a given source.

The aesthetic of redemption is theater. As Rosenzweig comments in his essay on "The New Thinking," God, world, and man are "the cast, the theater program, which is . . . not a part of the drama itself and which one nevertheless does well to read beforehand" (*NT*, 81). Indeed, the entire *Star of Redemption* is itself operatic. An "about-face into life," all that goes into the work of dramatic art stimulates the spectator, from whom it "spills over into life." And then, to repeat the sentiment, "The door of the personal realm of art opens and discloses the way into life" (*SR*, 248). The terrified human subject, her pride broken before God's command to love Him, joins the choral fugue. As the song falls silent, she stands redeemed from death's terror before the silent face of God as the gates at its border swing back into daily life. On a smaller scale, the synagogue was seen as providing an applied stage where the relationship between the silent, plastic figures of God, world, and person play out the drama between love and death through the verbal media of creation, revelation, and redemption.

And yet its centripetal character ultimately mars the understanding of the synagogue in *The Star of Redemption*. Instead of building out into the world, Jewish moral vision is forced to contract in upon itself. "The whole constriction of direct, naïve Jewish consciousness consists in [its] ability to forget that there is anything else in this world, indeed that there is any world outside of the Jewish world and the Jews" (*SR*, 403). Clearly on the defensive, Rosenzweig underplays the danger of particularism, claiming that the most narrow reflects, in truth, the broadest universal. "[I]n truth our dangers represent no danger at all for us in the final analysis" (407). They constitute a threat only to the individual Jew, not to Judaism writ large (408). This confidence rests on the notion that "the Jew simply cannot descend into his own interior without at the same time ascending to the Highest" (407). In Jewish mysticism, Rosenzweig explains, the narrow world of law relates to the world at large as its very pillar. Jewish law thereby acquires a "supra-Jewish sense." It expands and "points beyond itself" (409–10). "The most constricted expands has all expanded into the whole, the All. . . . The merely Jewish feeling has been transfigured into world-redemptive truth" (411).

The apologetic dovetails with a cultural polemic that was part of a profound wartime alienation from all things German. In a 1914 letter to his parents, Rosenzweig professed that he had never known "how entirely and completely I do not feel myself German since the outbreak of the war. Were I not materially to a certain degree also in the position of having to want to wish for a German victory, I am not sure why I should want the Germans, Austrians, and Turks to win and not the French, Russians, and Japanese" (*BT*, 174). In 1917, he wrote: "I do not know this Germany any more. I was born in it and can do nothing about it" (424). Ambivalence extended to his own given name, to which he claimed to have no relation. His parents had picked it out like something in a shop window. It was nothing, "nothing inherited, no memory, history, not yet once an anecdote, hardly even a whim, only a matter of taste" (432). Renouncing Hermann Cohen's fusion of "Germanism and Judaism," he complained to his parents that Cohen's Germanism was a spiritual caricature, just as theirs was a social one, restricted to other German Jews, déclassé bohemians, professed liberals, German converts to Judaism, and Germans dependent on Jewish families (444–45). In the end, Judaism and Germanism do not occupy the same kind of space. As he expressed it in a 1915 review of Cohen's essay, they do not lie on the same plane (*GS3*, 173).

The Jewish plane was narrow indeed. Based upon cultural clichés dividing time from space and Jew from gentile, Judaism was restricted to a mental ghetto that no "supra-Jewish sense" can ever hope to overcome. Already at the goal, the Jew and Judaism were confined to bloodline (home, family) and synagogue. The narrow isolation it imposed was not a stance typically associated with German Jewish liberalism. While Cohen understood the need to secure a distinct congregational, even national, existence, he and liberals like him sought to advance Judaism across the widest possible spectrum of German public life. Rosenzweig's position had more in common with cultural Zionism. As scrutinized by Eleonore Lappin, the claim that the Jew needs to withdraw from "history" and power politics, from German and gentile society, was shared by many of the left-leaning Zionists assembled around Buber at the journal *Der Jude* after World War I.[12] In Rosenzweig's case, the embrace of Judaism and Germanism grew liberal to the degree to which it opened itself to secular Zionism just when the Zionism of Buber came to embrace Cohen's internationalism.

Tel Aviv

Modernism evinced a more expansive impulse, before which any narrow conceptions of synagogue-space inevitably paled, one that did not draw back from the built environment into which it fed. In "An Introduction to Painting the Metropolis" (1914), Ludwig Meidner announced that it was now time to paint "our real homeland, the metropolis that we all love so much." He inveighed against impressionist cityscapes that set urban life in the soft tonality of colored light and shadows. Should one paint "strange and grotesque structures as gently and transparently as you paint streams; boulevards like flower beds!?" The city signified "Life in all its fullness: space, light and dark, heaviness and lightness, and the movement of things." In the city, "The light seems to flow. It shreds things to pieces. Quite clearly we experience light scraps, light streaks, and light beams. Whole groups undulate in light and appear to be transparent—yet in their midst, rigidity, opacity in broad masses." Big-city landscapes are "battlefields filled with mathematical shapes. What triangles, quadrilaterals, polygons, and circles rush out at us in the streets."[13] The city street melts solid matter into the quick geometry of spontaneous motion.

There was, however, no German Jewish street. In a May 1927 letter to Benno Jacob, a leader of the liberal, anti-Zionist Jewish community in Germany, Rosenzweig had Tel Aviv in mind when he claimed:

"[Religion] needs spontaneity. And when I consider what has sponta-
neously arisen in Palestine, I must admit that nowhere in the world
have the demands of religious liberalism been met, even today, as
fully as there." "[T]ake the observance of Sabbath!" Zionists smoked,
wrote letters, and arranged sporting events on the Sabbath. Even if the
Orthodox regarded this as *hillul Shabbat*, a desecration of the Sabbath,
Rosenzweig could not feel that way. "As for Tel Aviv, the 'town of spec-
ulators,' which most Zionists view as a questionable Zionist achievement—I cannot help but be impressed by the fact that all stores there
close from *kiddush* to *havdalah*, and that thus, at any rate, the mold into
which the content of the Sabbath can flow is provided." Secular Zionism more than held its own against Diaspora Judaism. "Where do we
have that here?" Referring to the secular *Reali* school in Haifa, Rosenzweig remarked how pupils read the Bible in Hebrew, which made him
"shudder at the mere thought" of religious instruction in Germany
(*FR*, 356–57; trans. modified).

Rosenzweig was drawn, not to the hoary image of sanctified Jerusalem or to the utopian socialism of the kibbutz movement, but to the
symbolic fulcrum of secular Zionist culture and commerce. His letter
to Jacob highlights an urbanity that undermines the dogmatic anti-
Zionism set out in *The Star of Redemption*. A signal to Rosenzweig's
own spontaneity of expression, synagogue and Sabbath, no longer a
strict monopoly of their Orthodox interpreters, remain open to the
saeculum. The appeal of Sabbath sporting events had already been anticipated by remarks about gesture, processionals, and physical movement in *The Star of Redemption*, but never in relation to Judaism. A new
look at Zionism thus marked for Rosenzweig a radical shift toward a
space broader than the limited parameters of diasporic congregational
life. Against any ideological extreme, Zionist or anti-Zionist, the letter
to Jacob reflects the in-between juncture where life "gravitates back to
earth" (*FR*, 358).

In coming back to earth, the kingdom no longer constitutes a utopian no-place whose ideal locus lies in the distant future. It must stand
here and now. The gritty realism at stake in this messianism undercuts
any combination of liberal idealism and romantic yearning. One cannot pray for something one considers impossible from the very outset.

The future envisioned by the prophets was a "future Zion on earth." Rosenzweig reminded Jacob of a story he had once told about Hermann Cohen in his Judah Halevy commentary. Already over seventy years old, Cohen had confessed to him that he still hoped to experience the beginning of the messianic era. When the much younger Rosenzweig replied that he did not think that he himself would live to see the day, Cohen pressed, "But when do you think then?" Not having the heart not to name a date, Rosenzweig suggested that it would only be after hundreds of years. Cohen misunderstood him to have meant only after a hundred years and cried, "Oh, please say fifty!" Quoting Halevy, Rosenzweig now insisted to Jacob: "What is not to come save in eternity will not come in all eternity" (*FR*, 358; *H*, 259–60).

Fixed on time, not space, Cohen's pathos rides upon a conception of messianic place that recedes further and further into the future. It lacks the solid dimension found in the letters to Jacob. In an earlier communication, also from May 1927, Rosenzweig had tried to mediate between Cohen's anti-Zionism and Buber's Zionism. Jerusalem is a messianic symbol, but for a symbol to become more than an arbitrary appendage, it must somewhere and somehow reflect an unsymbolic reality. Against the Zionists, he observed, "Warmth is not only to be found where there is sunlight—that is a Zionist superstition—but wherever I have a good stove." Rosenzweig counterclaimed that his own "Frankfurt wisdom"—a play on the rabbinic expression "Greek wisdom"—depended upon the Land of Israel, not just the land that had been, but the one that would be, and contemporary Palestine, which linked the two. "[T]he coal and the wood which warm me today could not have grown . . . if there were no sun. . . . The real sun!" Life requires a real point set in space, "[n]ot merely a painted symbol, no matter how attractive the painting!" (*FR*, 354–55). In still another letter from the same month and year, Rosenzweig explained to Jacob that the messianic vision of a convocation of nations and world peace would entail a miraculous transformation of human nature. This faith came from Jewish prayer books, the *Siddur* and *Mahzor*, and he could not tear Zion from it. He did not know how big and how modern Jewish Palestine might one day become, but he did not begrudge it its factories and highways (*BT*, 1145).

About the actual conflicts roiling modern Zionism, one notes a nearly complete inability to read the political map. Rosenzweig's letters to Jacob ignore animosity based on religion or international conflict. No one at the time could have foreseen the success with which the Orthodox and ultra-Orthodox streams of Judaism have since overwhelmed religious life in the state of Israel after the Holocaust; or the deep resentments their political monopoly would engender on the part of the less- and nonobservant majority. Rosenzweig innocently presumed that Reform Judaism would dominate religious life in Palestine, without realizing how alien it was to the politically radical young Jews from eastern Europe and their sabra children spearheading early Zionist culture. As for the Arab-Jewish conflict, one of his last letters before his death refers to the 1929 Hebron riots, his fear for the future of Zionism, and his worry about an *English-Muslim* war (*BT*, 1228). Focused on the idea of a broader civilizational clash between the Western world and Islam, Rosenzweig overlooked the immediate threat of Arab-Jewish enmity, a danger Buber clearly understood already in the early 1920s.

The Freies Jüdisches Lehrhaus and the Law

If Jewish life in the Diaspora were to express the free spontaneity enjoyed by the inhabitants of Tel Aviv, it would have to hinge upon a new approach to the space of education and law. An open letter from Rosenzweig to Cohen in 1917 entitled "Zeit ist's" outlines an ambitious program of study for secondary school students within the German educational system. A second essay, written in 1920 under the title "Bildung und kein Ende," indicates the spirit brought to adult education at the Freies Jüdisches Lehrhaus in Frankfurt. The confidence expressed in both essays revolves around the ideal of formative education essential to the constitution of culture and character. Jewish existence requires Jewish *Bildung*, immersion in the Hebrew language and literary sources. Yet the difference between the two essays could not be more complete. The anti-German model of Diaspora in the first essay falls back into the same closed circle that marks *The Star of Redemption*. The second essay reflects a more thoroughly liberal disposition. Revelation acquires a spatial orientation, the energy of which propels a platform out and over into the modern metropolis with triangular verve.

In "Zeit ist's," Jewish space stands embattled by the urban environment pressing down upon it. Jewish high-school students, who would have normally had to study religion as part of the German school curriculum, left gentile society, as it were, for two lessons each week, with time found to visit the synagogue on Saturday. They entered into a Jewish educational apparatus. Static, a circle sat within a circle; an outside environment encircled the outer circle (the classroom, described as an anteroom) that formed around an inner circle (the synagogue). The prayer book created a "Jewish world," understood as an "inner life." One might possess this Jewish world, but one was "surrounded by another one, the non-Jewish world" (*JL*, 29). The border between inside and outside seemed immutable, demonstrating none of the later desire to translate Hebrew into German. "[O]f the language of Hebrew prayer we may state quite categorically: it cannot be translated," Rosenzweig writes. In this earlier view, the autonomy and integrity of Judaism is set apart from and over against the gentile world. "Our own Jewish world," he insists, "ought not to be experienced as a mere preliminary stage to that other world" (30).

Big-city space proves more copious in the second essay, "Bildung und kein Ende." Jewish educators need to "[exploit] the big-city public's insatiable hunger for lectures" (*JL*, 67). In this essay, *Gesellschaft*/society and *Gemeinschaft*/community do not contradict each other as much as the one animates the other. The space construction is more open and gregarious, less antagonistic and insular than that in "Zeit ist's" and *The Star of Redemption*. The image of a "platform" and the use of words like "corner," "alongside," and "outside" are key to the dynamic space now framing Jewish life, lore, and law. Rosenzweig recognized that the historical entry of the Jews into gentile society with Emancipation had fragmented the integrated architecture of home, synagogue, and law prior to the modern period. With its scope and validity called into question, Jewish law no longer created community as much as it rent it. "Today the Law brings out more conspicuously the difference between Jew and Jew than between Jew and Gentile" (61). The home had also lost its dominance. At best, it had become merely "one thing" at the side of and outside of "another thing," one's occupation and public activities. And the synagogue, reduced to "religion," had become merely "a little corner."[14]

The reconstruction of Jewish life at the Lehrhaus starts modestly with a single and simple room, an open and empty space, with no preconceived blueprint. "Any 'plan' is wrong to begin with, simply because it is a plan. The highest things cannot be planned" (*JL*, 65). Rosenzweig opposed a Juda-"ism" based on "a canon of definite, circumscribed 'Jewish duties' (vulgar orthodoxy), or 'Jewish tasks' (vulgar Zionism), or—God forbid—'Jewish idea' (vulgar liberalism)." Recipes create caricatures of people. The only recipe for making a Jewish person is to have no recipe (66). The Jewish person has only to remain ready. "Those who would help him can give him nothing but the *empty forms* of preparedness, which he himself and only he may fill." Space and time provide empty forms in which "something can happen." "Really nothing more is needed: a space in which to speak [*ein Sprechraum*] and a time in which to speak [*Sprechzeit*]" (67; trans. modified). The Lehrhaus is an "empty form" (67, 68). The radically simple quality of the single discussion room at the center of the Lehrhaus recalls the discussion of Church architecture in *The Star of Redemption*: a perfect purity of space in which a group gathers. No single content, nothing more and nothing less than desire joins diverse people together in that single room.

The Freies Jüdisches Lehrhaus was inviting. At its inauguration, Richard Koch welcomed all Jews, anyone of goodwill, regardless of politics—liberals, Orthodox, Zionists, assimilationists, and also the non-Jewish world. Moving past the position staked out in *The Star of Redemption*, Rosenzweig understood that the Jewish people lives not just alongside the nations, but rather belongs to them (*BT*, 689). As expressed by Rosenzweig in "Bildung und kein Ende," Jewishness does not know "limitations inside the Jewish individual. Nor does it limit the individual when he or she faces the outside world." A Jewish person represents an all-embracing individuality. "His Judaism must, to the Jew, be no less comprehensive, no less all-pervasive, no less universal than Christianity is to the Christian human, or paganism to the pagan humanist" (*JL*, 57; trans. modified). The Lehrhaus stood for a new learning, not one that "starts from the Torah and leads into life, but the other way around: from life, from a world that knows nothing of the Law, or pretends to know nothing, back to the Torah." Jews should neither "give up anything, nor renounce anything, but lead everything back to Judaism. From the periphery back to the center; from the outside, in" (98). One must bring a "maximum of what is alien" back into Jewish life (99). The outlook explicitly contradicts that of *The Star of Redemption*, according to which Judaism "constantly divests itself of un-Jewish elements in order to reproduce out of itself ever new remnants of archetypal Jewish elements" (*SR*, 404).

A broken platform in "Bildung und kein Ende," Jewish law creates a virtual edifice in "The Builders" (1925). Publishing the piece as an open letter to Buber in *Der Jude*, Rosenzweig stood up for Jewish law against one of its chief detractors. It was he, Buber, who had broadened their conception of "Jewish teaching" beyond the narrow boundaries set for it by nineteenth-century liberal Jews like Abraham Geiger. After Buber's pioneering work, one knew better now than to reduce Jewish teaching to some rational essence, idea, ideal, or content. What would make a future idea or teaching Jewish? The path to it led through "the knowable" but was itself not knowable. Radically inclusive, Jewish teachings thrust toward a future that could never be known in advance. As for the law, Buber had stranded it, leaving it to the nineteenth-century neo-Orthodox Samson Raphael Hirsch and his followers. But law extended beyond the constricted sphere of "doable" Orthodox duties and expressly forbidden activities over against the narrow range of extralegal, non-Jewish activities deemed "permissible" by the modern Orthodox. All extra-Jewish aspects were to be brought into Jewish life. "Not one sphere of life ought to be surrendered" (*JL*, 83). In Rosenzweig's view of the law: "Nobody should be allowed to tell us what belong to its spheres, as nobody was allowed to tell us what belonged to the sphere of teaching." One cannot know or prescribe in advance what one might do within its frame of reference (86).

Porous barriers between inside and outside, forbidden and permissible, Jewish and non-Jewish defined the space of Jewish law. "Even what is within that sphere of demarcations, within that inner realm of Judaism, will be influenced by the fact that it is no longer separated from the [non-Jewish] realm of the merely 'permissible'" (*JL*, 83). Walls have been rendered ambiguous. "Thus the demarcation line is broken: the two worlds, the one of the Jewishly forbidden and the one of the 'permissible' extra-Jewish, flow into one another" (84). "We do not know the boundary, and we do not know how far the pegs of the tent of the Torah may be extended, nor which one our deeds is destined to accomplish such widening." Could anything remain outside the law permanently? If so, "the boundary would assume a character it should not have; as rigid and as fixed as the distinction between the forbidden and the permissible, which had been discarded" (87). Law allows a more subtle interplay between inside and outside that does not shut one off from the world. The view from within turns out into the surrounding environment, not unlike Gropius's use of glass in the Bauhaus building in Dessau.[15]

Decidedly urban, the distinction between inside and outside is pragmatic, maintained only in order to account for shifting perspectives. From the outside, the center looks variegated, including different points of view. The Lehrhaus curriculum was based on temporal-historical divisions (classical, historical, and modern) and genre contrasts (Torah and prophets, halakha and aggadah). From the inside, these different points of view merge into a whole. Inseparably intertwined in the center, "all of this hangs together. More than that: it is one and the same within itself" (*JL*, 100–101). Centers do not obstruct pluralism. In a long letter from March 1922 to Rudolf Hallo, Rosenzweig empathized with all who wanted to go their own way. He observed the individual and her thousandfold paths. One learned what connected another's path with one's own. They all came to a common landscape through learning. The Talmud itself had once provided the Jewish people with one common road—albeit one with a plurality of side streets, bridges, and little towns. Since the Emancipation, this no longer existed. Jewish life was now split into countless streets, not one big road. One day there would be a main road, or rather a "system of streets," for which, in the meantime, individual streets were the right preparation (*BT*, 763–64).

A system of streets, Lehrhaus, and law created a quintessentially modern space participating in the new space conception crystallized at the Bauhaus. Opposite tendencies were brought into a network of contrasts, craft and technology, the range of visual and performing arts, what Moholy-Nagy called "an intense and penetrating concentration of action."[16] In its own way, the Lehrhaus combined all the ideological strains that shaped the Jewish community in Weimar Germany. Like the Bauhaus, it located itself in the midst of the modern metropolis. Its founders did not see it as providing a retreat from real life. In contrast to the sanitarium in Thomas Mann's *Magic Mountain*, it was no sick-house world closed off from the outside world. The Lehrhaus design was open to the world and well aired. Ernst Simon recalled the atmosphere given to Jewish education, something aristocratic, audacious, high-spirited, playful, and secure, its big city air (*Großtadtluft*).[17] Just as the members of the Bauhaus looked forward to the salubrious effect of modern design upon industrial society, the Lehrhaus worked for the renewal of a Jewish person redeemed from the limiting confines of pre-modern ghetto life, the rigid sectarian sphere of creedal confession, the narrow notion of "essential teachings," and rigid legal borders separating Jewish and non-Jewish.

In one crucial respect, the Lehrhaus could never match the Bauhaus. Able to move and transform itself ideologically, the Bauhaus was not bogged down in one narrow circle. It survived the early Itten years, the departure of Gropius, and new leadership under the socialist Hannes Meyer and then under Ludwig Mies van der Rohe. And when Hitler rose to power and closed the Bauhaus, its leading lights moved to Harvard and to Chicago. In retrospect, the Lehrhaus ultimately failed to live up to its initial success. Its founders had hoped to attract a large attendance by means of lectures, while fostering more intensive study-groups. Rifts between intellectuals and the general public soon belied this grandiose plan. Rosenzweig's own lectures were a definite failure, too abstruse, demonstrating a distinct inability to communicate with ordinary people. And the study-groups never extended beyond the small group that formed around him. By 1926, it was realized that the Lehrhaus had turned into a "great Potemkin village" (*BT*, 1083). As one scholar has noted, it never lost the character of a narrow circle, based more upon personal relations than upon a successful social interface. Its founders failed to transcend the narrow *Gemeinschaft* character of a small private clique formed around a concept.[18]

Translation

Rosenzweig's thoughts about the Lehrhaus and Jewish law were of a piece with his and Buber's translation work. The language and

translation of meter, rhyme pattern, and word choice signal the problems of identity, multiple identities, and the transformation of identity. Believing that the good Lord wanted him to live, Rosenzweig
refused the torture of a bifurcation that would have split him in two,
separating the Jewish from the German. It was an operation he could
not survive. "I have indeed perhaps a special safeness [*Harmlosigket*]
vis-à-vis the problem Germanism and Judaism," he wrote in a 1923
letter to Hallo, "I believe that becoming a Jew [*die Verjudung*] has
made of me, not a worse, but a better German" (887). Loosening the
boundary separating Jew from German, the letter preserves the one
between Jew and Christian. While Judaism remains an "enclave,"
both the letter and the translation work look past the narrow division
of labor set out in *The Star of Redemption*. But like the Lehrhaus, the
task of translating Judaism into German collapsed under the brutal
weight of historical circumstance.

In translating Scripture into German, Judaism occupied the inside,
Christianity the outside of a structure whose differences Rosenzweig
sought to span. In a 1923 letter to Buber, Rosenzweig asserted that the
Halevy translation project was intended for Jews *and* Christians, "even
though and because it speaks so Jewish" (*BT*, 890). Inside/outside and
the possibility of transformation dominate the project. Can the source
language of the original, entering the outside world, retain its own dis-
tinctive identity in the act of translation? What happens to the identity of the target language? The translation theory assumes the same
breakdown of rigid boundaries separating inside and outside, foreign
and familiar from the letters to Benno Jacob and the Lehrhaus and law
essays. The goal in translating Hebrew poetry into German was not to
Germanize that which was foreign. That would be like mechanically
rendering a letter from a Turkish friend into German. The translation
might be accurate enough and German enough, but it would not be
Turkish enough. One would miss the friend's person, his tone, meaning, and heartbeat (*H*, 170). The point, however, was not so much to
preserve an original identity as to have the foreign element transform
what was familiar. Looking past the specific example of Hebrew poetry, Rosenzweig noted that translations of Shakespeare, Isaiah, and
Dante did not leave German untouched, insofar as, along with them-

selves, poets imported a new language spirit into the target language (170–71).

Rosenzweig's translation work depends upon a wide-open and future-oriented spatial orientation. Like Walter Benjamin's version of the same theory in "The Task of the Translator," the notion that there is only one language does not purport to describe reality as one knows it now or may have once known it in the paradisiacal past. Rosenzweig presumed that linguistic traits were shared, a structural affinity that makes it possible to translate one language into another. Voiced in the imperative, the act of translation forms around the *"commandment"* of "universal human mutual understanding." It anticipates "the day of that harmony of languages which can grow only in individual languages (*H*, 171). Words like "commandment," "day," and "growth" are messianic. The space is one that expands at the expense of national isolation (173). Indeed, the highpoint in translating is architectural, "when the dividing wall between poetry and translation falls down, if only for a moment" (182).[19]

The translation, like the Lehrhaus, provides an overlapping geometry to the local problem of Judaism and Germanism and to the broader problem of religion and secularism. The idea was to free the former plane from the narrow confine of "religion" and the latter from nationalism. Translation redeems words such as "grace," "resurrection," and "kingdom" from "religion" by bringing them into the workweek. The voice of the Bible transcends any enclosed space, be it a church or a language. It wants to remain free (*ST*, 56). A Bible translation must "[engage] all spheres of life. There is no 'religious sphere.'" Conversely, German culture needs Hebrew cosmopolitanism. It is that which brings Germanism into world history, into the broader world shape (*H*, 177). It contributes by teaching wholeness. Along with Christianity, it would be a factor in the salvation of Germany and Europe by introducing "super-European, superhuman powers" into them, but only upon the understanding that the "[e]ternity of these powers is confirmed in their capacity to be secularized ever anew (*BT*, 888–89). Translation thus signals the back-and-forth transposition of two distinct but interpenetrating worlds, one fleeting, the other eternal, one natural, the other supernatural. With the scriptural word, another world thrusts itself in front of the surrounding world, downgrading its status to an appearance or parable (*H*, 177).

This translation project is one in which revelation shifts out into the surrounding *secularium*, one in which the walls that separate "x" from "not x" collapse, if only for a moment. It is a model whose vulnerability rests upon the extent to which the surrounding society was itself already open to that foreign presence. Recognizing this utopian element, Scholem called the Buber-Rosenzweig Bible translation a *Gastgeschenk*, the gift of a guest, which German Jewry gave to the German people, the "tombstone of a relationship."[20] If tombs are earthbound, it was its innocent weightlessness that betrays Rosenzweig's entire conception of space. In *The Star of Redemption*, Judaism is a haughty structure composed of blood and time that hovers above the street's historical trajectory, untouched by the dangers that threaten it from without. Gradually, it opens out to the other, turning into glass and floating back to earth, where it seeks to expand out into the milieu. A fragile gesture, it never touches ground. Unreciprocated, the scheme lacked substance. As Scholem observed in 1962, there was no deep German Jewish dialogue, no historical German Jewish symbiosis. If Rosenzweig's project "ran its course" in "the empty realm of the fictitious," this was a testimony less against the larger project of cultural translation and spiritual transformation and more to the unfeasibility of doing so in Germany.[21]

II

Whereas Rosenzweig always kept to closed circles, Buber's lifelong political activity and the attention he paid to the dangers of Jewish particularism lent his understanding of "community" more political ballast. Already at the start of the century, he was engrossed in Zionist politics from the vantage point of an opposition. Prior to the Fifth Zionist Congress in 1901, he joined Ahad Ha'am and Haim Weizmann against the political Zionism of Herzl and Nordau. In the 1920s and throughout the 1930s and 1940s, he opposed the mainstream Zionist establishment in order to support the creation of a binational state in Palestine. The position, as so many have argued, may have been naïve, especially as Arab-Jewish relations in Palestine began to deteriorate in the 1920s. Yet Buber demonstrated a keen sensitivity to the dangers posed by narrow Jewish nationalism. The abiding sophistication of his position lay in its basic tensions. A Zionist critic of Zionism opposed to narrow nationalism, he worked within a movement dedicated to national renewal. The confident bromides offered by Rosenzweig regarding the "essential universalism inherent in the deepest particularism" do not compare to Buber's critique of a *Gemeinschaft* whose interests he actively promoted.

Buber's worldview reflects upon a deep spatial groundlessness. He recalled how, as a fourteen year-old boy, reeling from one possibility to the other, threatened by madness and thoughts of suicide, he had sought "again and again" to imagine the edgelessness of time and space. "Salvation" came a year later in the guise of Kant's *Prologemena to all Future Metaphysics*. Now he understood that space and time are forms of human intuition used to organize a chaotic manifold of sense impressions, and that being transcends human concepts like finitude or infinity (*BMM*, 136). From Nietzsche, he learned the importance of human will, the power to project oneself heroically into the world of flux, to bridge the abyss according to one's own measure and standard. For the early Buber, a spatial center forms out of the individual human body and the subject's own intuitive grasp of the world.[22] In his mature work, that orienting point is a shared center, the form of true community. The image of a spatial center, at first relatively simple and then increasingly complex, allows an individuated figure or group of figures to emerge out of the chaos over which they continue to hang.

Body

The centrality of spatial coordinates starts with the one most basic to human existence: the physical body. As understood by the early Buber, the world was one in which the objective spatial order dissolved, where up and down, left and right, bear no sense. The nodes around which the subject orients itself are not exhausted by *völkisch* and mystagogical sentiment, Dionysian *ecstasis*, promethean acts of will, and subjective states of consciousness. More fundamentally, orientation works around the body, itself an *objective* datum. Ethical life remains inextricably impacted within the world of space, the human body, and physical sensation as they cross out of the abyss of raw, unfiltered *Erlebnis*. The abyss of world war, the intensifying conflict between Jewish and Arab nationalism in Palestine, and the rise of fascism throughout the 1920s would soon scuttle the mystique of extension. Prior to the war, Buber was drawn to the image of community, but not yet attuned to how physical centers lend themselves to serious abuse. In short, the spatial and corporeal signifiers in the early work are not just "aesthetic," but they are not quite ethical.

Uneasy tensions between ethics and aesthetics appear in the early hasidica. The *zaddik* "dwells in the kingdom of life." A dynamic space, this kingdom is one in which "all walls have fallen, all boundary-stones are uprooted, all separation is destroyed" (*LBS*, 32). This allows the Besht to travel through vast space at the blink of an eye. In one story, on his way to Jerusalem, the sea dissolves (85). Another story relates how the Besht travels a great space in no time in order to get to Berlin, where he resurrects a dead bride. "Place and time were not fetters to the will of the master as to one of us" (98). Having nullified the reality of space, the Besht enjoys complete freedom of movement. The *zaddik* is a "brother" to all creatures. He feels their glance as if it was his own, their blood through his own body. Ultimately, however, ecstasy trumps ethics. The *zaddik* "makes his body the throne of life and life the throne of the spirit and spirit the throne of the soul and the soul the throne of the light of God's glory." There "the light streams round about him, and he sits in the midst of the light and trembles and rejoices" (32). While vision does not preclude service (*avoda*), ethical sympathy has been left behind at the height of *hitlahavut*, an ecstasy compared with which any return to this world pales.

The preoccupation with spatial extension found in *The Legend of the Baal Shem* reappears in three short essays on art from 1914, which express the same core idea about spatial orientation and the act by which a central figure extends itself out from the surrounding abyss of undifferentiated space. In "Productivity and Existence," Buber likens the creative act to lifting an image out of the stream of perception. The subject inserts the image into its memory as "something single, definite, and meaningful in itself" (*PW*, 9). Devoting the essay "Altar" to Matthias Grünewald's masterpiece at Isenheim, Buber argues that no living unity undergirds the phenomenal world. "Our world, the world of colors, *is* the world" (17). In the Resurrection panel of Grünewald's Isenheim altarpiece, all the manifold colors come together in the unified figure of Christ. The essay concludes verbatim on "our world, the world of color." We may not be able to "penetrate behind the manifold to find living unity. But we can create living unity out of the manifold" (19). The same thought reoccurs in "Brother Body," on Nijinsky, how individual gestures form into "one single image in time, a totality, uninterpretable, untranslatable, unique and unrelated." The image is not disinterested. It is the truth of a living unity that cannot be stated, but only shown. "To divulge the mystery . . . [means] to 'dance it out'" (23).

The corporeal imagery in "Brother Body" and "The Altar" creates a perfect complement to the *zaddik*'s "throne-like" body in *The Legend of the Baal-Shem*. It is key to the metaphor of island and bridge in *Daniel*, its picture of the hero who, in the face of grief at a loved one's death, reconstitutes a unified sense of self around the image of his own body, in which he finds an island projecting out from the torrent of annihilations. Its firm being rests bound and formed amidst chaos. Daniel has discovered the essential twofold quality of his own being: half-alive and half-dead, the surging blood of life and the compulsion to pass away, a movement of formation and disintegration. Demanding unity, his body automatically performs this one simple deed on its own: his two arms raise themselves, hands bending to each other, in a gesture that protrudes out into space. Over all horror arches "the God-powerful bridge" (*Dn*, 134–35). Daniel does not desire in the end to overcome the world of extension in its duality and appearance. He must now find unity as just this human body, which lives the whole surging duality of sensation, dancing it out.

Between

If in Buber's early work human subjects orient themselves in a formless chaos around the relatively simple gesture of their own physical extension, the model of spatial orientation grows far more complex and open to the other in *I and Thou*. The former space-conception remains limited to the simple contrast between two fields: a vast, empty space and a stylized figure. A third element, a formally empty point set between two subjects, will gradually take one beyond the individual's plastic gesture toward community. In his introduction to the *Die Gesellschaft* series from 1912, Buber had already referred to the *zwischenmenschliche* (the interhuman). "*Das Zwischenmenschliche* is that which occurs between men" that "cannot be fully ascribed or reduced to personal experience. For [the interhuman] can only properly be apprehended and analyzed as the synthesis . . . of two or more individuals . . . each finding in this abiding tension opposition and complementarity" (Z, 127). Mendes-Flohr has called "the between" a "zone of interaction."[23] Highlighting the complex plastic character of *Gemeinschaft*, it already indicates the space that will subsist between I, YOU, and IT in Buber's magnum opus.

The space created by this zone is oriented, nonsubjective, antisentimental, and postromantic. According to Buber, "True community does not come into being because people have feelings for each other . . . but rather on two accounts: all of them have to stand in a living, reciprocal relationship to a single living center, and they have to stand in a living, reciprocal relationship to one another" (*IT*, 94). The form of true community plots a stable point in space, one that his critics have frequently overlooked. While the I-YOU relationship represents a radically singular encounter in time, Buber understood that "the moments of supreme encounter" have to represent more than "mere flashes of lightning in the dark." In this way, the "genuine guarantee of spatial constancy consists in this, that men's relations to their true YOU, being radii that lead from all I-points to the center, create a circle. Not the periphery, not the community comes first, but the radii, the common relation to the center. That alone assures the genuine existence of a community" (163).

In *I and Thou*, the image of the circle does not ride roughshod over the individual, since it is not community as such that constitutes the circle's axiological center. Buber's understanding of community departs from the one advanced by Ferdinand Tönnies, a model of community based upon the tension between the center and periphery of a circle, one specific to the fondly imagined peasant structure of nineteenth-century

Germany. In that model, a paterfamilias and a group of elders sit firmly ensconced in the middle, surrounded by concentric circles defined by descendents and servants at the outermost periphery. Buber's arrangement is much less hierarchical. The community as a whole occupies the periphery, not the center. Not the community and its structure and standards, but rather "presence," a formally empty focus of value, occupies the circle's axiological center. The shape of a community, the ability to create a common periphery, depends on the individuality of each member-unit and his or her unique relationship to an open center.

The ideal of a community predicated upon an in-between zone contributes to the broader theoretical "program" set out in *I and Thou*. Buber strips existence down to its most fundamental essence: the relationship between an I and IT, between an I and YOU, and the space in between. This space constitutes an elemental and empty container that can accommodate different types of relationships (I-YOU, I-IT), different types of content (presence, object), and all possible combinations thereof. The in-between space that fills the gap between I and YOU or I and IT lacks determinate nature. This makes for a dynamic space whose content can change at any moment, even as it retains its basic form. Not one thing or the other, but radically different types of "substance," be it presence (*Gegenwart*) or object (*Gegenstand*), can constitute the space between the I and the other who stands over against it. Neither this nor that, the in-between space between two parties remains radically porous.

In *Pathways in Utopia* (1947), Buber plots the "image of perfect space" as one composed of lines that allow no fixed definition, the zone between the individual and collective constantly recalibrated according to the free creativity of its members. "The relationship between centralism and decentralization is a problem which . . . cannot be approached in principle, but . . . only with great spiritual tact, with the constant and tireless weighing and measuring of the right proportion between them." A "social pattern," utopia is based on a constant "drawing and re-drawing of lines of demarcation" (*PIU*, 137). The Jewish village commune in Palestine (i.e., the *kvutza*, kibbutz, and moshav), an "experiment that did not fail," owed its success to the pragmatism with which its members approached the historical situation, to their inclination toward increased levels of federation, and to the degree to which they established a relationship with the society at large. Single units combined into a system or "series of units" without the centralization of state authority (142–48). "Nowhere . . . in the history of Socialist movement were men so deeply involved in the process of differentiation and yet so intent on preserving the principle of integration" (145). They discovered "[t]he right proportion, tested anew every day according to changing conditions, between group-freedom and collective order" (148).[24]

At the turn of the century, in an unpublished address on "the new community," Buber had already opposed the instrumentalist nature of "the old *Gemeinschaft*," which reduced community to a means to economic and religious ends. Rejecting the argument that instinctual immediacy was presocial, he would have no truck with the pessimism then current regarding the future of community.[25] The purpose of community was the reciprocation of community itself; to live new things, to create a new life, a "life in which the creative power so glows and throbs that life becomes an artwork, so radiant in form, so resounding in victorious harmony, so rich in sweet secluded magic power as none ever before" (*ANG*, 50, 55). Buber's political thought gradually grew out of itself. In the 1912 introduction to the *Gesellschaft* series and then again in *I and Thou*, the in-between assumes a more dynamic locus. By 1929, that locale belongs, not to the face-to-face *Gemeinschaft* form per se, but to big-city life and society. And while Buber never quit using the language of community, the turn toward an urban locus proved more conducive to the spontaneity of the I-YOU relationship. What Meidner called "our true homeland," the "new *Gemeinschaft*" is itself *Gesellschaft*, a complex, multipart whole based upon a free, formal center of value.[26]

City Space

Fundamental bivalence marks the value of the city in the broader culture of German modernism. On the one hand, the city offered a sinister antithesis to nature, to garden settings in George and Rilke's poetry, to the never-never land of Kandinsky's *Riding Couple* (plate 9), to the primitivism roiling the work of Emil Nolde, and to the bathing scenes painted by members of the Brücke group of expressionist painters. The city is the world of alienated sex in Kirchner's *Street, Berlin*, full of menace in the poetry of Georg Heym and Meidner's apocalyptic landscape; which is why, on the other hand, the city creates an exciting and cosmopolitan center full of tumult and energy, an explosive motion captured by the artist's studio and the café, the automobile, and the tram. After the collapse of expressionism in the early 1920s, any ambivalence regarding the city all but disappeared. No alternative landscape challenged its dominant position in the work of Bertolt Brecht, Georg Grosz, and Walter Benjamin. Buber's work played out the same trajectory. The 1912 *Daniel* exhibits the Jugendstil and expressionist tension between dynamic city life and idyllic mountain scenes, quiet gardens, and seascapes; just as the 1929 essay "Dialogue" reflects the new objectivity, the Neue Sachlichkeit.

Daniel's negative regard for city life is fundamentally resolved by transforming an urban hell into the "kingdom of God." From high above and away from the city, one first hears voices as they "tug" and "shriek" like "sick hounds," raging "against and through one another" (*Dn*, 61). Shocked by compassion for the nameless crowd, Daniel retreats to a garden bench lonelier than before (62–63). Against the unreal spirit of the age, he looks past house, factory, urban wares, and refuse toward the millions of men, "naked underneath their clothes, bleeding under their skin" whose united heartbeat would drown out the voice of their machines (74–77). In the next dialogue, Daniel describes a wanderer who comes into the outermost street of an unfamiliar city. He walks for hours into a darkness "filled to the rim with strange threatening life. The houses stand like vague monsters with staring eyes and insidiously open jaws." One type of person longs for security, wanting to know his whereabouts so as leave this sinister place. The other wanders through the city with "wide-open senses, with opened spirit." He doesn't care what city he is in or where the street leads. "Now he is truly in it." He does not fear, "for he is not always at the same place but is ever at the new, ever at the uttermost," ever at God (88–91). The city is "the kingdom of danger and of risk, of eternal beginning, and of eternal becoming, of opened spirit and of deep realization, the kingdom of holy insecurity" (95).

No longer uncanny, city space in Buber's mature work exhibits a more unremarkable serendipity. The life of dialogue that constitutes revelation has as its focus an ordinary space, nothing extraordinary. Dialogue now takes place in and through haphazard events of daily street life. "I would rather think of something unpretentious yet significant—of the glance which strangers exchange in a busy street," Buber writes (*BMM*, 5). Or two men sit beside one another on a train without speaking or looking at one another. They know nothing of each other and do not share their thoughts. But something all of a sudden happens, without word, a silent communication at a moment of unreserve (3–4). Such incidents are commonplace. "I am not concerned with the pure," Buber proclaims; "I am concerned with the turbid, the repressed, the pedestrian, with toil and dull contrariness." There is nothing apocalyptic or "catastrophic" about the breakthrough between one person and another. It now appears in the "clanking of routine," as something "homely and glorious." Dialogue and revelation bear no all-or-nothing pathos.

City life now constitutes a locus of interpersonal revelation, the old idea from *I and Thou* that "something happens." Dialogue overcomes the barriers between this street corner and that, one train seat and another, one desk and the next, house and work, "man" and machine. It forms into a web, skips from one point over to the next. "No factory and no office is so abandoned by creation that a creative glance could not fly up from one working-place to another, from desk to desk, a sober and brotherly glance which guarantees the reality of creation which is happening." New meaning was given to the "unsentimental and unreserved exchange of glances between two men in an alien place." At the same time, the workplace was not irrevocably alien. Opposed to the division of life into separate zones, into alien "work" and home "recovery," Buber understood that work increasingly stamped time at home in the evening and on Sundays. To be real, dialogue had to happen here, where even lifeless things like machines were to be drawn into its orbit. A worker should experience his relation to the machine as one of dialogue, as when a compositor says he understands the machine's hum as a "merry and grateful smile at me for helping it to set aside the difficulties and obstructions which disturbed and bruised and pained it, so that now it could run free" (*BMM*, 36–37). Long before the advent of artificial intelligence, Buber underscored the even more radical idea that a machine can suffer.

Assuming broader social and political consequence, the locus of revelation and redemption forms into a modern *Gesellschaft* type, whose promise informs Buber's mature approach to Zionism and to the Arab-Jewish conflict over Palestine. In the late essay "Two Peoples in Palestine" (1947), he proposed economic-technical and political-spiritual action. "Politics" refers to the platonic sense according to which one "builds and gives form to society and state." "Technical" signifies the spiritual will to create an "all-encompassing, fruitful, and lasting peace among the peoples on the face of the earth." As a way to stimulate "the whole of Palestine," economic development, especially a huge irrigation enterprise, would increase arable land and supply energy to local industry. "From being a divided territory made up of a dynamic Jewish element and an Arab element that is still fundamentally static, it would come to be a united land humming with intense productivity" (*LTP*, 200). A land that hums—the image presupposes a sonorous plastic form. A machine image, it speaks to a technical project whose end is to sustain two people in one elastic place. Buber foresaw the spiritual-political task in Palestine in terms of a binational state. Viewed more broadly, he envisioned a "supra-national authority" to mediate disputes. All of this—the turn to technology, the expansion of space, the unification of a space around national difference, the creation of international institutions as a way to settle conflict—ultimately brings the kingdom of God out of *Gemeinschaft* and into *Gesellschaft*.

Politics

It was Hermann Cohen, not Buber, who first sought to adapt Judaism to a modern *Gesellschaft* form, namely, the state, which for Cohen constitutes the "hub of all human culture, that nexus that objectifies the "'I' of man" through political self-consciousness." In a 1916 public debate over "concepts and reality" in relation to "Zion, State, and Humanity," Cohen had argued against Buber that "the moral world, as it evolves in history is our true promised land . . . the entire historical world as the future abode of our religion. And it is only this future that we acknowledge as our true homeland." Against Cohen's idealism, Buber had sought to ground the service of God in the *Gemeinschaft* of

Jewish blood and "the firm sod" of Palestine." He was quick, however, to articulate the following paradox. "For me, just as the state in general is not the determining goal of mankind, so the 'Jewish state' is not the determining goal for the Jews." "Today only this," Buber wrote Stefan Zweig in 1918, "I do not know anything about a 'Jewish state with canons[,] flags, and military decorations,' not even as a dream" (*LTP*, 36). The difference, then, between Cohen and Buber was one that was destined to fall apart. Cohen continued to favor the preservation of the Jewish "nationality" (*Nationalität*) on the basis of religion, whereas the spiritual Zionism of Buber was anti-nationalist, increasingly internationalist, and to that degree, fundamentally liberal.[27]

Buber's support for a binational state in Palestine went against the efforts to create a majority Jewish state pursued by David Ben-Gurion and the more uncompromising stance taken by right-wing revisionists under Vladimir Jabotinsky and Menachem Begin. Buber's political stance was based upon a logic that struck a delicate balance between open space and limit. The Jewish people requires a social space of its own, the claim to which is limited by the need to share it with other people. A 1939 letter to Gandhi in defense of Zionism argues the simple point that land is an insufficient but necessary condition upon which to build a just society: "[S]uch a way of life . . . can be realized not by individuals in the sphere of their private existence but only by a nation in the establishment of its society: communal ownership of the land, regularly recurrent leveling of social distinctions [etc.]" (*LTP*, 118). While "Jews and Arabs both have a claim to this land . . . these claims are in fact reconcilable as long as they are restricted to the measure which life itself allots and as long as they are limited by the desire for conciliation" (123). In response to the 1948 War of Independence, Buber was to write: "Thus against my will I participate in it with my own being, and my heart trembles like that of any other Israeli. I cannot, however, even be joyful in anticipating victory, for I fear lest the significance of Jewish victory be the downfall of Zionism" (223).

The peculiarity of Buber's politics stemmed from the anomalies of Jewish life and his own social idealism. At the reincarnation of the Frankfurt Lehrhaus in 1934, Buber addressed the general insecurity that marks human existence as a whole and Jewish insecurity in particular. The Jewish people fits into no social type, and he rejected any attempt to classify it into a confessional or national type. He therefore opposed the position, dating back to the Jewish Emancipation in France, according to which Judaism constitutes a "religion," not a community. Against the attempt to fit Judaism into categories at play in the society at large, Buber argued, "the urge to conform became a cramp." Nor does the Jewish people compare to a merely national type. Buber therefore resisted the politics that turns a people into an idol, an end in itself, ranked hierarchically over and against other national forms, that only knows the rule of power without any due regard to a higher spiritual and moral authority (*IW*, 171). On the left fringe of Zionist politics, Buber identified with the nascent Jewish state, whose creation in the form it took he always rejected. Caught constantly in the space between, he rejected both Diaspora life and Jewish nationalism and the even more deadly cramp posed by the totalitarian left and right in Europe throughout the 1920s.

The challenge to create a space free from religious confession and narrow nationalism while at peace with the Palestinian Arabs was beset by problems from the very start. In the essay "The National Home and National Policy in Palestine" (1929), Buber complained, "We have not settled Palestine together with the Arabs but alongside them. Settlement 'alongside' [*neben*] when two nations inhabit the same country, which fails to become settled 'together with' [*mit*] must necessarily become a state of 'against.' This is bound to happen here—and there will be no return to a mere 'alongside'" (*LTP*, 91). In its broadest stroke, the analysis is fundamentally compelling. Two separate parties that sit side by side, one barely tolerating the other, will eventually come to an enmity from which it is impossible to return. In his opposition to the call for Jewish statehood officially adopted at the 1942 Biltmore Program, Buber was right to claim that "[s]hort-term politics does not go well with morality, while long-term politics merges with morality at certain crucial junctures" (*LTP*, 163). Tracing back to *I and Thou*, the naïveté that clings to his politics stems from the deep philosophical conceit that sets the life of dialogue apart from the quantifiable order of number; whereas the fate of European Jewry and the struggle over Palestine irrevocably revolved around the demographics of majority-minority status.

The same spatial analysis of "alongside" and "with" that Buber brought to the conflict in Palestine in 1929 was applied to the internecine, ideological conflicts in Europe. While moving toward a common goal, the members of a "community" experience a "dynamic facing of the other, a flowing from *I* to *Thou*" (*BMM*, 31). In contrast, "collectives" do not bind, but bundle individuals packed together, armed, and equipped. The distinction between community and collective was generational, meant to contrast the late Wilhelmine era youth movements—the German *Wandervogel* and the German Jewish *Blau-Weiss*—with the new ideologies that wracked the Weimar Republic. The pseudo-objectivity of the collective had soon surpassed the pseudo-subjectivity of the youth movement. Their members did away with "the self" and gave themselves over to orders. "Dialogue and monologue are silenced. Bundled together, men march without *Thou* and without *I*, those of the left who want to abolish memory, and those of the right who want to regulate it: hostile and separated hosts, they march into the common abyss" (32–33).

Buber was aware that refusing to enter into relationship will collapse the struggle for "perfect space" back into the nonspace of violent chaos. In light of the increasing threat to Jewish life in Europe, his political prognosis for Palestine missed the mark, but the diagnosis did not. He vociferously rejected the tragic view of two irreconcilable national claims, understanding that the ultimate success of Zionism requires peace with the Arab world. A binational state would have guaranteed free Jewish immigration and Arab rights simultaneously in the same place. This particular scheme was doomed from the start. As one British commentator observed: "I personally think Buber's solution, the so-called binational State is the figment of the constitutional imagination. If [Jews and Arabs] work together, you don't need it, and if they don't work together the constitution doesn't work" (*LTP*, 206). While no doubt a fiction, Buber's program rests upon a pragmatic conception of space whose formal parameters continue to hold. It demands an *expansive* notion refusing to bifurcate person from person, community from community, morality from politics, and spirit from power; and a concurrent *narrowing* according to which each party to this space makes do with basic needs, forfeiting the surplus that comes at the other's expense.

III

Gesamtwerk

The realization of utopia, the kingdom of God is a plastic form into which everything and everybody can fit. Even the author of *The Star of Redemption*, who treated Judaism as a thing apart, lent it the dimension of a closed complex whose walls miraculously expand. The basilica idea of a simple space was very much in sync with the main threads of expressionist image and rhetoric, exemplified by the "cathedral of socialism" on the cover of the Bauhaus manifesto. Into the 1920s, the utopianism in art and architecture looked increasingly away from the cathedral toward technology and the everyday facts of practical life in the here and now. Buber and Rosenzweig participated in the same basic movement at the Lehrhaus, in the translation theory, in their approach to modern urban life, and in Buber's understanding of the political crisis in Palestine and in Europe. The open plastic character given to the space of revelation remained a type of *Gesamtkunstwerk*—a total work whose design combines different social and spiritual parts under one single rubric.

Except in its earliest incarnations, in Buber's first conception of the new *Gemeinschaft* in his early hasidica and Zionism, the modern space of revelation did not proceed from before mountain vistas or seascapes. The scene staged between God, person, and community assumed a distinctly architectural locus fraught by the dissonance of extreme peril. The problem was not the *Gesamtwerk* per se, but rather Wagner's conception of it. In *Feste des Lebens und der Kunst (Festivals of Life and Art)* (1900), Peter Behrens, an influential architect and Gropius's mentor, underscored the difference between Wagnerian and anti-Wagnerian stage design. While he also conceived of theater space as a *Gesamtwerk* coordinating color and tone, Behrens worked toward a distinctly unnatural effect. He mocked the nineteenth-century realist stage for its brittleness. Its trees wobbled, rocks appeared soft as down pillows, a cave as high as a castle. A new stage conception, an amphitheater design that wraps around a flat stage, was meant to replace the neat division between stage and spectator and the illusion of perspectival depth. Against the illusion of nature, Behrens sought to conjure up on stage that which is sublime over it, the elevation through art above raw nature.[28]

The idea that Judaism is alien to beauty and the arts, expressed by Wagner in "Judaism and Music," was symptomatic of the reactionary, anti-cosmopolitan cast in German culture. Unlike Herder, Kant, and Hegel, who made room, if not for the contemporary expression of Judaism per se, then at least for the sublimity of Hebrew poetry, the Wagnerian *Gesamtwerk* overwhelms the individual element, allowing no space for even an iota of Jewish difference. In his essay "On Stage Composition," Kandinsky accuses Wagner of subordinating music to the libretto in his effort to link protagonists with specific musical motifs or to represent iron hissing in water or the beating of a smith's hammer musically, for example. Wagner used language to express a musical thought, which the orchestra then drowns out (*BRA*, 196–97). For Kandinsky, the modern work of art allowed for the separate independence of each element, without which there is no true combination. Buber and Rosenzweig's *Gesamtwerk* conception of revelation and redemption remained anti-Wagnerian to the same extent as Kandinsky's. Building upon difference, they tried to introduce incompatible elements into a single space.

The generous utopianism at work in early German modernism plays upon the free coordination of separate elements. Architecture combines with nature in Klee's *Memory of a Garden* (fig. 3). Grid-blocks and marks create a spiritual complement to the physical and to the organic. Sharing the same place in the picture plane, each subsists in its own right. Klee later imagined a work of "really great breadth, ranging through the whole region of element, object, meaning and style," "[c]ombining and again combining, but, of course, always preserving the culture of the pure element." Its ideal remained as dreamy as cosmopolitan Jewish life in Germany or a binational state in Palestine. "Nothing can be rushed," Klee declared, "We have found parts, but not the whole! We still lack the ultimate power, for: the people are not with us. . . . We began over there in the Bauhaus. We began there with a community to which each one of us gave what he had. More we cannot do" (*MA*, 54–55). This was the dream that drove Buber and

Rosenzweig in their attempt to juxtapose God, world, soul, I, YOU, IT, Arab, German, and Jew under an open spatial rubric. The plan never gelled. The people were not with them. They gave what they had and could do no more.

Figure 8. Egon Schiele, *Self-Seers II (Death and Man)* (1911).
Oil on canvas. Leopold Museum, Vienna.
Photo courtesy Galerie St. Etienne, New York.

Six Eros

In the rabbinic imagination, the renewal of Jewish life in the Land of Israel and the rebuilding of the Temple after the Babylonian captivity immediately recall the danger of idolatry. Rav Judah (others say R. Jonathan) recounts how "the shape of a fiery lion's whelp issued from the Holy of Holies and the prophet said to Israel, *That is the Tempter of Idolatry.*" The people imprisoned it in a lead cauldron and then proceeded to do the same with the spirit of sexual immorality, "the Tempter of Sin." But the world cannot stand without eros, so they blind the Tempter of Sin to protect themselves from the desire for incest, and then they set it free (b. Sanhedrin 64a). This erotic current thrives as a signal fixture in early twentieth-century Jewish thought, a critical counterpart to ethical idealism and bourgeois religion. In their appeal to what Buber called the life of boiling sensation, he and Rosenzweig brought revelation under the rubric of aesthetic judgment, that moment when a person declares a palpable image, act, or place to be beautiful or sublime. In this move toward physical perception and corporeal presence, they pulled Judaism away from a one-sided emphasis upon the dull work of ethical community, moral duty, and meaningful purpose.

In the culture of German modernism, the erotic image undergoes a fundamental transformation in shifting from Jugendstil to expressionism. The difference between Gustav Klimt and Egon Schiele is a case in point. Klimt's *Salome* depicts the New Testament villainess as an exotic, black-haired, half-naked menace. A doubled, ornamental white curve frames the white curve of her upper torso. A bejeweled mosaic of colors patterns the flow of her black dress. Yellow patterns spiral on the orange background, red bangles are set off by her dress. Schiele broke with his mentor's use of decorative disguise. The younger painter was most known, infamous, for the erotic images that dominate his work. Image after image on top of blank backdrops uncovers an overpowering panoply of human sexual behavior, bodies stripped bare to show skin, bone, and muscle tissue. No decorative device softens the image of exposed bodies, some of which lie prone, while others gaze directly at the viewer.

If I have chosen Schiele's *Self-Seers II (Death and Man)* (1911) (fig. 8) as a touchstone for this chapter, it is to make a point, not about early twentieth-century eroticism, but about the naked image, the use of personae, and the spiritual in art. In Schiele's *Self-Seer* series (1910–11), a doppelgänger always accompanies the figure: the self-seer, the prophet, the hermit. Jane Kallir notes how the images convey clairvoyance, the ability to probe "inner revelatory truths."[1] In *Self-Seers II*, that inner truth is the artist's masklike face stripped of flesh, revealing drawn-out reddish tissue stretched taught across the skull, embraced from behind by a dead white figure, who looks out to the left. On Schiele's self-identification with the Suffering Servant and St. Sebastian, Klaus Albrecht Schröder has argued the basic point that the role of other people was used to transform the identity of the artist.[2] Schröder claims, not quite convincingly, that this self-identification contributes to an *ars humilis*, and he goes on to suggest that in Schiele's work, "As soon as form lurches rudely into ugliness, the category of moral goodness implicit in beauty also disappears."[3]

In contrast to Schiele's especially gross rejection of conventional morality, the play of images and eros in the Buber-Rosenzweig corpus stands, not so much against, but to the side of ethical idealism. Unsullied by imagination and emotion, reason for Hermann Cohen constituted the organon of thought that generates the idea of a unique God and the idea of a messianic humanity based on social justice. It is affect, however, that caps his philosophy of religion. The virtue of peace with which the *Religion of Reason* concludes refers back to the feeling of being moved (*Rührung*) and the feeling of joy introduced in the *Ästhetik des reinen Gefühls* (Aesthetics of Pure Feeling) (1912), the last completed part of Cohen's philosophical system. To be moved refers "to an appearance of the good in the human world, without this good being actually embodied in any individual man." What truly moved Cohen was the ideal image of a good deed. It "brings a tear into my eyes. . . . Peace comes over me and animates me, even if I only hear of an invented action of goodness, which a man allegedly achieved."[4] Regarding joy, a good deed occurred that involves no advantage to me, yet "I am moved by this alleged fact as if it concerned my own life." It elevates the value of my own life "so that I am filled with joy about it."[5] "[J]oy shines in my eyes at the mental image [*Vorstellung*] of a good deed."[6] Full of promise, holiday life anticipates an equal share in "science, its inquiry and knowledge, as well as in the labor for their daily bread."[7]

Buber and Rosenzweig did not share Cohen's dewy sentiment. To be sure, the eroticism in their work comes across nowhere as boldly as it does in graphic works by Klimt or Schiele. Like the rabbis, Buber and Rosenzweig ultimately sought to mutilate the eros in their work. Against modern eroticism, Buber drew heavily on Kant's *Critique of Practical Reason* to argue that one must not treat other people as means to an end, but always as an end in their own right. The choral cry in *The Star of Redemption* declares God's goodness and reiterates Micah's call "to do justice and to love mercy and to walk humbly with your God." But this does not mean that ethics dominates Buber's and Rosenzweig's work. Whereas the idea and image of a good deed moved Cohen to tears, it was the sensate image of the divine *Gestalt* and the performance of ritual cult—thickened, as it were by gold (beauty), black (death), and red (sex)—that first attracted Rosenzweig to Judaism. A brighter luster illuminated Buber's attention to images. Like the sapphire blue underneath God's feet at Sinai, this conception of revelation was palpable, based upon the human body and its sense of touch, animal life, and iconic personae taken from Zionist politics, hasidic legend, the Hebrew Bible, and the power of his own personal presence. Immersed in Jugendstil and expressionist culture, modern Jewish thought intensified the erotic conditions of possibility upon which religious truth and ethics depend.

I

Persona/Charisma

Among its many virtues, Weber's analysis in *The Protestant Ethic and the Spirit of Capitalism* identifies the role played by charisma in a modern culture defined by the decay of traditional patterns of authority and the rise of bureaucratic modes of right.[8] Ecclesiastical authorities no longer control the lives led by society's individual members. No longer traditional but disenchanted with the bourgeois religion developed in the previous century, champions of the new Jewish *Moderne* turned to real-life and textual personae; to the image of Theodor Herzl and Hermann Cohen, to a boy named Immanuel Noah whom Rosenzweig had met during the war while stationed near Uskub, Macedonia; to literary stock figures such as the Shulamite from the Song of Songs, the prophet, and the Hasidic sage; and to the legendary figures of Rabbi Nachman, the Baal Shem Tov, and Judah Halevy. Transformed into icons, they were emblems that personified the presence attracting a certain kind of modern Jew to Judaism. With the exception of Cohen, these figures were steeped first and foremost in strong expression and spiritual judgment, in myth and poetry, not morality.

As the literary critic Robert Elliott points out, the Latin term *persona* originally referred to the use of masks to conceal and transform the subject wearing them, to embody a completely fictional dramatis persona, or to manifest the highest reality of all. Elliot explains how the word "I" used by poets is itself a persona. The "I" within a poem is not identical to the poet's own empirical self. In "writing 'I,' poets present themselves not in a personal way, but insofar as they represent mankind."[9] However, the obverse can also happen. "He" or "they" can mean "I." Buber and Rosenzweig used the personal charisma of Herzl and Cohen to provide a larger presence with which to model spiritual life. Hasidic *zaddikim*, the Shulamite, or Judah Halevy crystallized their own understandings of spiritual encounter and religious life and magnified their force. For both Buber and Rosenzweig, to cite a biblical, medieval, or eastern European text was to wear its perceived essence. I assume their identity without obviating my own modernity. Using masks to conceal my personal presence, I recreate myself in their image even as I create them in my own.

At one level of analysis, the biblical, hasidic, or poetic persona is a fetish. Fundamentally totemic, the turn to a "usable tradition" smacks of an idolatry that was by no means unique to the culture of modern Judaism. The painter August Macke began his article on "Masks" in the *Blue Rider Almanach* by listing, among other things, a sunny day, a Persian spear, a holy vessel, a pagan idol, a wreath of everlasting flowers, a

Gothic cathedral, the bow of a pirate ship, the word "pirate," the word "holy," an Egyptian sphinx, a landscape by Cézanne, the whirring of a propeller, and the whistle of a steam engine. The mask designates changing graphic and verbal forms through which "incomprehensible ideas express themselves" (*BRA*, 85). "Does Van Gogh's portrait of Dr. Gachet not originate from a spiritual life similar to the amazed grimace of a Japanese juggler cut in a wood block?" Macke asked. He concluded that the "grotesque embellishments found on a mask have their analogies in Gothic monuments and in the almost unknown buildings and inscriptions in the primeval forests of Mexico" (89).

The pose, craft, and farce endemic to the production of culture complicate the relation between two parties: the one who wears a mask and the person or force embodied by the mask. Putting on the mask transforms both parties, reflecting one's identity on the basis of an other as the mirror of one's own desire. The mask itself slips on and off. Recounting how members of his family had mixed up each other's Hebrew names, Rosenzweig explained that his own Hebrew name should not have been Levi, but Judah, and thus identical "with the name of the great man whose mid-sized reincarnation I am by way of *Ibbur*: Judah Halevy's" (*BT*, 1216). The mohel had asked for a name, his father was confused, and someone shouted out a name, which his father repeated. (The "tragic comedy" continued: Rosenzweig engraved the wrong Hebrew name on his father's gravestone.) Assuming another person's identity allows one to explore modern religious life at a distance, permitting claims about creation, revelation, and redemption that one could never make on one's own authority. The persona conceals the author's own charismatic presence, allowing the author to create that very authority on a hermeneutical basis. If caught, one can always fall back upon the humor with which the association is expressed.

II

Sensation

Depending upon the impulse to see, hear, and touch, the spiritual renewal advanced by the Jewish renaissance was at root sensational, its task the renewal of perception. In Buber's "Address on Jewish Art"

at the Fifth Zionist Congress, he railed against "ghetto sentimentality" in the face of an exile that had robbed the Jews of "the ability to
behold a beautiful landscape and beautiful people" (*FB*, 48). Zionism,
it was claimed, would cultivate a new Jewish art, a "new, strange, never
before seen garden," a teacher for a living perception of nature and
people, by means of which "[w]e will behold and recognize ourselves"
(51, 52). In a 1905 essay, "The Jewish Cultural Problem and Zionism,"
Buber locates the origins of the Jewish renaissance and its critique of
"religion" in Hasidism and *Haskalah*, the Jewish variant of eighteenth-
century Enlightenment. The liberation of feeling and of thought, they
together broke the rigid grip of law on Judaism (177). In still another
essay from the same period, Buber bemoans: "Religion has lost its
power to take souls into its arms and to deposit them at the heart of the
world. Today it lies to life and violates your boiling senses" (142).

The life of boiling, physical sensation is heightened by the introduction of revelation into the matrix binding "man" and world. In *I and
Thou*, Buber insisted: "There is no need to 'go beyond sense experience.'" Against philosophical idealism, Buber made sure to add, "Nor
need we turn to a world of ideas and values—that cannot become present for us" (*IT*, 125). The concentration of forces when I encounter
YOU "does not consider our instincts as too impure, the sensuous as
too peripheral, our emotions as too fleeting—everything must be included and integrated" (137). While presence "by its nature cannot be
grasped," at least not as "a sum of qualities" (160), the forms called up
at the moment of encounter remain sensual. "More certain for you than
the sensations of your senses," the event of pure relation is "embodied
in the whole stuff of life" (159, 163). Revelation has this base, one that
includes obvious appeals to sight and sound, the sound of thunder and
the color blue, the "holy basic word," no "mere flash of lightning," but
steady like "a rising moon in a clear starry night" (163).

Touch moves revelation deeper into raw corporeal expression. A
more fully realized erotic element, far more primitive in its biological
constitution and primary orientation than sight and sound, it spreads
like a nerve. Buber located the origin of relationship in "a drive for tactile contact," which, from the human side of "I," proves to be passive
(*IT*, 79). While YOU itself cannot be surveyed, it comes to fetch you.

"It does not stand outside you, it touches your ground" (82). At the nadir of human existence, YOU stand on reserve. "No, it does not stand
ready, it always comes toward them and touches them." But the people
are impervious. "O living finger," Buber pronounced, "upon an insensitive forehead" (92). When revelation reappears, it will do so again as
touch. "The purpose of relation is the relation itself—touching the You.
For as soon as we touch a You, we are touched by a breath of eternal
life" (112–13). "The eternal source of strength flows, the eternal touch is
waiting, the eternal voice sounds, nothing more" (160). The human element "waits to be touched by one who will touch it." Revelation works
to "seize" the ready human element in all its suchness (166).

Physiologically, touch affirms the experience of direct, immediate
sensation said to lie at the heart of revelation. As clarified by Sander
Gilman, its sensation is not limited to the eye's fixed-point perspective.
The organ of touch is the skin. Covering the entire body, the sensation
it stimulates is more ambient than sight or sound, a powerful corporeal
dimension with no determinate, locatable shape.[10] Invisible, touch is
breathlike. Its presence eludes the stability of sight, whose visual impression endures regardless of the distance separating one from its object. Evoking the image of breath, it recalls the sound of God's *ruah*, a
divine wind or spirit, a surge of tumult and rustle. Supplying bookends
to his own text, Buber states twice, once in part 1 and then practically
verbatim in part 3 of *I and Thou*, that in everything that becomes present to us, "we gaze towards the train [*Saum*] of the eternal YOU; in
each we perceive a breath [*Wehen*] of it" (*IT*, 57, 150). Kaufmann identifies the word *Saum* with the skirts of God's robe glimpsed by the
prophet Isaiah as the edge of God's infinitely sublime presence fills the
Temple in Jerusalem (Isa. 6:1). Combining sight with the touch of a
garment and wafting breath lends a splendidly tactile sense to the image of God's presence. We perceive God's breath indexically through
sight and sound, in the shake and rustle of a garment or tree branch,
but we sense it most directly upon our own flesh.[11]

Animals

In the Pentateuch, domestic animals are an everyday piece of equipment at the basis of pastoral economy, ritual cult, and social gestures of

welcome. In Psalms, Job, and Jonah, wild animals gauge the sublimity of divine power, a sovereignty extending far beyond the limits of human care. In modern Jewish thought, the life of encounter includes raw sensation. Religious thought thus participates in what Marc called "the animalization of art," a line he traced from Delacroix, Millet, Cézanne, and Van Gogh to unnamed French artists, presumably Picasso, Braque, and Delaunay. For both Buber and Marc, animal life is bound up with judgment. In *Horse in a Landscape* (plate 13), the "inner trembling animal life," the circuit of blood, is expressed through the multifarious parallelism and waves in line (*S*, 98). For Buber, the judgment conveyed by animal life is expressed by a wordless glance or by touch. The animal is a persona manifesting the spiritual sensation that animates the sensible world. Beasts reflect a trembling life that looks toward and makes demands upon the human person who comes near to them.

Animals embed a down-to-earth sensuality into human companionship and moral judgment. The young Besht slips away from the cramped and unpleasant confines of the traditional Jewish schoolroom "as softly as a cat." He is left alone in the forest, where he grows up "under the speechless modes of the creatures" (*LBS*, 52). On the mode of speechless communication, Buber professed in *I and Thou* that the "eyes of an animal have the capacity of a great language." Without sound or gesture, they communicate an anxiety between plantlike security and spiritual risk (*IT*, 144). "I sometimes look into the eyes of a house cat." We hear its "truly 'eloquent' glance" as it turns its glance upon "us brutes." The cat "began its glance by asking me with a glance that was ignited by the breath of my glance." It demands to know, "Can it mean that you mean me? Do I concern you? Am I there for you? Am I there? What is that around me? What is it about me? What is that?!" (145). Just as suddenly, the stammering glance reverts to speechless anxiety (146).

The animalization of religion and art, the cat's command of moral judgment, is a complex sensation that burrows deep beneath the surface of everyday human communication and rational discourse. To entertain the possibility that the cat's eyes have a great capacity for language is to join sight and sound into wordless expression. Touch suggests that an animal glance meeting my glance maintains the breathlike power to ignite. In his own art, Marc conveyed judgment through animal perception, the way in which nature appears to the eye of an animal, a comparison that renders our own conceptions paltry and soulless (S, 99). *I and Thou*, *Horse in a Landscape*, *Yellow Cow*, and *The Fate of the Animals* privilege raw animality over against impoverished, instrumental human reason. A severe act of judgment, the stammering eye of a beast turns the human person into a brute.

Conferring on animals the capacity to pass judgment upon human life, Buber describes himself as a young child on his grandfather's estate, recalling how he had gone to stroke the neck of "my darling," a broad-backed dapple-gray horse. Unsullied by self-consciousness and intellectual cognition,

> what I experienced in touch with the animal was the other, the immense otherness of the other, which, however, did not remain strange like the otherness of the ox and the ram, but rather let me draw near and touch it. When I stroked the mighty mane . . . and felt the life beneath my hand, it was as though the element of vitality itself bordered on my skin, something that was not I, was certainly not akin to me, palpably the other, not just another, really the other itself; and yet it let me approach, confided itself to me, placed itself elementally in the relation of *Thou* and *Thou* with me.

Gently raising its massive head, ears flick, a quiet snort, the signal from the beast, "and I was approved." But once he grew self-conscious about his own hand, contact was ruined. The horse did not raise its head to the boy's touch. "[A]t the time I considered myself judged" (*BMM*, 23). Bound up in the revelation of the other's presence, the moral authority to judge has been given over to a horse, by whose most forceful and elemental authority a human being is accepted or rejected.

Theodor Herzl

At best moody and subarticulate, animal sensations do not form into a complete "image." In this, they are surpassed by art and politics. In 1905, apropos of a series of etchings by Hermann Struck, Buber addressed the need to visualize Palestine: "Do we really see it, and then again, do we see it according to our mood?" (*FB*, 196). And was there "enough energy to transform . . . mood into an image, an image that would grasp and mesmerize others?" Buber understood that the most direct way to create an image is not through words but through pictures. Struck gave modern Judaism its first glimpse of Palestine: young blossoming settlements, expressive like human beings; a lonely palm tree reaching upward in a hazy landscape, clear and firm under a cloudless sky; a somber well near Jaffa beneath dark cypress trees; Absolom's strange, fantastic sepulcher, Rachel's tomb "frozen in structure and dome, a petrified accusation." Struck's art recreates a neoromantic mood transformed into empty and atmospheric volumes, clear outlines, and dark figures, a power not merely to mesmerize, but to judge (*FB*, 197).

Itself already an icon, the figure of Theodor Herzl was one such mesmerizing image in early Zionist culture, a unifying center around which a life gathers. His powerful presence looks out across the Rhine in Ephraim Moshe Lilien's famous photograph from Basel. Combining farce and eros, Lilien's portrayal of a naked, sexually aroused Herzl in *The Creation of a Poet* (plate 2) is brooding angelic flesh. Despite the eventual fallout in their own relationship, Buber continued to recognize the enormously charismatic draw of the Zionist leader, for good and for bad. In his considered opinion, Herzl was a second-rate novelist, whose own best image was that of himself. Here was a form-giving achievement (*FB*, 162). Buber referred to his "crystallizing manliness," his "beautiful greatness and superiority." A whole man, albeit not a whole Jew, he had come to the Zionist movement at a moment of great ferment, when a thousand things were in the making, but when everything was unclear. Herzl introduced clarity. His hand, a sure but insensitive hand, gave the unformed spiritual mass of Zionism form. "How many noble possibilities were killed! But it was an artist's hand, nevertheless. The Zionist movement was formed," crystallized into a party (160, 162).

Herzl represented the ultimate art nouveau object, a Nietzschean superman in the modern Jewish renaissance.[12] For Buber no less than for Lilien, the vitality of his shape stands out in a clear outline over against the formless swirl of a thousand things and noble possibilities. The attention paid by Buber to Herzl's hand was not fortuitous. In its sheer physicality, it lends an erotic appeal to the subject. The power and authority of his personality was the form around which the Zionist movement shaped itself. He gave his people "an image [*Bild*], not the image of a real person, an ideal image, a sincere, encouraging model [*Vorbild*]. This is the way poets in their works create their own wishful ideal" (*FB*, 163, trans. modified). Adding to the figure of Herzl's hand, Buber looked toward the head in order to complete his image. "Living, building, erring, . . . he created an image, a model [*Bildsaule*] for the people, to which they gave his name, a model without flaws and mistakes, only with the pure features of the genius, his forehead aglow with the brightness of the messiah. This is a gift of illusion, a gift of grace" (164).

The charismatic hand and forehead act with equal attraction and repulsion. In an article laced with criticism, Buber referred to the strength of the "heartfelt irony and the lyricism of the gesture" in Herzl's *Palais Bourbon* (*FB*, 147). Despotically charismatic, Herzl "loved the genuine, truly beautiful gesture more than almost anything else." He had the ability to win people over, to dominate, and use them. He epitomized the centralized authority who knows how to give orders, the power of a dictator (151). Still, there was "something captivating about him that was nearly irresistible." Buber understood the impression Herzl made upon the Jewish masses, why the "popular imagination wove a loving legend around him." The failed attempt to create a Jewish homeland in Uganda did not diminish his power. "Even his opponents were left with the image of a sunlike, harmoniously united being" (153). Buber's essay ends with Herzl's own words: "There are, in the life of a people, unparalleled individuals. . . . They have to live their personality, damage, contribute, dazzle the people . . . they must spread falsehoods across the land like a fertile Nile flood, for a distant purpose" (153). Herzl was a sublime figure, sunlike, unparalleled, damaging and dazzling.

Hasidism

Buber's early attraction to Hasidism was part and parcel of his attraction to Zionism, a self-consciously modern political movement. It was image more than ethics and ethos that drove Buber to both. Like the masks in Macke's essay, the spiritual reality of Hasidism testified against industrialization, urbanization, bureaucratization, and other modern ills (*HMM*, 39). It offered wholeness, the hallowing of everyday things like food and sex (28–32). Yet Hasidism as a distinct way of life had no attraction whatsoever for Buber. At play is the pivotal image of a holy person, whose very existence constitutes an embodied sign. Buber would later say the same about the prophets, that signs cannot be translated and replaced by words. Charismatic sign-acts are performative. "[B]ody and image do not let themselves be paraphrased" (*OMH*, 162). A "bodily representation in the most exact sense of the term," the religious virtuoso "does not merely act out a sign, he lives it. Not what he does is ultimately the sign, but while he does it he himself *is* the sign" (163; emphasis added).

A charismatic, living icon, the *rebbe* is an image of the perfected man. This interest in perfection underlies the otherwise innocuous opening sentence of the autobiographical essay "My Way to Hasidism" (1918), which reads, quite simply, "The Hebrew word 'Hasid' means a pious man" (*HMM*, 47). The sentence highlights not so much the life of community as the charismatic person at its center. Recounting his own childhood impressions in Galicia, Buber regrets how the legendary greatness of the grandfathers had disappeared among present-day Hasidim. He nonetheless recalls having sensed that "[A]ll their carryings on cannot darken the inborn shining of their foreheads, cannot destroy the inborn sublimity of their figure." Their sublime figure, the impression of their forehead, recalls the description of Herzl's forehead back in 1904. As for the *zaddik*'s followers, a "shudder of profoundest reverence seizes them ever again when the *rebbe* stands in silent prayer or interprets the mystery of the Torah in hesitating speech at the third Sabbath meal." Buber insists, "This I realized at that time, as a child, in the dirty village of Sadagora from the 'dark' Hasidic crowd that I watched—as a child realizes such things, not as thought, but as image and feeling—that the world needs the perfected man and that the perfected man is none other than the true helper" (52).

A sublime image, the *zaddik*'s impression from 1918 stimulated the same presentiments of charismatic authority that simultaneously attracted and repelled Buber to Herzl back in the early 1900s. One notes the importance of perception, the repulsion and the shudder of reverence, a radiant forehead amidst dark surroundings. The showy splendor of the *rebbe*'s palace "repelled" young Buber. The prayer house seemed "strange." But "when I saw the rebbe striding through the rows of the waiting, I perceived [*empfand*] 'leader,' and when I saw the hasidim dance with the Torah, I perceived, 'community'" (*HMM*, 53; trans. modified). A similar dynamic characterizes Buber's approach to hasidic literary documents. Buber describes himself as a young man of twenty-six reading hasidic source material after a university hiatus from Judaism, "at first ever again repelled by the brittle, ungainly, unshapely material, gradually overcoming the strangeness." But then one day reading *Zevaat Ribesh*, a compendium of legends about the Besht, "The words flashed toward me." The power of the hasidic soul left him "overpowered in an instant." And then an "image out of my childhood, the memory of the *zaddik* and his community, rose upward and illuminated me: I recognized the idea of the 'perfected man' and became aware of 'the summons' to proclaim it to the world" (59).

This description from 1918 speaks more to the style of Buber's late hasidica than to the Jugendstil-inspired style from the period recalled in the essay. Buber compares his own early hasidica to the work of a painter who "takes into himself the lines of the models and achieves the genuine images out of the memory formed of them" (*HMM*, 61–62). He had turned crude, clumsy material into "autonomous fiction" (63). Buber later turned to a new form, "the legendary anecdote," a more faithful way to represent the original hasidic source material. It was supposed to reflect a *nonliterary* way to "create a verbal expression adequate to an overpowering objective reality," the reality of exemplary lives. Like an explosion, the anecdote "communicates an event complete in itself" (26). It does so in images, not concepts (33), in this case, the *rebbe*'s "image-making vision and image-making memory" (41). There is, of course, an art to the "legendary anecdote," even as it rejects "art."

By 1922, Buber's hasidica aspired to the rougher shapes of expressionism, identified by the art historian Peter Selz in works by Schiele, "their acrid aspect, their withered surfaces." So unlike Gustav Klimt's decorative elegance, Schiele's castrated, undeveloped bodies are the "antipode of culture and luxury." In his interpretation of the figures in *Self-Seer I* (cf. fig. 8), Selz interjects, "their gestures seem meaningful—

but of what? Is it a desire for self-revelation or a concealment of the self behind a mask?"[13] The appearance of Rabbi Baruch in the introduction to *The Great Maggid and His Followers* (1922) also breaks with the flowing line and hazy reverie of Jugendstil composition. An antipode to culture and luxury, the *zaddik* "shunned 'beautiful,' deliberate human speech." In response to a learned man who asks to hear "words of teaching; you speak so beautifully!" Rabbi Baruch retorts: "Before I speak beautifully . . . may I become dumb and spoke no further." At the third Sabbath meal, he "usually speaks the teaching only sparingly and disconnectedly" (*OMH*, 147; trans. modified).

Falling short of Schiele's intensity, the image of Rabbi Baruch is better conveyed by the dissonance described by Klee when he wrote: "For my kind of composition, it is essential that the disharmonies (profane imponderables, defects or roughness) in the values be brought back into equilibrium by counterweights, and that the harmony regained in this way not be wanly beautiful but strong" (*DPK*, 197). He goes on to argue: "To emphasize only the beautiful seems to me to be like a mathematical system that only concerns itself with positive numbers." He repeats: "The compositional harmony gains character by dissonant values (roughness, imperfections), which are brought back into equilibrium by means of counterweights" (198). The imperfect, dissonant value expressed by Rabbi Baruch's sparing and disjointed speech constitutes a counterweight to the soft song enveloping his Sabbath table. The beauty is robust, not pale.

The Bible

Like his interest in Zionism and Hasidism, Buber's early interest in the Hebrew Bible revolved around images of the perfected human person. In his contribution to the *Jüdische Künstler* series (1903), Buber commended Lesser Ury for presenting "[b]iblical material in a new non-biblical way." Adam and Eve are young world conquerors. They want to know with sense and soul, to live according to the law of their own being, not according to strange laws. Adam stands self-assured and proud. Eve trusts, ready to act. Above them "in the shining heavens, is [a] song of songs of colors; in their shining souls is a song of songs of human energy and human love" (*FB*, 78–79). Ury's *Jeremiah* (1897) (plate 8) broods powerfully under "a broad night sky, . . . above a small, ugly piece of earth." He "reflects the blue of the universe. . . . His mouth is tightly shut; we can see his struggle with a superhuman pain." No lamenting figure, Jeremiah is "the lone powerful one for whom prophecy was a burden and an inspiration." He is the "strong one" whom the Lord fashioned into a "strong iron wall," who, "in the pain of his calling, rebels against his master and thinks, 'Well I will no longer think of him and preach his name' and in whom the word, nevertheless, jumps and vibrates like a fiery stream that he cannot resist" (80–81).

Bourgeois ethical categories of good and evil are not trumped so much as jumbled by the influence of Jugendstil and Nietzsche in the un-biblical Bible read by Buber into Ury's paintings. Kantian ethical categories—in particular, the distinction between autonomy and heteronomy—are also scrambled. The atmosphere identified by Buber throughout the pictures is ambient. In the landscapes, color blends objects into one another. In the biblical portraits, defiance and erotic surrender commingle. Beyond good and evil, the image in Buber's description of Ury's picture drips with a pronounced allusion to "the song of songs of human energy and love." Adam and Eve are modern youth who obey the law of their own hearts to the degree to which they give themselves up. The mix-up between defiance and submission, autonomy and heteronomy is intractable. As an autonomous subject, Jeremiah rebels against the sublime prophetic word whose vibration he is powerless to resist. A starry night sky and the "blue of the universe" hang over the image. The prophet's brow stands out, the same image of strength ascribed by Buber to Herzl.

Aesthetics and moral truth are inseparable in this attempt to open up a fresh approach to biblical material. In the essay "Herut" (1919), Buber maintains that, "God's mercy" is an "abstract statement." He therefore counsels: "[T]o penetrate the religious truth that lies beyond it, we must not shrink from opening the Bible to one of its most awful passages, the one where God rejects Saul, His anointed . . . because he spared the life of Agag, the conquered king of the Amalekites. Let us not resist the shudder that seizes us, but let us follow where it leads as the soul of the people struggled for an understanding of God" (*OJ*,

162–63). The prophet Samuel cuts Agag into pieces, a terrible image before which the soul must shudder (1 Sam. 15:32–33). In working through this passage, Buber turned to a rabbinic tradition tracing the ancestry of Goliath back to Agag. In Buber's reading, God will express joy in Goliath's soul and seek one day to bond it with David's in friendship (Sanhedrin 105a). An act of terrible violence thus conditions the otherwise bloodless truth of divine mercy.

No less than "divine mercy," the term "purity of soul is an ethical concept." Buber continues: "Nevertheless, let us not recoil from reading the third book of Moses, the paragraphs that describe purification by the blood of sheep and doves as well as the great purification through the scapegoat. And when our hearts tremble under the impact of the great, ancient, but also alien symbol, let us follow the way people's soul took as it struggled for its purity . . . to Akiba's liberating cry: 'God is the purifying bath of Israel'" (OJ, 162–63). While the divine "outgrows old symbols and blossoms forth into new ones" (150), the new symbol circles back to the old. Once again, "the awareness of [religion's] suprarationality" means that ethical worldview cannot be separated from its source in animal substance and sensation. An initial recoil at the sight of blood turns into moral confidence as the eye is led from blood to water.

This is the grisly, fluid stuff that circulates through religious truth and ethics. Years later in a series of "Autobiographical Fragments," Buber was to remember his own response to the story of Samuel and Agag quite differently. In this later account, he recalls once meeting an observant Jew on a journey. Speaking of our biblical passage, he told the latter: "I have never been able to believe that this is a message of God. I do not believe it." The conversation hemmed back and forth. "So, you don't believe it?" "No, I do not believe it." And then Buber declared, "I believe that Samuel has misunderstood God," to which his interlocutor replied, "Well, I think so too." The story proved to Buber that when an observant Jew of this nature is forced to choose between the Bible and God, he will choose God. Scripture combines understanding and misunderstanding, the word of God and the word of man, the received and the manufactured (AF, 31–33; cf. ST, 207). But this is just an apologetic move intended to free the divine word from human violence. The earlier position staked out in "Herut" was far more courageous. Even as they work through it, the earlier embrace of morally ambiguous scriptures holds onto the violent, symbolic quality of religious expression, "the awareness of [religion's] suprarationality," "a more inspirited, but also a more primitive, variation of a metaphysical or ethical ideology" (*OJ*, 161).

"Buber"

While Buber posed as a modern-day prophet or sage, he was too great an ironist to ignore the humorous disconnect between image and reality. In "My Way to Hasidism," he recounts how one night he went out with a group of students after a public appearance, like a *rebbe* at the center of his followers. A "well-built Jew of simple appearance" approached the table. It was M., the brother of his father's former steward. The man attended the philosophical conversation with a "devotion" that resembled "that of the believers who do not need to know the content of a litany since the arrangement of sounds and tones alone give them all they need, and more than any content could" (*HMM*, 64–65). Later, they spoke separately. M. asked for advice regarding a match for his daughter. The young man was a law student, but he wanted to know if he was a steady man. Should the suitor become a judge or a lawyer? Buber swore he could provide no information, not knowing the young man in question. At which M. looked at him half-complaining, half-understanding, and said in an indescribable tone of sorrow and humility, "Doctor, you do not *want* to say—no, I thank you for what you have said to me" (66).[14]

The encounter with M. is told as a farcical mix-up. Buber twice called this a "droll event" (*HMM*, 67), "a humorous and meaningful occurrence" (63, 66). While humor cushions the audacity of the comparison, Buber nonetheless proceeded to claim that the chance meeting afforded him new insight into Hasidism based on the image of the *zaddik* he had received as a child. "I, who am truly no *zaddik*, no one assured in God, rather a man endangered before God, . . . experienced from within for the first time the true *zaddik*, questioned about revelations and replying in revelations." Here was a measure of how the *zaddik* "moves, he talks, he looks, and each of his movements, [how] each of his words, each of his glances causes waves to surge in the happening of the world" (67). Despite his own disclaimer, Buber revealed his own dramatis persona, how he tried to turn himself into an image reflecting something great and true: an exemplary, perfected life marked by portentous mystery.

As observed with Robert Elliot, the poetic I is not the biographical I. Buber of course was no *zaddik*, no saint, which he himself recognized. His encounter with M. was one such collision between man and image. Buber was devoted to the pursuit of his own reflection, as testified by the photographs on so many paperback editions of his work. The long beard and direct gaze are supposed to project the very picture of a prophet or sage. It was an image that took no little cultivation. In his autobiography, Nahum Glatzer relates a story told to him by the publisher Salman Schocken about how he once caught Buber preparing a public address by writing the text beforehand and committing it to memory. The audience was led to believe that here was the famous man struggling with ideas and recalling quotations and allusions as if they had just occurred to him at that very moment. "Everything was planned in advance, the text, the phrases, the quotations, the allusions, the spontaneity, and the inspiration." To finish the thought, Glatzer adds, "If this is theater it is at least good theater."[15] Buber projected a powerful image of himself, a persona that might attract others to his own presence and to the life of revelation it embodied. An egoist of religious dialogue, he had but one serious competitor among his peers.

III

"Rosenzweig"

The continuing allure of his life and thought would have no doubt delighted an author profoundly aware of the effect he wanted to have on others. At work on *The Star of Redemption*, Rosenzweig wrote Hans Ehrenberg that he would rather be infamous than be a nobody (*BT*, 635). In another letter, he spoke of wanting to publish the book as it was, despite his own lack of credentials in the academic field of Jewish studies, as a way to make a reputation for himself (639). Reintroducing himself to Buber in 1919, Rosenzweig asked him to read a manuscript version of the text. Since one day it would gather a circle of readers, Buber might as well read it now (645). On completing *The Star of Redemption*, Rosenzweig bragged about having created a truly eternal work. Comparing it to *Faust*, he said that at the age of thirty-two, he had accomplished what had taken Goethe eighty-two years (718–19). Despite the saintly aura that still clings to him, "the sage of Frankfurt" devoted himself to the creation of his own image with considerable confidence.

A dark aesthetic imbued Rosenzweig's first intellectual passions. In a frequently cited 1920 letter to his mentor, the historian Friedrich Meinecke, Rosenzweig explained why he had turned down a university lectureship. Referring to a fellow student, Rosenzweig wrote, "I remember how sinister my insatiable hunger for 'forms' [*Gestalten*]—a hunger without goal or meaning, driven on solely by its own momentum—then appeared to him. The study of history would have only served to feed my hunger for forms [*Gestaltenhunger*], my insatiable receptivity. History to me was a purveyor of forms, no more. No wonder I inspired horror in others as well as in myself" (*FR*, 95). These intellectual appetites presumed no extrinsic purpose apart from their own movement. Linking the study of history to aesthetics, Rosenzweig continued to explain, "Scientific curiosity and aesthetic appetite [*Stoffhunger*] no longer fill me today, though I was once under the spell of both, particularly the latter" (97). By his own admission, Rosenzweig was something of a "vampire," a vile creature overwhelmed by insatiable hungers.

It was false modesty when Rosenzweig told Meinecke that *The Star of Redemption* was "just a book." And he never broke the spell of aesthetic form-hunger, no matter what he said here or elsewhere. Revelation made him no less grotesque. Ethics never trumped aesthetics. Abandoning historical research and "aesthetic appetite," he went to Judaism, to "the vaults of my own being" and its "ancient treasure chest." The occasions when he had gone there before had been "the supreme moments of my life." But cursory inspection no longer satisfied him. Now his hands dug deeper into the bottomless chest. He went away with "treasure," with "as much as his arms could carry." Now he claimed to possess his own talent, mastering it, whereas previously it had possessed him. In fact, the letter shows no such mastery. Now a philosopher, his life had fallen under "the rule of a 'dark drive' which I'm aware that I merely *name* by calling it 'my Judaism.'" The pull toward Judaism was every bit as daemonic as the one that had drawn him to historical form and aesthetic appetite. The moral difference between "stuff," "form," and "treasure" proves unclear. The object of the same dark hunger, nothing changed, except the menu.[16]

The Erotic

Writing for the expressionist journal *Der Sturm*, the poet Paul Hatvani considered all experience (*Erlebnis*) erotic, insofar as creative artists form a sexual relation to their material and as such to the world overall. The ideal creator exhibits the highest manliness.[17] This includes what Rosenzweig called "my Judaism." Like ejaculate, eternity shoots over the death-crowned world into which it bursts. An image of Israel, fire from the core of the star burns incessantly. Requiring no fuel from without, the star "must produce its own time, and reproduce itself forever." Sexual reproduction thus shifts revelation from the astral plane back down to earth and eros. Eternity is the bearing of children across the span of generations. The "son is born so that he may bear witness to his father's father. The grandson renews the name of the forebear." Citing God's promise to Abraham, Rosenzweig pointed back up to "the star-strewn heaven of the promise" that burns above "the darkness of the future." God swears, "So shall thy seed be" (*SR*, 298). Male issue transforms into and out of starlike substance. Sticky stuff enjoys supernatural status, revelation at its most raw.

In this paean to reproductive power, there is only one crude reference to women: to their wombs (*SR*, 299). Apart from this brief biological form, the more generalized absence of women is used to ascribe a thick, masculine potency to revelation. A widespread notion about gender, it goes back to Winckelmann and the neoclassical idealization of Greek sculpture in the eighteenth century, an "image of man" that demands moral proportion and the control of passions.[18] As sketched by George Mosse, men were supposed to steel themselves by means of martial culture, gymnastics, and Christian morality and by separating themselves from women.[19] Identical exclusions mark the masculine ideal and the absence of women from Rosenzweig's formulation of God's promise of seed. Women are said to be "simpler" than men. Once touched by eros, they are already prepared for what it might take a man one hundred years to achieve. Touched and passive, she is "ready for the final encounter—strong as death." Having thus idealized women, Rosenzweig would exclude them from the central dramas defining revelation. In the words of Richard Koch, his Judaism was "free, manly, invigorating, and beautiful" (*BT*, 1011).

Undermining the bourgeois moral order of normative manliness based on restraint and control, the emphasis placed on passion and eros by the German youth movement and German expressionism broke the bounds of conventional respectability. At the same time, Mosse comments, even the avant-garde upheld the virtue of decisiveness and willpower, male activity against female passivity.[20] Referring to the act of artistic creativity as a "genesis," Klee wrote from Tunisia, "In the beginning the motif, insertion of energy, sperm." Form "in the material sense" constitutes the artwork's "primitive female component" against which "form-determining sperm" constitutes a male counterpart. His own drawings belong to the male realm (*DPK*, 310). But Marc complained that "our *Erotik*" was still sentimental and feminine. The knowing, severe new European would be a male type, one that required no little gender trouble. To create this new type, to put an end to the feminization of "our *Erotik*," required the awakening of manly drives in women. "We stand today in the midst of the age old Amazon-problem" (*S*, 211).

Rosenzweig's eroticism, with its starry-eyed look back to Genesis and male issue, was active, severe, and violent. In his account, pagan self-creation forms around the violence of an assault. "This speechless, sightless, introverted *daimon*," the image of one's defiant self, "assaults man first in the guise of *Eros* . . . until the moment when he removes his disguise and reveals himself to him as *Thanatos*" (*SR*, 71). The event of revelation displays no more tenderness. "Against whom does love display its strength? Against *him* whom it seizes. . . . It originates in the lover. The beloved is seized, *her* love is already a response to being seized" (156; emphasis added). The switch in gender is deliberate. God's "untrammeled passion" bursts forth "into the light of the new day" (159). It assumes the guise of a "fateful domination over the heart in which it stirs" (160). Revelation is a "shock." The beloved soul is "moved," "gripped," "seared" (179). "Love is as strong as death." The eros of revelation is violent. The death-crowned world of creation "is conquered" and "laid at the feet of love." Death and the netherworld "collapse before the strength of love" and "the hardness of its zeal" (202).

The violent form of Rosenzweig's literary expression comports with love's zeal in its relation to death. The agon is dramatized in exclamatory, declarative pathos. The subject terrified by death creeps like a worm "into the folds of the naked earth" before "the fast-approaching volleys of a blind death from which there is no appeal." An image of violent death, "Let him sense there, forcibly, inexorably" that "his I would be but an It if it died." At which we hear the subject's own declarative "roar" of "Me! Me! Me!" (SR, 3). Love sounds no less declamatory. "Where are You?" (175). "Love me!" "You are mine" (175, 177, 183). "I have sinned," "I am a sinner," "I am thine," "my god, my God" (179, 180, 182, 183, 184). The violent expression forms around pronouns—I, you, he, the repetition of sin and of the phrase "my God" building up the pressure. As Mosse so keenly put it, "death was the final sensuous experience, the necessary climax of a fully lived life."[21]

The contest between love and death in revelation is rooted in sublimated human aggression. Unapologetic, Rosenzweig never denied that psychoanalysis lends itself to the interpretation of Scripture and midrash (Abraham, Terah, Isaac, and the conflict between fathers and sons; Abraham and Sarah in Egypt and the problem of incest). In his view, however, psychoanalysis refutes "paganism," not faith. In faith, he argued, one knows nothing "about" God. One receives revelation simply as it comes to one, projecting nothing onto it. Even the experience of the father (Vatererlebnis) constitutes genuine revelation. Rosenzweig only opposed the idolatry that turns the father into a totem, calling him God. Subjective experience and physical sensation do not preclude revelation. With a quick nod to Freud, Rosenzweig expressed it this way in a letter to Ernst Simon: "There is nothing simply subjective. Not even erroneous ideas, not even dreams. . . . Everything subjective has a relation to something objective," even the false gods of idolatry (*BT*, 1114). This includes violent erotic personae wearing deathlike masks.

The Homoerotic

The relative place of men and women in Rosenzweig's life and thought was itself fraught. A woman's presence means nothing in either *The Star of Redemption* or the recently published letters sent by Rosenzweig to his lover Margarit (Gritli) Rosenstock-Huessy and to her husband, Rosenzweig's beloved friend Eugen Rosenstock (*GB*). The real tensions occur, not between men and women, but between men. What Rosenzweig came to call "my Judaism" was a homoerotic compact marked by four features that are basic to fin de siècle homoeroticism: intensive homosocial circles, overwhelming male authority, open erotic discourse, and self-conscious devotion to beauty. All these justify a look at "the role of the erotic in male society"—the title of a 1920 text by Hans Blüher—to shed new light upon images of male presence, young boys, and the appearance of an exceptional female figure in the cast of characters crowding the body of Rosenzweig's writing.

Blüher's text in particular highlights male compacts (*Männerbünde*) centered around a predominant male figure. He based his analysis on the German youth movement, of which he was a leading member, and the men's huts used by indigenous people in the South Sea Islands. As he understood it, the *Männerbund* is a highly differentiated product of "male-male eros" (*mannmännlichen Eros*).[22] This male-male eros is bisexual, caught between wife and home, on the one hand, and the community of men, on the other. Although erotic life between husband and wife perpetuates the species, a fully formed, richly developed collective life, in all its forms, political and religious, depends on the erotic attachments formed between men. The *Männerbund* has no primary purpose apart from men wanting to be with each other. Every other purpose, political or religious, that devolves from that primary basis represents mere rationalization.

That *The Star of Redemption* is itself a *Männerbund* from which women are effectively excluded is only strengthened by the appearance of the Shulamite. In Rosenzweig's reading of the Song of Songs in the discourse on revelation, she is the figure from the "grammar of eros" who declares herself to God. An extraordinary female figure, she assumes a major place, midpoint in the entire book. A centrally located persona, she masks the author's own presence. The Shulamite is *not* Gritli, to whom Rosenzweig ostensibly dedicated part 2 of *The Star of Redemption*. The Shulamite is Rosenzweig himself, a female avatar of his own eros, his passion for male authority, passive receptivity, his own desire to be a woman with the force of her own character. Unlike the "womb," her passivity is not unambiguous. The Shulamite's eros is like the young boy's described by Blüher in the *Männerbund*, equally vinous, radiant, and possessive (*weinhaft, strahlhaft, besitzergriefend*).[23]

As a figure, the Shulamite's identity undergoes a series of subtle textual transpositions. Her first appearance is in female form. She is the beloved soul in part 2 in a subsection to the chapter on revelation entitled "atonement," which accompanies the "grammar of eros." She then appears in the analysis of the Song of Songs at the end of the conclusion of the chapter. However, when the Shulamite reappears in part 3, she does so in altered form. A subsection with the identical title, "Atonement," heads the depiction of Yom Kippur in the Judaism chapter. In part 2, the Shulamite declares her love for God. Now in part 3, the community of men reenacts her avowal. Linked by "atonement," their eros is her eros. In the final transposition, the oblique reference to God's face in part 3 ("the eyes of his judge") anticipates the consummate appearance of God's face with which Rosenzweig concludes his text. From the Shulamite, the text proceeds to the homosocial Yom Kippur crowd of men, to God kissing Moses mouth to mouth.[24]

The exceptional female mask that is the Shulamite reinforces the strong emphasis upon men, the paterfamilias, and the relationship between old men and young boys. Like Blüher's analysis of male eros, "my Judaism" swings back and forth between home and the community of men. Its account of the Sabbath shifts from the synagogue service to the father at home. Six days he has worked, attending to his affairs. Now the manservant and maidservant must also rest. "All the house" is free from noise. As for the festivals of Passover, Shavuot, and Sukkot, while the meal is eaten at home in a family setting, it compares, not to occasions when men and women mingle, but to those enjoyed in exclusively male fellowship at a monastery, lodge, club, or fraternity. "The sweet, fully ripened fruit of humanity craves the community of man with man" (*SR*, 316, 315). Afterward, guests from the previous night greet each other in the street. The gesture of greeting evoked by Rosh Hashanah and Yom Kippur is matched up to such all male venues as the military parade, saluting the flag, in review before the commander-in-chief (322–23). The collective meal and greeting have turned a heterosocial community into a *Männerbund*.

Charismatic male authority runs throughout the entire Rosenzweig oeuvre. His beloved Uncle Adam, the Orthodox rabbi and Goethe aficionado Nehemia Nobel, and Hermann Cohen drew Rosenzweig to Jewish life. Regarding his uncle, he wrote that it was "through him and only though him that he received a glance into and a bit of an entry into . . . a 'Jewish world'" (*BT*, 506). In reference to Cohen, he explained: "How did I come to the Lehranstalt [*für die Wissenschaft des Judentums*]? Because I wanted to come to him and the way to him passed through that institution and past its blackboard" (446). And then there was Heinrich Wölfflin, "the god of my youth." In the discussion of male reproduction, grandfathers are privileged over fathers. At the *havdalah* ceremony closing the Sabbath, a young boy holds the candle lit by an old man and drinks from a cup with his eyes shut (313). Uncle Adam, Nobel, and Cohen were "the gods" of Rosenzweig's turn to revelation. Like the elders of a *Männerbund*, their presence pertains to the structure of memory. Witness and memory skip a generation; they miss a beat. Ignoring the intermediary figure of the father heightens the gap between the old man and young boy, a prototype of the absolute difference between God and "man."

Youth exercised its own erotic authority. With Rosenzweig, one follows young Immanuel Noah through Uskub. Writing home to his parents, Rosenzweig tells how he had been looking for a synagogue when he ran into a group of children. Noah spoke French and German and is described as "thin and well dressed." In the letter, Rosenzweig recalled how he had appealed to him ("Er gefiel mir sehr") and how he had invited the boy to visit him at the home of local acquaintances, the Navarros, who, as it turned out, were distant relatives of the boy's. At this point in the letter, Rosenzweig goes on to describe a Passover seder that he and F. had celebrated with a group of German and Russian Jewish soldiers. Rosenzweig suspected that the almost beastly vitality of the latter had something to do with the rape of Jewish women by Russian peasants; "great strong people" from Minsk, Odessa, and Galicia, they seemed to belong to another race. The account then shifts back to the meal enjoyed at the Navarros', after which Rosenzweig went to look for Noah, who had not shown up as promised. He went to the boy's home, but eventually found him with a group of friends.

As the two walked through the city, and here the account intensifies, Rosenzweig observed with pleasure the contempt with which Noah judged those local families, five in number, who opened their shops on Jewish holidays. He then began to ask questions. The dialogue goes back and forth in German and French. Noah wanted to know why Rosenzweig wrote for non-Jews. It was "as if the people itself interrogated me" (*BT*, 393). Rosenzweig responded feebly. Noah then demanded to see what Rosenzweig knew about Moses, David, and Jacob. He demanded to know why Rosenzweig's father had not tried to get him out of the army or given him pages of psalms to protect him from harm. If anything were to happen to Rosenzweig because of the war, the boy scolded, it would be God's will. This "mixture of solemnity and the childlike" drove our author close to tears. Had they not been in the street, he would have embraced this "little 'representative of the people.'" It was the first time that a child had ever spoken to him like that, just like an old man (394).

Rosenzweig here fleetingly resembles Gustav Aschenbach in Thomas Mann's novella *Death in Venice*, who falls in love with a young Polish boy. As described by Mann's anonymous third-person narrator, what starts as a "fatherly" attraction turns into something else, and loss of control renders Aschenbach "unmanly." Rosenzweig roams through Uskub in pursuit of a boy, just as Aschenbach wanders through Venice. In contrast to the bourgeois ancestral world and manly ideals, Noah is a haughty symbol of purity. A young boy with the authority of an old man, to whom Rosenzweig must answer, but cannot, he stands between the animal vigor of the Russian and Galician Jews and the diluted Jewishness of the German Jewish middle class, calling into question attempts to straddle the worlds of Judaism and German culture. Rosenzweig struggled in vain to make plausible the symbiosis personified by his own parents, mainstream *Centralverein deutscher Staatsbürger jüdischen Glaubens*, and Hermann Cohen. Immanuel [Noah] was "not so much the old '*Volk*' as the young 'direction,' and as such certainly to take seriously, but in fact also already sufficiently to be taken seriously by me" (*BT*, 448; cf. 530). The boy stimulates a pleasant crisis of consciousness that allows the author to create a break between his world and that of his parents.

The picture of Rosenzweig wandering around Uskub in search of the boy calls attention to itself, even if there is no reason to suspect him of Aschenbach's folly. The same is not true of his relationship with Eugen Rosenstock. It was a harrowing encounter with him in 1913 that forced the young Rosenzweig to come to terms with revelation. It was Eugen, along with Rosenzweig's cousins Hans and Rudolf Ehrenberg, who sought his conversion to Christianity. Eugen's very humanity (*Menschlichkeit*), Rosenzweig said, "tore up my roots" (*GB*, 105). While Gritli is the more obvious sexual focus, the letters testify to Eugen's magnetic power over Rosenzweig. In an early letter from 1917, Rosenzweig explained to Gritli how for more than seven years, his "noxious friendship" (*böses Freundschafterlebnis*) with Eugen had eaten at him. He averred that although he had felt free from it over the past few years, one became new only with new people—meaning Gritli (17–18).

Nevertheless, her husband's presence dominates the letters even to Gritli, confirming Eve Kosofsky Sedgwick's insight that "gender asymmetry and erotic triangles" intensify erotic attachments between men. In response to Eugen's discovery of the affair in June 1918, Rosenzweig wrote to Gritli: "[I] have never before loved without any creator-feeling [*Schöpfergefühle*]; I have had at no moment with you the feeling of having *made* something in you, let alone *of* you; I have only *found* you, entirely finished, entirely 'already made.' And because you are surely made and somebody must have made you, so have I loved in you your creator, he who is in heaven and he who is on earth, Eugen." It was Eugen's humanity, not her own, that overflowed to Rosenzweig when her love gave itself to him, and it was only since meeting her that Rosenzweig's love for Eugen had become complete (*GB*, 105). A few days later, he insisted, "Eugen must know that he is the master of our love, that it would fall into the abyss were he to turn away" (106). And then, a few more days later, Rosenzweig sought to describe how he and Eugen had come to lose sight of each other. He had always felt that "in writing to [Gritli] I was writing to him" (108; cf. 113).[25]

Gritli was not the "mistress" of Rosenzweig's heart ("my heart has no mistress and only one master, and against him it rebels") (*GB*, 505). In a letter dated December 26, 1919, he explained to Gritli how for him, his cousin Gertrud Oppenheim had come to replace his mother, a difficult and psychologically unbalanced woman whose relationship with her son was strained by bouts of jealousy. In his love for Gritli, he saw first and foremost the feeling for a sister, his "sister soul," with whom he had grown and suffered (509). Writing soon after his engagement to Edith Hahn, Rosenzweig professed in a letter from January 7, 1920, that his love for his fiancée was "not at all sisterly. The love reaches out over a chasm. Here stands a man and there a woman." To Gritli, he alleged: "I never felt with you that I am a man or that furthermore you are a woman, so much do our hearts beat as one. Edith and mine beat not at all at the same time. It is painful for me to listen to hers; it must no doubt be painful for her to see mine beat, so must my heart run over in order to wash over hers and so must hers grow . . . in order to be contained in mine" (524).

By his own admission, there was something unconventionally "manly" in Rosenzweig's erotic entanglements, not just with Gritli but with Judaism as well. In one crucial respect, the arhythmic relationship with Edith, defined by unbridgeable antinomies, mimicked the one with Eugen and his mother, both of whom were jealous of Rosenzweig's active embrace of Judaism and other women. Eugen was not at all pleased by Rosenzweig's engagement to Edith. In his letter to Eugen from January 15, 1920, Rosenzweig suspected that for Eugen, his engagement to Edith repeated his earlier refusal to convert to Christianity (although it may just be that, as Rosenzweig went on to suggest, both Eugen and his mother noticed the same lack of visible joy in his relationship with Edith) (*GB*, 528–29). The same painful distance characterized Rosenzweig's relationships with both Eugen and Edith, the same inability of one heart to make room for another. With Eugen and Edith, Rosenzweig was a "man." But not with Gritli. In the letter to Gritli from January 7, Rosenzweig proceeded to explain that it was Judaism that allowed him and Edith to go step in step, an explanation that deepens the suspicion that what bound Gritli and Rosenzweig together was the jealous master whom they shared.

"My Judaism" was subject to lines, in this case the one between Gritli and Eugen, between "homoeroticism" and "homosexuality," which, in the end, as Mosse and Sedgwick point out, remain impossible to control.[26] Strongly drawn to the image of men, Rosenzweig advanced a Judaism that was openly erotic and intensely homosocial, the precise combination that constitutes the homoerotic element to his thinking. The death shroud worn by men in this world directed him away from women, who do not wear it. At his wedding and at the seder, it is the man, not his wife, who "challenges death and becomes as strong as death." The exclusion is even more emphatic at Yom Kippur and the sight of man "utterly alone on the day of his death . . . lonely and naked, straight before the throne of God," the "united and lonely pleading of men in their shrouds, men beyond the grave" who constitute "a community of souls" (SR, 327). This community of men has been made possible by the exclusion of women, who are taken for granted, their presence effaced.

In a gendered body of work, from which actual women are explicitly excluded, "man" is more than a generic brand of human community. "Only man needs to be aware that the Torah is the basis of life," Rosenzweig insisted. "When a daughter is born, the father simply prays that he may lead her to the bridal canopy and to good works. For a woman has this basis of Jewish life without having to learn it deliberately over and over, as the man who is less securely rooted in the depth of nature is compelled to do. According to ancient law, it is the woman who propagates Jewish blood" (SR, 326). The woman determines the Jewish character of blood; her blood and womb carry the man's seed. But for Rosenzweig she does so invisibly and utterly passively—the standard excuse used to justify the exclusion of women from the all-important active center of Jewish religious life, the study of Torah and its commandments, which requires constant deliberation "over and over."

Perhaps it was not that Rosenzweig hated women—there is surely no indication of that—but that he loved men more.

Mitzvah

The power of sensation, the pull of men, death, and intense aesthetic and erotic appetite constitute the dark drive to Rosenzweig's approach to revelation and ritual observance. Touching upon the entire gambit of sensual perception is a tactile world of men in their *talit*, in their shrouds, a young boy leading an utterly charmed soldier-tourist though exotic Uskub, the eros of sexual reproduction, creating a community out of its own viscous substance combining seed and blood. Leora Batnitzky has called attention to the fact that, in contradiction to the profound understanding of aesthetic life that runs through his work, Rosenzweig did not think Judaism needed art. A dubious claim on Rosenzweig's part, it ignores the more profound understanding of aesthetic life that runs throughout the body of his own work. The ritual act is a plastic art, the life of mitzvah aesthetic in the structure of its sensual performance. Indeed, Batnitzky's analysis makes this salient point. According to Rosenzweig, too, prior to Enlightenment and Emancipation, Judaism had itself been a piece of art, not art for art's sake, but wholly art, beautiful life, understood as such, uncanny, self-contained.[27]

That was the only *compelling* reason to observe mitzvot today. "From Mendelssohn on, our entire people has subjected itself to the torture of this embarrassing questioning: the Jewishness of every individual has squirmed on the needle point of a 'why.'" Piling midrash on top of midrash, aggadah on top of aggadah, Rosenzweig countered: "No doubt the Torah, both written and oral was given to Moses on Sinai, but was it not created before the creation of the world?" And was it not written on black and white fire? Was not the world created for its sake? [Was it not] [s]tudied by Adam's son Seth? Observed by the patriarchs? Given in seventy languages? It has 613 commandments "a number which . . . mocks all endeavor to count what is countless." Did it not include everything that later generations have come to interpret? Did not its vast scope allow later scholars to interpret the ornamental crownlets and tips of letters, outdoing the comprehension of Moses? Concluding, this interrogative barrage ends with an exclamation point: "The Torah, which God himself learns day after day? And can we really fancy that Israel kept this Law, this Torah, only because of [the one fact] that the six hundred thousand heard the voice of God on Sinai?!" (*JL*, 78–79; trans. modified).

Beauty and sublimity establish the mitzvah's charisma. Against Samson Raphael Hirsch, the founder of modern Orthodox Judaism, Rosenzweig contested the "pseudo-historical theory of its origin" and the "pseudo-juristic theory of its power to obligate." That is, ritual authority does not lie in the supposed fact that once upon a time, at a particular place, God "commanded" it to the Jewish people. Also rejected is the "pseudo-logical theory of the unity of God" and the "pseudo-ethical theory of the love of one's neighbor" espoused by the liberal Judaism of Abraham Geiger. The so-called essence of Judaism has less to do with the logical rigor of its monotheism or the purity of its ethic, or with the priority of community and the need for meaning. The system of Jewish life sketched in the "Builders" does not constitute a means toward a social good. It is its own purpose. As Rosenzweig expressed it, "miracle does not constitute history, a people is not a ju-ridical fact, martyrdom is not an arithmetical problem, *and love is not social*" (*JL*, 80; emphasis added).

I observe the Torah and its commandments because I love their height and structure, because they are beautiful and sublime, because their number "mocks the endeavor to count what is countless." Rosen-zweig heaped midrash on top of midrash to form one great rhetori-cal question. Why observe the law? The image of black and white fire shimmers. Like a work of art as understood by Kant, it has no instru-mental or extrinsic purpose outside its own remarkable edifice. With-out a doubt, the social world was created for its sake, not the other way around. The concluding question: "And can we really fancy that Israel kept this Law, this Torah, only because . . . the six hundred thousand heard the voice of God on Sinai?!" is carried by an exclamation point in the wake of the questions that precede it, a judgment, as if to con-firm, "How divine!" Builders are architects. Samson Raphael Hirsch had used history and law as "the foundation of a rigid and narrow structure, unbeautiful despite its magnificence" (*JL*, 80). The Judaism whose radiance Rosenzweig sought to construct on the foundation of "law" would be the polar opposite: free, open, and beautiful.

Reflecting an acute intersection between ritual and visual aesthetics, Rosenzweig wrote to his parents in 1917 about going to the Orthodox Hildesheimer synagogue for the High Holidays of Rosh Hashanah and Yom Kippur in 1914 because it offered the most beautiful service in Berlin (*BT*, 446–47). A 1922 letter to Joseph Prager notes the "great joy" taken in a marvelously beautiful (*wunderschön*) Yom Kippur service arranged for him at his home. The attention to interior design is pronounced: the blue room of the family apartment bedecked by a colossal display of cloth and candles, a white and gold cloth spread over a cabinet. Rosenzweig went on to recount that the next day, the lighting was natural because the ceiling light had gone out the day before and "fortunately" could not be repaired in time. And that evening, "another lucky accident," the final recitations of the *Shema* were preceded by a full five-minute silence because the closing *neilah* service that precedes them had concluded some five minutes too soon (*FR*, 120–21).

Rosenzweig's account of Yom Kippur recalls a unique combination of halakha and happenstance, the tactile feel of cloth, the shimmering glow of candle and natural light, the intermingling of a ritual commandment with silence. At the simplest level, the letter is full of color, light, cloth, and sound. More technically, it suggests that the mitzvah's beauty consists in the way it combines necessity and accident. According to the traditional standard of interpretation, the law forbids Jewish people to turn electricity on and off during Sabbaths and holidays. And the law demands that the congregation conclude Yom Kippur by reciting the *Shema* at dusk. These are the structures that combine with circumstance to create intense beauty. An everyday annoyance of an electric light happening to go out the night before creates a Yom Kippur space lit by fading, natural light. The inconvenience of the service ending five minutes too soon forced a drawn-out silence. The beauty of the system lies in the way it orders the accidental element into a lovely sensory pattern.

First and foremost, then, ritual space is a place of perception. As pictured by Rosenzweig, the holiday cycle forms into what Kalman Bland calls "a fully engaged, well-tempered sensorium."[28] It takes in at least four of the five senses. Taste: "Every mouthful of bread and every sip of wine tastes just as wonderful as the first we ever savored" (*SR*, 312). Taste underlies that "very act of renewing the life of the body" ritualized in the common festival meal (316). Touch: the Yom Kippur costume—the death shrouds traditionally worn by men under the shawl, "the chiton and tunic of antiquity"—is nothing less than the "wholly visible sign" of eternity in time (325–26). A tactile sign, cloth brushes up against male flesh (327). Sight: "the eyes of his judge," no longer guilty before man, all sins pardoned, a merciful divine face. Sound: the soul "bursts out," an "exultant profession," "'The Lord is God:' this God of love, he alone is God!" The holiday system extends perception from the fleshy to the spiritual. Smell is the only sense neglected by Rosenzweig.

The complete truth is perceived only at the end—at the end of life, and at the end of Rosenzweig's text. Viewed from the vantage of this sensorium, the face of God as it finally appears in full is a theatrical mask. The three "receptive organs" (ears and nose) form its base. "[T]hey are the building blocks, as it were, which together compose the face, the mask." Rosenzweig exclaimed: "The Star of Redemption is become countenance [glancing] at me and out of which I glance." God's truth has put on a human mask. Enmeshed in living form, [He] turns to look at me. And wearing the same mask, the soul peers out at [Him]. The mask-work is now complete. Face-to-face, the subject anticipates the great consummation, like Moses at his death. "Thus does God seal" the truth, with a kiss, "and so too does man." That is, the truth is conceived not as a concept, but rather perceived as gesture and artifice.

This truth is part of a highly staged and choreographed expression, anticipated in the synagogue, week in and week out, year after year. Rosenzweig explicitly compares the synagogue to the theater and concert hall in a 1917 letter to his cousin Richard Ehrenberg concerning the creation of the Academy for the Science of Judaism proposed in "Zeit ist's," Rosenzweig's open letter to Hermann Cohen that same year. In the communication to Ehrenberg, Rosenzweig argues that German youth go to school and then to the theater and concert hall. The latter serves as a "magnified object lesson," which projects what they learned at school onto a broader scale. The synagogue should likewise function as a place to project the language and literature learned at school writ large. Clearly, it was not "religion," not simply moral community, that lured Rosenzweig to religion. Otherwise, he would have compared the synagogue to a church, not to a theater and a concert hall.

IV

Aesthetic Judgement

Aesthetic judgment is the medium for sorting through spiritual expression in modern Jewish thought. "How dissonant the I of the ego sounds!" Buber proclaims, "When it issues from tragic lips, tense with some self-contradiction that they try to hold back, it can move us to great pity. When it issues from chaotic lips that savagely, heedlessly, unconsciously represent contraction, it can make us shudder" (*IT*, 114). Buber rejected the I-IT world as seen through the darkest lens of German expressionism. In contrast, Socrates, Goethe, and Jesus are said to represent the life of dialogue lived, respectively, in relation to the human, to nature, and to God. "But how beautiful and legitimate the vivid and emphatic I of Socrates sounds!" "How beautiful and legitimate the full I of Goethe sounds!" With Jesus, however, the aesthetic frame of reference lurches from beauty to the sublime—and back to expressionism. His image is "powerful, even overpowering" (115–16). Both Buber and Rosenzweig understood that the life of dialogue and revelation is "marked by its essential and indissoluble antinomies" (143). The passive sense that "I have been surrendered" sits alongside the active sense that "[i]t depends on me" (144).

This peculiar tension between passivity and activity informs the aesthetic base upon which Judaism is made to depend. We have seen it in the description of Yom Kippur in Rosenzweig's letter to Prager, and we find more of it in *Bildung und kein Ende*, his major text on adult Jewish education at Frankfurt's Freies Jüdisches Lehrhaus. Rosenzweig opposed the formulation of pedagogical plans, proclamations, and programs in favor of questions, doubt, and desire (*JL*, 70). "Wait," he counseled, "People will appear who prove by the very fact of their coming that . . . the Jewish human being is alive in them" (68–69). Who will come and why? Rosenzweig averred: "I can already hear voices saying: 'How vague, how undefined, how cloudy.' . . . I can also hear the voices of those who say, 'How little.' . . . But perhaps here and there someone will say longingly, 'How beautiful' and think hesitantly, 'If only such a thing only existed'" (71). Not "how true!" Not "how good!" Without the "'true ring' of dead-sure conviction," both the "program" of the Lehrhaus and the Judaism it represented remained intentionally pared down. Therein lay the very modern beauty of revelation.

It will no doubt be argued that image, eros, and the beauty of sheer expression provide no sure basis upon which to build religious life and thought. Other contributors to the Jewish renaissance in Germany voiced severe opposition to a form of literary Judaism that could not meet more demanding standards. Ernst Simon, who succeeded Rosenzweig at the Lehrhaus, makes this point perfectly clear in his critique of an article entitled "Traditionelles und nationals Judentum" (Traditional and National Judaism) published in the 1916–17 edition of *Der Jude*. The author of the original article had proposed an educational program that stressed the aesthetic form and feeling of Jewish customs and literature, not their religious content and intellect. Simon attacked the program some ten years later in the same journal under the title "Erziehung zur Tradition" (Educating Toward Tradition), arguing against educational programs based on religious fairy tales (*Storchmärchen*).[29] For their part, Buber and Rosenzweig struggled with their own artistic proclivities. Rejecting a narrowly conceived "aesthetic" of rarified art objects and mere beauty, they understood the difference between truth, goodness, and beauty even as they opposed the ideal of art as an independent value.

Those critics who think that art and aesthetics are too subjective to incur real obligation might recall with Kant that to judge something "beautiful" or "sublime" transcends mere "liking." The latter is always only personal. In contrast, the individual subject who comes to make an aesthetic judgment wants to share that judgment with other people and bind them to it. The vague Lehrhaus program, the free beauty of its form and its lack of fixed and rigid contents were meant to surprise, to enchant, to solicit a spontaneous response like the sudden inhalation of air. In the modern world, the charisma of religion and revelation depends upon aesthetic judgment—"How beautiful"—and wanting to share it with others. The pure beauties that had appealed to Kant at the end of the eighteenth century were nonmimetic patterned forms, like wallpaper design, presuming no objects in whose real existence the subject takes an interest. Buber and Rosenzweig belonged to a generation that broke with the conception of autonomous beauty radically divorced from the rigor of truth, ethics, spiritual encounter, and everyday life. Beauty is not always beautiful, nor aesthetics always "aesthetic." As against the art-for-art-sake beauty of impressionism, the attraction to erotically powerful images opened revelation to violent expression, harsh judgment, and dissonant sound, a beauty that was beautiful in spite of itself.

Aesthetics may not grant a single, stable standard upon which to build religious life. Nevertheless, powerful styles survive the passage of time. Great art and literature enjoy a longer shelf life than the scientific worldviews and social and moral mores that prevail at the time of their creation. Styles that once fell out of fashion come back into style long after their initial demise. Greek aesthetics resurfaced in the Renaissance, during the Enlightenment, and in nineteenth-century Greek-revival styles. The baroque fell out of favor in the eighteenth century, only to see renewed interest at the start of the twentieth. Expressionism collapsed in the early 1920s only to enjoy a renaissance first in the 1950s (abstract expressionism) and then again in the 1980s (neo-expressionism). Religious thought and philosophy are also kept alive by great style. It is always possible to rework a truth into a more precise, contemporary idiom. Great works of philosophy endure, not simply because their authors spoke a truth, but because the form in which they spoke that truth continues to fire human intelligence. As for Buber and Rosenzweig, I suspect that readers continue to read them today for the verve they introduced into religious truth and ethics.

Comparing Klimt and Schiele, Peter Selz comments that Klimt masked his erotic obsessions in nineteenth-century allegorical evasions, whereas Schiele maintained his openly. The fraught energy twisting it lends Schiele's pictorial universe a deliberate frankness. The viewer knows that he or she is looking at death, psychological extremis, and open erotica. Selz and Schiele suggest to us that it may be necessary to look at modern Jewish thought with two sets of eyes. Looked at one way, Buber and Rosenzweig are still contemporary in their insistence that an elemental root of religion and revelation lies in physical sensation and the creation of images. Looked at another way, the reader never quite gets the naked truth from them. When one looks at a photograph of Buber or Rosenzweig or reads books by them, there is the feeling that a persona is pretending to be a person, not vice versa. Because they were less straightforward than Schiele in their obsessions, there is always the danger that the image and eros in their work is just dressed up and weird.

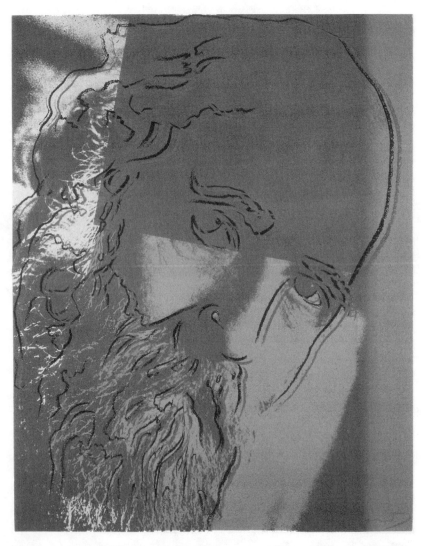

Figure 9. Andy Warhol, *Portrait of Martin Buber* (1980). Courtesy Ronald Feldman Fine Arts, New York. © 2005 Andy Warhol Foundation for the Visual Arts / ARS, New York.

Epilogue: Mutations

"The eclipse of God," Buber's symbol for the spiritual crisis in post-war Western culture, calls attention to a nadir in the history of the human imagination. It designates, not just moral collapse, but first and foremost the decline of the human heart's "image-making power." There once was a time, Buber surmised, when images, "absolute, partly pallid, partly crude, altogether false and yet true," opened out into a "glimpse of the appearance of the absolute" (*EG*, 119). In its allusion to the primitive past, this comment from 1952 recalls the arts and theology of expressionism in their heyday. Once upon a time, graphic signs and poetic images assumed uncanny animation, invested with the power to restore dead stuff to life. Marc's *Yellow Cow*, Klee's *Runner at the Goal*, the blue circle in Kandinsky's *Painting with White Border*, Judaism and the Jew, Hebrew Scripture, and the kingdom of God present themselves as living creatures. Disparate elements combine into patterns, powered by an invisible current—God's face, the spiritual in art—made visible through physical form's dark glass. Acquiring a closed-in tempo and expansive spatial shape, they were supposed to tug the modern subject into a parallel universe.

Among the varied forms of European modernism, German expressionism was the only one that left room for crude, pallid spiritual expression: Jewish and Christian theology, theosophical speculation, and messianic utopianism based on loose combinations of Bible, Marx, and Nietzsche. Open to every gradation between the material and immaterial, expressionism created visual and poetic conditions of possibility for the emergence of new religious discourse. The demise of its image-making power in the 1920s rendered religion and revelation culturally incongruous, out of sync with the new realism in painting and the fascination with technology, and drowned out in the clash between

245

fascism and totalitarian communism. The acid clarity exhibited by critics like Siegfried Kracauer on the left and Leo Strauss on the right, and
by Oskar Schlemmer at the Bauhaus, exemplified a more exacting modernism. Based upon unambiguous commitments to the visible and the
profane, there was no place for revelation. If the spiritual in art and the
"theological feminism" opposed by Strauss survived "the new sobriety,"
they did so altered by postmodernism, a cultural condition more at ease
in the hermaphrodite space between reason and sensation.

Life

Straining against the limits of reason, the wild and wooly conception
of the artwork in expressionism bordered on magic and spirit possession. Klee believed that ideas "which no longer correspond wholly to
the artist's will" insinuate themselves into the work (*MA*, 31). Living
creatures inhabit the picture frame. They take on their own existence
vis-à-vis their creator, the painter. The objects in the picture "look out
at us, serene or severe, tense or relaxed, comforting or forbidding, suffering or smiling" (33). They have "become realities—realities of art
which help to lift life out of its mediocrity. For not only do they . . .
add more spirit to the seen, but they also make secret visions visible"
(51). The same independent pulse powers Kandinsky's pictures. In
his essay "Painting as Pure Art," he called the beautiful work of art
a "spiritual organism." No dead object, "[t]he work of art becomes a
subject" (*CWA*, 350). A living "spiritual subject," it constitutes "a realm
of painterly, spiritual essences (subjects)" by which "spirit can speak to
spirit" (353).

The fancy that art constitutes the uncanny medium through
which spirit "speaks" to spirit reflects an overriding orality unique to
expressionist painting, particularly in the polemic waged against impressionism and Jugendstil. As averred by Hermann Bahr in his 1916
monograph *Expressionismus*, the impressionist has "another set of ears,
but no mouth. . . . [He] listens to the world, but does not breathe upon
it. . . . The Expressionist, on the contrary, tears open the mouth of
humanity. . . . [O]nce more, it seeks to give the spirit's reply." Art does

more than beautify life, the purpose of art nouveau. It must create life. "Art must bring Life, produce Life from within, must fulfill the function of Life as man's most proper deed."[1] Breath brings to life. Marc invoked "that mysterious moment in our work in which the work begins to breathe. It falls off from us and starts its own life. At first we were the master of the picture. Now, we become at this moment its slave. It watches us alien, large, admonishing, compelling." An artist's merely mortal will pales before the artwork's immortal being. "Why should we not believe," Marc asked, "that an archangel did not paint [such works] upon the wall of heaven, things from its kingdom, through the hand of our friend Kandinsky?" (S, 139–40).

Why not indeed? Bright color, jagged line, and flattened picture planes take on their own autonomous life, disorienting the material impression in order to redirect perception around new spiritual values. Angels, saints, and riders dissolving into nothing, villas, gardens, and runners rearranged according to a foreign geometry, a red horse, blue deer, and yellow cow, the melting face of a prophet, a young man flattened by apocalypse, and erotic disfigurement are in no wise "natural." Like revelation, the spiritual in art is caught in the ambiguous space between worlds. The intensity of color and line shoots past their everyday appearance to create a visual context in which their physical characteristics rivet consciousness, but where material values are possessed by an unspeakable surplus.

The verbs *beleben* (to animate, enliven) and *beseelen* (to animate, ensoul) unlock spiritual presence. Like electrical current, Jewish renewal for Buber was "sudden and immense," not gradual. Quoting Isaiah 64:17, he intoned, "I create new heavens and a new earth" (OJ, 35). A jolt of energy, Jewish religiosity constitutes a *Gegenstand*, an object or thing, whose "upsurging blaze would restore it to new life [*beleben*] and whose total extinction would deliver it to death" (79). We have seen that in Buber's early work, the creative human deed made the divine reality real. In the mature work, the subject encounters a presence beyond its ken in the living form of an I-YOU relationship. *The Star of Redemption* concludes "into life." Love and choral expression redeem transient substance by means of the mouth. Rosenzweig writes: "Thus love turns the world into a world animated with a soul. . . . The world knows only that all that lives must die. . . . Only when and where the animating breath of the love of the neighbor wafts over the limits of this growing living being will these gain . . . what life itself could not give them: animation, eternity" (SR, 240).

The theological expression, this Jewish *Lebensphilosophie*, was in tune with a broad interest in the occult at work in the culture well into the 1920s. Folktales such as those of the Golem and Dybbuk were popular among Jewish and non-Jewish novelists, dramatists, and filmmakers imbued by French symbolism, German expressionism, Russian cubo-futurism, and Hebrew literary revival. In these stories, supernatural powers animate the physical matter with which they forcibly intermingle. To protect the Jewish community, Rabbi Loew, the legendary Maharal of Prague, called a consummate modernist by Noah Isenberg, creates a golem out of earth, a "mystical technological wonder," inspirited by the word "truth" inscribed upon its forehead.[2] The golem comes to life only to run amuck, its autonomy uncanny, a destructive dynamo acting out against the express wish of its creator. Its autonomy is uncanny. For its part, the dyybuk is the dead soul of a once-promising student named Khonen, returning to inhabit the body of Leah, his true beloved. An alien force, it takes control of the subject's body, moving her like a puppet.

In the postreligious culture of early modernism, the supernatural feeds upon the social and psychological clash between young love and the world of tradition, Jews and gentiles, the individual and the collective, personal happiness and national survival, "man" and machine. Shai Ansky called his theatrical rendition *Der Dybek* "a realistic drama about mystics."[3] Reading Gustav Meyrink's *Der Golem*, Rosenzweig wrote his parents that the least successful part of the novel was the "already always metaphysical" (das "schon so wie so Metaphysische"), as opposed to the metaphysicalization of the ordinary (*Metaphysierung des Gewöhnlichen*), which he found splendid (BT, 342). After having completed the book, he praised it as "completely magnificent." His parents did not understand it. They took a murder/rape scene too literally. It was "only a symbol (for the hermaphrodite, which can then only develop when the sex act is absolutely and uniquely unrepeatable; the 'second time' is already 'adultery' to the first)." In Meyrink, such "transitions from apparently crass reality through the grotesque into the symbolic," "the station of the spiritual between the grotesque and the symbolic," are "inimitably beautiful" (344).

Dead

The intellectual ferment in Weimar Germany after World War I had no place for any such vestiges of occult supernaturalism. Despite a "sharply critical view of existing society and individuals, and a determination to master new media and discover new collective approaches to the communication of artistic concepts," the "new sobriety" contributed to a crippling polarization, a cynical resignation that, as Peter Gay notes, became a self-fulfilling prophecy.[+] I have chosen to focus on Schlemmer, Kracauer, and Strauss because they exhibit patterns of thought that testify to both sides of the new realism, mapping profound shifts toward the optical, the technological, and the profane in modern culture. Kracauer and Strauss were illiberal thinkers who forced their readers to choose between extremes of absolute atheism and absolute orthodoxy, whereas Schlemmer was more ambivalent about such choices. Under the gaze of the new realism, the weird spiritual growths cultivated in the hothouse of early German modernism withered. The new realism choked off the warm air in which revelation and the spiritual in art had previously flourished.

Schlemmer's work provides an excellent platform from which to view the death of expressionism. In a publicity pamphlet for "The First Bauhaus Exhibition in Weimar, July to September 1923," he looked back to the school's first days: "The *Staatliches Bauhaus*, founded after the catastrophe of the war, in the chaos of the revolution, and in the era of the flowering of an emotion-laden, explosive art, becomes the rallying-point of all those who, with belief in the future and with sky-storming enthusiasm, wish to build the 'cathedral of socialism.'" Chronicling the new guard's emergence, Schlemmer heralded "the next faith" at the Bauhaus, its reliance on reason, science, mathematics, structure, mechanization, power, and money, and the influence of Dada, the court jester, and "Americanisms transferred to Europe, the new wedged into the old world." Mocking the pretensions of expressionism, Schlemmer proclaimed: "Man, self conscious and perfect being, surpassed in accuracy by every puppet, awaits results from the chemist's retort until the formula for 'spirit' is found as well."[5]

Puppets were the cipher to the faith in machines, theater, and dance at the Bauhaus, a counterpoint to the romantic legacy that the new sobriety sought to overcome. In Heinrich von Kleist's essay "The Marionette Theater," the puppet and God are the two extremes of unconsciousness and superconsciousness between which the hapless romantic falls. "Paradise is locked and barred and the Cherub is behind us." Burdened by the laws of gravity and the limits of self-consciousness, no dance can match the "ease, grace and pose," the "balance, agility, lightness" of the marionette or any other mechanical device. Unlike us, they need "only *glance* upon the ground, like elves, the momentary halt lends the limbs a new impetus." Far surpassing human capacity, "in dance, only a god was a match for matter; and that was the point where the two ends of the round earth met." Grace will return to human movement only after consciousness has passed through infinity, "most purely present in the human frame that has either no consciousness or an infinite amount of it, which is to say either in a marionette or in a god."[6]

Against the ideal of natural grace, Schlemmer sought to surmount the gap between puppet and human. By setting the physical body within the order of architectural space or in robotic, doll-like costumes, he transformed it into an abstract art figure. In *Bauhaus Stairway* (1932) (plate 18), a group of female students ascend and descend the steps in front of the large glass windows inside the Dessau Bauhaus building. As observed by Karin von Maur, the image combines human and architectural figures, the staircase neatly structuring the picture into Euclidean order.[7] The curvature of the female body is juxtaposed to the vertical, straight-edged, architectural line. With their short hair, the young women appear androgynous and puppetlike. They are but one step removed from the costumed figures of the *Triadic Ballet* (1922) (plate 19).[8] With no plot apart from movement through space, Schlemmer's theater transfigures human form into abstract geometry. Fantastic and machinelike, the body defies gravity. Costumes and mechanical devices, automatons and marionettes, precision machines, glass, artificial limbs, and outfits designed for deep-sea divers and modern soldiers expand the human capacity they simultaneously restrict.[9]

The desire to transform material limit links Schlemmer to the romanticism of Kleist and to the expressionism mocked in his Bauhaus pamphlet. On the one hand, he was drawn to art and painting, which he associated with religious and metaphysical values. On the other hand, there was the new spirit represented by theater, dance, and technology. The expression in his letters and diaries oscillates between romanticism and classicism, Grünewald and van Eyck, Van Gogh and Cézanne, primitivism and cubism, Itten and Gropius, India and America, the divine and the human.[10] What distinguishes his work from expressionism is the emphasis placed upon the optical. As early as 1913, he declared: "I believe in the world of the visible. I believe in the painter's mode of vision, i.e. abstraction won of familiarity with nature" (*LD*, 13). In 1942, shunned by the Nazis and no longer enamored of "Picasso-style abstraction," Schlemmer experienced "with unfamiliar intensity the mystic force that resides in the optical effects of nature." He found "the world of the visible opening up to [him] in a remarkable fashion, in all its density and surrealistic mystique" (399).

Kracauer evoked the same commitments to the visible to assail religion, mysticism, and metaphysics. Having finished reading *The Star of Redemption*, he wrote Leo Lowenthal: "I despise this kind of philosophy, which makes of the hymn a system . . . and twaddles on about creation, revelation, and redemption in such excited tones as to move a dog to pity."[11] His tendentiously partisan review of the Buber-Rosenzweig Bible reflects the new objectivity in its complete hostility to Jugendstil, expressionism, and religious renewal. The new translation was compared to the poetry of Stefan George: aesthetic, unreal, not of the age. Kracauer was unable to grant that all this twaddle was not unmodern, if only because neoromantic and expressionist bathos belonged to the history of twentieth-century art styles upon whose carcass the new sobriety fed. To see this, however, would have required greater critical care and hermeneutical charity than Kracauer was prepared to give in 1926.[12]

The formal choice that propelled Kracauer was the one between "common" public life and private spiritual/intellectual experience, reality and "aesthetics," everyday life and exotic constructs, rigid oppositions staked between "x" and "not x," self-consciously understood as two equally extreme and disagreeable options. This homogenizing logic played out throughout nearly all his articles from the 1920s collected in *The Mass Ornament*. In the collection's title essay, critical reason stands opposed to "the mythological delusions that have invaded the domains of religion and politics" (*MO*, 80). The brilliant "Hotel Lobby" sets pure, empty immanence against the house of God's absolute transcendence. Opposed to religious renewal *tout court*, Kracauer accused Max Scheler of simultaneously embracing relativism and Catholicism. "By creating this hermaphrodite of natural religion, Scheler has now really fallen between two stools" (208). In "The Crisis of Sciences," Kracauer showed how Ernst Troeltsch failed to reconcile the contingent relativism of historical research with the intuition of absolute values, "an Archimedean point outside the historical process" (218).

Kracauer's ultramodern nihilism brooked no compromise. Parodying Buber, Kracauer argued that "reality can be reached *only* by means of a path that leads through the 'unreality' of the profane" (*MO*, 200), a sentiment that repeats itself at the conclusion of the review: "For today access to truth is by way of the profane" (201). A prelude to catastrophe, the word "only" admits nothing other than its own narrow grip. Kracauer therefore rejected Walter Benjamin's work as "a type of thinking that is foreign to current thought. Such thinking is more akin to talmudic writings and medieval tractates for, like these, its manner of presentation is interpretation. Its intentions are of a theological sort" (259). The new sobriety excluded, not just theology and Judaism, but foreigners and interpretation, restricting not just the renewal of religion but modernity as well. Against interpretation, it programmatically strangled each and every attempt to open spiritual life out into the modern world, while confining modernity to the deadest plane of immanence.

Kracauer knew very well that hotel-lobby modernism is a suffocating dead-end space. A person can "vanish into an undetermined void, helplessly reduced to 'a member of society as such'" (*MO*, 179). "The desolation of *Ratio* is complete only when it removes its mask and hurls itself into the void of random abstractions that no longer mimic higher determinations. . . . The only immediacy it then retains is the now openly acknowledged nothing, in which, grasping upward from below, it tried to ground the reality to which it no longer has access" (180). As in a tale by Kafka, the modern world is an architectural universe composed of seamlessly constructed, impermeable, and impenetrable dungeons and burrows. *"The more systematically they plan it, the less they are able to breathe in it,"* Kracauer observed (268; emphasis added). Built piecemeal, open and permeable, the "Great Wall of China" in the tale told by Kafka is a counterimage of the true ideal. And yet Kracauer still believed that even though the "sought after solution is unattainable," it was "at the same time attainable here and now" (277). He called it "the place of freedom" without explaining, as it were, how one gets from the hotel lobby to the Great Wall of China (278). No less beholden to the archaic and exotic, the call for a *"real transformation of our entire essence"* (223) was even vaguer and less clear-cut than the so-called romanticism for which he ridiculed Buber and Rosenzweig.[13]

The center vanished under attacks by the likes of Kracauer from the political left and by those like Strauss from the right. While Kracauer sought to radicalize Enlightenment with more Enlightenment, Strauss was anti-modern, "which is precisely what renders [him] inner-modern" (*EW*, 5). The same either/or logic between the sacred and profane defined both thinkers. In *Philosophy and Law* (1935), Strauss counterposed a radical form of revelation and orthodoxy to modern philosophy, political Zionism, and atheism. "The contemporary situation seems to allow no way out," he averred (*PL*, 19). And like Kracauer, Strauss rejected all attempts to find one. He consequently took Cohen, Buber, and Rosenzweig to task for having not *"unreservedly* [returned] to tradition" (8; emphasis added), for abandoning literal belief in "the existence of God, an existence that is entirely indifferent to human existence and human need" (EW, 69). In sync with the Neue Sachlichkeit return to optical objects in painting, Strauss insisted that others embrace dogmatic *content*. The religion of reason and empty encounters was too mixed up with human correlates, and thus unable to meet the high standard Strauss set for pure revelation.

No less than Kracauer in his critique of religion, Strauss rejected the very idea of "interpretation" in his search for the original significance of revelation. Living under an "open sky," he said, modern theology "[stretched] the meaning of words to the point that they retain barely any of their original sense." Perhaps Strauss was right. Reason, presence, and eternity are vague abstractions, "merely an unreal shadow and no longer the powerful personality of religious doctrine," "unworthy of belief" (*PL*, 76–77, 207). Except that the "enclosed world of the past" (70) and the indifferent God invoked by Strauss in no way jibe with the theological tradition whose virtues he supposedly espoused. A caricature of revelation, the creation of "an entirely closed world" resembles much more the modernity pictured by Kracauer, with its seamlessly constructed dungeons and suffocating burrows.

The appeal to an "absolute and immutable" revelation (*PL*, 7) only helped to undermine the religion it was intended to buttress. In *Philosophy and Law*, Strauss forced revelation to legitimate "unambiguous commands to philosophize" (40), the "*unconditional* superiority of medieval over modern philosophy" (52), a "total order" (53), a "perfect society," the "perfection of man" that only obedience to prophets can promise (100), "direct knowledge of the upper world" (104, 105). It was a religion Strauss himself was unable to adopt. By the time he came to write his eulogy for Weimar German Judaism (in the preface to the 1965 translation of his 1930 book *Die Religionskritik Spinozas*),[14] the conflict in his thought between reason and revelation, Athens and Jerusalem, had ground to a standstill. Seen as a belief system in its own right, the quest for certain truth in rationalist philosophy is an act of will, no less than religious faith. Reason cannot refute belief in an omnipotent and unfathomable God. And if such a God exists, then anything is possible. Impossible to *know* philosophically, *belief* in revelation, Mosaic authorship of the Pentateuch, and biblical miracles remain theoretically possible (*JP*, 170–72).

Just not for Strauss. Still demanding a radical choice between extreme orthodoxy and extreme secular modernity, he chose neither. Strauss explained to a young American critic, "I rejected . . . all attempts to interpret the Jewish past," and not just the Jewish past, but revelation itself, "in terms of culture. Therefore the emptiness of which you complain. In other words, for me, the question is: truly either the Torah as understood by our tradition, or, say, unbelief" (*JP*, 343). Strauss's critique of modern Judaism and all its projects was total: the liberal state (the private sphere permits discrimination), political Zionism (an empty shell without Jewish content), cultural Zionism (a gross distortion of Judaism into high culture), and modern Jewish philosophy (imagistic, subjective, selective) (142–53, 318–20). Insisting that religious Zionism was the only clear solution to "the crisis" of modern Judaism, he rejected it as "not feasible, humanly speaking, for all Jews." Not much remained to revelation except ancestral fidelity, the symbolism of unredeemed existence, and the vague sense that "being is radically mysterious" (320, 327, 328).[15]

The nothing left by Strauss to Judaism is a mirror image of the nihilism reflected in Kracauer's Weimar-era writings. On the irresolvable tensions that drove Strauss, Michael Zank writes: "Once the extreme opposites are seen as equally grounded in irrational assumptions, and once the reconciliation of such assumptions is excluded, only one alternative [remains]: the philosopher who articulates this insight gloating in the heroism of the ability to stare back at the Gorgon's head of—absolutely nothing" (EW, 27). Strauss rejected the precarious and imperfect "something" represented by modern democracy and liberal Judaism for the false choice between everything and nothing. The choice compares poorly to the spiritual and ideological capaciousness worked by Rosenzweig and his collaborators into the Lehrhaus, and also to Buber's consistent opposition to left-wing totalitarianism and to right-wing nationalism in Europe and in British Mandate Palestine. Buber and Rosenzweig sought to extend revelation by opening Judaism to that which is alien to it. Staining his early writings on Judaism, Strauss's association with the political theorist Carl Schmitt and German ultraconservative politics of the late 1920s and early 1930s was part of a general cultural propensity to shut down the difference represented by excluded middles.

Politics is the pivot around which revelation was supposed to trump reason in these writings on Judaism from the 1920s and 1930s. According to Strauss, the modern emphasis upon inwardness and self-consciousness provides no basis upon which to civilize human community (PL, 13). Yet the Orthodoxy advanced in Philosophy and Law was only a rhetorical foil. Strauss only upheld the "form" of revelation, being less drawn to ritual observance than to the prophecy of direct perception. The prophet "knows more, and more directly than the philosopher . . . blinded by the all too bright unaccustomed light" (89). He occupies the highest rung of human consciousness, "the stage of the *blissful*; the men of this stage see the thing in itself; they see, as it were, the light itself. In their seeing there is absolutely nothing seeming; they themselves become the thing they see" (105). Only this lends the basis upon which to create an ideal state, to mandate the freedom of philosophy, and to ensure the survival of humanity (99). The order for which the early Strauss longed was immutable, absolute, unconditional, and authoritarian. "The health of the world of the senses" and the survival of the political world was forced to rest upon direct perception of the supernal world (104). An overpowering light applied directly to the optical nerve, an appeal to a concentration of order and authority two years after the rise of Hitler, it leaves one breathless.

This Jerusalem is a polis barely fit for human habitation—in contrast to the alternative space that Cohen, Buber, and Rosenzweig sought to build between the absolute bind of unbending orthodoxy and atheism, between that which belongs to God and that which belongs to "man." Neither everything nor nothing, the sensation that revelation reflects the glimmer of a bare "something" lends more give-and-take to religious reality than the all-or-nothing approach advanced by early critics like Kracauer and Strauss. The caricatures were unfair. Buber and Rosenzweig never abandoned the public interest or restricted revelation to subjective consciousness. On the contrary. Their only fault was the human inability to anticipate the future: the murder of European Jewry, the dropping of the atomic bomb, Jewish majority status in the state of Israel, the rise of global capitalism, and the hegemony of American popular culture. Kracauer and Strauss survived the war in the United States, where they remained. Gropius moved to Harvard, Mies van der Rohe and Moholy-Nagy to Chicago. Symbolized by the skyscraper, the modernism they advanced into the 1940s and 1950s was the one pilloried in postmodernism: sleek and cool, homogeneous and corporate, the eclipse of God and of the spiritual in art.

Next

In postmodern philosophy and contemporary theory of religion, the language of trace, gift, aporia, and absence seep into the logic previously lent to revelation by abstract art and the discourse of eternity, spirit, and presence. Passing from modernism to postmodernism, art and revelation lack any clear-cut power to transcend material existence, fix the social order, and redeem physical suffering. As they enter into the current imaginary, the gestural acts and historical memory that circumscribe art and religion refract in the light cast by television, neon, movie projectors, and computer screens. Buber and Rosenzweig were in that sense naïve, too close to a Judaism of their own invention, which they trusted too much. Their work is uninformed by the self-critical ironies that absence can bring to religion. Every word, no matter how odious, was to them potentially a revelation. They could not see how the play of signs has no final resting point or any single moral significance; how the form of revelation marks a presence irretrievably out of sync with itself.

Neither Buber nor Rosenzweig ever seemed to suspect that revelation is a *pharmakon*, what Derrida calls a "medicine" or " philter, which acts as both remedy and poison. . . . This charm, this spellbinding virtue, this power of fascination, [which] can be—alternately or simultaneously—beneficent or maleficent."[16] Derrida associates the *pharmakon* in Platonic philosophy with writing, painting, pictorial color, and perfume. Socrates rejected writing as an aid to memory and wisdom, arguing that it aggravates the forgetfulness it purports to remedy. With no innate value, the written must be confirmed or disconfirmed by authority, the father, God, the good about which one cannot speak directly.[17] Radically ambiguous, the same, single word associates one thing and its very opposite. "The *pharmakon* has no ideal essence or identity; it is aneidetic, firstly because it is not monoeidetic (in the sense in which the *Phaedo* speaks of the *eidos* as something simple, noncomposite: *monoeides*)," Derrida comments. "We will watch it . . . endlessly vanish through concealed doorways that shine like mirrors and open onto a labyrinth."[18]

The rabbis in the Talmud were more cautious about this medicine. Conceived of as a *pharmakon*, Torah is dangerous. Comparing the ideal scholar to the Tabernacle ark, Raba observes that both must be covered by gold from within and from without, saying "Any Torah scholar whose inside is not like his outside is not a Torah scholar." Reflecting great anxiety, Samuel b. Nahmani exclaimed in the name of R. Yonathan: "Woe to them, the enemies of the scholars who occupy themselves with the Torah, but have no fear of heaven!" Without fear of heaven, the scholar is compared to a gate without a courtyard. He leads out into nothing. To this R. Joshua b. Levi relates: "What is the meaning of the Scriptural verse: *And this is the law which Moses set [sam] before the children of Israel?*—If he has merit it becomes for him a medicine [*sam*] of life, if he has no merit it becomes for him a medicine of death. That is what Raba [meant when he] said: If he used it skillfully [*'uman*] it is a medicine of life unto him; [for him] who does not use it skillfully, it is a deadly medicine" (Yomah 72b).

The sound of redemption also requires careful calibration. The hymnic rhythms of *I and Thou* and the violent lyric in *The Star of Redemption* echo the mordant librettos, the harsh percussion, and trumpet blasts, the sudden and lingering silences in works by Mahler, Schoenberg, and Stravinsky. A more contemporary sound is the introduction of nonmusical sounds, noise, and silence into the compositions of John Cage, the smaller voice of Steven Reich and Phillip Glass in minimalist music, a trilling wind machine combined with trumpet in Olivier Messiaen's *Des canyons aux étoiles* (1971–74). Buber and Rosenzweig never seem to have suspected the dangers to which their own discourse is subject, that religion represents a grave toxin when it fails to pitch the sound of revelation and redemption lower than the gigantic, all-tones of modern music and pseudo-redeeming polyphony.

Burnt out by renewal and revolution, the "new" has lost its edge in a culture where ideas and images circulate with no great moral urgency. Religious fundamentalism and international terrorism, fanatics of revelation, currently constitute the only serious challenge to "the cultural logic of late capitalism."[19] The reality and rhetoric of community continue to bear upon contemporary society, but under transformed economic conditions. Church communities, the Jewish community, the black community, the gay community, the art community, online communities present lucrative niche markets. An iron cage with satellite television and wireless Internet, the "spirit of capitalism" has intensified the conditions for proliferating art and religious expression. Prints and posters, ritual objects and decorations, academic and coffee-table books, web sites, college curricula and adult education programs, the supernatural in popular film, religious and cultural performance, pilgrimage and tourism, public-speaking forums, geegaws, coffee mugs and T-shirts are brought to the broadest possible public. At once naïve and cynical, markets never judge, and they thus permit art and religion to flourish at the intersection between elite and kitsch culture.

This concluding nod to postmodern surface is a prefatory note to further study. Modernism has entered the historical archive. The first quarter of the twentieth century and its cultural expression in central Europe are situated at a profound remove from contemporary art, religion, and philosophy. With each passing year, such masterworks of modernism as *I and Thou*, Kandinsky's *Composition VIII*, Mies van der Rohe's Seagram building in New York (1954–58), and Tel Aviv Bauhaus slip further into the historical past. This has only recently been the case, however. Buber was still alive when émigré scholars introduced him and Rosenzweig to a new generation of readers in the United States and Israel. Along with Hermann Hesse, his reputation was revived among these younger readers, no doubt, thanks to 1960s drug culture and the beginnings of New Age spirituality (basic tenets of which he himself rejected).[20] Buber's face was ubiquitous, staring out at the reader from the front cover of so many paperback editions of his works.

But modern Jewish thought is no longer contemporary. In Andy Warhol's late screenprint of Buber for the Jews of the 20th Century Portfolio (1980) (fig. 9), it is already a gimmick, an electric pop icon. The entire series originally opened at the Jewish Museum in New York. In addition to Buber, Warhol included Sara Bernhardt, Louis Brandeis, Einstein, Freud, Kafka, Gershwin, Golda Meir, and Gertrude Stein. In each image, the heads from well-known photographic portraits have been lifted out and superimposed with intersecting blocks of bright color. As art, the images are mechanical, even for Warhol. Bluma Goldstein notes that the Jews of the 20th Century Portfolio was widely panned by the critics for its crass, commercial opportunism. In her own analysis of Warhol's Kafka, she faults the portrait for suspending important points of historical, social, and biographical reference.[21] Of course, this is precisely the point missed by the historically minded critic. Detached from its original time and place, Kafka's and Buber's direct, frontal gazes are now filtered through masks of color and geometric shapes.

Caspar David Friedrich's romantic *Monk by the Sea* (plate 1) stands alone, facing the sea, which dwarfs him, and the viewer of the figure gazing at the sea is correspondingly magnified. Warhol's photographic image of Buber—identical in form to Emil Nolde's *Prophet* (plate 16), that icon of German expressionism—has the opposite effect: unlike Friedrich's diminutive figure, Buber's enormous face fills the entire composition, diminishing the viewer. The revelation that occurs through dialogue, in the in-between space of the interhuman, is supposed to be unmediated and unique. With the wide dissemination of photographic technologies, in Warhol's rendition, it threatens to turn into a good-natured joke. Always one step removed from the original, the reprocessed image highlights the self-conscious production of a religious gesture—just as by 1980, critics were right to suspect that Warhol's original flare had turned into a weak imitation of itself.

My point in this critique is not to rebuff Buber, Rosenzweig, religion, or revelation. For Warhol, "Pop art is liking things."[22] And there is every reason to "like" Buber and Rosenzweig. Even at a distance, they continue to mark out a powerful place for religion and religious thought in contemporary culture, the zone between one person and another where the human and the divine intermingle. This was the position rejected out of hand by Kracauer and Strauss. Postmodernism simply provides a new visual and conceptual lens, far removed from the calamity that was Weimar Germany, through which to consider and reconsider that presence of revelation and the spiritual in art and the claims made about them. Warhol's silkscreens, like the woodcut technology used by Nolde, make for easy dissemination. The blue and purple superadded by him bring new color to what is otherwise a black and white image. Alongside the suspicion that artifice inevitably engenders, that revelation does not exist apart from appearance, Buber's and Rosenzweig's own attempts at self-creation may only further endear them to postmodern readers, who have come to embrace artifice.

In the epilogue to his 1992 book *Correlations in Rosenzweig and Levinas*, Robert Gibbs identifies a group of rubrics with which to organize contemporary Jewish philosophy: a nonexclusive, undogmatic universalism; the primacy of ethics; cooperative community; prophecy and messianic politics; material existence and the body; devotion to Jewish law; and a critique of the state.[23] While these rubrics remain essential building blocks for contemporary religious thought, they are not postmodern topoi. They belong to early German modernism, to Hermann Cohen and Walter Benjamin, not to American postmodernism. In actual fact, a robust postmodern aesthetic of copies and fakes, semblance and artifice, has barely begun to make an impact on contemporary Jewish thought. The oversight creates the false impression that religion and revelation stand outside "the society of spectacle." Our own visual culture calls attention to the following: religion is indeed steeped in figures; revelation is appearance and the semblance of appearance; end-time pathos has burnt itself out; the closed quarter of community opens out into larger circuits, human creation is polymorphous and perverse. If something continues to happen in contemporary culture that looks and sounds like revelation, it does so as an image-mediated form, not as a voice, but as the daughter of a voice (*bat kol*). In distinct contrast to Buber and Rosenzweig's heavy reliance on Scripture, contemporary religious thought that builds off their efforts will come to resemble Talmud.

Hocus-Pocus

"Signs happen to us," Buber wrote in 1929. We try to ward them off with the assurance that "nothing is directed at you, you are not meant; it is just 'the world,' you can experience it as you like. . . . We have turned off our receivers" (*BMM*, 10–11). But is it really God who speaks to us "out of that decisive hour of personal existence" (14)? By now, I hope to have shown that revelation and the spiritual in art do not occur outside the play of signs, the world of illusion and appearance, a trick of the eye and ear, the power of art, the arts, and social convention. And this renders them immediately suspect. Revelation depends upon the world of creation at the base of communication. Buber knew the comparison was gauche when he went on to say that "all we know of the poet is what we learn of him in the poem" (15). Understanding that "in our age especially, it appears extremely difficult to distinguish the one from the other," he asked in 1952: "Are you really addressed by the Absolute or by one of his apes?" (*EG*, 119). Human discourse is all we have, and the possibility of divine revelation makes claims about the reality of revelation no less patently fraudulent.

Is the image of the "absolute," the word of God, pure hocus-pocus, a make-believe imaginary? The rabbis were alert to the possible deception broached by Buber when they asked about this statement from Scripture: "As Moses spoke, God answered him in thunder" (Exod. 19:19). The prophet's communication precedes the divine utterance. A master magician out of Egypt, Moses speaks first and then God responds. On the defensive, the rabbis explain that the text "merely teaches that Moses was endowed with strength and force and that God was helping him with His voice so that Moses could let Israel hear the same tone [*neimah*] which he himself heard" (*Mekhilta de Rabbi Ishmael*, tractate *Bahodesh*, chap. 4). Although modest, Moses was a man of strength and force. The sensation of God's presence depends upon a combination of elements, sensual media drawn from the world of creation. What the rabbis fear without wanting to admit is that revelation has to be as such that even when the people's receivers are on, it is still not clear whose value it communicates.

Like any article relating to religious faith, revelation and the spiritual in art are not subject to strictly empirical or phenomenological investigation. Sympathetic readers are caught before a hermeneutical choice. Signs are conceivably everywhere. According to a skeptical philosophical realism, any physical sign remains just a sign, manifesting nothing beyond itself and its relation to other empirical signs. In the romantic view, signs constitute symbols in which revelation—the "surplus" in autonomous art that Adorno called the "crackling noise . . . in which the more of the phenomenon announces itself in opposition to this phenomenon"[24]—at first partial, grows increasingly manifest. A seal inscribed with a lion embodies power. A finite sign imbeds the infinite. A scripture reflects the mind of God, a work of art the quintessence of humanity. The essence of the one participates in the essence of the other, a stance freighting expression with significance that no sign can carry for too long in the face of critical scrutiny.

Both realists and romantics, Buber and Rosenzweig invoked an elusive presence fundamentally foreign to the artful sign-combinations into which it is manifested. There and then not-there, this null presence hovers over the individual sign upon which it will glance, insinuating itself into the empty space between two signs. "My beloved is like a gazelle or like a young stag. There he stands behind our wall, gazing through the window, peering through the lattice" (Song of Songs 2:9). A mutant motion, its presence disappears before one can reach it in language. Visual marks, sonic combinations, tactile impressions and their interface with the human subject's perceptual, mental, and technological apparatus: signs are just signs, a product of the natural order writ large and the human hand writ small. They are themselves neutral with no inherent status prior to revelation. The discombobulation of elements through technics of repetition, this relief from historical context and realist reference, is a second-order moment in which a not-just-physical charge is wrapped about what Rainer Crone in his study of Klee calls "the deliberate combination of two discontinuous systems."[25]

Something is said to appear, but the referent is obscure. The suspicion remains that we have been tricked by magic powers brought to image and word.

Such tricks proliferate around death and violence. In Salman Rushdie's *The Satanic Verses*, the reluctant Indian film star Gibreel Farishta is transformed into the archangel Gabriel. He comes to Mahound. "It happens. Revelation. Like this: Mahound, still in his notsleep, becomes rigid, veins bulge in his neck, he clutches at his centre. No, no, nothing like an epileptic fit, it can't be explained away that easily; what epileptic fit caused day to turn to night, caused clouds to mass overhead, caused air to thicken into soup while an angel hung, scared silly, in the sky . . . held up like a kite on a golden thread? The dragging again the dragging and now the miracle starts in my our guts, he is straining with all his might at something, forcing something, and Gibreel begins to feel that strength, forcing something, and Gibreel begins to feel that strength that force, here it is *at my own jaw* working it, opening shutting; and the power, starting within Mahound, reaching up to *my vocal cords* and the voice comes." Gibreel proceeds to qualify, "Butbutbut God isn't in this picture."[26] "Halfway into sleep, or halfway back to wakefulness,

Gibreel Farishta is often filled with resentment by the non-appearance, in his persecuting vision, of the One who is supposed to have the answers, *He* never turns up, the one who kept away when I was dying, when I needed needed him."[27]

Revelation and the spiritual in art bet that an immaterial surplus lurks in patterns conjured by human expression. Hebrew Scripture is not coy with the dynamite this brings to revelation. "You shall not wrong a stranger or oppress him, for you were strangers in the land of Egypt. You shall not ill-treat any widow or orphan" (Exod. 22:20–21). But also: "Remember what Amalek did to you . . . you shall blot out the memory of Amalek from under heaven" (Deut. 25:17–19); "If your brother, your own mother's son, or your son or daughter, or the wife of your bosom entices you in secret. . . . Show him no pity or compassion, and do not shield him; but take his life" (Deut. 13:7–10); "When the Lord your God . . . dislodges many nations before you . . . you must doom them to destruction" (Deut. 7:1–2); "tear down their altars, smash their pillars, cut down their sacred posts, and consign their images to the fire (Deut. 7:5). Both sets of discourse are parts of a precarious historical trust that is its own interpretation. Critical readers, even sympathetic ones, might no longer be certain that Scripture is either good or true, but there is no other place to see this shape as it comes into and out of view, "under His feet . . . the likeness of a pavement of sapphire" (Exod. 24:10), "the appearance of the semblance of the glory" (Ezek. 1:28).

Reference Matter

Notes

Preface: Revelation and the Spiritual in Art

1. Walter Benjamin, *The Origin of the German Tragic Drama*, trans. John Osborne (London: Verso, 1998), 27.

2. On the vexed relationship between art and art history, on the one hand, and theory (especially theoretical statements made by artists about their own work), on the other, see Reinhard Zimmermann, *Die Kunsttheorie von Wassily Kandinsky*, vol. 1 (Berlin: Gebr. Mann, 2002), chap. 1.

3. My description of Klee's painting relies heavily upon Marcel Franciscono, *Paul Klee: His Work and Thought* (Chicago: University of Chicago Press, 1991), 182–84.

4. Ibid., 173–74. See also James Elkins, *On the Strange Place of Religion in Contemporary Art* (New York: Routledge, 2004). Like many art critics and art historians, Elkins finds himself caught. Paraphrasing Maurice Blanchot, he writes, "The name of *God* does not belong to the language of art in which the name intervenes, but at the same time, and in a manner that is difficult to determine, the name *God* is still part of the language of art even though the name has been set aside" (116). Elkins shows marked hostility not only to organized religion but to any overt religious symbol and any reference to the "spiritual in art," including Kandinsky's, which he seeks to alter, pare down, and burn (88). At the same time, he is almost drawn to the negative theology in works by Derrida, Levinas, Mark C. Taylor, and John Caputo, although claiming that their theories have no influence on contemporary art (105–12). He then turns to Slavoj Žižek, whose idiosyncratic interest in Christianity is relegated to the very last footnote of the book (132n26). Elkins's discussion of the spiritual in art is less crimped in his earlier book *What Painting Is: How to Think About Oil Painting, Using the Language of Alchemy* (New York: Routledge, 2000), in which he implores his fellow art historians to consider painting in its spiritual capacity as alchemy, as "hypostasis"—i.e., the infusion of thick, painted, oily objects with life, spirit, etc.—and demonstrates warm regard for the mystical pretensions of Kandinsky and Emil Nolde.

5. Immanuel Kant, *Critique of Pure Reason*, trans. Norman Kemp Smith (New York: St. Martin's Press), 93. The circularity between perception and intellection receives more fundamental consideration in Rudolf Arnheim, *Visual Thinking* (Berkeley: University of California Press, 1969). In contrast to Kant's binary scheme, Arnheim's model of perception, indebted to Gestalt psychology, is itself active and already endowed with intelligence.

6. Terry Eagleton, *Ideology of the Aesthetic* (Cambridge: Basil Blackwell, 1990), 16.

7. Alexander Baumgarten, *Reflections on Poetry* (Berkeley: University of California Press, 1954), § 43.

8. Mark C. Taylor, *Disfiguring: Art, Architecture, Religion* (Chicago: University of Chicago Press, 1992), 6.

9. Clement Greenberg, "Avant-Garde and Kitsch," in id., *Art and Culture: Critical Essays* (Boston: Beacon Press, 1961), 10.

10. See Paul Tillich, "Aspects of a Religious Analysis of Culture," "The Nature of Religious Language," and "Protestantism and Artistic Style," in *Theology of Culture* (New York: Oxford University Press, 1964). See also id., "Art and Ultimate Reality," in *Art and Architecture*, ed. John Dillenberger and Jane Dillenberger (New York: Crossroad, 1987). The problem persists in essays by Phillip Blond and Catherine Pickstock in John Milbank, Catherine Pickstock, and Graham Ward, eds., *Radical Orthodoxy* (London: Routledge, 1999), and in Jean-Luc Marion, *The Crossing of the Visible*, trans. James K. A. Smith (Stanford: Stanford University Press, 1996), and *The Idol and Distance: Five Studies*, trans. Thomas A. Carlson (New York: Fordham University Press, 2001). Unlike the more liberal Tillich, these conservative radicals combine a heavy premium on religious authority with an almost intense disregard for visible (secular) phenomena. The latter are always made to conform to the inflexible standards set by the former.

11. Gotthold Ephraim Lessing, *Laocoon: An Essay upon the Limits of Painting and Poetry*, trans. Ellen Frothingham (New York: Noonday Press, 1957). Lessing's interpretation, made to suit rules of classical sculpture and poetry that he himself had invented, hardly squares with the image itself. Contrary to Sophocles' pathos-laden account, Lessing does not allow the sculpture to convey suffering; he finds in it only the stoic heroism of a steady, composed, serene soul.

12. Ibid., 17.

13. Georg Heym, *Dichtungen und Schriften*, vol. 3 (Hamburg: Heinrich Ellermann, 1960), 140, 159. See also Heinz Rölleke, "Georg Heym," in Wolfgang Rothe, ed., *Expressionismus als Literatur: Gesammelte Studien* (Bern: Francke, 1969), 363. According to Rölleke, this uniquely expressionistic style is more easily accomplished in painting than in poetry.

14. W. J. T. Mitchell, *Iconology: Image, Text, Ideology* (Chicago: University of Chicago Press, 1986), 46. Cf. pt. 2.

15. Wendy Steiner, *The Colors of Rhetoric: Problems in the Relation Between Mod-*

ern Literature and Painting (Chicago: University of Chicago Press, 1982); id., *Pictures of Romance: Form Against Context in Painting and Literature* (Chicago: University of Chicago Press, 1988). Rainer Crone and Joseph Leo Koerner, *Paul Klee: Legends of the Sign* (New York: Columbia University Press, 1991), 32, 79. See also Will Grohmann, *Paul Klee* (New York: Harry N. Abrams, 1954), 150.

16. Hermann Cohen, *Religion of Reason, out of the Sources of Judaism*, trans. Simon Kaplan (1972; 2d ed., Atlanta, Ga.: Scholars Press, 1995), 57. Originally published as *Religion der Vernunft aus den Quellen des Judentums* (Leipzig, 1919).

17. Ibid., 57–58.

18. Hermann Cohen, *Ästhetik des reinen Gefühls*, in id., *Werke* (Hildesheim: Georg Olms, 1977), 2: 404–5. Cf. 2: 322–24; 1: 337–38.

19. Moshe Barasch, *Icon: Studies in the History of an Idea* (New York: New York University Press, 1992), chap. 1. Recent work in Jewish studies regarding visual experience in rabbinic and medieval Jewish thought further undermines Cohen's reading of the second commandment. See Vivian B. Mann, *Jewish Texts on the Visual Arts* (Cambridge: Cambridge University Press, 2000), 74–75; Daniel Boyarin, "The Eye in the Torah: Ocular Desire in Midrashic Hermeneutic," *Critical Inquiry* 16 (1990): 532–50; Elliot R. Wolfson, *Through a Speculum That Shines: Vision and Imagination in Medieval Jewish Mysticism* (Princeton: Princeton University Press, 1994); Kalman Bland, *The Artless Jew: Medieval and Modern Affirmations and Denials of the Visual* (Princeton: Princeton University Press, 2000); Moshe Halbertal and Avishai Margalit, *Idolatry*, trans. Naomi Goldblum (Cambridge, Mass.: Harvard University Press, 1992), 262n22. The earliest strata of rabbinic text and law tend to take a more conservative stance vis-à-vis plastic art, but as Barasch demonstrates, the same is true in Christian patristics. Mostly the sources are too ambiguous to hazard any sweeping judgments with absolute certainty. One finds a comprehensive ban on all images in the early midrashic compilation *Mekhilta de-Rabbi Ishmael* (commentary on Exod. 20:4) and also in the twelfth-century responsum of Elyakim b. Joseph of Mainz. Conversely, tractate *Avodah Zarah* of the Babylonian Talmud, the *Mishne Torah* of Maimonides, and the *Shulkhan 'Arukh*, the authoritative code of Jewish law from the sixteenth century, provide far more leeway. In either case, it is important to note that those authorities who banned the use of all images generally objected to their appearance within the synagogue. In addition to the second commandment, they cited custom, the importance of not distracting worshippers, and reluctance to follow gentile habits. Those authorities who granted more leeway showed intense opposition to certain cases; for instance, David ibn Zimra's opposition to placing a crowned lion inscribed with the seal of a prominent family on top of a Torah ark in the synagogue of Candia (Iráklion), Crete.

20. Steven Schwarzschild, "The Legal Foundations of Jewish Aesthetics," in Menachem Kellner, *The Pursuit of the Ideal* (Albany: State University of New York Press, 1990), 114. See also 112, 115–16. Schwarzschild cites *Shulkhan 'Arukh, Yoreh*

De'ah, chap. 141.

   21. Ibid., 115.

   22. Ibid., 112.

   23. Ibid., 114.

   24. Mitchell, *Iconology*, 10.

Introduction

   1. Paul Mendes-Flohr, "The Berlin Jew as Cosmopolitan," in Emily D. Bilski, ed., *Berlin Metropolis: Jews and the New Jewish Culture, 1890–1918* (Berkeley: University of California Press, 1999), 27. For an in-depth analysis of the link between the modern Jewish renaissance, the work of the cultural historian Jakob Burkhardt, and the Italian Renaissance at the fin de siècle, see Asher Biemann, "The Problem of Tradition and Reform in Jewish Renaissance and Renaissancism," *Jewish Social Studies* 8, no. 1 (2001): 58–87. See esp. Michael Brenner, *The Renaissance of Jewish Culture in Weimar Germany* (New Haven: Yale University Press, 1996).

   2. My reading of romantic subjectivity relies heavily upon Philippe Lacoue-Labarth and Jean-Luc Nancy, *The Literary Absolute: The Theory of Literature in German Romanticism*, trans. Philip and Cheryl Lester (Albany: State University of New York Press, 1988), esp. 30–35, 55–57, 70–71, and 121–22.

   3. In disassociating Rosenzweig and, especially, Buber from romanticism, I follow Alexander Altmann, who contrasts the soft, romantic pathos of infinity with the hard-edged, anti-romantic moral pathos of a suprahuman absolute. See Altmann, "Theology in Twentieth-Century German Jewry," *Leo Baeck Institute Yearbook*, no. 1 (1956): 203.

   4. In addition to primary sources, my reading of neoromanticism relies heavily upon Robert Schmutzler, *Art Nouveau* (New York: Harry N. Abrams, 1962); Helmut Seling, *Jugendstil: Der Weg in 20. Jahrhundert* (Heidelberg: Keyser, 1959); Jacques Le Rider, *Hugo von Hofmannsthal: Historismus und Moderne in der Literatur der Jahrhundertwende* (Vienna: Böhlau, 1997); and Theodore Ziolkowski, *The View from the Tower: Origins of an Antimodernist Image* (Princeton: Princeton University Press, 1998).

   5. Robert Rosenblum, *Modern Painting and the Northern Romantic Tradition: From Friedrich to Rothko* (New York: Harper & Row, 1975), 14.

   6. Ibid., 13.

   7. Meyer Schapiro, *Theory and Philosophy of Art: Style, Artist, and Society* (New York: George Braziller, 1994), 54.

   8. G. F. Hartlaub, *Kunst und Religion: Ein Versuch über die Möglichkeit neuer religiöser Kunst* (Leipzig: Kurt Wolff, 1919), 16–17.

   9. Ibid., 82–83, 87–88.

   10. Ibid., 37–39.

11. Ernst Ludwig Kirchner in Victor H. Miesel, ed., *Voices of German Expressionism* (Englewood Cliffs, N.J.: Prentice-Hall, 1970), 19.

12. Max Pechstein, "Creative Credo," ibid., 180.

13. Hartlaub, *Kunst und Religion*, 39.

14. This sketch depends heavily on Franciscono, *Paul Klee*, 193–96, and Rainer Crone, "Cosmic Fragments of Meaning: On the Syllables of Paul Klee," in Crone and Koerner, *Paul Klee: Legends of the Sign*, 17–20. I follow most of the critics who view Klee as in opposition to romanticism. For a contrasting position, see Jürgen Glaesemer, "Paul Klee und die deutsche Romantik," in Carolyn Lanchner, ed., *Paul Klee: Leben und Werk* (Ostfildern-Ruit, Germany: Hatje Cantz, 2001), 13–29.

15. Cf. Frederick S. Levine, *The Apocalyptic Vision: The Art of Franz Marc as German Expressionism* (New York: Harper & Row, 1979), 52, 77, 66.

16. Wolfgang Rothe, *Expressionismus als Literatur* (Bern: Franke, 1969), 7.

17. Wilhelm Worringer, *Abstraktion und Einfühlung: Ein Beitrag zur Stilpsychologie* (Neuwied: Heuser, 1907), trans. Michael Bullock as *Abstraction and Empathy: A Contribution to the Psychology of Style* (New York: International Universities Press, 1963); id., "Current Questions on Art," cited in Rose-Carol Washton-Long, *German Expressionism: Documents from the End of the Wilhelmine Empire to the Rise of National Socialism* (Berkeley: University of California Press, 1993), 285, 286.

18. Iwan Goll, "Expressionism Is Dying," cited in Washton-Long, *German Expressionism*, 289.

19. G. F. Hartlaub, preface to the catalogue of the Neue Sachlichkeit exhibition, Mannheim, 1925, cited in Washton-Long, *German Expressionism*, 291.

20. Dennis Crockett, *German Post-Expressionism: The Art of the Great Disorder, 1918–1924* (University Park, Pa.: Pennsylvania State University Press, 1999).

21. Walter Benjamin, "Walter Benjamin Conversations with Brecht," in Ernst Bloch et al., *Aesthetics and Politics* (London: Verso, 1977), 89–90.

22. Christopher Fynsk, *Heidegger: Thought and Historicity*, rev. ed. (Ithaca, N.Y.: Cornell University Press, 1986), 28. Fynsk suggests that the other is a topic that must be "forced" into the interpretation of Heidegger.

23. Jacques Derrida, *Of Spirit: Heidegger and the Question*, trans. Geoffrey Bennington and Rachel Bowlby (Chicago: University of Chicago Press, 1987), 14–17, 23.

24. Ibid., 87–98. See also esp. 28–29, 33.

25. The description of Rovner's work is drawn from essays by Sylvia Wolf and Michael Rush and from Leon Golub's interview with the artist in *Michal Rovner: The Space Between* (New York: Whitney Museum of American Art, 2002). A catalogue to a mid-career retrospective, it is an up-to-date and comprehensive introduction to her work.

26. Walter Benjamin, "The Work of Art in the Age of Mechanical Reproduction," in id., *Illuminations: Essays and Reflections*, trans. Harry Zohn (New York: Schocken Books, 1968), 222, 233.

27. Ibid., 236.

28. Nissan Perez, "Waiting for . . . ," in Michal Rovner, *Michal Rovner: One-Person Game Against Nature* (Jerusalem: Israel Museum, 1994), 3. For a nearly identical description, see Steven Henry Modoff, "In the Zone of Transition," in Sylvia Wolf, *Michal Rovner* (Chicago: Art Institute of Chicago, 1994).

29. Roberta Smith, "Technology as Muse: A Hazard and an Ally," *New York Times*, August 16, 2002, E31. Smith's negative review is unfair only to the extent that the "pandering" she finds in Rovner's work is more "metaphysical" than the political clichés to which she reduces her work.

30. The figure of Plato in early twentieth-century discourse that appears in this study represents a partial truth about platonic philosophy, a caricature at best. The focus on the parable overlooks the importance of sensation and the imagination in other platonic dialogues, as well as other passages in the *Republic* itself.

Chapter One: Form

1. Cited by Rose-Carol Washton Long, *Kandinsky: The Development of an Abstract Style* (New York: Oxford University Press, 1980), 11. See also *The Life of Vasilii Kandinsky in Russian Art: A Study of "On the Spiritual in Art,"* ed. John E. Bowlt and Rose-Carol Washton Long, trans. John Bowlt (Newtonville, Mass.: Oriental Research Partners, 1980).

2. Friedrich Schiller, *On the Aesthetic Education of Man in a Series of Letters*, trans. Reginald Snell (New York: Continuum, 1965), 106.

3. Ibid., 127.

4. Georg Simmel, *Grundfragen der Soziologie*, 2d ed. (Berlin: Göschen, 1920), trans. Kurt H. Wolff in *The Sociology of Georg Simmel* (New York: Free Press, 1950), 11. Italics in the original, published in 1917.

5. Ibid., 44. Simmel's influence on Buber is not lost on Paul Mendes-Flohr, *From Mysticism to Dialogue: Martin Buber's Transformation of German Social Thought* (Detroit : Wayne State University Press, 1989), esp. chaps. 1–2.

6. See Georg Simmel, "Religion," in *Essays on Religion*, ed. and trans. Horst Jürgen Helle in collaboration with Ludwig Nieder (New Haven: Yale University Press, 1997), 65–66, 137–213. See also esp. 140, 165, 213.

7. Ibid., 213.

8. Phillip Hammond, ibid., vii.

9. Kandinsky, "On the Spiritual in Art," *CWA*, 170. Kandinsky's composition theory eludes the critique of Peter Bürger and others that a hegemonically conceived organic whole annihilates the individual figure. See Peter Bürger, *Theory of the Avant-Garde*, trans. Michael Shaw (Minneapolis: University of Minnesota Press, 1984), 86. Cf. Richard Murphy, *Theorizing the Avant-Garde: Modernism, Expressionism, and the Problem of Postmodernity* (Cambridge: Cambridge University Press, 1998), 12–16.

10. Robert Kudielka, *Paul Klee: The Nature of Creation. Works, 1914–1940* (London: Hayward Gallery), 104.

11. Immanuel Kant, *Critique of Judgment*, trans. Werner S. Pluhar (Indianapolis: Hackett, 1987), 108–9.

12. Crone and Koerner, *Paul Klee*, 65–69, 79.

13. Rivka Horwitz has translated most of the letter in her *Buber's Way to "I and Thou"* (Philadelphia: Jewish Publication Society, 1988), 226–29. My translation departs from hers where noted.

14. Buber's approach to *Form* is inconsistent. Contradicting the rhetoric with which he began the essay, the piece on Ury concludes with Buber calling it an interconnection that awakens one thing to another (*FB*, 82). Unlike this ambivalence about artistic form, the reflections on law never lost their own unbending, polemical character.

15. See Zachary Braiterman, "Martin Buber and the Art of Ritual," in Michael Zank, ed., *Martin Buber: New Perspectives/Neue Perspektiven* (Tübingen: Mohr Siebeck, 2006). The article collects material from various chapters in this book, including this one, but reformulates it more explicitly around ritual.

16. Steven Katz, *Post-Holocaust Dialogues: Critical Studies in Modern Jewish Thought* (New York: New York University Press, 1983), 20–21.

17. Unlike Buber's other critics, Norbert Samuelson notes the IT-world's degenerate shape in part 2, in contrast to its appearance in parts 1 and 3. See Norbert M. Samuelson, *Introduction to Modern Jewish Philosophy* (Albany: State University Press of New York, 1989), 194–201.

18. Kaufmann translates *aufnehmen* as "accept" and *verspüren* as "feel." Neither translation does justice to the epistemological and aesthetic weight of this particular passage, and both make Buber sound romantic.

19. Hermann Cohen, *Logik der reinen Erkenntnis*, in id., *Werke* (Hildesheim: Georg Olms, 1977), 6:52–62.

20. Ibid., 324, 347.

21. Ibid., 338–50.

22. Glatzer translates *sinnliche* and *unsinnliche* as "corporeal" and "non-corporeal" (*OJ*, 102).

23. For a complete analysis of the *Kriegsbuber*, see Mendes-Flohr, *From Mysticism to Dialogue*, 93–101.

24. Magdalena Dabrowski, *Kandinsky Compositions* (New York: Museum of Modern Art, 1995), 47–48.

25. Avraham Shapira, *Hope for Our Time: Key Trends in the Thought of Martin Buber*, trans. Jeffrey Green (Albany: State University of New York Press, 1999), chap. 6, 203n6.

26. Hermann Bahr, *Expressionism*, trans. R. T. Gribble (1916; reprint, London: Frank Henderson, 1925), 96.

27. Nahum Glatzer calls Buber "metanomian." See Glatzer, "Frankfurt

Lehrhaus," *Leo Baeck Institute Yearbook*, no. 1 (1956): 121.

28. Annemarie Mayer-de Pay, "Rosenzweig's Stellung zur Kunst," in Wolfdietrich Schmied-Kowarzik, ed., *Der Philosoph Franz Rosenzweig, 1886–1929* (Freiburg: Karl Alber, 1988), 2: 957–98. See Seling, *Jugendstil*, 1959), 11.

29. The position taken here directly contradicts the view of Emmanuel Levinas, who saw in Rosenzweig a precursor of his own postwar critique of totality. See Levinas, *Totality and Infinity*, trans. Alphonso Lingis (The Hague: Martinus Nijhoff, 1979), 28; id., *Difficult Freedom: Essays on Judaism*, trans. Seán Hand (Baltimore: Johns Hopkins University Press, 1990), 188–89, 199–200. While I agree with Eric Santner that *The Star of Redemption* resists a traditionally romantic part/whole harmonization, I believe that he overstates the weight placed on the individual element. If the first interpretation makes Rosenzweig read too much like a postmodernist, Santner's interpretation makes him seem too much like Walter Benjamin. See Santner, *On the Psychotheology of Everyday Life: Reflections on Freud and Rosenzweig* (Chicago: University of Chicago Press, 2001), 136, 142.

30. Cordula Hufnagel, "Das Volksspiel als johanneischen Fest," in Schmied-Kowarzik, ed., *Der Philosoph Franz Rosenzweig*, 981.

31. Rosenzweig never named the painting, but the letter describes *The Tempest* in perfect detail.

32. Heinrich Wölfflin, *Principles of Art History: The Problem of the Development of Style in Later Art*, trans. M. D. Hottinger (Mineola, N.Y.: Dover, 1932), 14–17. The exact status of the aesthetic and its place in Rosenzweig's thought remain unclear in the secondary literature. Giancarlo Baffo has argued that scholarship has paid too much attention to epistemological questions and not enough to aesthetics. Even Rosenzweig's best readers have not done justice to his "theory of art." I am not sure, for instance, why Stéphane Mosès placed his own discussion of Rosenzweig's aesthetic theory, material that appears throughout part 2 of *The Star of Redemption*, in the chapter where he analyzes Rosenzweig's understanding of Christianity, which appears in part 3 of Rosenzweig's text! Mosès has thus marginalized the aesthetic character of *The Star of Redemption* (even in its aural form) by relegating his analysis of it to the back pages of his own work—a superb study that, with this glaring exception, scrupulously follows the unfolding order of Rosenzweig's system. In my view, the "aesthetic theory" belongs not just to the proto-world of paganism of part 1 nor to the world of Christianity in part 3. Placed in part 2, it cuts to the center of revelation. The aesthetic sections threading through part 2 are not the disjointed bastard units that they might otherwise appear to be. Instead, they form a coherent, integrated nexus in which the elemental parts of Rosenzweig's system form an animated totality. See Giancarlo Baffo, "Die ästhetische Dimension im Denken Rosenzweigs," in Schmied-Kowarzik, ed., *Der Philosoph Franz Rosenzweig*, vol. 2, 965; Stéphane Mosès, *System and Revelation: The Philosophy of Franz Rosenzweig*, trans. Catherine Tihanyi (Detroit: Wayne State University Press, 1992), 237–50.

33. Benjamin, *Origin of the German Tragic Drama*, trans. Osborne, 54–55

34. Ibid., 28–29, 161, 178.

35. Georg Wilhelm Friedrich Hegel, *The Philosophy of Fine Art*, trans. F. P. B. Osmaston (New York: Hacker Art Books, 1975), 2: 175.

36. Ibid., 179.

37. Ibid., 262.

38. Ibid., 3: 121–22.

39. Ibid., 139–41.

40. Ibid., 223–24.

41. Wölfflin, *Principles of Art History*, 124–26.

42. Ibid., 15.

43. Ibid., 157.

44. Ibid., 174.

45. Ibid., 174–75.

46. Samuelson, *Introduction to Modern Jewish Philosophy*, 214, 216–17.

47. Wölfflin, *Principles of Art History*, 155–56; emphasis added.

48. Ibid., 156.

49. Leora Batnitzky takes Rosenzweig's critique of art at face value, which I think is profoundly problematic, but my own analysis here of the relation between aesthetics and truth accords with hers. See Batnitzky, *Idolatry and Representation: The Philosophy of Franz Rosenzweig Reconsidered* (Princeton: Princeton University Press, 2000), 86. Cf. Zachary Braiterman, "Der Ästhet Franz Rosenzweig: Beautiful Form and Religious Thought," *Journal of Jewish Thought and Philosophy* 10 (2000): 145–69.

50. Cf. Walter Sokel, *The Writer in Extremis: Expressionism in Twentieth-Century German Literature* (Stanford: Stanford University Press, 1959), 49–51. Sokel notes the technique in Trakl and Kakfa.

51. See Peter Eli Gordon, *Rosenzweig and Heidegger: Between Judaism and German Philosophy* (Berkeley: University of California Press, 2003), chap. 5. Gordon's analysis of Buber and Rosenzweig's use of the word *Dasein* is of particular interest (258–62).

52. Friedrich Schlegel, "Ideas," in id., *Philosophical Fragments*, trans. Peter Firchow (Minneapolis: University of Minnesota Press, 1991), no. 95.

53. Georg Wilhelm Friedrich Hegel, *Hegel's Science of Logic*, trans. W. H. Johnston and L. G. Struthers (London: George Allen & Unwin), 38–39.

54. On the reception of the Bible translation, see Martin Jay, "Politics of Translation: Siegfried Kracauer and Walter Benjamin on the Buber-Rosenzweig Translation," *Leo Baeck Institute Yearbook*, no. 21 (1976): 3–24; Lawrence Rosenwald, "On the Reception of Buber and Rosenzweig's Bible," *Prooftexts* 14 (1994): 141–65; Siegfried Kracauer, "The Bible in German: On the Translation by Martin Buber and Franz Rosenzweig," in id., *The Mass Ornament: Weimar Essays*, trans. Thomas Y. Levin (Cambridge, Mass.: Harvard University Press, 1995), 189–201.

55. Robert Alter, *Partial Magic: The Novel as a Self-Conscious Genre* (Berkeley: University of California Press, 1975), 153.

Chapter Two: Abstraction

1. For analyses of *Composition V* and the tension between reference to objects and pure abstraction, see Will Grohmann, *Kandinsky: Life and Work* (New York: Harry N. Abrams, 1958), 124, and Günter Brucher, *Kandinsky: Wege zur Abstraktion* (Munich: Prestel, 1999), 414–31.

2. Katz, *Post-Holocaust Dialogues*, 25–46.

3. The reference is in relation to Scholem and Kafka. Robert Alter, *Necessary Angels: Tradition and Modernity in Kafka, Benjamin, and Scholem* (Cambridge, Mass.: Harvard University Press, 1991), 109. For the correlation between abstract art, the philosophy of Ernst Cassier, and modern theoretical sciences, see Rainer Crone and David Moos, *Kazmir Malevitch: The Climax of Disclosure* (Chicago: University of Chicago Press, 1991), esp. chaps. 6–7.

4. For a recent work on revelation without content, see Norbert Samuelson, *Revelation and the God of Israel* (New York: Cambridge University Press, 2002).

5. Theodor W. Adorno, *Aesthetic Theory*, trans. Robert Hullot-Kentor (Minneapolis: University of Minnesota Press, 1997), 86.

6. Theodor W. Adorno, *The Jargon of Authenticity*, trans. Knut Tarnowski and Frederic Will (Evanston, Ill.: Northwestern University Press), 16.

7. Ibid., 17.

8. On stylization in Lilien's work, see M. S. Levussove, *The New Art of an Ancient People: The Work of Emphraim Moshe Lilien* (New York: B. W. Huebsch, 1906); Lothar Brieger, *E. M. Lilien: Eine künstlerische Entwicklung um die Jahrhundertwende* (Berlin: Benjamin Harz, 1922).

9. Kant, *Critique of Judgment*, trans. Pluhar, 135.

10. Hegel, *Philosophy of Fine Art*, 2: 103.

11. Worringer, *Abstraction and Empathy*, trans. Bullock, 18.

12. Siegfried Wichmann, *Japonisme: The Japanese Influence on Western Art in the 19th and 20th Centuries* (New York: Harmony Books, 1980).

13. Jacques Derrida, *Of Grammatology*, trans. Gayatri Chakravorty Spivak (Baltimore: Johns Hopkins University Press, 1974), 98.

14. Ibid., 155.

15. Ibid., 244.

16. Ibid., 255.

17. Kant, *Critique of Judgment*, trans. Pluhar, 122–23.

18. Hugo von Hofmannstahl, *The Lord Chandos Letter*, trans. Russell Stockman (Marlboro, Vt.: Marlboro Press, 1986).

19. Maurice S. Friedman notes the affinity between Rilke and Buber in his introduction to Martin Buber, *Daniel: Dialogues on Realization*, trans. Maurice S.

Friedman (New York: Holt, Rinehart & Winston, 1964), 15–18.

20. See Theodore Ziolkowski, *The View from the Tower: Origins of an Antimodernist Image* (Princeton: Princeton University Press, 1998).

21. The relevant passages are scattered throughout the section. I have paraphrased the material while retaining Buber's own choice of words.

22. Cited in Derrida, *Of Spirit*, trans. Bennington and Bowlby, 98.

23. Novalis, *Henry von Ofterdingen*, trans. Palmer Hilty (New York: Frederick Ungar, 1964), 118.

24. Stefan George, "The Seventh Ring," in *The Works of Stefan George Rendered into English*, trans. Olga Marx and Ernst Morwits, 2d ed. (Chapel Hill: University of North Carolina Press), 174, 258.

25. Schmutzler, *Art Nouveau*, 260–72.

26. John Rupert Martin, *Baroque* (New York: Harper & Row, 1977), 224–50.

27. Ibid., 223.

28. Norbert Samuelson, "The Concept of 'Nichts' in Rosenzweig's *Star of Redemption*," in Schmied-Kowarzik, ed., *Der Philosoph Franz Rosenzweig*, vol. 2, 646–47. Cf. Franz Rosenzweig, *Understanding the Sick and the Healthy: A View of World, Man, and God*, ed. N. N. Glatzer (Cambridge, Mass.: Harvard University Press, 1999), 54–59, 76–78.

29. Kant, *Critique of Judgment*, trans. Pluhar, 68.

30. See esp. Dabrowski, *Kandinsky*, 34–35, 38.

31. Grohmann, *Kandinsky: Life and Work*, 112.

32. Adorno, *Aesthetic Theory*, 87.

33. Ibid., 1.

34. Ibid., 39–40.

35. Ibid., 5–6.

36. Ibid., 9.

37. Ibid., 177.

38. Kant, *Critique of Pure Reason*, trans. Norman Kemp Smith, 523.

39. David E. Wellbery, *Lessing's Laocoon: Semiotics and Aesthetics in the Age of Reason* (Cambridge: Cambridge University Press, 1984), 4–5, 23–24, 31–35. See Alexander Gottlieb Baumgarten, *Reflections on Poetry*, trans. Karl Aschenbrenner and William B. Holther (Berkeley: University of California Press, 1954), nos. 45 and 48. Moses Mendelssohn, "On the Sublime and Naive in the Fine Sciences," in id., *Philosophical Writings*, trans. and ed. Daniel O. Dahlstrom (Cambridge: Cambridge University Press, 1997), 208–10. See Rainer Maria Rilke, *Letters on Cézanne* (New York: North Point Press, 2002); Jacques Le Rider, *Hugo von Hofmannsthal: Historismus und Moderne in der Literatur der Jahrhundertwende*, trans. Leopold Federmair (Vienna: Böhlau, 1997), 199–228.

40. Meyer Schapiro, *Modern Art: 19th & 20th Centuries*, Selected Papers, vol. 2 (New York: George Braziller, 1978), 229.

41. Ibid., 224.

42. Johanna Drucker, *Theorizing Modernism: Visual Art and the Critical Tradition* (New York : Columbia University Press, 1994), 151–53.

43. Max Scheler, *On the Eternal in Man*, trans. Bernard Noble (Hamden, Conn.: Archon Books, 1972), 126–27.

44. Adorno, *Aesthetic Theory*, 60.

45. Ibid., 78.

46. Ibid., 79.

Chapter Three: Pathos

1. Stefan Zweig, "Das neue Pathos," and Rudolf Kayser "Verkündigung," in Paul Pörtner, *Literaturrevolution, 1910–1925: Dokumente, Manifeste, Programme*, vol. 1 (Darmstadt: Hermann Luchterhand, 1960), 231–35, 259–63.

2. Douglas Kahn, *Noise, Water, Meat: A History of Sound in the Arts* (Cambridge, Mass.: MIT Press, 1999), 2.

3. Ibid., 1–3, 16.

4. Arnold Schoenberg, *Theory of Harmony* (1911), trans. Roy E. Carter (1978; reprint, Berkeley: University of California Press, 1983), 19.

5. Paul Mendes-Flohr, *Divided Passions: Jewish Intellectuals and the Experience of Modernity* (Detroit: Wayne State University Press, 1991), 253, 268.

6. Theodor W. Adorno, *Mahler: A Musical Physiognomy*, trans. Edmund Jephcott (Chicago: University of Chicago Press, 1992), 6.

7. For the critical response to the Buber hasidica writ large in its relation to Hasidism as a historical phenomenon, see Gershom Scholem, "Martin Buber's Interpretation of Hasidism," in id., *The Messianic Idea in Judaism* (New York: Schocken Books, 1971); Steven Katz, "Martin Buber's Misuse of Hasidic Sources," in *Post-Holocaust Dialogues: Critical Studies in Modern Jewish Thought* (New York: New York University Press, 1985). Rivkah Schatz-Uffenheimer focuses on hasidica from the 1940s. See Schatz-Uffenheimer, "Man's Relation to God and World in Buber's Rendering of the Hasidic Teaching," in Paul Arthur Schilp and Maurice S. Friedman, eds., *The Philosophy of Martin Buber* (La Salle, Ill.: Open Court, 1967). In contrast, scholars whose own primary interest is German Jewish culture at the turn of the century tend to focus on the early hasidica, and do so with much greater sympathy. See Steven E. Aschheim, *Brothers and Strangers: The East European Jew in German and German Jewish Consciousness, 1800–1923* (Madison: University of Wisconsin Press, 1982), chap. 5. See esp. Paul Mendes-Flohr, "Fin de Siècle Orientalism, the *Ostjuden*, and the Aesthetics of Jewish Self-Affirmation," in id., *Divided Passions*. Mendes-Flohr notes the Jugendstil character of Buber's early work, especially his hasidica. See also Mendes-Flohr, *From Mysticism to Dialogue*, 83–86, 91–92. The counterarguments posed by Kepnes and Silberstein to Katz and Scholem appear in Steven Kepnes, *The Text as Thou: Martin Buber's Dialogi-*

cal Hermeneutics and Narrative Theology (Bloomington: Indiana University Press, 1992), 10–40; Laurence J. Silberstein, *Martin Buber's Social and Religious Thought: Alienation and the Quest for Meaning* (New York: New York University Press), chap. 2. By and large, Silberstein objects more strenuously to Scholem's historicist approach, whereas Kepnes suggests a middle position that would seek to bridge the gap between Buber and his critics. In part this may result from the regard with which Kepnes holds the "text" in relation to the individual interpreter.

8. Rainer Maria Rilke, [1907] *New Poems*, trans. Edward Snow (New York: Farrar, Straus & Giroux, 1984), 87.

9. Kahn, *Noise, Water, Meat*, 206.

10. Although the tension between form and content has bedeviled Buber's hasidica from start to finish, it is important to contrast the early and the later work. Compared to the early hasidica, the tales from after the war lack the art nouveau beauty. Expressionism encouraged Buber to stay true to the rough form of the original source material. In terms of philosophical content, however, the latter tales reflect a this worldly spirit at odds with important tenets of hasidic mysticism. Ironically, the early neoromantic work, so foreign in style to the original material, actually resonates with the mystical bent in hasidic theology in ways that the later work does not. This tension between form and content plays out in the critical, typically hostile reception in the secondary literature. Scholem, Katz, and Schatz-Uffenheimer focus their critique almost exclusively on the later body of work, which allows them to complain that Buber obscured the mystical element in Hasidism. Yet even Scholem admits that the early hasidica retain a mystical spirit. He calls the introductory essay to the Baal Shem Tov book ("The Life of Hasidim"), which was reprinted in *Hasidism and Modern Man*, "justly famous." See Gershom Scholem, "Martin Buber's Interpretation of Hasidism," 231, 240–44. See also Katz, "Martin Buber's Misuse of Hasidic Sources," 87.

11. Gershom Scholem, "At the Completion of Buber's Translation of the Bible," in id., *Messianic Idea in Judaism*, 316.

12. See Siegfried Kracauer, "The Bible in German." Kracauer detects the influence of Wagner and Stefan George. But in its deliberate primitivism, the choice of words lacks the former's sonority or the latter's slickness. The harsh and awkward effect have more in common with expressionism.

13. Walter J. Ong, *Orality and Literacy: The Technologizing of the Word* (London: Methuen, 1982). Ong includes a broad, albeit partisan, review of the scholarly literature regarding the priority of oral culture over written culture. For a more phenomenological approach, see Walter J. Ong, *The Presence of the Word: Some Prolegomena for Cultural and Religious History* (New Haven: Yale University Press, 1967), the epigraph to which cites Rosenzweig's friend Eugen Rosentock-Huessy, indicating a genealogy that includes subjects of the present book. Ong's approach is relentlessly "oralist" in its privileging of sound over against script. In both books, Ong makes claims regarding the originally oral character of the

Hebrew Bible. For a more systematic argument regarding the impact of oral culture on the written biblical word, see Susan Niditch, *Oral and Written Word: Ancient Israelite Literature* (Louisville, Ky.: Westminster John Knox Press, 1996). See in contrast the work of James Watts, who in his study of biblical law argues against the oralists. Watts argues that biblical legal lists first took shape as a literary form meant to be read aloud. "Only in its Mosaic origins is biblical law depicted as the transcription of orally proclaimed law . . . and even then, its core is received in writing," he contends. See James W. Watts, *Reading Law: The Rhetorical Shaping of the Pentateuch* (Sheffield: Sheffield Academic Press, 1999), 23. As for the interplay between oral and written culture in rabbinic and medieval Judaism, see Martin S. Jaffee, *Torah in the Mouth: Writing and Oral Tradition in Palestinian Judaism 200 BCE–400 CE,* (Oxford: Oxford University Press, 2001), and Yaakov Elman and Israel Gershoni, eds., *Transmitting Jewish Traditions: Orality, Textuality, and Cultural Diffusion* (New Haven: Yale University Press, 2000).

14. Kahn, *Noise, Water, Meat,* 70; and see 70–71 in general.

15. Ibid., 70.

16. Ibid., 4, 360n3.

17. Ibid., 75.

18. Cited in Peter-Klaus Schuster, *Franz Marc: Postcards to Prince Jussuf* (Munich: Prestel, 1988), 25.

19. Klaus Lankheit, *Franz Marc: Sein Leben und seine Kunst* (Cologne: DuMont, 1976), 78; Levine, *Apocalyptic Vision,* 60.

20. Cited in Levine, *Apocalyptic Vision,* 77.

21. Ibid., 100.

22. Cited by Bryan R. Simms, *The Atonal Music of Arnold Schoenberg, 1908–1923* (Oxford: Oxford University Press, 2000), 151–52.

23. Max Brod, *Paganism, Christianity, Judaism: A Confession of Faith* (1921), trans. William Wolf (University, Ala.: University of Alabama Press, 1970), 5.

24. Karl Barth, *Epistles to the Romans* (London, Oxford University Press, 1933). Rudolf Otto, *The Idea of the Holy,* trans. John W. Harvey (New York: Oxford University Press, 1958), esp. chap. 5. For a critique of Barth, see Rosenzweig, *Briefe und Tagebücher,* 875 (*BT*). For Buber, God remained other, but not "wholly other." He wrote against Otto's approach in *I and Thou,* 127 (*IT*), and in "Replies to My Critics," in Schilpp and Friedman, eds, *Philosophy of Martin Buber,* 712.

25. Rosenzweig, *Understanding the Sick and Healthy,* 101–2. See also Else-Rahel Freund, *Franz Rosenzweig's Philosophy of Existence: An Analysis of "The Star of Redemption"* (The Hague: Martinus Nijhoff, 1979), 3–5. In line with Glatzer, Freund has argued that "from death into life" constitutes the entire meaning of Rosenzweig's "existential analytic." See esp. Stéphane Mosès, "Franz Rosenzweig in Perspective: Reflections on His Last Diaries," in Paul Mendes-Flohr, ed., *The Philosophy of Franz Rosenzweig* (Hanover, N.H.: University Press of New England, 1988), 191–93. My analysis coincides with that of Mosès in all but one respect.

Mosès also characterizes Rosenzweig as a quietist for whom love gives only spiritual life and mystical vision. However, he does so on the basis of Rosenzweig's latest and unpublished diary entries. Mosès concedes that realism and terrestrial life constitute the ultimate word in *The Star of Redemption*. It is not a concession I would make. See Zachary Braiterman, "'Into Life'? Franz Rosenzweig and the Figure of Death," *AJS Review* 23, no. 2 (1998): 203–21. Elliot Wolfson has anticipated most of my remarks as they relate to death in "Facing the Effaced: Mystical Eschatology and the Idealistic Orientation in the Thought of Franz Rosenzweig," *Zeitschrift für neuere Theologiegeschichte* 4 (1997): 39–81. A scholar of kabbalah, Wolfson exhibits much greater ease than most modern Jewish philosophers with the appearance of death and the acosmic element. As evidence, his analysis includes many of the passages drawn from the Rosenzweig corpus that appear in my own.

26. See Wolfson, "Facing the Effaced," 64–70. Against Scholem, Wolfson locates Rosenzweig within the apocalyptic tradition. In this view, Rosenzweig's notion of redemption takes from the neoplatonic notion of *apokatastasis*, according to which all things ultimately return to their source in the One (70).

27. In his translation, Hallo renders *Triumphsgeschreit* as "triumphal shout." He thereby misses the transformation that the word *Schrei* undergoes. For a contrasting view to mine, see Robert Gibbs, *Correlations in Rosenzweig and Levinas* (Princeton: Princeton University Press, 1992), 101–4. While Gibbs correctly notes the sensitivity to human suffering, the *Schrei* remains short-lived, unable to outpace the *Triumphsgeschrei* at the end of redemption. Martin Kavka has perhaps best understood the degree to which the chorus drowns out suffering. According to Kavka, the soul as depicted by Rosenzweig never really talks to its neighbor. In my view, this is has not a little bit to do with all the death-pathos in Rosenzweig's text. For Kavka, this represents an ethical problem, although I myself understand how the contemplation of death might come to overwhelm everyday ethics. The problem is not ethical so much as acoustic. See Martin Kavka, *Messianism and the History of Philosophy* (New York: Cambridge University Press, 2004), chap. 4.

28. On the asymmetry of judgment, see Batnitzky, *Idolatry and Representation*, esp. 155–62.

29. See the discussion of this letter in Stéphane Mosès, "Franz Rosenzweig in Perspective," 191–92. See also Werner Marx, *"Die Bestimmung des Todes im 'Stern der Erlosung,'"* in Schmied-Kowarzik, ed., *Der Philosoph Franz Rosenzweig*, 612–15.

30. Wolfson, "Facing the Effaced," 80.

31. Gibbs, *Correlations in Rosenzweig and Levinas*. Cf. Stéphane Mosès, *System and Revelation* and "Franz Rosenzweig in Perspective." Richard A. Cohen, *Elevations: The Height of the Good in Rosenzweig and Levinas* (Chicago: University of Chicago Press, 1994), 70–71.

32. Russell A. Berman, *The Rise of the Modern German Novel: Crisis and Charisma* (Cambridge, Mass.: Harvard University Press, 1986), 204.

33. For the idea of Yom Kippur as "the apex of Jewish existence," see Emil Fackenheim, "The Systematic Role of the Matrix (Existence) and Apex (Yom Kippur) of Jewish Religious Life in Rosenzweig's "Star of Redemption," in Schmied-Kowarzik, ed., *Der Philosoph Franz Rosenzweig*.

34. See Mosès, *System and Revelation*, 284–86; Cohen, *Elevations*, 241–67. Wolfson, "Facing the Effaced," 74–81.

35. *Tanhuma va-ethanan* 6, Deuteronomy Rabbah 11:10, and Moses Maimonides, *Guide of the Perplexed*, III: 53.

36. Nahum Glatzer, *Franz Rosenzweig: His Life and Thought* (New York: Schocken Books, 1953), 115.

37. For a similar opinion see Barbara Ellen Galli, "Placing the Halevi Book, Rosenzweig, and the *Star*," in id., *Franz Rosenzweig and Jehuda Halevi*, 289 (*H*).

38. See Zachary Braiterman, *(God) After Auschwitz: Tradition and Change in Post-Holocaust Jewish Thought* (Princeton: Princeton University Press, 1998), chap. 3.

39. Novalis, *Hymns to the Night*, trans. Dick Higgins (Kingston, N.Y.: McPherson, 1978), 15 (my trans.).

40. Ibid., 31.

41. Ibid., 37.

42. In his study *An Episode of Jewish Romanticism: Franz Rosenzweig's "The Star of Redemption"* (Albany: State University of New York Press, 1999), 68–85, 144–53, Ernest Rubinstein links these themes first to Leo Baeck's broadside against "romantic religion" and then to Schelling.

43. Karl Barth, *Protestant Theology in the Nineteenth Century: Its Background and History* (London: SLM Press, 1959), 380.

44. Schoenberg, *Theory of Harmony*, 29–30.

45. Ibid., 309.

46. Ibid., 421–42.

47. Ibid., 239.

48. Thomas Grochowiak, *Ludwig Meidner* (Recklinghausen, Germany: Aurel Bongers, 1966), 180.

Chapter Four: Time

1. William Rubin, "Modernist Primitivism: An Introduction," in id., ed., *"Primitivism" in 20th Century Art: Affinity of the Tribal and the Modern* (New York: Museum of Modern Art, 1984), 1:11. See also E. H. Gombrich, *The Preference for the Primitive: Episodes in the History of Western Taste and Art* (London: Phaidon Press, 2002). Gombrich traces the "lure of the primitive" back to Plato and the revival of Platonism in eighteenth-century English and German aesthetics. The primitive represents the elemental, the sublime, and the spiritual in the struggle against the corrupting influence of illusion, beauty, and culture.

2. Peg Weiss, *Kandinsky in Munich, 1896–1914* (New York: Solomon Guggenheim Museum, 1982), 78–79. For a more general discussion of Kandinsky's relation to St. George, see Peg Weiss, *Kandinsky and Old Russia* (New Haven: Yale University Press, 1995), 76–77, 145–53. See also, Günther Brucher, *Kandinsky: Wege zur Abstraktion*, (Munich: Prestel, 1999).

3. The quotations are from Charles Baudelaire, "The Painter of Modern Life," in *The Painter of Modern Life and Other Essays*, trans. and ed. Jonathan Mayne (Greenwich, Conn.: Phaidon, 1968), 9, 12, 13, 15.

4. In chapters 3 and 4 of *Natural Supernaturalism: Tradition and Revolution in Romantic Literature* (New York: Norton, 1971), M. H. Abrams locates the theme of the circuitous journey in Plotinus, Proclus, Goethe, Novalis, Schelling, Hegel, and Holderlin. In *Radical Hermeneutics: Repetition, Deconstruction, and the Hermeneutic Project* (Bloomington: Indiana University Press, 1987), John Caputo builds upon Nietzsche's eternal recurrence, Kierkegaardarian repetition, Husserl's analysis of time-consciousness, and Heideggerian historicity and appropriation.

5. Walter Benjamin, "Theses on the Philosophy of History," in id., *Illuminations*, 261. Robert Gibbs, "Lines, Circles, Points: Messianic Epistemology in Cohen, Rosenzweig and Benjamin," in Peter Schäfer and Mark Cohen, eds., *Toward the Millennium: Messianic Expectations from the Bible to Waco* (Leiden: Brill, 1998), 363–82.

6. Georg Simmel, *The Conflict in Modern Culture and Other Essays*, trans. K. Peter Etzkirn (New York: Teachers College Press, 1968), 25. The identification of Simmel with impressionism belongs to David Frisby, *Sociological Impressionism: A Reassessment of Georg Simmel's Social Theory* (New York : Routledge, 1992).

7. Georg G. Iggers, *The German Conception of History: The National Tradition of Historical Thought from Herder to the Present* (1968; rev. ed., Middletown, Conn.: Wesleyan University Press, 1983), 295–98nn1, 4, and 5. On anti-historicism in modern Jewish thought, see David N. Myers, *Resisting History: Historicism and Its Discontents in German-Jewish Thought* (Princeton: Princeton University Press, 2003).

8. Jörn Rüssen, *Geschichte des Historismus* (Munich, C. H. Beck, 1992), 141–46; Charles R. Bambach, *Heidegger, Dilthey, and the Crisis of Historicism* (Ithaca, N.Y.: Cornell University Press, 1995), 22; Iggers, *German Conception of History*, 124–27.

9. Wilhelm Dilthey, *Introduction to the Human Sciences*, ed. Rudolf A. Makkreel and Frithjof Rodi (Princeton: Princeton University Press, 1989), 238.

10. See Iggers, *German Conception of History*, 124–34, 139, 152. Cf. Bambach, *Heidegger, Dilthey, and the Crisis of Historicism*, 22–26, 40.

11. Max Weber, *The Protestant Ethic and the Spirit of Capitalism*, trans. Talcott Parsons (New York: Scribner, 1958), 181–82. See also id., "Politics as a Vocation" and "Science as a Vocation," in *From Max Weber: Essays in Sociology*, trans. H. H. Gerth and C. Wright Mills, (New York: Oxford University Press, 1946).

12. Oswald Spengler, *The Decline of the West*, trans. Charles Francis Atkinson (New York: Knopf, 1937), 6–7, 31–39.

13. Donald Gordon, *Expressionism: Art and Idea* (New Haven: Yale University Press, 1987), 25.

14. See *OMH*, 234–. In this late essay, Buber criticized Zen Buddhism for rejecting history. However, the argument affirming the importance of history does not obviate the basic anti-historicist argument. Historical context does not restrict the value of historical forms, which remain subject to regeneration and renewal.

15. Mosès, *System and Revelation*, 170–75.

16. Paul Mendes-Flohr, "Rosenzweig and the Crisis of Historicism," in id., ed., *Philosophy of Franz Rosenzweig*, 159. Paraphrasing Rosenzweig, Alexander Altmann states: "God must redeem man not through history but—there is no alternative—through religion." Altmann, "Franz Rosenzweig on History," ibid., 132.

17. Kaufman translates *gegenseitig* as "mutuality." The proper English translation overlooks the tension suggested by the German prefix. See Buber's 1928 essay "The Baal Shem Tov's Instruction in Intercourse with God," reprinted in *Hasidism and Modern Man*, where the author identifies "standing over against" with "real mutuality" (*HMM*, 180).

18. Wolfgang Rothe, *Expressionismus als Literatur: Gesammelte Studien* (Bern: Francke, 1969), 83.

19. Pörtner, *Literaturrevolution*, 1: 184.

20. Margaret Mahony Stoljar, ed. and trans., *Novalis: Philosophical Writings*, (Albany: State University of New York Press, 1997), 137–52.

21. Peter Szondi, "Friedrich Schlegel and Romantic Irony, with Some Remarks on Tieck's Comedies," in *On Textual Understanding and Other Essays* (Minneapolis: University of Minnesota Press, 1986), 57, 58, 63–64. Jochen Schulte-Sasse's critique of Paul de Man is of interest here. Schulte-Sasse agrees with de Man that romantics recognized the inevitable and even permanent cleft between ideal and representation, subject and object. But they never renounced the *desire* for the infinite, even if it remained neither reachable nor representable. Undetermined and unstructured, the infinite is that which creates a common point of stability and unity. In this way, acts of reflection that surpass "distance and difference" supplement romantic allegory and irony. See Schulte-Sasse, ed., *Theory as Practice: A Critical Anthology of Early German Romantics* (Minneapolis: University of Minnesota Press, 1997), 22–25, 41.

22. Hermann Obrist, *Neue Möglichkeiten in der bildenen Kunst* (Leipzig: Eugen Diederichs, 1903), 32–35.

23. Ibid., 49–54.

24. Ibid., 96–97. See also Henry van de Velde, *Vom neuen Stil* (Leipzig: Insel, 1907).

25. The first comment is by Carl Georg Heise in "Begegnung mit Emil Nolde" in the journal *Brücke-Archiv* and the second by Jenns Howoldt. Both are cited in Jenns Howoldt, "'Weckruf des großen Aufbruch' Emil Noldes religiöse Bilder als Leitbilder des Expressionismus," in *Emil Nolde, Legende,*

Vision, Ekstase: Die religiösen Bilder, ed. Annabelle Görgen (Cologne: DuMont; Hamburg: Hamburger Kunsthalle in Zusammenarbeit mit der Nolde-Stiftung Seebüll, 2000), 24.

26. Emil Nolde, *Jahre der Kämpfe* (Berlin: Remandt), 108.

27. On the eclectic mix of borrowed styles informing expressionist art, see Gordon, *Expressionism*, 70.

28. Jill Lloyd, *German Expressionism: Primitivism and Modernity* (New Haven: Yale University Press, 1991), 47–48.

29. Ludwig Meidner, "An Introduction to Painting the Metropolis," in Washton Long, *German Expressionism*, 104.

30. Lloyd, *German Expressionism*, 177, 179–80.

31. While Daniel Breslauer has argued that one cannot understand Buber's text apart from its relation to Jewish tradition, he notes the "ambiguous content" and calls *I and Thou* a "prologue" to Judaism. S. Daniel Breslauer, *The Chrysalis of Religion: A Guide to the Jewishness of Buber's I and Thou* (Nashville, Tenn.: Abingdon, 1980), esp. 9–24. Likewise, Walter Kaufmann notes in his introduction to *I and Thou* that "The book is steeped in Judaism" without quite showing where, apart from general references to the second commandment and to the idea of return (*IT*, 32, 32–37). His running notes that follow the text are more instructive.

32. Kepnes, *Text as Thou*, 150. Cf. 22.

33. Mosès, *System and Revelation*, 170.

34. Gilles Deleuze, *Difference and Repetition*, trans. Paul Patton (New York: Columbia University Press, 1994), 90.

35. Judah Halevi, *The Kuzari (Kitab al Khazari): An Argument for the Faith of Israel*, trans. Hartwig Hirschfeld (New York: Schocken Books, 1964), 140.

36. Mosès, *System and Revelation*, 170–72, 223.

37. Deleuze, *Difference and Repetition*, 17.

38. Jacques Derrida, *Limited Inc* (Evanston, Ill.: Northwestern University Press, 1988), 12.

39. Søren Kierkegaard, *Fear and Trembling/Repetition*, ed. and trans. Howard V. Hong and Edna H. Hong (Princeton: Princeton University Press, 1983), 220–21.

40. Arthur Cohen, *The Natural and the Supernatural Jew: A Historical and Theological Introduction* (New York: Pantheon Books, 1962), 294, see esp. chaps. 3–4. For more of the same, see Abraham Joshua Heschel, *God in Search of Man* (New York: Farrar, Straus & Cudahy, 1955), chap. 21; id., *Israel: An Echo of Eternity* (New York: Farrar, Straus & Giroux, 1969), chap. 4; Abba Hillel Silver, *Where Judaism Differed* (New York: Macmillan, 1956), chap. 2, "Will"); Will Herberg, *Judaism and Modern Man* (New York: Farrar, Straus & Young, 1951), chaps. 15–16; Robert Gordis, *A Faith for Moderns* (New York: Ktav, 1973), chap. 7.

41. Theodor W. Adorno, *Philosophy of Modern Music*, trans. Anne G. Mitchell and Wesley V. Blomster (1973; reprint, New York: Continuum, 2003), 160.

42. Gershom Scholem, *From Berlin to Jerusalem: Memories of My Youth*, trans. Harry Zohn, (New York: Schocken Books, 1980), 140.

43. Berman, *Rise of the Modern German Novel*, 280–82.

44. Ibid., 222–25.

45. Deleuze, *Difference and Repetition*, xx.

Chapter Five: Space

1. Sigfried Giedion, *Space, Time, and Architecture: The Growth of a New Tradition*, (1941; 5th ed., Cambridge, Mass.: Harvard University Press, 1966), 493–97.

2. Simmel, "Religion," in *Essays on Religion*, 200.

3. Ferdinand Tönnies, *Community & Society* (New York: Harper & Row, 1963), 229.

4. Ibid., 227.

5. If only at the most superficial level, Buber's work appears to lend itself to Tönnies's conception. The YOU-world would seem to correspond to that intimate social space formed by *Gemeinschaft,* while the IT-world jibes with impersonal *Gesellschaft.* For its part, the social ideal set out in *Paths of Utopia* (1947) is based on "small and ever smaller communities," a "community of communities," suggesting a *Gemeinschaft* ideal (*PIU*, 136, 137). Rosenzweig's understanding of Jewish community (family, congregation, *Lehrhaus*) seems to fit the same narrow mold. In contrast, Mendes-Flohr indicates the degree to which, from early on, Buber's notion of a new *Gemeinschaft* was quite unlike the notion of community in Tönnies. He notes in particular the absence of a common symbolic center in Buber's conception as laid out in the early essay, *"Alte und neue Gemeinschaft."* See Mendes-Flohr, *From Mysticism to Dialogue,* 76–82 and esp. 163n274. On the close connection between Buber and Tönnies, see Silberstein, *Martin Buber's Social and Religious Thought,* 32–35, 182–83.

6. Walter Gropius, "Program of the Staatliche Bauhaus in Weimar," in Hans M. Wingler, *The Bauhaus* (Cambridge, Mass.: MIT Press, 1969), 31. For a basic discussion of the Bauhaus and its antecedents, see Frank Whitford, *Bauhaus* (London: Thames & Hudson, 1984).

7. Gropius quoted in Whitford, *Bauhaus,* 120.

8. Hermann Obrist, *Neue Möglichkeiten in der bildenden Kunst* (Leipzig: Eugen Diederichs, 1903), 4–5, 35–37, 48–49, 141, 167.

9. Ibid., 167–68.

10. Henry van de Velde, *Vom neuen Stil* (Leipzig: Insel, 1907), 14–15.

11. Ibid., 46.

12. See Eleonore Lappin, *Der Jude, 1916–1928* (Tübingen: Mohr Siebeck, 2000), 131–33, 219, 371, 408. Among others, Lappin cites Hugo Bergmann, Gershom Scholem, David Koigen, and A. D. Gordon.

13. Ludwig Meidner, "An Introduction to Painting the Metropolis," in Washton Long, *German Expressionism*, 101–3.

14. "Bildung und kein Ende" was published in 1920, *The Star of Redemption* in 1921. Despite the earlier publication date, the essay on the Freies Jüdisches Lehrhaus reflects the more open spirit that informed Rosenzweig's writings in the 1920s. For its part, *Star* reflects the period of its literary gestation, the years 1918–19, following World War I, and thus the more closed-in conception found in the earlier essay "Zeit ist's" (1917).

15. On the crystal shrines designed by the expressionist architects Bruno Taut and Paul Scheerbart, see Timothy O. Benson, ed., *Expressionist Utopias: Paradise, Metropolis, Architectural Fantasy* (Berkeley: University of California Press, 2001).

16. László Moholy-Nagy, "Theater, Circus, Variety," in Walter Gropius, ed., *The Theater of the Bauhaus*, trans. Arthur S. Wensinger (Middletown, Conn.: Wesleyan University Press, 1961), 68. Originally published as *Die Bühne im Bauhaus* (Munich: Albert Langen, 1924).

17. Cited by Lappin, *Der Jude*, 411.

18. Wolfgang Schivelbusch, *Intellektuellendämmerung: Zur Lage der Frankfurter Intelligenz in den zwanziger Jahren* (Frankfurt: Insel, 1982), 40.

19. Walter Benjamin, "The Task of the Translator," in id., *Illuminations*, 69–82.

20. Scholem, "At the Completion of Buber's Bible Translation," in id., *Messianic Idea in Judaism*, 318.

21. Gershom Scholem, "Against the Myth of the German-Jewish Dialogue," in *On Jews and Judaism in Crisis* (New York: Schocken Books, 1976), 64.

22. See Mendes-Flohr, *From Mysticism to Dialogue*, chap. 3.

23. Ibid., 46.

24. See Paul Mendes-Flohr, "The Desert Within and Social Renewal: Martin Buber's Vision of Utopia," and Gregory Kaplan, "Response to Paul Mendes-Flohr's Commentary," *Religion and Culture Web Forum*, University of Chicago Divinity School, February 2003, http://marty-center.uchicago.edu/webforum/022003/response_kaplan.shtml (accessed September 17, 2006).

25. Mendes-Flohr, *From Mysticism to Dialogue*, 76–78, 112.

26. Ibid., 113–19.

27. Martin Buber and Hermann Cohen, "Martin Buber and Hermann Cohen: A Debate on Zionism and Messianism," in Paul Mendes-Flohr and Jehuda Reinharz, eds., *The Jew in the Modern World: A Documentary History* (New York: Oxford University Press, 1980), 448–53.

28. Peter Behrens, *Feste des Lebens und der Kunst: Eine Betrachtung des Theaters als höchster Kultursymbols* (Leipzig: Eugen Diederichs, 1900), 14–15, 17–18.

Chapter Six: Eros

1. Jane Kallir, *Egon Schiele: Love and Death* (Ostfildern-Ruit, Germany: Hatje Cantz, 2005), 78.

2. Klaus Albrecht Schröder, *Egon Schiele: Eros and Passion* (Munich: Prestel, 1995), 58–60.

3. Ibid., 90.

4. Cohen, *Religion of Reason*, 455.

5. Ibid., 456.

6. Ibid., 457; trans. modified.

7. Ibid., 458.

8. See esp. "Politics as a Vocation" and "The Sociology of Charismatic Authority" in Max Weber, *From Max Weber: Essays in Sociology* (New York: Oxford University Press, 1953), 78–9, 245–300. Cf. Berman, *Rise of the Modern German Novel*, 58. Berman calls the baroque novel traditional, the nineteenth-century novel bureaucratic, and the modernist novel charismatic.

9. Robert C. Elliott, *The Literary Persona* (Chicago: University of Chicago Press, 1982), 5.

10. Sander Gilman, *Inscribing the Other* (Lincoln: University of Nebraska Press, 1991), 31.

11. Many thanks to David Bakan, Daniel Breslauer, and Gesine Palmer for help with this material and its German.

12. For a discussion relating the impact of Nietzsche upon young Zionists at the turn of the century, particularly Buber and Berdichevsky, see Steven E. Aschheim, *The Nietzsche Legacy in Germany, 1890–1990* (Berkeley: University of California Press, 1992), 104–12. On the use of Herzl in Lilien's image, see Michael Stanislawski, *Zionism and the Fin de Siècle: Cosmopolitanism and Nationalism from Nordau to Jabotinsky* (Berkeley: University of California Press, 2001), 112–13.

13. Peter Selz, *German Expressionist Painting* (Berkeley: University of California Press, 1957), 157.

14. As Steven Aschheim remarks, Buber pulled a broad, sophisticated readership into the magical orbit of Judaism, the crème de la crème of German letters— Georg Simmel, Walter Rathenau, Gustav Landauer, Oswald Spengler, Hugo von Hofmannsthal, Rainer Maria Rilke, and Arnold Zweig—not to mention members of the younger generation of Jewish intellectuals. Aschheim, *Brothers and Strangers: The East European Jew in German and German Jewish Consciousness 1800–1923* (Madison: University of Wisconsin Press, 1982), 127–35.

15. Nahum N. Glatzer, *The Memories of Nahum N. Glatzer*, ed. Michael Fishbane and Judith Glatzer Wechsler (Cincinnati: Hebrew Union College Press, 1997), 101.

16. Eric Santer points to the letter to Meinecke as a mark of the author's turn away from the vampire-life of academic scholarship and aesthetic pleasure back to the world of everyday, ethical life and its picayune details. Eric L. Santner, *On the Psychotheology of Everyday Life: Reflections on Freud and Rosenzweig* (Chicago: University of Chicago Press, 2001), 15–19.

17. Cited in Pörtner, *Literaturrevolution*, 1: 175.

18. George L. Mosse, *The Image of Man: The Creation of Modern Masculinity* (Oxford: Oxford University Press, 1996), 39.

19. Ibid., 53–55, 102.

20. Ibid., 94–95.

21. George L. Mosse, *Nationalism and Sexuality: Respectability and Abnormal Sexuality in Modern Europe* (New York: Howard Fertig, 1985), 44.

22. Hans Blüher, *Die Rolle der Erotik in der männlichen Gesellschaft: Eine Theorie der menschlichen Staatsbildung nach Wesen und Wert* (Jena: E. Diederichs, 1917–19), 2: 38.

23. Ibid., 39.

24. Maimonides used the image of the kiss (*Guide of the Perplexed* III: 51) to symbolize the philosophically perfected soul at its death as it unites with the Active Intellect. His use of the image speaks *against* sensation. Any sexual trace has been so radically sublimated as to bear no reference to any human facet.

25. Eve Kosofsky Sedgwick, *Between Men: English Literature and Male Homosexual Desire* (New York: Columbia University Press, 1985), chap. 1. See esp., too, Michael Zank, "The Rosenzweig-Rosenstock Triangle, or, What Can We Learn from *Letters to Gritli*? A Review Essay," *Modern Judaism* 23 (2003). In his thorough and excellent analysis of the letters, Zank notes the "virtual exchangeability of the [parties]" (80). For more on the crucial role played by Eugen Rosenstock in the affair, see ibid., 79–84. See also the introduction by Reinhold Mayer and Inken Rühle to *GB*, vi, and Harold Stahmer, "The Letters of Franz Rosenzweig to Margrit Rosenstock-Huessy: 'Franz,' 'Gritli,' 'Eugen,' and 'The Star of Redemption,'" in Schmied-Kowarzik, ed., *Der Philosoph Franz Rosenzweig*, vol. 1, 121–26.

26. Mosse, *Nationalism and Sexuality*, 60, 67; Sedgwick, *Between Men*.

27. Batnitzky, *Idolatry and Representation*, 90–101.

28. Kalman P. Bland, *The Artless Jew: Medieval and Modern Affirmations and Denials of the Visual* (Princeton: Princeton University Press, 2000), 91.

29. Cited by Lappin, *Der Jude*, 400–401.

Epilogue: Mutations

1. Bahr, *Expressionism*, 85–87.

2. Noah Isenberg, *Between Redemption and Doom: The Strains of German-Jewish Modernism* (Lincoln: University of Nebraska Press, 1999) 82.

3. Shai Ansky, "From a Letter to Khaim Zhitlovsky," in *The Dybbuk and the Yiddish Imagination: A Haunted Reader*, ed. and trans. Joachim Neugroschel, (Syracuse, N.Y.: Syracuse University Press, 2000), 1. For the performance of *The Dybbuk* by Habima, see Emanuel Levy, *The Habima—Israel's National Theater 1917–1977: A Study of Cultural Nationalism* (New York: Columbia University Press, 1979. Levy notes that Ansky's original version relates to the struggle of a soul between two worlds, earthly and heavenly, within a religious order. The Habima

performance from the 1920s was more political, reflecting the revolt against traditional values, children against parents, and the poor against the rich. For a similar interpretation, see Freddie Rokem, "Hebrew Theater from 1889 to 1948," in Linda Ben-Zvi, ed., *Theater in Israel* (Ann Arbor: University of Michigan Press, 1996), 62–70. For more on the Russian context of the performance, see Avram Kampf, "Art and Stage Design in the Jewish Theaters of Moscow in the Early Twenties," in *Tradition and Revolution: The Jewish Renaissance in Russian Avant-Garde Art, 1912–1928* (Jerusalem: Israel Museum, 1987), 132–35. Kampf's analysis emphasizes the cubo-futuristic elements in Natan Altman's original stage design from 1922. As for the reception of the Habima performance in Germany, see Bernhard Diebold, *Habima: Hebräisches Theater* (Berlin: Heinrich Keller, 1928). Diebold's analysis and the photographic plates highlight expressionistic elements. For discussions of Wegener's *The Golem*, see Lotte H. Eisner, *The Haunted Screen: Expressionism in German Cinema and the Influence of Max Reinhardt* (Berkeley: University of California Press, 1969), 56–59, 64–74. See also Noah Isenberg, *Between Redemption and Doom: The Strains of German-Jewish Modernism* (Lincoln: University of Nebraska Press, 1999), 77–104. Isenberg's interpretation lays greater stress on social elements: the golem as an emblem for city life and the problem of "myth based, caricatured constructions of Jewishness" as seen in Wegener's representation of the Jewish masses (89). For an interpretation of German cinema that lays greater stress on the supernatural, see Paul Coates, *The Gorgon's Gaze: German Cinema, Expressionism, and the Image of Horror* (Cambridge: Cambridge University Press, 1991).

4. The first view comes from John Willett, *Art and Politics in the Weimar Period: The New Sobriety, 1917–1933* (New York: Pantheon Books, 1978), 11. Gay's more cautious comment can be found in Peter Gay, *Weimar Culture: The Outsider as Insider* (Westport, Conn.: Greenwood Press, 1968), 2, 122.

5. Hans M. Wingler, *The Bauhaus* (Cambridge, Mass.: MIT Press, 1969), 65–66.

6. Heinrich von Kleist, *Selected Writings*, ed. and trans. David Constantine (London: J. M. Dent, 1997), 413–16.

7. Karin von Maur, "The Art of Oskar Schlemmer," in Arnold L. Lehman and Brenda Richardson, eds., *Oskar Schlemmer* (Baltimore: Baltimore Museum of Art, 198), 74.

8. On Schlemmer's theater work, including the *Triadic Ballet*, see Nancy J. Troy, "The Art of Reconciliation: Oskar Schlemmer's Work for the Theater," in Arnold L. Lehman and Brenda Richardson, eds., *Oskar Schlemmer: The Baltimore Museum of Art* (Baltimore: The Museum, 1986), 127–47.

9. Oskar Schlemmer, "Man and Art Figure," in Gropius, ed., *Theater of the Bauhaus*, esp. 28–29.

10. See Troy, "Art of Reconciliation," in Lehman and Richardson, eds., *Oskar Schlemmer*, 127–48.

11. Cited by Leo Lowenthal, "As I Remember Friedel," *New German Critique*, no. 54 (1991): 9.

12. As Lawrence Rosenwald notes, Kracauer had at his disposal only "the bare text" of the first Genesis translation, without benefit of the later commentaries that Buber and Rosenzweig penned in response to critics. Lawrence Rosenwald, "On the Reception of Buber and Rosenzweig's Bible," *Prooftexts* 14 (1994): 149.

13. For a more sympathetic approach, see Miriam Hansen, "Decentric Perspectives: Kracauer's Early Writings on Film and Mass Culture," *New German Critique*, no. 54 (1991): 47–76. Hansen argues that Kracauer's apocalyptic understanding of modern culture participates in the discourse of modern Jewish messianism, insofar as he invokes a community of contemporaries who share his alienation and capacity for critical self-reflection (71–75). While his thoughts on "The Great Wall of China" support that thesis, they do nothing to dispel their inherently vacuous character when compared to the forcefulness of his critique.

14. Leo Strauss, *Spinoza's Critique of Religion*, trans. E. M. Sinclair (New York: Schocken Books, 1965). Originally published as *Die Religionskritik Spinozas als Grundlage seiner Bibelwissenschaft: Untersuchungen zu Spinozas Theologisch-politischem Traktat*, Veröffentlichungen der Akademie für die Wissenschaft des Judentums, Philosophische Sektion, 2 (Berlin: Akademie-Verlag, 1930).

15. See Kenneth Hart Green, *Jew and Philosopher: The Return to Maimonides in the Jewish Thought of Leo Strauss* (Albany: State University of New York Press, 1993), and David Novak, ed., *Leo Strauss and Judaism: Jerusalem and Athens Critically Revisited* (Lanham, Md.: Rowman & Littlefield, 1996). Werner Dannhauser suggests that filial piety, i.e., "love of one's own," is the only reason why Strauss never explicitly embraced Athens over Jerusalem (Novak, ed., *Leo Strauss and Judaism*, 169–70). In contrast, Hart Green calls Strauss a "cognitive theist." But the fact that he chose to place a "brief and allusive" statement regarding the author's religious belief in a footnote reflects quite strongly against the ultimate place of Strauss in Jewish philosophy. So too the fact that Strauss's chief preoccupation was political philosophy, not Jewish thought.

16. Jacques Derrida, "Plato's Pharmacy," in *Dissemination* (Chicago: University of Chicago Press, 1981), 70.

17. Ibid., 76–83.

18. Ibid., 126, 128.

19. Frederic Jameson, *Postmodernism, or, The Cultural Logic of Late Capitalism* (Durham, N.C.: Duke University Press, 1992).

20. See Yizhak Ahren and Jack Nusan Porter "Martin Buber and the American Jewish Counterculture," *Judaism* 29, no. 3 (1980): 332–39. See also Allen Ginsburg's interview with *Playboy* magazine, in which he recalls his own drug use, the exploration of sense perception, the expansion of consciousness, and his meeting with Buber. Thomas Clark's interview with Ginsberg is reprinted in *Writers at Work: The Paris Review Interviews, Third Series*, ed. George Plimpton (New York:

Penguin Books, 1967), 314.

21. Bluma Goldstein, "Andy Warhol: His Kafka and 'Jewish Geniuses,'" *Jewish Social Studies* 7, no. 1 (2000): 127–40.

22. Cited by Taylor, *Disfiguring*, 181.

23. Gibbs, *Correlations in Rosenzweig and Levinas*, 255–59.

24. Adorno, *Aesthetic Theory*, 79.

25. Crone and Koerner, *Paul Klee*, 48.

26. Salman Rushdie, *The Satanic Verses* (New York: Viking, 1988), 112.

27. Ibid., 111.

Index